D0609824

THE POLITICS OF
EVANGELICAL IDENTITY

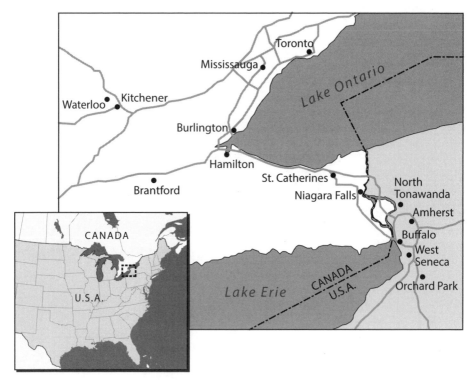

Buffalo, New York, and Hamilton, Ontario

THE POLITICS OF EVANGELICAL IDENTITY

Local Churches and Partisan Divides
in the United States and Canada

LYDIA BEAN

PRINCETON UNIVERSITY PRESS

PRINCETON AND OXFORD

Library of Congress Cataloging-in-Publication Data

Bean, Lydia, 1985–
The politics of evangelical identity : local churches and partisan divides
in the United States and Canada / Lydia Bean.
pages cm
Includes bibliographical references and index.
ISBN 978-0-691-16130-3 (hardcover : alk. paper)   1. Evangelicalism—
United States.   2. Evangelicalism—Canada.   I. Title.
BR1642.U5B43 2014
322′.10973—dc23
2013039985

British Library Cataloging-in-Publication Data is available

This book has been composed in Sabon

Printed on acid-free paper. ∞

Printed in the United States of America

1 3 5 7 9 10 8 6 4 2

CONTENTS

TIMELINE

	United States	Canada
1910	1910–15: *The Fundamentals* published by the Bible Institute of Los Angeles, defining Protestant orthodoxy against modernist threats 1914: Founding of Assemblies of God	1915–16: Saskatchewan, Manitoba, Ontario, British Columbia, Alberta, and New Brunswick enact prohibition laws with evangelical Protestant support 1917: Protestant churches rally Canadians for conscription in WWI; radical Anabaptists and some Pentecostals resist conscription 1918: Federal government bans interprovincial trade of liquor 1919: Founding of Pentecostal Assemblies of Cana da
1920	1920: Eighteenth Amendment begins Prohibition 1925: Scopes trial 1928: Fundamentalists mobilize against Catholic presidential candidate Al Green	1925: United Church of Canada founded as merger of Congregationalists, Presbyterians, and Methodists 1925: William "Bible Bill" Aberhart begins radio broadcasts that become "Back to the Bible Hour" 1927: Fundamentalist-Modernist controversy among Canadian Baptists; 77 churches split off to form Union of Regular Baptists
	1929: Great Depression Begins	
1930	1931: Carl McIntire forms American Council of Christian Churches 1933: Prohibition repealed	1932: Baptist minister Tommy Douglas founds Co-operative Commonwealth Federation (precursor to the New Democratic Party) 1935: William Aberhart's Social Credit Party wins Alberta election with evangelical support

continued

	United States	Canada
1940	1943: National Association of Evangelicals founded 1947: NAE forms National Association of Christian Schools	1944–61: Tommy Douglas becomes premier of Saskatchewan, introduces Provincial Medicare
1950	1950: Howard J. Pew funds Christian Freedom Foundation to promote free-market ideas in Christian language 1951: Bill Bright founds Campus Crusade for Christ with support from politically conservative, anti-communist businessmen 1952: Billy Graham rallies northern evangelicals in support of presidential candidate Dwight D. Eisenhower 1954: *Brown v. Board of Education* of Topeka, Kansas 1955: Carl McIntire begins using radio program as anti-Communist conservative platform 1955: Slaying of Emmett Till (August), Montgomery Bus Boycott (December) 1957: Founding of Southern Christian Leadership Conference	1953: Merger creates Fellowship of Evangelical Baptists in Canada, fundamentalist alternative to Canadian Baptist Federation 1953: Dutch Reformed immigrants found Christian Labour Association of Canada 1958: United Church of Canada hosts Billy Graham crusade
1960	1962–63: Supreme Court rulings limit school prayer (*Engel v. Vitale* and *Abington School District v. Schempp*) 1963: California white evangelicals mobilize against Fair Housing legislation 1963: Stonewall Riots; growing visibility of gay rights movement	1960: Quiet Revolution begins in Quebec; dramatic secular shift 1964: Evangelical Fellowship of Canada founded 1965: Implementation of the New Curriculum begins in the United Church of Canada 1967: Canada's centennial celebration, Protestants join in celebrating Canadian civil religion 1968–69: Therapeutic abortion and homosexuality decriminalized by Criminal Law Amendment Act, opposed by Fellowship of Evangelical Baptists

continued

	United States	*Canada*
1970	1971: Phyllis Schafly campaigns to block the ERA 1972: Tim and Beverly LaHaye launch Family Life Seminars 1973: *Roe v. Wade* strikes down abortion laws as unconstitutional 1973: White Presbyterians from Mississippi, Alabama, and South Carolina withdraw from PCUS, form National Presbyterian Church 1974: Southern Baptist Convention passes resolution affirming therapeutic abortion 1974: Network of right-wing activists found Third Way Publishers to link Christianity and right-wing politics 1974: Protests against new curriculum in Kanawha County, fuse concerns about sex, race, and secular humanism 1976: Jimmy Carter elected president 1976: Francis Schaeffer publishes *How Should We Then Live?* 1977: James Dobson founds media empire; Anita Bryant campaigns against Miami non-discrimination ordinance 1978: Campaign to defend tax status of private Christian academies 1979: Fundamentalists take over Southern Baptist Convention	1970: October Crisis begins when members of the Front de Libération du Québec kidnap two government officials; rise of the Québec sovereignty movement, crisis of Canadian national identity 1974: Ken Campbell founds Renaissance Canada
1980	1980: Ronald Reagan elected president with evangelical support 1987: Randall Terry founds Operation Rescue 1987: Elimination of the Fairness Doctrine in broadcasting 1988: Pat Robertson runs for Republican presidential nomination	1982: Charter of Rights and Freedoms adopted 1983: Founding of Focus on the Family Canada 1983: Evangelical Fellowship of Canada begins engaging in policy advocacy 1985: Supreme Court of Canada rules Lord's Day Act as unconstitutional

continued

United States	Canada
1980, cont'd	1987: Reform Party founded by Preston Manning with prominent evangelical leadership 1987: Founding of Christian Heritage Party 1988: Supreme Court of Canada strikes down federal abortion law as unconstitutional 1988–89: Canadian members of Operation Rescue block access to abortion in Ontario
1990 1992: Pat Buchanan gives Republican Convention speech on "Culture War" between liberals and conservatives 1996: Defense of Marriage Act 1998: Dr. Barnett Slepian murdered by anti-abortion activist	1990: Vote to replace Abortion law fails 1990–92: Bans on Sunday shopping lifted in Ontario 1998: Canadian Family Action Coalition founded as U.S.-style Christian Right group 1998: Attempt to murder Hamilton-area doctor who performed abortions
2000 2000: George W. Bush elected president with Christian Right support 2004: Focus on the Family steps into political role 2004: Re-election of George W. Bush with evangelical support; Bush promises to push constitutional amendment against same-sex marriage 2008: Proposition 8 in California bans same-sex marriage	2000: Stockwell Day defeated in federal election, after attacks on his evangelical faith, alleged creationist beliefs, and moral conservatism 2003: Conservative Party of Canada formed, as merger between Canadian Alliance and Progressive Conservative Party 2004: Supreme Court of Canada rules in favor of marriage equality for same-sex couples 2006: Conservative Party wins federal election, its evangelical leader Stephen Harper becomes prime minister

Preface and Acknowledgments

To honor the many people who made this book possible, I want to share how they have shaped my perspective on American religion. I have struggled to be as objective and systematic as possible, but one's choice of research questions is always guided by a particular perspective. The reader will naturally ask if I am a cultural insider or an outsider to American evangelicalism. The answer is neither. I was raised in an evangelical-inspired faith that was idiosyncratic to my family—what sociologists call a microculture. When I became an adult and stepped out to face America's religious landscape on my own, I felt like an alien discovering a foreign world. My own perspective on American evangelicalism is inevitably shaped by that particular history.

My parents, Alan and Nancy Bean, met at Southern Theological Seminary in Louisville, Kentucky. My mother came there answering a call to the ministry—a call that was even more controversial in 1977 than it was today. My parents recognized in each other a common passion for what they called the Kingdom of God: a holistic vision that included justice, discipleship, and personal transformation. My mother was from Texas, my father from Canada. But their own family histories had converged on this overlap between faith and justice.

My father's parents, Muriel and Gordon Bean, were blue-collar Canadian Baptists who joined the charismatic movement in the 1970s. My father, Alan, was raised in strict Christian home where television watching was forbidden on Sunday. Growing up, his father Gordon told him about his hero and former pastor, T.C. Douglas. T.C. Douglas is now known as the father of the Canadian Medicare system, voted the Most Important Canadian of all time by Canadian Broadcasting Corporation viewers in 2004. But in the 1930s, he was my grandfather's pastor at Calvary Baptist Church in Weyburn, Saskatchewan. Grandpa often talked about his hero Tommy Douglas, who modelled every Christian's responsibility to "stand up for the little guy."

My Grandpa Gordon was a New Democratic Party supporter who read the Bible literally and insisted that Prohibition could have worked, if Canada had only given it more time. My Grandma Muriel was active in her Baptist church and Women's Aglow International, a nondenomina-

tional charismatic women's ministry. Returning from a charismatic conference in the United States in the mid- 1980s, my grandparents reported
to my father that strange political trends were going on south of the
border. They loved Pat Robertson's preaching, but they found his political ideas bizarre.

After high school, my father attended an unaccredited Bible college,
the Baptist Leadership Training School, where he discerned a call to the
ministry. He had never really thought about college, but he headed to the
University of Alberta because it was a prerequisite for seminary. Then he
moved to Louisville, Kentucky to attend the Southern Baptist Theological
Seminary, then one of the most academically respected Baptist schools in
North America.

There he met my mother, Nancy Kiker, the daughter of a Baptist minister. Her parents, Charles and Patricia Kiker, were from a tiny farming
community in Swisher County in the Texas Panhandle. When my grandfather answered the call to ministry, he became the first boy in his family
to go to college, and ultimately earned a Ph.D. in Old Testament Studies.
Nana became a teacher and Grandad pastored American Baptist churches
in Colorado, Idaho, and Kansas City, Kansas. Throughout his ministry,
he was a strong voice for justice and civil rights, and he paid a steep cost
for his courage. My Grandpa taught me about the Hebrew prophets and
their cry for social justice, and he always amazed me by using words and
phrases in the original Hebrew. In Kansas City, Kansas, he led an aging,
white congregation to reach out to their predominantly black and Hispanic neighborhood. When his integration efforts began to succeed, the
resulting conflict ended in his early retirement.

Growing up, my parents ministered in Baptist churches across western
Canada and the United States. My parents had a strong, shared vision for
what the church was called to be, and they often came into conflict with
laypeople who saw things differently. I was born in Medicine Hat, Alberta, and grew up in whirlwind of small cities: Edmonton, Alberta;
Peachland, British Columbia; Glenrock, Wyoming; Pueblo, Colorado;
Derby, Kansas. My two brothers and I received an intense, round-the-
clock religious education that went far beyond Sunday school and worship. Most of my Biblical education took place around the dinner table,
reading Scripture aloud and discussing the text's relationship to everyday
life and current events. Between church and home, my parents surrounded
us with an idiosyncratic brand of Christianity that combined evangelical
piety with a strong commitment to social justice. Even though my parents
imparted to us a clear, countercultural set of values, they gave us room to
ask hard questions. Growing up, I never felt a conflict between critical
thought and faith, or between science and the Bible.

In 1989, my father went back to get his Ph.D. at the Southern Baptist Theological Seminary in Louisville, Kentucky. But the seminary had changed dramatically since the late 1970s, when he had last attended there. Shortly after he arrived, the school was taken over by a well-organized movement of theological conservatives. Professors were forced to sign a statement that they opposed the ordination of women. The faculty began to resign in protest. My middle-school friends were the sons and daughters of seminary professors, and we often talked about Southern Baptist politics over lunch. In 1991, I was baptized at Crescent Hill Baptist Church, a moderate Southern Baptist church that was subsequently expelled from the denomination. By my twelfth birthday, the denominational culture that I knew best no longer existed.

In 1998, my parents decided to move back to my mother's hometown of Tulia, Texas, to be closer to my maternal grandparents after they retired there. In 1999, we read in the paper about a massive drug sting in our tiny town of 5,000 people. A police task force had arrested forty-seven people based on the testimony of an undercover cop, thirty-nine of them African-American. We started to ask questions: how could a town of 5,000 people support forty-seven drug dealers? Why did the sting pick up only black people and people closely associated with the black community? My parents and grandparents joined with the defendant's families and other citizens to make sure the defendants got a fair trial. We called our little group the Friends of Justice.

Friends of Justice met on Sunday nights to worship, read the Bible, and plan strategy. Ultimately, we were able to draw in national allies to help us bring the Tulia drug sting to national attention. It turned out that the cases were built on the faulty testimony of an unsupervised undercover agent named Tom Coleman, who likely invented cases and pocketed police money to pay off old debts. We won: negative media coverage and a public outcry forced Governor Rick Perry to pardon the Tulia defendants. The Texas Legislature passed the Tulia Corroboration Bill, which has led to the exoneration of dozens of innocent people by raising the evidentiary standards for undercover testimony.

After our victory, my parents started getting letters from all over the country, asking about how to fight back against similar problems in other cities. We incorporated Friends of Justice as a nonprofit and started organizing across Texas and the South. Learning from our experience in Tulia, we helped affected communities hold public officials accountable in places where due process had broken down. This was a formative experience for me, as a scholar and as a person. Many of my research questions come out of my practical experiences organizing for justice in places like Texas, Louisiana, and Mississippi.

When I first arrived at Harvard University to start a Ph.D. in sociology, I actually expected to write a dissertation on the politics of mass incarceration. My interest in American evangelicalism emerged after the 2004 election. Suddenly, people around me were bewildered and threatened by people who I considered entirely ordinary. Evangelicals, conservatives, people in small and medium-sized cities, people in the so-called flyover states. The kind of people that I knew best. Where did this mutual miscomprehension come from? Why had the battles lines hardened in these particular ways? And so I became part of a second generation of scholars who sought to explain and interpret the Culture Wars, a generation who came of age at the height of partisan conflict over abortion, sexuality, and religion.

I come to these topics from a peculiar vantage-point, as neither an insider nor an outsider to evangelicalism. I didn't exactly grow up in the evangelical subculture—I grew up in the vibrant, countercultural world of evangelical piety that my parents created together. I'm not exactly a product of the liberal Mainline Protestantism either. Many of my mentors were strong liberal Protestant activists like Rev. Henry Bucher, my Presbyterian chaplain at Austin College, who participated in the civil rights movement and sued the Selective Service in opposition to the Vietnam War. I appreciate the liberal Protestant openness toward science, experience, historical scholarship, and the ordination of women. But when I try to make the Mainline Protestant tradition my own, gatekeepers inform me that I'm doing it wrong. Liberal Protestantism is a good tradition, but it is quite different from the one that I was raised in.

This is why I am so grateful to the people and communities who sustained me through the writing of this book. The last decade has made me painfully aware that strange perspectives are too much to bear without social support. I am grateful to the people who made me feel a little less strange, including Jeff and Tara Barneson, Susan Chamberlain, Madeleine Currie, Andrew Friedman, Alison Jones, Lauren Rivera, Christina Salib, and Lisa Thiebaud. Sylvia Keesmaat, David Krause, Matt Thompson, and Brian Walsh kept me grounded in community during my fieldwork. I also thank my thought-partners at the intersection of evangelicalism and organizing, including Rachel Anderson, Aaron Graham, Troy Jackson, and all the amazing folks at the PICO National Network. In addition to my parents and grandparents, I owe a debt to my younger brothers, Adam and Amos Bean. Finally, I want to thank my husband, Norman Lee, who shares my conviction that the moon is a cabbage. Thank you for being my helpmate and best friend.

I am grateful to the many people who provided feedback on this manuscript, including my editor Fred Appel and three anonymous reviewers at Princeton University Press. From the neighboring field of political science, Steven Teles has been a valuable thought-partner and collaborator. My wonderful colleagues at Baylor University gave feedback and support along the way, including Candi Cann, Victor Hinojosa, Mark Long, Jerry Park, Chris Pieper, and Lenore Wright. Nancy Ammerman, Jason Kaufman, Robert Sampson, and Theda Skocpol all provided pivotal feedback on the doctoral dissertation, which bore fruit in a more ambitious book. Marshall Ganz deeply shaped my approach to both scholarship and organizing.

The writing of this book was made possible by a sabbatical from Baylor University and support from the Canada-U.S. Fulbright Award, the Canadian Embassy, the National Science Foundation, and grants from Harvard's Weatherhead Center, Hauser Center, and Center for American Political Studies. Chapter Five is reprinted with permission from the *Journal for the Scientific Study of Religion*, which appeared in the March 2014 issue under the title "Compassionate Conservatives?: Evangelicals, Economic Conservatism, and National Identity."

Most of all, I want to thank my research participants, who showed me such hospitality and generosity. Thank you for sitting down with me and sharing your lives.

THE POLITICS OF
EVANGELICAL IDENTITY

INTRODUCTION

[S]omewhere along the way, faith stopped being used to
bring us together. . . . Faith started being used to drive
us apart. Faith got hijacked.

—Presidential candidate Barack Obama,
quoted in the *New York Times*

On the 2008 campaign trail, candidate Barack Obama accused Christian Right pastors and television pundits of hijacking the evangelical Christian movement for partisan gain. Has evangelical Christianity been hijacked? This top-down explanation makes sense to Christians who feel marginalized by the Christian Right. Randall Balmer, Episcopal priest and historian, protests that the evangelical faith "has been hijacked by right-wing zealots who have distorted the gospel of Jesus Christ, defaulted on the noble legacy of nineteenth-century evangelical activism, and failed to appreciate the genius of the First Amendment."[1] Progressive evangelical Jim Wallis argues that "God is not a Republican or a Democrat."[2] These politically liberal and moderate Christians insist that evangelical beliefs do not naturally support a conservative agenda. Rather, a small minority of partisan activists have co-opted the language of faith to manipulate people in the pews. Since the 2004 election, Democrats have courted evangelical voters by framing their progressive agenda in moral and religious language.[3] A more diverse set of evangelical leaders and interest groups has emerged, attempting to mobilize evangelicals around other "moral issues" like poverty and care for the environment.[4]

But white American evangelicals remain remarkable in their political homogeneity. In 2004, 77.5 percent supported the Republican candidate for president,[5] and their support for the Republican Party was largely unchanged in 2008, 2010, and 2012.[6] Progressive faith outreach may have borne some fruit among under-thirty evangelicals, who voted for Obama 8 percent more than their elders in 2008. Even so, 70 percent of younger evangelicals voted for Senator John McCain in 2008 and a majority still identify as politically conservative.[7] For white evangelicals, it has not been enough for Democrats and progressive activists to make top-down appeals to religious faith. The coalition between evangelicals and the Republican Party is not just constructed from the top down, by political elites who frame conservative issues in religious language. In *The Politics of Evangelical Identity*, I show how this relationship is anchored from the bottom up within the worlds of local congregations. Setting American evangelicals in cross-national perspective, I show how political conservatives have reshaped what it means to be an evangelical Christian within everyday religious practice.

The hijacking metaphor paints a fundamentally distorted picture of *how* local evangelical churches have become politicized. Guided by this metaphor, scholars and pundits have looked for evidence that evangelical churches have been co-opted in top-down, heavy-handed ways. We imagine that politicized religion looks something like this: A corpulent, balding minister gets up in the pulpit and rails against the sins of Sodom, beads of sweat pouring down his brow. He shakes his finger at the faithful, framing his opposition to gay marriage in terms of the core values of the faith. The congregation listens obediently from the pews, nodding their heads in humorless disgust. Then all rise to sing the closing hymn: "Onward Christian Soldiers." The ushers distribute a Christian Right voter guide that identifies which candidates support a "Christian agenda." The self-satisfied flock pours out of the church doors and into the polls, commissioned to wage a culture war on gays, abortionists, and secularists.

But this image does not capture how most rank-and-file evangelicals experience the political climate of their local churches. Local congregations have a particular organizational logic that is different from the worlds of politicians and interest groups.[8] While Christian Right elites promote a coherent culture war ideology, evangelical congregations favor pragmatism, self-help, and local concern. Sermons on political topics and "moral issues" are rare in evangelical churches. According to the National Congregations Study, only 10 percent of evangelical congregations report distributing Christian Right voter guides.[9] For more than twenty years, a majority of evangelicals have distanced themselves from the "Christian Right" as a political movement, expressing negative attitudes toward Jerry Falwell, Pat Robertson, and the Moral Majority.[10] There is a large divide between the worlds of evangelical congregations and the conservative power brokers who speak for them.

Ironically, white evangelicals report that they engage in fewer political discussions at church than mainline Protestants Catholics, and Black Protestants.[11] Using the 1998 National Congregations Study, Kraig Beyerlein and Mark Chaves found that evangelical churches engaged in a fairly limited set of political practices, compared to mainline, Catholic, and Black Protestant churches. Mainline congregations tend to organize discussion groups around political issues and host political candidates. Catholic congregations organize demonstrations and marches and lobby elected officials. Black Protestant congregations register voters, open their doors to candidates, and distribute voter guides from sources other than the Christian Right. Evangelical congregations rarely engage in collective demonstrations and marches like Catholic parishes, sponsor discussions on political issues like mainline churches, or open their doors to candidates like Black Protestant churches.[12] In reality, the worlds of local evangelical congregations are far less overtly political than the worlds of Christian Right elites.

Yet the Christian Right is still winning the framing game. How do evangelical churches reinforce such a high level of political homogeneity? I find that evangelical churches have become politicized in more subtle ways that reflect the influence of the Christian Right. Even though evangelicalism is not defined by a shared, coherent political worldview, evangelical congregations still foster thin coherence between religious identity and partisanship.[13] Political influence does not work through explicit persuasion or deliberation about political subjects, but by defining evangelical identity in ways that are implicitly linked to partisanship. Ironically, these partisan cues have greater moral power because they are distanced from the dirty business of "politics."[14] Political conservatism takes on a sacred quality because it is woven into the fabric of everyday religious life.

Evangelicals and the Culture Wars

This book offers a new perspective on how white evangelical Christians have become an important constituency for the Republican Party in the United States. Robert Wuthnow has described this shift as part of a larger restructuring of American religion that took place within local congregations, denominations, and public life.[15] Before the 1960s, voters were socialized from birth into ethnoreligious communities—Protestant, Catholic, or Jewish—that instilled certain assumptions about party loyalty.[16] Protestants identified with the Republicans and Catholics with the Democrats. But since the 1960s, religious identity has become more voluntary and disconnected from tight-knit ethnic communities.[17] Americans are now divided by the values and lifestyles that they have chosen for themselves, rather than by inherited ethnoreligious loyalties. The important divides are no longer between Protestants, Catholics, and Jews, but between "modernist" and "orthodox" people within each religious group.

According to Wuthnow's account, this restructuring of American religion contributed to ideological polarization between liberals and conservatives in electoral politics. It also transformed the relationship between religious identity and partisanship, forcing political scholars to rethink traditional models of political socialization. In the older "ethnoreligious" world, people were socialized into an ascribed religious identity, which might then inform their political attitudes and party identification. The causal relationships were easier to model, because people were "assigned" to their religious group in childhood and then chose their political party later in life. We knew which came first. The restructuring of American religion complicates that picture, because people can choose the religious subculture that will socialize them politically, based in part on preexisting political commitments.[18]

Even as mainline Protestants and Catholics became divided between liberal and conservative camps, white evangelical Protestants became *more* united in their political vision. Evangelicalism is a Protestant movement that affirms the authority of the Bible, Christ's atoning sacrifice on the cross, the need for a personal commitment to Christ, and the need for all believers to participate actively in religious mission.[19] Throughout this book, I use the term "evangelical" to refer to a broad coalition of theologically conservative Protestants in North America, which includes groups like Southern Baptists, Pentecostals, charismatics, independent Bible churches, and Fundamentalists. Social scientists commonly refer to these groups together as "conservative Protestants." But to avoid confusion between the theological and political meanings of conservatism, I use the more popular term "evangelical" to describe the broad coalition of Protestants who have resisted theological modernism.[20]

At the start of the twenty-first century, white evangelicals stand out among traditionalists in all observant Christian groups as the most politically conservative.[21] Frequent attendance at evangelical churches is consistently identified as an important predictor of voting Republican in the United States.[22] The so-called God Gap is not just between more and less devout voters, compared in terms of a generic religious traditionalism or "orthodoxy." To predict political attitudes, it matters if voters belong to an *evangelical* church, ascribe to characteristic *evangelical* beliefs, and identify as an *evangelical* or born-again Christian.[23]

Previous scholarship has offered two competing explanations for this strong relationship between evangelicals and the Republican Party. James Hunter has argued that evangelicals' political behavior is primarily driven by a coherent moral worldview, which follows naturally from their shared theological beliefs. By contrast, Hunter's critics reject this notion that there is a thick coherence between evangelical religion and political conservatism.[24] That is, evangelicals are not inevitably attracted to conservative politics by the internal logic of a coherent religious worldview. Instead, critics claim that this sense of coherence was manufactured from the top down by political elites and advocacy groups. But both of these frameworks ignore a critical piece of the puzzle: how the Christian Right was able to exercise moral power within the evangelical movement, to invest conservative politics with authentic spiritual meaning for people in the pews.[25] By comparing evangelicals in the United States and Canada, I show how political forces have actually reshaped the content of American evangelical identity at the level of everyday religious practice, not just at the level of top-down political mobilization.

A Coherent "Orthodox" Worldview

James Hunter has famously argued that American politics has become locked in a culture war between "orthodox" and "progressive" visions of moral authority. In this account, evangelicals increasingly support the Republican Party because they subscribe to an "orthodox" worldview that privileges transcendent truth, while Democrats subscribe to a "progressive" worldview that privileges the individual as the arbiter of truth.[26] These different views of morality authority are expressed in two very different narratives of American national identity.

Within the orthodox narrative, America was founded as a Christian nation—or at least founded on generally Judeo-Christian principles—with a divine mission to spread freedom and justice. But American "freedom" is primarily imagined socially, as a society living free from external tyranny, enjoying the benefits of free-market capitalism. "Justice" is imagined individually, so that administering justice means punishing the wicked and rewarding individual righteousness. Accordingly, America's founding documents take on a quasi-sacred quality for orthodox activists, since these texts lay out God's unchanging plan for America's past, present, and future. Social change is only desirable if it allows America to more faithfully realize these founding principles. Likewise, gender roles and family relationships are held to a timeless standard of objective truth, and so feminism promotes deviation from God's ideal.

By contrast, the progressive narrative casts America as an ongoing experiment, founded as a mixture of religious values and humanist, Enlightenment ideas. "Freedom" is imagined individually, as a collection of individuals enjoying freedom of conscience, guided by their diverse notions of the good. "Justice" is imagined socially, as a collective struggle to foster inclusion and equality. For progressives, America's founding documents are works-in-progress, not sacred texts, and so collective understanding of national values should naturally evolve as part of this historical struggle for justice. Likewise, gender roles and family forms are not fixed by timeless truths, but change naturally over time, to allow for greater individual freedom and self-realization. Since America does not have a uniquely God-given destiny, progressives do not value national loyalty, but rather identify as citizens of the world.[27]

According to Hunter, these competing narratives resonate with different groups of Americans based on different patterns of moral perception and judgment, not based on class or social status. Hunter describes these patterns of moral judgment as *prepolitical*, or shaped by an individual's primary socialization in families and group subcultures.[28] In his account, the orthodox narrative resonates with evangelicals because they hold a high view of moral authority, apart from human reason and desire. Evangelicals judge sexual norms and gender roles by reference to an authoritative reading of scripture, a timeless source of truth that is not subordinate to reason or experience. By contrast, the progressive narrative resonates with people from secular and theologically liberal backgrounds, who locate moral authority within the individual and reconsider truth in the light of reason, science, and new cultural trends.

But the culture wars framework has also been extensively criticized. Within cultural sociology, Hunter's argument has largely been rejected on theoretical grounds. Hunter assumes that cultural systems can be treated as internally coherent, consensually shared within groups, and deeply internalized as values that motivate behavior.[29] But cultural sociology has increasingly rejected the notion that culture shapes the *ends* that people pursue. Following Ann Swidler, the field has re-conceptualized culture as a "toolkit" or "repertoire," which provides the *means* that people use within action and interaction.[30] This new paradigm explains why rank-and-file evangelicals are far more diverse, nuanced, and pragmatic than the political elites who claim to speak for them.[31] For example, evangelical couples often express symbolic support for the idea that women should "submit" to their husbands, but in practice, they draw on the notion of submission to justify quite egalitarian relationships.[32]

If any rank-and-file evangelicals ascribe to Hunter's coherent orthodoxy, we would expect to fit it among grassroots pro-life activists. But social movement scholars find this internal complexity even when they study the most the most highly mobilized, pro-life activists from evangelical backgrounds.[33] For example, Rhys Williams and Jeffrey Neal Blackburn found that evangelical Christian participants in Operation Rescue described their motivations in quite diverse terms despite their similar religious backgrounds.[34] Pro-life and pro-choice activists do not inhabit parallel moral universes; both groups value motherhood and the nurturant values associated with it, even as they clash over the meaning of women's lives.[35] It is also incomplete to describe the contemporary pro-life movement as a traditionalist backlash against the changing role of women, as Kristin Luker argued in her classic 1984 study of abortion politics.[36] Pro-life activists appeal to many of the same principles as pro-choice and secular political activists, but apply these concerns to consider the rights and dignity of the fetus within a constitutional framework of "life, liberty, and the pursuit of happiness."[37] Jon Shields concludes that the abortion conflict is not a war between clashing worldviews, but rather a disagreement about how to apply a *shared* repertoire of democratic discourse to evaluate this medical procedure.[38]

This basic critique is confirmed by a large body of political science and public opinion research, which finds that the U.S. general public does not appear to be polarized around two rival worldviews or systems of moral understanding.[39] When asked about abstract values, American evangelicals seem to share a broad set of national ideals with other Americans, valuing a balance of equality and freedom, moral standards and respect for diversity.[40] While political elites may think in terms of internally coherent moral worldviews, most people combine "orthodox" and "progressive" positions on different issues.[41]

Finally, comparative research shows that traditional moral beliefs do not always inform political behavior. For example, Black Protestants share theologically orthodox beliefs with white evangelicals, yet black Christians vote overwhelmingly Democratic.[42] Religious participation is associated with morally conservative attitudes on abortion, marriage, and homosexuality in all regions of the United States, Canada, and Britain; however, these attitudes are only associated with distinct voting patterns in the United States.[43] Cultural divides can remain differences of private opinion unless strategic political actors mobilize voters around them. Hence, we need to explain the circumstances under which white American evangelicals make these particular "moral issues" of abortion and homosexuality central to their political decision-making.[44]

Constructing Coherence from Above

In reaction to Hunter, scholars have argued that the U.S. culture wars are primarily driven by top-down political mobilization, rather than an inherent clash between orthodox and progressive worldviews. Candidates, political parties, interest groups, and social movements have played a critical role in linking religious belief and identity to political behavior.[45] This body of research has extensively documented how politicians, religious activists, and advocacy groups have strategically mobilized the general public around alleged cultural threats and moral conflict.[46] Political scientists Geoffrey Layman and John Green argue that there are three conditions under which religious divides become relevant to mass political behavior: (1) when religious perspectives are logically related to policy issues; (2) when communal experiences encourage these connections; and (3) when electoral actors emphasize and differentiate themselves on such matters.[47]

All three of these conditions have operated to make evangelicals the base of the Republican Party since the 1980s. Interest groups and networks of Christian activists have worked within evangelical churches to distribute voter guides and emphasize the differences between the two parties on the "moral issues" of abortion and same-sex marriage.[48] Evangelical pastors have embraced the mandate of a new "civic gospel" to influence public life by giving their congregation political cues.[49] And, as the Christian Right seized power within the Republican Party, they were able to nominate candidates that appealed to evangelicals using religious rhetoric.[50] The political mobilization framework calls our attention to how much strategic framing was required to organize evangelicals around moral issues like abortion and homosexuality.

At first glance, much of this work actually extends rather than discredits James Hunter's basic framework. Hunter has consistently stressed that "without doubt, public discourse is more polarized than the American public itself." The culture wars are primarily fought between two rival elites, opposing clans of knowledge workers who pursue greater ideological consistency than the general public.[51] But Hunter's central claim is that these new political alignments are primarily driven by underlying moral commitments, rooted in different religious or quasi-religious worldviews. By contrast, this work raises the possibility that not only does religious morality inform political conflict; political conflict can also shape the content of religious morality.[52] A particular formulation of evangelical orthodoxy may be the outcome of power struggles, driven by the exigencies of partisan coalition-building rather than theological deliberation.

Historical research provides some support for this view. For example, evangelicals hadn't always been uniformly pro-life. When the Supreme Court first ruled on *Roe v. Wade* in 1973, the Southern Baptist Convention praised the decision as a wise compromise. At the time, evangelicals saw the pro-life position as a distinctively Catholic one, and generally avoided taking a position on the procedure. Hence, it wasn't inevitable that evangelicals took on the abortion issue because of their commitments to a high view of biblical authority, as James Hunter claims. Rather, a small set of political activists articulated a new narrative of evangelical identity that made abortion newly central to the worldview.

Some scholars have argued that this shift was entirely manufactured by cynical Christian Right operatives, who took over the evangelical subculture to advance their political agenda.[53] There is some evidence for the view that right-wing activists co-opted key evangelical institutions.

During the 1980s, Christian Right activists took over the Southern Baptist Convention and forced out theological moderates who disagreed with their political agenda.[54] But there was more going on here than pure power politics. The problem with this hijacking metaphor is that evangelicalism had no central cockpit that could be stormed.

Evangelicalism has always been a decentralized, trans-denominational movement based in self-governing local churches.[55] Even the Southern Baptist Convention, the nation's largest Protestant denomination, was largely organized within autonomous local churches. Christian Right activists could gain some leverage by taking over the Southern Baptist Convention, but individual congregations could decide for themselves whether or not to recognize denominational dictates or even to pay their dues to the denomination. This religious movement had no central control room, no lever that political activists could pull to make all evangelicals think a certain way.

This leaves us with an important puzzle: how did the culture war narrative take root among rank-and-file evangelicals, who were entrenched in local congregations rather than the halls of power? For most evangelicals, religious identity is not primarily constructed during election seasons, nor in the context of direct political activism. Rather, their primary reference point is the mundane settings of lived religion: local congregations, family life, religious media, parachurch networks, denominational polities, and personal networks.[56] These local settings play a critical role in religious conversion and commitment, by providing social support for the plausibility of religious beliefs.[57] To explain the politics of evangelicals, we need to understand how this particular "moral values" agenda comes to be experienced as a natural—even sacred—expression of their faith.

To answer that question, I spent a year observing how evangelicals talk about politics in ordinary congregational settings. Using ethnographic methods, I asked how this political configuration becomes accepted as common sense within the everyday lives of rank-and-file evangelicals.[58] It is wrong to assume that evangelicals are "cultural dopes" who accept whatever political agenda elites foist upon them.[59] At the same time, a majority of white evangelicals feel that their faith compels them to support the Republican Party, on the basis of non-negotiable "moral issues" like abortion.[60]

According to James Hunter, evangelicals feel bound to political conservatism because of the internal logic of a coherent "orthodox" cultural system. But as a cultural system, evangelicalism has only thin coherence, potentially open to multiple political interpretations and applications.[61] As William Sewell argues, "when a given symbol system is taken by its users to be unambiguous and highly constraining, these qualities cannot be accounted for by their semiotic qualities alone." When stable patterns of interpretation emerge, it is because symbolic systems have become interlocked with practices and social structures.[62] Rank-and-file evangelicals are not free to relate their faith to politics in any way that seems logically coherent to them. There are limits to how individuals can legitimately interpret their tradition, if they want to be accepted within local congregations. This book reveals the social mechanisms that keep cross-cutting political concerns and political identities from being voiced within the evangelical subculture.

The evangelical tradition has always favored voluntary, populist forms of organization. It lacks formal ecclesiastical authorities that can hand down official doctrinal statements or excommunicate those who disagree. But local congregations still constrain how rank-and-file evangelicals interpret their tradition. In multi-level analysis, congregations have important contextual effects on political attitudes, controlling for individual characteristics. For example, the theological conservatism of a person's congregation is a better predictor of their moral conservatism and attitudes toward cultural out-groups than their own theological conservatism.[63]

Evangelical churches create self-enclosed social worlds, which fill people's leisure time with church activities and concentrate their relationships within the church.[64] A large body of work finds that dense, bounded networks contribute to cultural and political homophily.[65] But quantitative research has not explained how conservative politics become sacred and authentic for evangelicals—how the *content* of local church life creates these effects.[66] This book uses qualitative methods to look inside the black box of congregations, to reveal the mechanisms within local group interaction that produce contextual effects.

I spent a year observing in four evangelical congregations, listening to how faith was linked to political conservatism in religious practice and group interaction. To understand how this tradition has become politicized, I compared American evangelicals to a meaningful counterfactual: Canadian evangelicals, who share their theological beliefs but not always their conservative politics.

A New Approach: Comparing Evangelicals in the United States and Canada

In *The Politics of Evangelical Identity*, I compare how evangelicals talk about politics in everyday congregational settings in the United States and in Canada, a country where religion is less politicized. Since the 1960s, Canada experienced the same dramatic cultural shifts as the United States, but morality politics have never gained the same traction. Canadian evangelicals provide a theoretically interesting comparison, because they have the same theology and conservative moral attitudes as American evangelicals. Yet they have historically remained more centrist in their political ideology and partisanship than American evangelicals.[67] I spent 2006–2007 observing in two Baptist and two Pentecostal churches, matched on either side of the border in Hamilton, Ontario and Buffalo, New York.

Seymour Martin Lipset famously stated, "Knowledge of Canada or the United States is the best way to gain insight into the other North American country. Nations can be understood only in the comparative perspective."[68] Scholars often compare the United States to Europe, to note how religion and morality plays a much stronger role in U.S. politics than in more secular European democracies.[69] But Canada is a far better comparison, since this country has a substantial evangelical minority with a long history of political engagement. For example, Alberta's Social Credit party was founded by the Fundamentalist radio preacher "Bible Bill" Aberhart,[70] while the Co-operative Commonwealth Federation was founded by the Baptist minister Tommy Douglas, also known as the father of Medicare.[71] Since the 1960s, Canada experienced cultural changes similar to the United States, but without experiencing party polarization around culture war issues.

Canada is a particularly interesting case because it took a middle path of secularization and cultural change, falling between the United States and Europe. In the 1950s, Canada and the United States had similar rates of church attendance, but Canada's rates of religious participation have plummeted much faster since the 1960s.[72] Yet, as in the United States, Canadian evangelicalism continued to grow demographically during this period, even as mainline Protestantism and Catholicism declined.[73] In both the United States and Canada, secularization and evangelical religious vitality have both proceeded simultaneously.[74] Evangelical Protestants have always been a smaller minority in Canada: 10—12 percent of the population, as compared with 25—33 percent in the United States.[75] At the same time, Canada's evangelical subculture has continued to offer a much larger potential constituency for Christian Right politics than are present in most Western Europe countries.[76]

Canadian evangelicals are particularly relevant to the culture war debates, because this religious subculture shares the patterns of moral judgment and perception that Hunter identifies with an orthodox worldview. Like their American counterparts, this substantial religious minority has remained vital even as Canada has grown more secular and culturally diverse.[77] In a multi-method comparison of evangelicalism in the United States and Canada, Sam Reimer found that evangelicals in both countries maintain strong subcultural boundaries based on a shared set of theological beliefs and "strict" moral standards. Like their American counterparts, Canadian evangelicals practice what Christian Smith calls an "engaged orthodoxy": sustaining a dynamic tension with their sociocultural environment, while avoiding separatism.[78]

In both countries, the evangelical subculture is also associated with particular attitudes on political issues related to sexuality and the family. American and Canadian evangelicals are significantly more opposed to abortion and gay rights than comparable non-evangelicals in each country. Indeed, evangelicals in both countries are similar in the strength of their opposition on these moral issues.[79] But their "orthodoxy" does not extend to other political issues. For example, Canadian evangelicals are more concerned about economic inequality and more supportive of government's role in addressing it than are their American counterparts.[80]

Canada provides a particularly useful case to understand the relationship between partisan mobilization and the local construction of religious belief and identity. Even as Canada has grown more secular and religiously diverse since the 1960s, evangelicals have continued to play an important role in Canadian politics, a role that pundits have alternately ignored, underestimated, and misunderstood. This paradox is embodied by Canada's current prime minister, Stephen Harper, who identifies as an evangelical Christian but avoids talking about faith in public.

In recent years, political observers have expressed concern that Canada could see the rise of an American-style Christian Right, particularly since 2005, when the federal government legalized same-sex marriage.[81] The Conservative Party has been hesitant to use overt religious language, but there are signs that the political Right is using "dog-whistle politics" to appeal to evangelicals in ways that are invisible or incomprehensible to more secular voters.[82] The same-sex marriage debate brought sudden visibility to socially conservative interest groups in Canada who spoke for conservative Christians—some of them new, some of them well-established. My fieldwork took place during 2006–2007, a period when evangelical churches were making sense of same-sex marriage. Hence, I entered the field during a dynamic period in Canadian politics, which offered particular insight into the relationship between partisan mobilization and the local construction of religious identity.

Comparing across the border, I found that all four evangelical churches defined their subcultural boundaries through opposition to abortion and same-sex marriage. Furthermore, both U.S. and Canadian churches emphasized their responsibility to promote a shared sense of moral truth in the wider society by drawing on narratives of religious nationalism.[83] These uses of Christian nationalism were not *authoritarian*, since all four churches encouraged members to respect democratic norms and transform their nation through individual conversion and personal influence. It is more accurate to describe these churches as authority-*minded*, because they refused to privatize their moral beliefs and defended objective moral truths that applied to the nation as a whole.[84] Hence, both U.S. and Canadian churches emphasized distinctive patterns of moral judgment and perception that Hunter has associated with an orthodox worldview.

Yet this distinctive moral traditionalism does not, by itself, explain how white American evangelicals have become so tightly bound to the Republican Party. Comparing churches across the border, I also found important differences that help us understand how evangelicalism has become so tightly tied to conservative politics in the United States. Both American evangelical churches did more than foster a shared moral perspective and religious identity: they also linked them to *partisanship* in local church life, in ways that Canadian churches did not.

CROSS-NATIONAL DIFFERENCES: HOW RELIGIOUS IDENTITY WAS LINKED TO PARTISANSHIP

Previous scholarship suggests that partisanship and religious identity have become mutually constitutive identities in American public life, so that voting Republican is part of what it means to be a good evangelical Christian.[85] As the United States has become more polarized around a few culture war issues, there is a stronger correlation between political conservatism and religiously conservatism, and a stronger likelihood that political liberals will claim no religious identity.[86] In this book, I use cross-national comparison in order to understand how American evangelical identity has taken on a partisan meaning.

I found that both American churches did more than just signal the "right" positions for Christians to hold on the moral issues. They also signaled the "right" party identification: which party "we" support, and which party "we" oppose.[87] In this way, both churches signaled that voting Republican on these two issues was an important part of being a Christian. Religious identity became symbolically and socially inseparable from affiliation with the Republican Party and conservative ideology.[88] By contrast, both Canadian churches defined their subcultural identity in different terms, which were more easily separated from the cultural meanings of partisanship. In the United States, this strong linkage between morality, religious identity, and partisanship strengthened political conformity and silenced cross-cutting political identities.[89]

Here, I define partisanship as a group identity defined by reference to a cultural map of electoral politics.[90] In their classic study *The American Voter*, David Campbell and his collaborators argued that voters do not support candidates on the basis of a rational consideration of facts and policy goals. Rather, "[i]n casting a vote the individual acts towards a world of politics in which he perceives the personalities, issues, and the parties and other groupings."[91] Voters think about politics in terms of their "cognitive and affective map of politics," a sense of how *people like them* relate to particular parties and candidates. Political parties become objects of group identification in their own right, and these loyalties systematically bias how voters make sense of political information.[92] Even when voters cannot articulate a coherent political ideology, they can often describe a cultural map of what groups and issues go with what parties—and locate themselves on this map.[93] In the field of political science, Kathy Cramer Walsh has observed that partisanship is a broader concept than party identification, since the cultural meaning of partisan loyalties may change over a person's lifetime, even if their identification with a particular party remains stable.[94]

In both Canada and the United States, partisanship is a valuable lens through which to understand how voters make sense of politics in terms of in-groups and out-groups, not just in terms of a rational consideration of past performance, self-interest, or policy goals.[95] In the United States, an individual's map of partisanship may include party identification, or a psychological attachment to Democrats or Republicans as a group.[96] Partisanship also includes a related concept of ideological identity, or an affiliation with "conservatives" or "liberals" as a social group.[97] In Canada, voters choose among three major parties, and since parties may form coalitions, voters may also see one rival party as an adversarial out-group and another party as an acceptable coalition partner.[98] Throughout this book, I use this sensitizing concept of partisanship to ask how rank-and-file evangelicals locate themselves and "people like them" on a map of electoral politics.

Comparing evangelical churches in the United States and Canada, I found that political influence primarily worked by defining a shared map of political conflict, in ways that linked religious identity to partisanship. These partisan cues were not seen as political, because they were woven into everyday religious practice, rather than explicit electoral mobilization. Using participant observation, I identified three practices that linked religious identity and partisanship more strongly in American churches than Canadian churches.[99]

First, religion and partisanship became fused in the *narratives of Christian nationalism* that church members used to make sense of their responsibilities to a broader society. In both countries, evangelicals engaged in similar practices of public narrative: telling stories to motivate one another to engage with the outside world.[100] In the United States, evangelicals mourned the loss of America as a "Christian nation." In Canada, evangelicals mourned the loss of their country as "God's Dominion." In all four churches, these public narratives were not used for explicitly political goals, but to build a sense of urgency to engage in evangelism and community service outside of their local church.[101] But in both American churches, these narratives of Christian nationalism defined liberals as the villains of the story, as a political and cultural out-group responsible for America's "moral decline."[102] In both Canadian churches, I heard a rather different narrative, which blamed the loss of a "Christian Canada" squarely on the church itself.

Second, partisanship became linked to religious identity within everyday practices of *identity-mapping*. In all four churches, leaders and members spent a great deal of time drawing symbolic boundaries between "us" and "them," to strengthen a clear sense of subcultural distinction with diverse out-groups in their larger sociocultural environment.[103] In both countries, churches avoided "political talk," understood as explicit persuasion or deliberation about political subjects. Instead, politics was only addressed obliquely, through a practice that political ethnographer Paul Lichterman has called *mapping*. The most explicit partisan cues emerged in small group interaction, as members used words and gestures to draw a shared map of their national context, to define how "we Christians" should relate to other groups within this broader civic arena.[104] In both American churches, liberal politicians and political groups were frequently mapped as salient adversaries to "our" influence in society as Christians.

Third, I found that the most explicit partisan cues did not come from ordained clergy, but rather from a broad base of volunteer *lay leaders*. Within both American churches, I found that a broader set of key laypeople were "captains" for culture war politics within their congregation, who modeled a strong conservative or Republican political identity. These lay leaders did not identify as political activists or members of a Christian Right, yet they were still engaged in leadership projects that bridged religious and political fields.[105] In their capacity as church leaders, these respected laity also served as political opinion leaders, who helped less politically engaged peers to link evangelical identity to conservative politics.[106]

Throughout the book, I show how these local religious practices of *public narrative, identity-mapping,* and *local leadership* helped to strengthen political conformity in both American churches. Political conservatism took on a sacred quality because it was woven into the fabric of everyday religious life. This strong link between religious identity and partisanship worked to limit political diversity within American evangelical churches. By contrast, local religious practices did not conflate partisanship and religious identity in the two Canadian churches.

OVERVIEW OF THE BOOK

In the next chapter, I introduce two Baptist churches and two Pentecostal churches, matched on either side of the U.S.-Canada border. From August 2006 to 2007, I conducted participant observation in two evangelical churches located in Buffalo, New York—one Baptist and one Pentecostal. During the same period, I also observed in two Canadian churches located in Hamilton, Ontario, matched by denominational tradition, theology, and behavioral strictness. I describe the similarities across all four churches which reflect a shared, transnational evangelical subculture. But I also highlight differences between these two U.S. and two Canadian churches, which reflect the enduring role of national identity and national borders in the production of evangelical identity.

In the following chapters, I draw on ethnographic fieldwork to analyze how religion became linked to conservative politics within these four churches. I present my analysis in two parts. In chapters 3 through 5, I compare how U.S. and Canadian churches talked about politics in public church settings: worship, small groups, Sunday school, and informal conversations.

In chapter 3, I show that "political" talk was considered unspiritual and inappropriate in both American congregations, Northtown Baptist and Lifeway Assembly of God. But even though both churches avoided politics, they enforced an informal understanding that good Christians voted Republican. I describe how religion and partisanship became fused, as members mapped their subcultural identity and drew on narratives of religious nationalism.

In chapter 4, I contrast the two American churches with two similar congregations just across the border in Canada, which I call Highpoint Baptist and Grace Assembly of God. Both Canadian churches constructed their subcultural identity in ways that sounded similar to the two American churches. Like their American counterparts, Canadian evangelicals identified themselves as defenders of their nation's embattled Christian heritage and emphasized shared moral stances on abortion and sexuality. But Canadian evangelicals used Christian nationalism in more broadly civic and nonpartisan ways: to draw strong subcultural boundaries, but also to express solidarity with Canadians across cultural, religious, and partisan divides. Because Canadian evangelicals drew on different narratives of Christian nationalism, they also talked differently about poverty and the welfare state in church contexts.

In chapter 5, I evaluate the claim that evangelical Christians are predisposed toward economic conservatism because of their individualistic theology. In the United States, white evangelicals are more economically conservative than other Americans. Yet Canadian evangelicals are just as supportive of redistributive social policy as other Canadians, even though they share the same tools of conservative Protestant theology. To solve this puzzle, I compare how U.S. and Canadian evangelical congregations talked about poverty and the role of government. In both countries, evangelicals made sense of their religious responsibilities to "the poor" by reference to national identity. Evangelicals used their theological tools differently in the United States and Canada, because different visions of national solidarity served as cultural anchors for religious discourse about poverty.[107] To understand the political and civic effects of religion, scholars need to consider the varied ways that religious groups imagine national community within religious practice.

In chapters 6 through 8, I examine how religion and politics were linked at the individual level, by describing the personal meanings and biographical narratives that emerged in private interviews. Like other scholars, I highlight significant diversity within each church at the individual level, showing that the illusion of public consensus often concealed unvoiced private opinions. But this diversity was not equally distributed in social space. By comparing private interviews with public church interaction, I show how some political attitudes and identities were silenced or unsupported within an individual's congregational context.

In chapter 6, I find that in both U.S. churches, political influence operated through a broad set of opinion leaders, not just through ordained pastors or media elites. Previous research has identified local pastors as key opinion leaders who help bridge the gap between political elites and the general public, by preaching on political topics, sending partisan cues, or proclaiming official church stances on issues like abortion and gay marriage.[108] Other scholars argue that Christian Right elites increasingly reach individual directly, through targeted mailings, Fox News, and Christian radio, without the need to work through their personal networks and congregations. But previous work has largely ignored the political influence of volunteer, non-ordained religious leaders.

I find that a broad set of laypeople serve as opinion leaders, helping their less politically engaged peers to link evangelical identity to conservative politics. Local opinion leaders help define evangelical identity in partisan terms, such that voting Democratic is incompatible with being a Christian.[109] In chapter 7, I argue that these opinion leaders contribute to "thin coherence" between religious identity and partisanship, even for individuals in their church who subscribe to moderate, progressive, or ambivalent political attitudes.

In chapter 8, I compare the role of opinion leaders in the two Canadian churches. As in both American churches, Canadian lay leaders were expected to model orthodox positions on theology and moral issues, as part of their leadership role. But, unlike in the American churches, this moral conformity was combined with an acceptance of political diversity within the church. Both Canadian churches contained networks of conservative Christian activists who wished to mobilize the congregation around abortion and homosexuality. But politically conservative activists were unable to set the tone for the church's public life, since other prominent members held other political views. As a result, less politically engaged members did not receive clear cues about partisanship from the opinion leaders around them. In both Canadian churches, members picked up a sense of consensus around moral conservatism, but elaborated diverse perspectives about how these concerns related to electoral politics.

The Politics of Evangelical Identity offers a new perspective on Robert Bellah's concept of civil religion: generically religious constructions of national identity that provide consensual symbols of solidarity and moral guidance.[110] Bellah's critics have pointed out that civil religion is often a site of conflict, a means by which a particular religious group defends its dominant status in public life, rather than a unifying set of symbols. Indeed, Robert Wuthnow argued the culture wars have fractured America's civil religion into two competing liberal and conservative narratives.[111] Within American evangelicalism, civil religion often takes on an ideological, partisan meaning, which excludes liberals and other cultural outgroups from the nation.

Ironically, Canadian evangelicals have made the opposite shift. While the country's tradition of Christian civil religion has been pushed out of public life, Canadian evangelicals continue to draw on religious nationalism in more civic and nonpartisan ways: to draw strong subcultural boundaries, but also to express solidarity with Canadians across cultural, religious, and partisan divides. Their banal uses of nationalism were closer to Robert Bellah's consensual formulation of civil religion.[112] I found that both formulations of civil religion were correct, even within the same religious tradition—and even within the same church.

By comparing evangelicals in the United States and Canada, I find that American evangelicals are not bound to political conservatism by the content of their distinctive theology or moral worldview. Rather, the U.S. Christian Right has successfully defined evangelical identity in ways that delegitimize political diversity within the subculture.

BROADER IMPLICATIONS

In conclusion, the United States is not polarized because the two sides of the culture wars' lack shared values or moral concerns. Rather, America is polarized because these overlapping concerns and identities are systematically silenced as a basis for public action.[113] Other scholars have shown how these cross-cutting projects are pushed aside in the world of electoral politics and national discourse, by a polarized media climate, power dynamics within both political parties, and rival teams of interest groups, parachurch organizations, and think tanks.[114] This book shows how polarization has become entrenched within the American evangelical subculture, within the local worlds of lived religion.

These findings have clear implications for political strategy. Since 2004, pundits have asked what other political movements can learn from the evangelical voting bloc. The most common answer has been that parties and interest groups should frame their issues in the language of moral values. This book provides a different answer. If other movements want to replicate the strength of the Christian Right, it will not be enough to engage in top-down messaging about "moral values." They also need to find substitutes for the powerful identity-work that goes on every week in evangelical congregations. The Christian Right has not succeeded just because they framed the conservative agenda in the language of faith. When these frames resonate, it is because local congregations have woven them into everyday religious practices, reinforcing a powerful connection between religious identity and partisanship.

It will be critical to keep this insight in mind, as evangelical public discourse grows more pluralized in years to come. Political commentators have been too quick to proclaim that the United States has entered a post–Christian Right era. It is true that the Christian Right is no longer the only public voice speaking for evangelicals. Alternative leaders, ministries, and advocacy groups are stepping forward to broaden the Christian agenda beyond abortion and sexuality, to consider poverty, creation care, and racial reconciliation as equally important "moral issues." But this broadened political agenda will only gain traction with rank-and-file evangelicals if it informs the daily religious practices of local congregations. The challenge for young, dissenting evangelicals is not just to establish a public face for their political vision. They face a much greater challenge: to connect these new moral issues to the sacred within local religious practice. Disentangling evangelicalism from the Republican Party will take as much time, ingenuity, and internal conflict as it took to build this relationship in the first place.

CHAPTER 1

COMPARING EVANGELICALS IN THE UNITED STATES AND CANADA

During Canada's debate over same-sex marriage, many commentators wondered if evangelicals were mobilizing to fight an American-style culture war. Leaders like Charles McVety stepped forward, representing themselves as advocates for a united evangelical perspective on gay marriage. Canadians wondered how to respond. Did McVety speak for evangelicals? Did rank-and-file members of local churches share his Christian Right political vision? Most journalists took McVety's leadership claims for granted. But I saw a different picture, by watching how McVety engaged his self-proclaimed constituency.

One drizzly March morning in 2007, I joined a group of Ontario Baptists as they attended Mission Fest, a weekend-long celebration of global evangelism and domestic mission to reach Canada for Christ. We carpooled there in a van from Hamilton, a mixture of church elders and bleary-eyed young adults who complained bitterly about the early start on a Saturday.[1] Our trip was organized by Morton, a deacon in his late 60s who taught the New Member's Sunday school class. From morning to evening, we sampled from a dizzying array of workshops, worship events, and information fairs meant to equip us to share the gospel with Canada and "the nations." Mission Fest was not sponsored by any particular denomination or local church; it brought together a broad coalition of churches, denominations, and parachurch ministries under the wide umbrella of evangelical Christianity. Conspicuously missing were representatives from the United Church of Canada or from Anglican Church, the bastions of Canada's former mainline establishment. Nor did I meet representatives from the Catholic Church. Over the course of the day, I heard presentations led by Baptists, Pentecostals, charismatics, Christian Missionary Alliance, and a host of nondenominational Bible churches.

At the main plenary, we heard a message from Franklin Graham, the son of American evangelist Billy Graham, who shared his testimony and gave an uninspired presentation of the "plan of salvation."[2] Though

Graham himself did not address political issues, it became apparent that Christian Right activists hoped to use the event to rally attendees behind a conservative political agenda. After Graham spoke, he was thanked by Charles McVety, who rose to prominence in Canada's Christian Right during the fight against same-sex marriage, as leader of the *Defend Marriage Coalition* and president of *Canada Family Action*. McVety praised Graham as a model of evangelical orthodoxy, within a church that was losing its focus:

> Franklin Graham is a man of moral clarity. Our church is under unprecedented attack, an attack greater than at any time since the early church. . . . Our church has gotten involved in so many issues. Sometimes we get away from the Great Commission. But Franklin Graham has stayed focused.

Then, after presenting Graham with an award from Canada Christian College, McVety instructed us to "Please rise as we sing our Canadian National Anthem!" A Christian vocal trio called His Season led us in a pop version of the national anthem. McVety, a self-described leader of Canada's Christian Right, seemed to be in command of a crowd of thousands, as we stood and pledged to "stand on guard" for Canada. Were Canadian evangelicals rallying an army to fight a culture war?

Watching from the crowd, I could see that the picture was more complicated. On stage, I saw a lineup of white men, all older than fifty, calling on Christians to defend themselves and their nation from cultural threats. But in the crowd, I saw stunning racial and ethnic diversity, and a mixture of ages that was not represented on the stage. From the crowd, I saw that Charles McVety wasn't just waging war on external enemies: homosexuals, secularists, left-leaning causes. He was fighting for the soul of evangelicalism itself. When McVety talked about the church's involvement in "so many issues," he was implicitly attacking the tone of most of Mission Fest so far. After all, the day-long conference had featured a variety of Christian social ministries that hosted booths and organized workshops on domestic poverty, human trafficking, creation care, and refugee assistance. By contrast, McVety defined orthodox Christians as people of "moral clarity," who stayed focused on defending their religion from attack, instead of being distracted by these social concerns.

McVety's doom-and-gloom narrative of defense was strikingly out of touch with the dominant narrative of Mission Fest as a whole, which emphasized growing churches and multicultural missions. At the end of the day, we met at the closing worship service, hosted by David Mainse, host of the Canadian Christian television show *100 Huntley Street*. Mainse celebrated the ethnic diversity that we saw represented among workshop leaders and in the crowd around us. "The wealth of the world has come to Toronto! And we're blessed. Are we blessed?" he asked the crowd. The crowd roared back. The dominant narrative of evangelical identity was the celebration of the global, multicultural church: the Canadian church's unique mission to bring together Christians from all over the world.

An outside observer watching the crowd might have been terrified to see this Christian Right leader commanding a crowd of thousands of evangelicals to sing "Oh Canada." But looking more closely, Charles McVety's culture war rhetoric had fallen flat at Mission Fest, at least among members of Highpoint Baptist who attended that day. As we walked back to the van to return to Hamilton, Morton turned to me and shook his head, "Well, somebody should tell 'His Season' that the national anthem is not something you improvise on." I asked Morton if it was normal to end this kind of event with the national anthem. "No, that was highly unusual," said Murray, with great irritation in his voice. "We never sing the national anthem unless it's a Canada Day event or something," said his wife, Lori. Murray added, "But I would think that they'd end with a hymn or something to do with missions." It was clear that the event's awkward ending had rubbed Morton the wrong way. On the drive back, different members of our group shared the high points of Mission Fest, which for them included panels on outreach to immigrants, church planting among First Nations peoples, and global poverty.

It became evident that McVety was not just at war with secular Canadians; he was engaged in a cultural struggle with the evangelical movement itself. To rally Canadian evangelicals behind his American-style Christian Right agenda, McVety first needed to delegitimize the kinds of civic-minded social ministries that were already well-established within Canadian churches. The entire festival had been a day-long celebration of Canadian multiculturalism, where most speakers encouraged attendees using positive, forward-looking narratives about Canada's unique potential to "reach the nations." McVety seemed visually out of place: huddled behind the podium with a small group of aging white men, addressing a multi-ethnic audience that represented the racial and ethnic diversity of Toronto. For Murray, McVety's appeal seemed out of place because it distracted the focus from missions.

Since 2004, it has become increasingly obvious to American observers that the Christian Right is in a struggle with alternative evangelical voices. As a loose coalition, conservative Protestants have never had a centralized religious authority who could speak for the religious tradition, as the U.S. Conference of Catholic Bishops speaks for Catholics.[3] Christian Right leaders like Charles McVety represent themselves as the political arm of evangelicalism, characterizing this group's values and policy priorities in the public sphere. But it is never obvious who has the authority to speak for evangelicals, because this religious tradition is a loosely organized coalition within no single ecclesiastical authority. McVety is only one of a dizzying array of leaders who claim to speak for the evangelical tradition. And as he lamented, many of these leaders are not interested in fighting a culture war—they are too busy serving the poor, reaching out to refugees, and planting churches. At Mission Fest, McVety was desperately attempting to establish his moral authority to define the evangelical tradition by connecting himself to Billy Graham, framing his concerns as part of the core "gospel message," and disparaging other evangelical leaders who focused on "all these issues" that distracted Christians from the gospel.

This vignette illustrates that the Christian Right is a movement with two faces: one face that represents evangelicals in public debates and electoral politics, and another face that seeks to promote its particular vision of "orthodoxy" within the evangelical movement. The Christian Right does not just represent the self-evident values and policy priorities of evangelicals. It also functions as an internal movement to shape what these values and policy priorities should be. In the United States, this is readily apparent as an open struggle between the evangelical left, evangelical moderates, and the established Christian Right. But previous studies have understated the role of these internal struggles within evangelicalism as a critical dynamic in the culture wars. Previous work has explained how the Christian Right was able to mobilize resources and co-opt the religious institutions to build a political movement. But scholars have not asked how they were able to create a political consensus within evangelicalism, and keep alternative voices from gaining a following. Comparing the United States and Canada sheds light on the internal politics of evangelical identity: the ways that the Christian Right faced inward to wield power within their own subculture.

In this chapter, I compare the historical and institutional differences that made it more difficult to politicize evangelical identity in Canada than in the United States. These institutional differences set the context for local church life, leading to cross-national differences in how evangelical identity has been linked to politics in the United States and Canada.

THE POLITICS OF EVANGELICALS IN COMPARATIVE PERSPECTIVE

Before the 1960s, party conflict in both the United States and Canada pitted Catholics against Protestants. In the United States, Catholics have historically voted Democrat while Protestants have voted Republican. In Canada, Catholics have historically voted Liberal, while Protestants have favored the Progressive Conservatives.[4] In a variety of Western democracies, this kind of "ethnoreligious" cleavage between Catholics and Protestants was locked into place during the nineteenth century, during partisan conflicts over the consolidation of a national identity and church-state relations.[5] But in the 1960s, a wave of cultural change swept across the United States, Canada, and other Western democracies, a trend toward what public opinion researchers called "self-expressive"[6] or "libertarian" values.[7]

These cultural shifts were rooted in long-standing themes of modernity and liberal democracy, human equality and emancipation, but they were accompanied by new changes in gender roles, sexual behavior, and general orientations toward authority. Between the 1950s and the 1970s, sexual norms changed rapidly in both the United States and Canada, as women rejected double standards about premarital sexual behavior.[8] This sexual liberation was made possible by growing access to and use of oral contraceptives and other reliable birth control methods, which made it easier to decouple sexual intimacy from childbearing and marriage.[9] In both countries, women made rapid gains in higher education and workforce participation, and the feminist movement gained cultural visibility.[10]

Cultural changes went hand in hand with policy changes in the regulation of sexuality and reproduction. Empowered by the Stonewall riots of 1969, the gay rights movement entered the public sphere to challenge discrimination against homosexuals. From 1971 to 1983, American states began to abolish or reform their sodomy laws. Between 1973 and 1974, homosexuality was removed from the *DSM-II* as a psychological disorder.[11] In 1963, Colorado became the first state to legalize therapeutic abortion, and in 1973, *Roe v. Wade* struck down abortion laws nationwide as violations of the constitutional right to privacy.[12] In Canada, both homosexuality and abortion were decriminalized in 1968–69 by the Criminal Law Amendment Act. Prime Minister Pierre Trudeau defended the bill in terms of individual freedom, claiming that "there's no place for the state in the bedrooms of the nation."[13]

In both countries, these legal changes alerted religious leaders that they were losing authority in public life, as well as in the lives of individual citizens.[14] But initially, Catholics and Protestants were divided about how to respond. The Catholic Church immediately opposed the decriminalization of abortion, but mainline and evangelical Protestants supported these reforms out of concern for women's health. From the 1960s to the late 1970s, evangelical leaders spoke out publicly against gay rights, but agreed that therapeutic abortion was acceptable in some circumstances.[15] Abortion was still considered a narrowly Catholic issue.

But during the 1970s, American evangelicals began to think that Catholics were no longer the greatest threat to their Protestant Christian hegemony. Instead, their true enemy was "secular humanism," a shadowy set of elites who opposed their vision of a Christian America. Between 1973 and 1980, evangelicals embraced a hard-line position on abortion, as this issue became associated with secular humanism, feminism, and sexual license.[16] The Christian Right movement burst onto the national scene, to battle secular humanism by brokering an alliance between evangelicals and the Republican Party.

In this book, I use the term "Christian Right" broadly to refer to all the key actors who built a strategic coalition between evangelicals and a partisan conservative agenda, not just the advocacy groups and leaders who claimed this label. This broad definition is important because many key evangelical leaders like Billy Graham distanced themselves from the so-called Christian Right, even as they worked behind the scenes to mobilize evangelicals behind a conservative political agenda. In the United States, this Christian Right movement united a broad set of activists around a shared narrative of Christian nationalism, a diagnosis of "secular humanism" as the problem, and the Republican Party as the solution.[17] From 1980 to 2004, this national Christian Right movement took power within the Republican Party and unified rank-and-file evangelicals as a voting bloc.

By contrast, Canada did not experience the same kind of culture war polarization over moral issues from the 1970s through the 1990s, even though the Canadian public was privately divided in their attitudes toward abortion, sexuality, and gay rights.[18] During this period, Canada still contained a homegrown Christian Right, networks of activists who sought to build a coalition between evangelicals and right-wing politics.[19] As early as 1974, Baptist minister Ken Campbell founded Renaissance Canada to bring Canadian evangelicals into conservative politics and the pro-life movement. In the 1980s, Canadian evangelical activists founded two different political parties, the Reform Party and the Christian Heritage Party, which linked traditional morality to a broader conservative ideological agenda.

But Canada's would-be Christian Right failed to broker an American-style coalition for two reasons. Facing outward, social conservative activists found it more difficult to get their "moral issues" of abortion, homosexuality, and marriage policy onto the political agenda. Facing inward, Christian Right activists in Canada were less successful at pouring their national evangelical subculture into a partisan mold. For example, the Evangelical Fellowship of Canada was founded in 1964 as a parallel organization to the U.S. National Association of Evangelicals. While the EFC took a strong pro-life stance during this period, it also advocated on a broader set of issues, like poverty, that cut across partisan boundaries. Throughout the 1980s, the EFC deliberately defined their moderate, accommodating approach in opposition to the U.S. Christian Right. Gladys

Ganiel has described the EFC as "mediating evangelicals," because they worked to find common ground between evangelicals and other groups in an accommodating spirit.[20]

This contrast shows that the cultural shifts of modernity do not always force evangelicals to embrace a culture war model of public religion. Throughout the twentieth century, evangelicals in both the United States and Canada struggled with the same distinctively modern challenge: how to reformulate their constructions of orthodoxy to engage an increasingly pluralized public sphere.[21] In *Public Religions in the Modern World*, José Casanova concluded that modernity did not kill religion or relegate it to the private sphere, as many prophets of secularization had foretold. Instead, modernity undermined the ability of dominant religions to provide a taken-for-granted "sacred canopy" for public life. In response, religious traditions re-organized themselves to speak as one voice among many, to articulate a more explicit vision for public life in relationship to competing visions.[22] But waging a culture war was not the only way that American evangelicals might have reformulated their orthodoxy to engage a pluralized public sphere.[23] In Canada, evangelicals responded to the 1960s by developing new tools to engage their society in constructive ways as a cultural minority. Canadian evangelicals remained politically diverse, even as their society was rocked by the trends associated with modernity: urbanization, cultural pluralism, the sexual revolution, the growth of higher education, and the growth of "postmaterialist" forms of expressive individualism.

By comparing the United States and Canada, we can better recognize the historically contingent events that made the culture war narrative more powerful among U.S. evangelicals. As Nancy Ammerman has argued, the restructuring of American religion is better understood as a historically contingent outcome, driven by strategic action within religious institutions in response to the forces of modernity.[24] In the United States, the Christian Right was successful at getting its "moral issues" on the political agenda by seizing power in the Republican Party. But it was also successful as a movement within evangelicalism, a movement that created a new configuration of evangelical "orthodoxy" that linked this religious tradition to a broader conservative political movement.

POLITICAL CONSERVATIVES AND THE CONSTRUCTION OF U.S. EVANGELICAL IDENTITY, 1910–1990

To outside observers, the emergence of the New Christian Right in the 1980s came as a great surprise. How did a small network of political activists unite these diverse groups so quickly around a shared political vision? In fact, it took forty years for Christian Right activists to unite

American evangelicals behind a conservative political agenda. Their efforts often went unnoticed, because they were focused inward: on the task of forming evangelicals into political conservatives. Historians were wrong to characterize the Christian Right as an emotional backlash to the 1960s. In the United States, evangelicals initiated an alliance between small-government conservatives as early as the 1940s, long before Vietnam, Woodstock, or *Roe v. Wade.*

It is overly simplistic to claim that the Christian Right "hijacked" American evangelicalism, because evangelicalism has no central "cockpit" that can be stormed. American evangelicalism is best described as a coalition: a decentralized movement of local churches, denominations, parachurch ministries, and entrepreneurial media empires.[25] Before the 1980s, theologically conservative Protestants were fragmented into separate groups who viewed one another with suspicion: Southern fundamentalists, Northern fundamentalists, Northern neo-evangelicals, Southern Baptists, Pentecostals, charismatics, and theological conservatives within mainline denominations. Conservative Protestants have always been prone to fission and infighting, because *anyone* could lay claim to legitimate authority in a culture that valued scripture as the sole source of truth.[26] The challenge for the U.S. Christian Right was to overcome these fractious tendencies, to get these diverse religious streams to identify with an overarching, evangelical movement, united by a shared political agenda.

Instead of the hijacking metaphor, it is more helpful to think of evangelicalism as a fleet of ships, which the Christian Right gathered in open sea and turned to sail in the same direction. Conservative Protestants are known for three waves of political activism that occurred in the 1920s, the 1950s, and the 1980s.[27] But in between these periods, evangelicals never truly retreated from politics.[28] Instead, networks of politically conservative evangelicals continued to organize within their subculture in the 1940s, the 1960s, and the 1970s. During periods of abeyance, activists focused on the long-term task of crafting a shared narrative of Christian nationalism and socializing rank-and-file evangelicals into this narrative.[29] The "New" Christian Right was the culmination of more than forty years of continuous organizing by politically conservative evangelicals. By the 1980s, conservative elites were able to turn evangelicalism like a fleet of ships because they had spent the last forty years linking evangelical identity to right-wing politics.

In the nineteenth century, American evangelicals enthroned themselves as the nation's unofficial established religion, despite the formal separation of church and state. Protestants shared an optimistic narrative of Christian nationalism, a mandate to "Christianize" the social order through both evangelism and social reform.[30] Evangelicals waged crusades against slavery, vice, and alcohol, as part of their triumphalist, social gospel mission to build a more just and equal society. Politicians like William Jennings Bryan mixed moralistic crusades against the teaching of evolution with a populist economic platform.[31] Evangelical reformers ascribed to an optimistic, postmillennial theology: humanity would progress toward a golden age, ushering in the return of Christ.[32] But as fundamentalists split from mainline denominations between 1919 and 1936, they embraced a more pessimistic, premillennial view of the end-times, predicting that society would continue to get worse until Christ returned.[33]

In the 1920s, fundamentalists sensed that Protestants were losing the cultural hegemony that they had enjoyed in the nineteenth century, as Catholic immigration increased, the educational system became more secular, and the teaching of evolution spread. To preserve their "Christian nation" from divine destruction, fundamentalists organized to maintain Prohibition, combat vice, and to keep the Catholic Al Green from winning the White House in 1928. But Fundamentalists grew pessimistic in the 1930s as their political gains evaporated. President Franklin Roosevelt repealed Prohibition in 1933, and Catholics gained growing influence in Washington and across northern cities. During the Scopes trial, fundamentalists were ridiculed in the national press for trying to ban the theory of evolution from the public schools. The Scopes trial brought a bitter end to William James Bryan's career, and convinced many conservative Protestants that their society had turned against them.[34] In the 1930s, fundamentalists began building a new empire of Protestant institutions, to separate themselves from the world and modernist theological influences.[35]

But even as fundamentalists built separate institutions and disparaged social reform, they never completely withdrew from politics. Even in separation, fundamentalists continued to nurse their sense of responsibility for American culture—and their entitlement to preside over the nation's civil religion.[36] By the 1940s, theologically conservative Protestants were united by their moral crusade against communism. Since fundamentalists interpreted world events within the unfolding drama of global missions, Communism became the mortal enemy of Christianity, a plot by Satan himself to destroy the church.[37] Crusading against communism, some fundamentalist elites came to see small-government conservatives as allies. Though fundamentalists had been politically marginal during the Great Depression, their fatalistic end-times prophecies often had a partisan edge: for example, Roosevelt's New Deal was interpreted as part of Satan's communist plot to destroy America in the end-times. In 1931, northern fundamentalist preacher Carl McIntire formed an association of fundamentalist churches, the American Council of Christian Churches, which attacked mainline Protestant leaders in the National Council of

Churches as communist infiltrators. In 1955, McIntire began using his radio show to promote an anti-communist, political right agenda, along with many other right-wing and conservative Christian personalities.[38]

From its founding in 1943, the National Association of Evangelicals identified with the Republican Party, feeling that Democrats were too soft on communists and too closely allied with Catholics and other religious minorities. This "neo-evangelical" movement blamed their fundamentalist forebears for retreating too quickly from public life in the 1930s, ceding too much influence to mainline Protestants.[39] To build power, theologically conservative Protestants needed to overcome their sectarian divisions and stop dividing their votes along partisan lines. Though the NAE professed to be a nonpartisan organization, their public statements directly paralleled Republican campaign messages in their attacks on Democrats, Catholic influences, and domestic liberals with communist sympathies. In 1952, Billy Graham worked behind the scenes to rally northern evangelicals behind Dwight D. Eisenhower, based on his willingness to serve as high priest of this Protestant, anti-communist civil religion.[40] Neo-evangelicals like Graham and fundamentalists like McIntire disagreed over rhetorical tone and strategy, but they shared a common narrative of Christian nationalism: casting themselves as Christian patriots in a global struggle against godless communism and its domestic sympathizers.

But until the 1960s, conservative Protestants remained sharply divided along regional lines, as Southern evangelicals held fast to the Democratic Party. Even though Southern Fundamentalist activists like Billy James Hargis ranted against communism and its pink sympathizers in the Democratic Party, few Southern pastors were willing to preach against the party that had lifted their congregation out of the Great Depression.[41] The Southern Baptist Convention also refused to join northern evangelicals in their defense of school prayer and devotional Bible reading, in response to Supreme Court rulings in 1962 and 1963 that limited these traditional practices.[42] Unlike Northern evangelicals, Southern Baptists did not feel threatened by secularism as a rival ideology, since both of these rulings went largely unenforced in small-town Southern settings. Because Southern Baptists enjoyed unquestioned hegemony over regional public life, they saw the separation of church and state as a tool to combat Catholic interests in the public schools.[43]

Before the 1970s, Northern evangelicals were also hesitant to partner with Southern Fundamentalists because of their vocal opposition to the civil rights movement. Southern anti-communist crusaders like Bob Jones Jr. shared Graham's conservative politics, but they also shamelessly defended racial segregation. Responding to the civil rights movement, Billy Graham drew on his Southern roots and his Northern alliance to broker a moderate position on race that could bring Southern evangelicals along with an evolving nationwide consensus. In the late 1960s, Southern Fundamentalists softened their opposition to racial integration, while Northern evangelicals like Graham moved rightward, blaming the civil rights movement for sowing the seeds of urban violence.[44] In the 1970s, white evangelicals converged on a color-blind conservative stance: supporting racial equality in theory but opposing social policy measures to remedy racial inequality.[45] Once former segregationists like Jerry Falwell sang from the same hymnbook as racial moderates like Billy Graham, a truly national Christian Right movement could take shape.

Northern and Southern evangelicals began to elaborate a shared narrative of Christian nationalism, drawing on themes that first emerged in Southern California in the 1950s and 1960s. California became a crucible for right-wing politics after the Dust Bowl brought evangelicals from Texas and Oklahoma to work in the defense industry. These Southern migrants arrived as loyal Democrats who favored a mix of economic populism and traditional morality. But in the 1940s and 1950s, Sun Belt evangelicals clashed with California's fragmented culture, militant labor movement, and a Democratic establishment that despised their old-time religion and feared their provincial Southern ways. California's budding conservative movement recognized a strategic opportunity. From 1940 to 1960, California's economic conservatives and intellectual conservatives began working closely with moral conservatives to rally evangelicals behind a consistent small-government agenda. Together, this network of activists forged an updated narrative of Christian nationalism that defined a clearer partisan enemy. The old narrative had framed international communism as the primary adversary; the new narrative painted the domestic "liberal establishment" as the enemy of patriotic, godly Americans.[46]

Right-wing philanthropists began pouring financial support into California's evangelical ministries, leaders, and schools to promote this conservative vision of Christian patriotism.[47] Since World War II, right-wing philanthropists like J. Howard Pew and Richard DeVos had funded efforts to rally Christian support for free-market capitalism by articulating a philosophy of "Christian economics."[48] In the 1950s and '60s, right-wing businessmen adopted a new strategy: funding evangelical institutions that promised to make Christians into political conservatives as part of their primary religious socialization.[49] In 1951, Bill Bright raised money to launch Campus Crusade for Christ by pledging to convert California's university students into God-fearing, patriotic conservatives. Conservative patronage helped Pepperdine University grow from a small Church of Christ school into an ideological counterweight to California's liberal public universities. This investment paid off in the 1970s, as California's evangelicals built national Christian media empires that promoted their conservative Christian Americanism through television, radio, and books.[50]

In the United States, Christian radio played a critical role in promoting conservative politics among rank-and-file evangelicals. During the 1970s, entrepreneurial preachers like Pat Robertson and Jim Bakker expanded communications empires into radio, television, cable, and satellite. Likewise, psychologist James Dobson founded a media empire in 1977 that provided family and relationship advice from a Christian perspective. By 1984, Dobson's Focus on the Family had 400 employees and a daily 30-minute program heard on 400 radio stations. But in these early years of Christian radio and television, the Federal Communications Commission routinely invoked the Fairness Doctrine to rein in right-wing broadcasters.[51] After the Fairness Doctrine was eliminated in 1987 under President Ronald Reagan, religious broadcasters were allowed to engage in explicitly partisan political commentary, without regard for alternative viewpoints.[52] The Fairness Doctrine swept aside, the American Christian Right gained their own media platform to promote conservative politics to a broader evangelical audience.[53]

By the 1960s, evangelicals had also forged grassroots relationships with small-government conservatives through their public school activism and anti-vice crusades. As early as the 1950s, evangelicals began mobilizing to protect their children from hostile cultural influences: pornography, sexual education, homosexual teachers in the public schools, and "dirty books" in the curriculum that undermined "mainstream" values. These crusades were run largely by middle-class housewives, who feared that Christian parents were losing their ability to pass on their values to the next generation.[54]

When evangelical activists failed to reform the public schools, they began forming private Christian schools through their churches. In 1947, the NAE formed the National Association of Christian Schools as an affiliate board to oversee the evangelical school movement, and by 1965, the NACS had built a directory of 228 schools. Withdrawing into private Christian schools, white evangelicals emphasized that their primary concern was to pass on religious and moral values to their children. But in practice, parents' moral concerns were linked to inequalities of race, space, and class, since Christian schools were also a way to opt out of busing and school integration.[55] White evangelicals were fighting to shield their children from secularism, but also from cultural influences that they associated with downward mobility: drugs, countercultural youth movements, and contact with racial minorities.

Amid the turmoil of the 1960s, suburban churches and Christian schools became islands of security for white middle-class evangelicals, where they could shield their families from the dangers of the secular, multicultural city.[56] Soon, their private Christian empire was threatened by the specter of government power. In 1964, evangelicals in California mobilized against state-level fair housing legislation, claiming that it violated the sacredness of private property and gave government the dictatorial power to interfere with church properties and religious schools.[57] Defending their private Christian empires from civil rights legislation, white evangelicals began to link their moral concerns to the dangers of an activist liberal government.[58]

In the early 1970s, this seasoned army of school-based activists built a Christian women's movement to defend marriage and traditional gender roles.[59] Evangelical women were recruited into this Christian women's movement through new parachurch ministries that offered practical advice on marriage, parenting, and biblical motherhood.[60] These ministries brought together women from diverse theological backgrounds—Baptist, Pentecostal, charismatic, even Catholic—around a common identity as conservative Christian women. This "pro-family" women's movement gained national visibility as it collided with the feminist and gay rights movements. In 1971, Catholic conservative Phyllis Schafly built a state-by-state campaign to block the Equal Rights Amendment by recruiting from the ranks of this Christian women's movement, who had united across sectarian divides in their sisterhood of godly submission.[61] In 1977, the Florida housewife Anita Bryant became a national hero among evangelicals for her campaign to block a Miami city ordinance that would prevent schools from discriminating against homosexual teachers.[62]

In the late 1970s, New Right activists Paul Weyrich and Ed McAteer build a network that became known as the New Christian Right: Robert Grant's *Christian Voice*, Robert Billings' *National Christian Action Coalition*, Jerry Falwell's *Moral Majority*, and James Robison's *Religious Roundtable*. The network launched its first national campaign in 1978, when the IRS threatened to revoke the tax-exempt status of Christian academies that preserved de facto segregation. According to Christian Right architect Paul Weyrich, "what galvanized the Christian community was not abortion, school prayer, or the ERA. . . . I am living witness to that because I was trying to get those people interested in those issues and I utterly failed." Instead, Weyrich found that it was Jimmy Carter's intervention against the Christian schools that threatened evangelicals the most. While evangelicals were troubled about abortion, school prayer, and feminism, many preferred to respond by living faithfully within a separate Christian subculture. But when the federal government took action to regulate Christian schools, "suddenly it dawned on them that they were not going to be able to be left alone to teach their children as they pleased." At this stage, evangelicals had not yet identified abortion as a defining "moral issue"; instead, they united politically to defend Christian schools and oppose gay rights.

It was not until 1980 that evangelicals became united in their opposition to abortion, after a concerted campaign to attract greater Protestant support for the pro-life movement. In 1974, the Southern Baptist Convention passed a ruling to reaffirm their support for therapeutic abortion, and even many politically conservative fundamentalists like Rev. W. A. Criswell still praised *Roe v. Wade*. Frustrated by the lack of evangelical outrage, a network of political conservatives and pro-life evangelicals worked to rally their religious subculture against abortion. Their cause was aided by Francis Schaeffer, an eccentric Protestant intellectual who denounced abortion as an expression of secular humanism, the dangerous ideology that humanity was the measure of all things. Secular humanism, not communism, became the primary enemy for the nascent Christian Right, and abortion became the issue that most clearly dramatized the dangers of secular humanism.[63]

By the early 1980s, Christian Right activists had clearly defined abortion as a "moral issue" that defined the boundaries of evangelical orthodoxy. Their partisan narrative of Christian nationalism became a cultural anchor that defined the national evangelical movement. This narrative contained a clear diagnostic frame, placing the blame squarely on "secular humanism" and "liberals" for causing America's woes. It also contained a prognostic frame, that electing "godly leaders" through the Republican Party was the solution.[64] Along the way, the Christian Right had to overcome resistance within the evangelical subculture to their desired political coalition. In the 1970s, political conservatives contended with alternative evangelical voices who opposed an alliance between their faith and right-wing politics. These critics included theological moderates in the Southern Baptist convention, who wanted to preserve freedom of conscience on issues like abortion.[65] Other critics included an emerging evangelical Left, who supported the civil rights movement, opposed the Vietnam War, and gravitated toward the Democratic Party.[66] From the late 1970s to the early 1980s, the Christian Right deftly marginalized these alternative voices, by challenging their moral standing as "true" evangelicals.

When persuasion failed, the Christian Right wielded more coercive forms of power to silence political diversity within evangelicalism. In 1979, Fundamentalists launched a stunning takeover of the Southern Baptist Convention, which was orchestrated by two Christian Right power brokers, Morton Blackwell and Ed McAteer.[67] This victory was critical to enforcing political conformity among evangelicals, since the Southern Baptist Convention was the nation's largest Protestant denomination, with evangelicalism's most sophisticated network of seminaries and denominational media. Before the Christian Right takeover, the SBC took moderate positions on abortion and opposed school prayer. The denomination's Christian Life Commission focused its policy analysis on poverty and other social justice issues, as well as opposition to gambling and support for church-state separation. But after "ultra-conservatives" took over the denomination's infrastructure, the SBC abruptly changed its stance on these issues to fit Christian Right ideology.[68]

Under the new leadership of Richard Land, the Christian Life Commission became a mouthpiece for official evangelical stances on the "moral issues," and eliminated moderate or liberal-leaning social policy stances that conflicted with a broad conservative political agenda.[69] Conflict between Southern Baptist moderates and conservatives was as much about partisanship and competing views of church-state separation as it was about theological differences. After all, many of the "moderates" in the Southern Baptist Convention were as theologically conservative as Billy Graham, and many of them held morally traditional perspectives on sexuality and abortion as matters of personal conscience. The real problem with Southern Baptist moderates was that they supported the separation of church and state and opposed the combative tone of Christian Right politics.

Once these dissenting voices were silenced, the Christian Right narrative of Christian nationalism became a cultural anchor that united the national evangelical movement. From the 1980s to the 2000s, a variety of Christian Right leaders and interest groups rose and fell from the public eye: the Moral Majority of the 1980s, the Christian Coalition of the 1990s. In the late 1990s, some evangelical streams of the pro-life movement embraced more militant forms of pro-life direct action, when electoral politics failed. In the 2004 election, Focus on the Family stepped into a leadership vacuum, along with its affiliate, the Family Research Council.[70] Even though leaders and advocacy groups came and went, they all appealed to this narrative of Christian nationalism as a constitutive element of evangelical identity. This narrative served as a cultural anchor that bound the Christian Right together over time. By contrast, Canada's "mediating evangelicals" played a far more important role in the development of Canadian evangelical identity.

MEDIATING LEADERSHIP AND THE CONSTRUCTION OF CANADIAN EVANGELICAL IDENTITY, 1910–1990

Canadian evangelicals responded differently to the 1960s, in part because institutional differences within national Protestant life were already in place by the 1940s. In the late nineteenth century, Canadian Protestants were united by their mandate to transform "The Dominion of Canada into the Dominion of the Lord."[71] Inspired by this optimistic narrative of Christian nationalism, evangelicals rallied for evangelism, social service, and anti-vice crusades. By the 1910s, Canadian fundamentalists began to separate from mainline Protestant denominations, and built a distinct network of religious institutions to resist theological modernism, new historical criticism, and the teaching of evolution. But the boundaries between evangelicals and mainline Protestants remained fuzzier in Canada, as many moderate evangelicals continued to operate between both camps until the 1960s.[72] Canadian evangelicals never united around a rival narrative of Christian nationalism, framed in opposition to communism or liberal politics.[73] By contrast, anti-communism became a unifying moral crusade for U.S. evangelicals in the 1940s and 1950s, which bound their movement together across sectarian and regional divides. Because Canadian evangelicals did not forge an early alliance with right-wing politics in the 1940s, this period of institution-building set the stage for how evangelicals would respond to the 1960s.

At the turn of the twentieth century, many theologically conservative Protestants became skeptical of the social gospel and its optimistic narrative of Christian nationalism.[74] But Canadian evangelicals never rallied around an alternative civil religion, a counter-narrative of Christian nationalism that enshrined laissez-faire economics instead of the social gospel. In response to the Great Depression, Protestant leaders headed up two radical social experiments on the Canadian prairies. In 1935, the fundamentalist radio preacher William Aberhart helped found Alberta's Social Credit party, which proposed a simple solution to end the depression: to print and distribute new money. In 1932, Baptist minister Tommy Douglas helped found the Co-operative Commonwealth Federation, an alliance between farmers and organized labor that would later become the New Democratic Party. As premier of Saskatchewan, Douglas went on to implement the country's first socialized medicine program.

While Tommy Douglas was criticized by fundamentalist Baptists for his liberal theology, this mixture of religious and economic populism still found broad resonance among working-class and rural evangelicals across the Canadian prairies.[75] Canada's labor movement maintained a generally positive relationship with working-class religious traditions after World War II.[76] In 1953, Dutch Reformed immigrants to Ontario formed the Christian Labour Association of Canada, a Christian union based on principles of cooperation instead of class conflict. Though marginal to the broader labor movement, the CLAC influenced Canadian evangelicalism by making a theological case for unions from a non-Marxian, biblical perspective.[77] In 1955, Pentecostal lay preacher Sam Jenkins was elected president of the Marine Worker and Boilermakers Union, while simultaneously active as an evangelist for the Pentecostal

Association of Canada. Explaining his dual vocation, Jenkins stated, "I am my brother's keeper—against thieves, murderers, extortioners, and laws that discriminate against him. Therefore, I will join with him to fight a bad law. When I do so, I am helping to bear his burden, thus fulfilling the law of Christ."[78]

Until the 1960s, theologically conservative Protestants lacked a separate identity as "evangelicals," because the United Church of Canada remained the dominant voice for Canadian Protestants.[79] Founded in 1925 as a merging of Congregationalists, Methodists, and Presbyterians, the United Church brought together evangelical theology and social gospel optimism under one roof. This changed in the early 1960s, when denominational elites in the United Church of Canada rolled out a controversial "New Curriculum" for Sunday school and Christian education. The New Curriculum horrified many laypeople with its liberal theology, critical views of biblical authority, and progressive pedagogy. In the late 1960s, United Church denominational elites began to soften their opposition to premarital sex and advocate for legalized abortion.[80] Theologically conservative Protestants began forming groups to represent "evangelicals" as a distinct voice, since the United Church of Canada could no longer be trusted as the Protestant standard-bearer.[81]

Even so, many of these new groups took a more thoroughly nonpartisan approach than the Christian Right, working as mediating leaders to find common ground between evangelicals and other groups.[82] For example, the Evangelical Fellowship of Canada was founded in 1964 as a parallel organization to the U.S. National Association of Evangelicals. In 1983, the EFC hired its first full-time executive director, Brian Stiller, who pushed the organization to publish statements on policy issues and meet with public officials.[83] While the EFC took the same pro-life, pro-family stances as the NEA, it also advocated on a wider set of issues that included poverty and homelessness.[84] Their mediating approach was apparent in a 1990 vote on abortion, when the EFC broke with the pro-life movement to support a compromise bill, concerned that an all-or-nothing approach would leave Canada with no abortion law at all.[85] Likewise, Focus on the Family Canada was established in 1983 in British Columbia as an offshoot of James Dobson's American organization. During the 1980s and 1990s, FOFC carefully branded itself as a distinctively "Canadian" group, by adopting a less combative tone, focusing on education, and avoiding policy advocacy that might associate it with the U.S. Christian Right.[86]

To justify their mediating approach, the Evangelical Fellowship of Canada appealed to well-established narratives in Canadian Protestant life. Unlike their American counterparts, Canada's Protestants had always been forced to recognize that their nation had two traditions of civil religion: the Anglo, Protestant nationalism of Ontario, and the Franco-phone, Catholic nationalism of Quebec. In many provinces, this dual civil religion was institutionalized in separate, state-funded Catholic school systems. Multiculturalism did not threaten Anglo Protestants because it was historically defined in opposition to Quebec nationalism; hence, it validated the rights of Protestant minorities in a Catholic-dominated context. During Canada's centennial celebrations of 1967, Protestants joined in public expressions of civil religion that enshrined multiculturalism as part of Canada's evolving national identity.[87] Thus, Canada's Protestant civil religion had long been more pragmatic and accommodating, more influenced by the priestly Anglican narratives of the British Empire than the prophetic jeremiads of the frontier preacher.[88] Militant fundamentalists also composed a smaller share of the Canadian evangelical coalition, and a larger share came from theologically moderate Baptists, Mennonites, and Reformed denominations.[89]

Through the 1980s and 1990s, mediating evangelicals played a greater role in Canada, while their American counterparts were drowned out by polarizing right-wing leaders. In the United States, the moderate National Association of Evangelicals was pushed aside in the 1980s, by Christian Right leaders like Jerry Falwell, Pat Robertson, and James Dobson, who spoke directly to the rank-and-file through their own Christian radio and television empires.[90] Since the NAE represented a network of denominational elites and parachurch organizations, they had no direct influence on congregations or laypeople.[91] By contrast, the Evangelical Fellowship of Canada remained the primary national voice for evangelicals through the 1990s, even though multiple provincial and national organizations sprung up to mobilize evangelicals behind a "pro-family" agenda.[92] Right-wing Christian activists in Canada did not have their own TV and radio empires that would enable them to speak directly to people in the pews, because religious broadcasting had been systematically blocked by federal regulation.[93]

The U.S. Christian Right was also able to promote their policy agenda through Christian TV and radio, in ways that were legally impossible in Canada. For example, Pat Robertson founded the National Legal Foundation in 1985, the Christian Coalition in 1989, and the American Center for Law and Justice in 1990. These interest groups freely promoted their ideology and policy goals through Robertson's own Christian Broadcasting Network. In 1988, Robertson also used this TV and radio platform to promote his failed bid for the Republican presidential nomination.[94] Because Canada lacked these Christian media empires, the Evangelical Fellowship of Canada played a more important role through the 1990s than their American counterpart, the National Association of Evangelicals.

THE CHRISTIAN RIGHT FACES OUTWARD: GETTING MORAL ISSUES ONTO THE PARTY AGENDA

In both the United States and Canada, socially conservative movements have sought to get "moral issues" on the political agenda in both countries. But Canadian political institutions made it much more difficult for Christian Right activists to advance their issues through electoral politics.[95] As a result, Canada's major political parties failed to mobilize the electorate around culture war divides, and these issues were kept outside the boundaries of politics.[96]

In part, "moral issues" were kept out of electoral politics because Canada followed a different pathway of political development.[97] Although both the United States and Canada are federal systems, the Canadian federal government and Supreme Court had greater jurisdiction to strike down abortion laws and anti-sodomy codes on a more final basis.[98] In Canada, the gay rights struggle was more decisively national, because anti-sodomy codes and marriage rights were federal issues.[99] After Canada adopted the Charter of Rights and Freedoms in 1982, such issues were often decided by courts, with few opportunities for electoral mobilization.[100] In the United States, social conservatives could fight national trends on a state and local level.[101]

Canada's lack of a culture war also reflected differences in party strategy. Demographic differences between the countries made it riskier for politicians to appeal to religious traditionalism. Canada has a smaller proportion of evangelicals than the United States, and lacks a regional stronghold of religious conservatism like the South. Moreover, the median voter in the United States is more religious and morally conservative than in Canada, even when evangelicals are combined with traditional Catholics and observant members of other faiths.[102] Because Canada secularized more rapidly than the United States, politicians during this period always had to consider backlash from nonreligious and less religiously observant voters if they appealed to sectarian identities.[103]

These different political strategies were also shaped by power struggles within the conservative movement itself. In the 1980s, the U.S. Christian Right conducted a hostile takeover of the Republican Party, pushing aside a moderate, pro-choice establishment that sought compromise on divisive cultural issues.[104] During this same period in Canada, the Progressive Conservative establishment was more successful at marginalizing social conservatives that did not fit their party's moderate center-right strategy. Some of these elites identified with Canada's Red Tory tradition, which sought to balance free enterprise with strong national institutions that served the common good.[105] In Canada, these party leaders fought off social conservatives by drawing on institutional rules that favored party discipline and invoking cultural norms that ruled "issues of conscience" outside the boundaries of politics.[106] Thus, Christian Right and pro-life activists were able to infiltrate the Republican Party in the 1970s and '80s in ways not possible under the Canadian system.

This is particularly clear in the case of abortion, which never emerged as a salient political issue in Canada as it did in the United States. In 1988, the Supreme Court of Canada declared the country's abortion law to be unconstitutional in its entirety, as a breach of the woman's right to security of the person under the Charter of Rights and Freedoms. The Progressive Conservative government then introduced a compromise bill to restore federal restrictions on abortion, and both Conservatives and Liberals freed their members to vote their conscience, except for cabinet ministers. The 1990 parliamentary vote on abortion did not break down partisan lines, and so neither Progressive Conservatives nor Liberals became associated with pro-choice or pro-life politics after the bill was defeated in the Senate.[107]

Since then, Canada has gone without federal restrictions on abortion, besides the standards of healthcare providers and provincial Medicare. Even among developed countries with permissive abortion laws, Canada stands out for refraining to regulate late-term abortions after the point of viability. This is not because Canadians are unusually libertarian in their beliefs about abortion: though a majority of Canadians were pro-choice in 2012, a vast majority preferred some restrictions on abortion over no laws at all.[108] Rather, it is because Canada's major parties have refused to let the issue come up for a vote since 1990. Abortion did not fuel partisan polarization in Canada because pro-life activists have been consistently thwarted in getting this issue onto electoral politics.[109]

Canada came close to party conflict around "moral issues" in the 1990s, after a Western populist movement gave birth to the Reform Party. Many of the key figures in the Reform Party were evangelical Christians, including its leader, Preston Manning. But Manning actively downplayed abortion as a policy priority, promising to represent the views of his constituents rather than his own moral beliefs.[110] As Reform attempted to win national representation in the late 1990s, party leaders tried to avoid public association with an evangelical constituency. When party leaders like Preston Manning and Stockwell Day made passing references to religion, they were pilloried in the media and punished by voters.[111] "Moral issues" were even further marginalized after the Reform Party merged with a group of Conservatives to form the Canadian Alliance in 2000.

Since the 1990s, Canadian public opinion has only shifted further toward libertarian or self-expressive values, favoring more liberal policies on abortion and homosexuality.[112] But unlike many European countries, Canada retains pockets of moral conservatism that can be mobilized politically. Indeed, many morally conservative voters were attracted to the Reform and Alliance Parties from 1996 to 2000, despite the lack of public rhetoric around morality.[113] During the same period, the older Catholic-Protestant cleavage also continued to shape voting patterns, as Canadian Catholics still voted Liberal in large numbers.[114] Political rhetoric about religion and morality was largely excluded from electoral politics, yet religion continued to matter in Canadian politics. The challenge for candidates, parties, and interest groups has been to appeal to moral conservatives without provoking backlash from secular voters.

Until the early twenty-first century, it seemed clear that Canadian evangelicals had followed a more politically moderate path than their American counterparts. Scholars generally agreed that Canada had avoided a culture war, and that an American-style Christian Right could not take root on Canadian soil. But this contrast between the United States and Canada broke down in 2004, when the Supreme Court of Canada affirmed that same-sex marriage legislation was constitutional under the Charter and under the jurisdiction of the federal Parliament. For the first time in decades, Liberals and Conservatives took opposing stances on a "moral issue" with potential salience to traditional religious voters. The Liberal Party moved to legalize same-sex marriage and enforce a clear partisan stance on the issue. In 2005, Liberal prime minister Paul Martin introduced a same-sex marriage bill, and expelled a junior minister from cabinet for voting against it.[115] Then in opposition, the Conservatives did not enforce a party position, but nearly all Conservative MPs opposed the bill. In the 2004 election, the Liberal Party attacked Stephen Harper and his party as right-wing religious extremists, puppets of the un-Canadian Bush administration.[116]

The gay marriage debate gave new visibility to more overtly partisan Christian Right leaders and groups in Canada, who wished to rally evangelicals behind a broader conservative agenda. During the 1990s, Canadian evangelicals had formed a variety of advocacy groups, but groups like the Evangelical Fellowship of Canada generally took a moderate and nonpartisan approach to meeting with all parties. Since its founding in 1983, Focus on the Family Canada had avoided the kind of overt political advocacy that might associate it with the U.S. Christian Right. But prior to the 2004 election, Focus on the Family Canada released reports on MP's votes on marriage issues and launched an advertising campaign in major Canadian newspapers to rally evangelicals in support of traditional marriage. In early 2006, Focus on the Family Canada established an Ottawa office, called the Institute on Marriage and Family Canada.[117]

The gay marriage debates also helped boost openly right-wing interest groups like the Canadian Family Action Coalition, founded in 1998 to mobilize Christians as a political bloc using American-style "moral issues."

During the 2004 election, CFAC's founder Charles McVety coordinated a network of ideologically conservative organizations that worked together to rally evangelicals behind the Conservative Party. From the early to mid-2000s, an entrepreneurial set of evangelical leaders founded new interest groups to rally evangelicals against same-sex marriage: Tristan Emmanuel founded Christians in the Public Square, Craig Chandler expanded Concerned Christians Canada, and Faytene Kryskow launched 4MYCanada as a revival movement of "conservative" youth. Unlike the Evangelical Fellowship of Canada, many of these newer groups unabashedly identified themselves with the American Christian Right. For example, Charles McVety invited the former head of the Christian Coalition Ralph Reed to speak at a 2005 event in Toronto, an act that shocked the national media.[118]

Between 2000 and 2008, it seemed that Canada's Christian Right was successfully building a coalition between evangelical voters and the Conservative Party. Unlike in the United States, Canadian right-wing politicians generally avoided divisive appeals to religion and social conservatism, which had proved to be so politically damaging in the 1990s. Instead, these overtly religious appeals came from this new network of Christian Right interest groups that claimed to be distant from partisan politics, but sent clear partisan cues. The strategy was successful in building evangelical support for the Conservative Party. In 2000, Christians who believed the Bible was the literal word of God supported the right-wing Alliance Party to the Liberals by a margin of 15 points. In 2003, the Alliance merged with the Progressive Conservatives to unite the right under a new Conservative Party. By 2008, Canadians who were biblical literalists preferred Conservatives to the Liberals by a margin of 50 points.[119]

Between 2000 and 2008, Canada's political Right crafted a new strategy to mobilize religious conservatives without alienating more secular voters. Before 2000, the conservative movement had been divided between far-right and center-right, and uncertain about the place of social conservatism within their agenda. But after 2000, social conservatives found a new ally in Stephen Harper, an evangelical Christian who was formed by the Reform Party tradition of right-wing populism. In a 2003 speech, Harper called for a new alliance between "neo-cons" and "theo-cons" to blend fiscal and moral traditionalism within a shared right-wing agenda.[120] Unlike previous generations of Progressive Conservative leaders, Harper recognized religious conservatives as valuable allies.[121] At the same time, Harper was determined to avoid the missteps that had derailed other evangelical politicians like Stockwell Day.

In 2006, the Conservative Party came to power in a stunning upset that ended twelve years of Liberal rule. The new prime minister, evangelical Stephen Harper, had campaigned on the vague promise to bring same-sex marriage to an open vote while safeguarding the rights of gays and lesbians.[122] Even though Harper largely avoided culture war rhetoric, his victory was partly driven by religious factors: strong support from evangelical Protestants and morally conservative voters, and higher-than-normal support from Catholics, who were normally the base of the Liberal Party. Once in office, Harper took little substantive action on a Christian Right agenda, but he engaged in symbolic politics to appeal to morally traditional Canadians at little or no political cost.[123] After winning the 2006 election, the Harper government dodged both same-sex marriage and abortion as political issues. Conservatives held a parliamentary vote on whether to revisit gay marriage legalization, and after the vote was defeated, the government declared the matter settled. Harper's government has also refused to raise the abortion issue, following keeping this issue outside of the boundaries of politics as prior conservative leaders had done.

Even as Harper seemed to govern from the center, he also made more ideological moves calculated to stoke culture war politics.[124] For example, Harper's government proposed to deny tax credits to films with objectionable content, and then cancelled funding for Gay Pride parades.[125] In 2010, Harper's government excluded abortion from new funding to international maternal health development. The Conservative government has also made polarizing statements in support of Israel, thus currying favor with Christian Zionists like Charles McVety. In 2008, the Harper government raised the age of heterosexual consent from fourteen to sixteen, while retaining the age of homosexual consent at eighteen. Stephen Harper was able to represent himself as a strict father figure, laying down the law to protect innocent youth from "sexual predators."[126]

When gay marriage became a partisan issue, this created an opening for more partisan Christian Right interest groups in Canada.[127] Canada's would-be culture warriors faced a more unfavorable political opportunity structure, which made it more difficult to mobilize resources, get their issues onto the political agenda, and fight back against unfavorable court rulings.[128] As a result, the United States and Canada diverged sharply on gay marriage in the early 2000s. In 2004, eleven American states banned same-sex marriage, and George W. Bush won re-election with help from high turnout from evangelical voters in critical states like Ohio.[129] During the same period, Canadian social conservatives failed to influence public debate or defeat same-sex marriage, which became federal law in 2005.[130] Yet, while Canada's Christian Right failed to block gay marriage, they succeeded in uniting moral traditionalists and economic conservatives to elect Stephen Harper. In the 2000s, the Conservative Party won over a significant bloc of Canadian evangelical voters, by appealing to religious identity and traditional morality in targeted ways that avoided backlash from the broader electorate.

But despite the best efforts of conservative interest groups, Canada has not yet seen a complete culture war realignment. In a 2009 report from the Evangelical Fellowship of Canada, Don Hutchinson and Rick Hiemstra argued that evangelicals are not as strongly wedded to political conservatism as in the United States. The evangelical exodus to the Conservative Party may have been partly driven by the 2004 sponsorship scandal, a misuse of government funds that tarnished the Liberal Party's reputation. Hutchinson and Hiemstra found that each time Canadians went to the federal polls in 2004, 2006, and 2008, the Liberals only managed to hold on to roughly half of the evangelical voters they had had at the previous election. But about one-third of these evangelical voters actually moved *left*, to support the social-democratic NDP instead of the Conservative Party. In 2006, the NDP became the second-choice party for evangelical voters in Ontario and the Atlantic provinces.[131]

These trends show that many Canadian evangelicals do not view politics through a culture war lens, despite Conservative dog-whistle appeals to traditional morality and "pro-family" campaigns by Christian Right interest groups. By contrast, American evangelical support for the Republican Party remained strong through 2012, even as Democrats and alternative evangelical advocacy groups worked hard to frame progressive issues in religious and moral language. Top-down political mobilization is only half of the story. The U.S. Christian Right was more successful not just facing outward to shape electoral politics, but also facing inward to shape the evangelical subculture itself.

CONCLUSION

Comparing the United States and Canada, we see how different political institutions shaped the historical timing, form, and even tone of evangelical activism in the two countries.

These cross-national differences are consistent with the political mobilization account of the culture wars. To understand the different timing and shape of the culture wars in Canada, we must look to political party strategy, interest groups, and media rhetoric rather than to underlying divides in morality. Why did culture war politics break out in Canada in the first decade of the twenty-first century, after forty years of rapid cultural change in relative peace? The Canadian public did not suddenly become more culturally polarized. Rather, Canada's political parties were finally distinguishing themselves on same-sex marriage, after years of excluding such "moral issues" from electoral politics.

But political mobilization is only half of the story. By recognizing the Christian Right's two faces, we can better understand why the evangelical tradition has fueled very different political practices in different national contexts.[132] Throughout forty years of institution-building, U.S. Christian Right activists defined a core narrative of American evangelical identity in terms of a conservative political agenda. During the 1960s and 1970s, this partisan narrative of Christian Americanism was challenged by internal critics, like Southern Baptist moderates who advocated a mediating approach to cultural diversity. But from 1980 to the mid-2000s, the Christian Right effectively silenced and marginalized internal diversity within the religious subculture. By contrast, Canada's "mediating evangelicals" played a far more important role in the development of Canadian evangelical identity. Even though advocacy groups have emerged in Canada to mobilize evangelicals behind the Conservative Party, these efforts did not build on the same forty-year effort to define Canadian evangelical identity in partisan terms. Before the U.S. Christian Right could mobilize rank-and-file evangelicals, conservative activists had to engage in symbolic and material struggles within the religious field itself.[133] These efforts to define evangelical identity were not directly connected to particular election cycles, but they were still guided by a long-term strategic vision to create a new partisan coalition.[134]

To reshape the meaning of evangelical identity, elites had to bridge the divide between local lived religion and the halls of power. Evangelicalism remains a decentralized, entrepreneurial movement, where no single figure or organization can claim to speak for people in the pews. Christian Right elites have been successful to the extent that they can connect directly with a rank-and-file constituency and their local religious worlds. In this book, I compare local congregations in the United States and Canada, to explore how evangelical identity becomes linked to politics within the everyday religious life.

CHAPTER 2

THE BOUNDARIES OF EVANGELICAL IDENTITY

To understand how religious identity becomes linked to conservative politics, I spent a year observing in two Baptist and two Pentecostal churches, matched on either side of the U.S.-Canada border. Entering these churches as an outside observer, I learned a great deal about how theologically conservative Protestants define the boundaries of their religious subculture. Social scientists have vigorous debates about who is, and who isn't, an evangelical. Should survey researchers identify evangelicals based on theological beliefs, church affiliations, or particular practices? How important are historical divisions between Pentecostals, fundamentalists, and neo-evangelicals? But gaining entrée to local church life, I learned that the boundaries of evangelical identity were quite straightforward from the perspective of practitioners. I introduced myself as a social scientist interested in how religion informs public life, and asked their permission to observe. Pastors and laypeople had only one question: Had I made a personal decision for Christ?

My honest answers were never quite satisfactory. In my first visit to a small Pentecostal congregation in Buffalo, New York, a young woman asked me if I was a believer. She had approached me after the service, to welcome me as a fellow single woman to her church. I informed her about my research goals, and so naturally she wanted to know if I was studying her church as an insider or an outsider. I gave a long and rambling account of my own religious background, growing up as the daughter of a Baptist minister. I rattled off a list of the kinds of churches that I had attended: American Baptist, Southern Baptist, United Methodist, Presbyterian. This wasn't what she wanted to know. "So . . . you've made the decision then?" she asked, looking me up and down. My denominational background and current religious participation were irrelevant. She wanted to know if I was saved.

In these churches, there were only two kinds of Christians: born-again Christians who had made a personal decision for Christ, and nominal Christians who lacked this personal relationship with Christ. Other denominational or sectarian differences were meaningless to rank-and-file members, even though conservative Protestants once divided themselves rigidly between charismatics, Pentecostals, fundamentalists, and culture-engaging evangelicals. In both Pentecostal churches that I studied, believers were encouraged to speak "in tongues," but it was not required for salvation. Likewise, both Baptist churches avoided such "gifts of the spirit" in worship, but members were welcome to speak in tongues in their own prayer life, as long as it didn't impinge upon public worship. All four churches even disregarded the historical boundary between Catholics and Protestants; even Catholics could be sorted neatly into saved and unsaved on the basis of their personal relationship with Christ.

All four of these churches shared a sense of subcultural identity as "born-again" or evangelical Christians, which transcended the historical divisions between Baptist and Pentecostal worship and theology. In Baptist and Pentecostal churches, believers looked for the same clues to recognize whether or not I was a "true" Christian, who had made a personal decision for Christ. To be accepted as a true, evangelical Christian, it was not *really* enough to describe a born-again experience. Pastors and laypeople looked for more tangible clues that the born-again experience was real. In all four churches, a "true" conversion would naturally manifest itself in a specific set of theological beliefs, ways of reading the Bible, personal piety, and adherence to certain norms about family, gender, and sexuality.

Because the born-again experience was so private and subjective, churches used these outward signs of "true" salvation to police their subcultural boundaries. Before I could start my research at a Baptist church in Buffalo, I had to sit down with a group of deacons and answer detailed questions about my theology. I was asked to share my personal testimony, to explain why I deserved to get into heaven, and whether there were multiple paths to salvation. During my fieldwork, worshippers regularly glanced down at my Bible, or asked me which translation I preferred. I carried a copy of the New Revised Standard Version—the most common translation used by mainline Protestants, a signal that I might subscribe to liberal interpretations of the Bible. But on the other hand, my Bible was well-worn and full of bookmarks. After a few months in the field, members started to ask whether I would like to be introduced to a godly man they knew. As a single Christian woman in my late twenties, presumably I was anxious to find a husband and start a family. I did not describe myself as a born-again or evangelical Christian; I simply answered questions about my religious beliefs and background as participants inquired. Based on my answers, I was never accepted as a "good" evangelical: the kind of model believer who could be trusted to teach Sunday school. But neither was I viewed as an outsider.

This blurred insider-outsider identity gave me a valuable lens on local religious practice.[1] While I did not study the evangelical subculture as an uncritical insider, research participants showed confidence that I was saved, and hence, not a target for conversion. At a Baptist church in Buffalo, two women approached me after a church dinner, to ask whether I was a Christian. When I answered affirmatively, they erupted in delight. "We had been praying for you! We thought you were an atheist!" they confessed. "But your advisor's not a Christian?" the woman asked, implying strongly that he could not be. As a Christian in the secular Ivy Leagues, I was assumed to be embattled. I did not fit their stereotype of a hostile, secular academic, and so I was treated as an ally in the battle against secularism. As a result, participants spoke openly with me about their views of non-Christians and other out-groups, and felt comfortable using the term "we" in small group settings, implying that all present were believers. If I had presented myself as a religious outsider, I would not have learned how evangelicals map their group in social space; rather, I would have learned how evangelicals map themselves in relationship to unsaved, secular academics. My liminal status proved critical to the ethnographic findings that follow.

RESEARCH METHODS

From July 2006 until October 2007, I conducted participant-observation within two Baptist churches and two Pentecostal churches in middle-class, suburban areas of the Hamilton, Ontario and Buffalo, New York metropolitan areas. I chose to study congregations in Hamilton, Ontario and Buffalo, New York because this comparison has a straightforward theoretical interpretation: these cities are part of the same Niagara region, yet are nested within different national institutions. Buffalo, New York and Hamilton, Ontario are both medium-sized rust belt cities with similar economic and cultural profiles.[2] Indeed, during my fieldwork, I found that several of my research participants frequently traveled across the border or had family members in the other country. Studying these border cities can be considered a conservative test of cross-national differences in evangelical identity, since I would expect these differences to be larger, not smaller, in other parts of the United States and Canada.

Given the internal complexity of North American evangelical life, no two congregations could be chosen as "typical." Hence, my goal was not to compare the characteristics of all Canadian or U.S. churches based on a sample of two congregations in each country. Rather, I used these sites to rebuild theory by identifying local mechanisms within lived religion that explain how theologically similar churches produce different political orientations in the laity. Large-N survey research can only speculate about these mechanisms. To address questions of generalizability, I place these case studies in a broader context by comparing my findings to broader survey studies of American and Canadian evangelicals.[3]

To isolate the effects of cross-national differences, as opposed to differences between churches, I matched two congregations in each city as closely as possible along a number of important dimensions. Sociologists of religion have documented how religious tradition, denomination, race, national origin, socioeconomic class, lifestyle, level of strictness, size, and internal organization can serve to distinguish institutions in a multi-congregational field.[4] In choosing congregations, I carefully matched two Baptist and two Pentecostal churches from comparable denominational traditions. I chose to focus on Baptist and Pentecostal churches because Southern Baptist and Assembly of God churches have been critical bases of Christian Right organizing in the United States.[5] Furthermore, both of these denominations could be matched with similar sister denominations in Canada.[6] It is important to study both groups because they have historically organized in distinct political streams.[7] There is also a need to understand the public role of Pentecostals in international perspective, since they are the fastest-growing Christian group in the United States and the world.[8]

PORTRAITS OF FOUR CONGREGATIONS

Here, I provide a brief portrait of the four congregations that I observed during my fieldwork, highlighting ways that their unique history and identity shaped the interactions that I observed.[9] Even when congregations are matched by theological beliefs, demographic characteristics, and denominational tradition, this local particularity still matters.[10] Denominations do not foster the same degree of local homogeneity as they did in the 1950s. As a transdenominational movement, evangelicalism has become increasingly influenced by nondenominational and independent churches, as well as a dizzying array of generic "Christian" parachurch ministries.[11] Evangelical congregations often have a rather flexible relationship to their denominations, drawing music and Sunday school materials from a wide mix of generic evangelical publishers.[12]

Furthermore, Penny Edgell has shown that local congregations favor different cultural models of what local church life is all about. Some local churches think of themselves as one big "family," while others imagine themselves to be a participatory "community," a "leader" in the civic realm, or a "house of worship."[13] Conflict within congregations is often shaped by notions of "how we do church here" as much as by theological disputes.

Northtown Baptist

Northtown Baptist is allied with the Southern Baptist Convention, America's largest Protestant denomination.[14] But research participants repeatedly told me, "We're not your typical Southern Baptist Church!" They meant various things by this. First, most members did not grow up in the distinctive Southern Baptist denominational culture, having either switched from other evangelical, fundamentalist, or mainline traditions, or having converted from Catholicism. Second, Northtown's worship used contemporary music, including electric guitars and bongos, and it was not unusual for members to raise their hands in worship. I often heard it remarked that they had a more charismatic worship style that would have scandalized more traditional Southern Baptists.[15] This congregation was more open to distinctively charismatic practices like speaking in tongues, which Southern Baptist churches have historically condemned. These practices did not occur in worship, but the head pastor and several laypeople told me that they had spoken in tongues in other settings. On the other hand, I observed the distinctive markers of Southern Baptist life all around me. Most of the Sunday school classes used official Southern Baptist curriculum, although several small groups used non-denominational materials. The church also conformed to Southern Baptist beliefs about male leadership: only men were allowed to serve as elders or pastors, although there was a female "missionary" on staff.

Northtown Baptist was organized around a "community" model of congregational life, which emphasized close interpersonal relationships, widespread participation, and inclusive and democratic decision-making.[16] They also emphasized close interpersonal relationships, hosting many small groups and regularly socializing within the church. Northtown also prided itself on helping members live out their faith in the larger community.[17] Laypeople were involved in a dizzying array of ministries directed outside the congregation, which they had organized independently but with the encouragement of church leadership. Some of these ministries had become officially sponsored by the church. For example, a small group of mothers had felt called to launch a ministry to children with special needs, and undertook special training through a national parachurch organization. They convinced the pastor that Northtown should develop a special ministry for children and adults with developmental disabilities. By the time of my fieldwork, the whole congregation had embraced this ministry. Another group of laypeople were involved with a campus ministry to international students, and the congregation gave financial support to this ministry out of its budget. A third group of laypeople were involved with a "crisis pregnancy" ministry, which helped mothers to carry their pregnancies to term. This group was also working to encourage adoption within the congregation—especially adoption of children with special needs—as an expression of their pro-life commitments. Finally, Northtown hosted a ministry to people "struggling" with "same-sex attraction," which I will discuss further in chapter

4. Demographically, this was a young church, with most of the leadership in their forties and fifties. There were few people over sixty-five, because all the older members had left during a period of church conflict about fifteen years ago, under a previous pastor. There were many young families, and an overflowing nursery.

Lifeway Assembly

Lifeway Assembly is allied with the Assemblies of God, the nation's largest Pentecostal denomination. These denominational ties could be seen in the church's mission partnerships, which rallied the congregation in support of Assembly of God missionaries and church planters around the world. During my fieldwork, the church was renewing its local chapters of "Royal Rangers" and "Missionettes," youth leadership programs sponsored by the Assembly of God.[18] Lifeway Assembly also emphasized distinctive Pentecostal practices: glossalalia, miraculous healing, prophetic visions, and other personal experiences of the Holy Spirit. They also practiced expressive worship, with extended periods of contemporary praise songs, often sung with hands raised. On most Sundays, a group of five to ten people would dance "in the spirit" at the front of the auditorium, often waving large, brightly colored flags. On some Sundays, someone in the church would share "a word" or prophetic vision they had received from the Lord: usually a word of encouragement in times of trial, an assurance of God's love, or a call to greater commitment. The church taught that all believers were meant to receive the gift of tongues, and regularly offered opportunities for people to receive "more of the Holy Spirit." For example, one morning in Sunday school class, where the teacher asked if anyone in the room had not yet spoken in tongues but wished to. One young man raised his hand, and the group huddled around him to pray for an infilling of the Holy Spirit.[19] Speaking in tongues wasn't considered necessary for salvation or lay leadership, although not having that gift would have been a barrier to ordained pastoral leadership.

At the same time, many individuals in this church identified as more broadly "evangelical" or "born-again," rather than with Pentecostalism or the Assemblies of God. Many members had converted from Catholicism, and were averse to defining their faith in denominational terms—now that they had been freed from the bondage of "religion," they just wanted to follow the leading of the spirit rather than "man-made" institutions. Compared to Northtown Baptist, Lifeway members were involved with some of the same generically "evangelical" parachurch ministries and events, like the Christian music festival "Kingdom Bound" and the Cornerstone ministry to women in crisis pregnancies. Yet I often noted ways that their perceptions of "evangelical" often included prophetic and charismatic ministries that Northtown Baptist avoided. For example, Lifeway Assembly often promoted events from a broader charismatic and Pentecostal field outside of the Assemblies of God, like regional youth rallies and conferences on biblical prophesy. These events were rarely labeled as Pentecostal, charismatic or spirit-filled, even though they clearly were. In sum, Lifeway members perceived themselves to be part of a broader evangelical subculture, and did not emphasize the boundaries of Pentecostalism as opposed to other forms of evangelicalism. But this was largely because Pentecostal and charismatic traditions largely defined their notions of what constituted "generic" evangelicalism. Most laypeople were so immersed in this particular stream of the evangelical subculture, that they were only vaguely aware that their stream was only one of many.

Lifeway Assembly was organized around a "family" model of congregational life. I often heard members say that they were like a big family, and this was more than a metaphor. It was seen as desirable for children to grow up at Lifeway Assembly, marry someone from the church, and then raise their children there. Several intergenerational families there had followed just this path. The church operated its own Christian school and encouraged homeschooling, although parents were also encouraged to send their children to public schools as a way to witness to the larger community. Lifeway Assembly did not preach strict separation from the outside world; their support of homeschooling was part of a more positive emphasis on intensive Christian parenting.[20] Unlike Northtown Baptist, Lifeway Assembly did not support the same variety of ministries directed outside the congregation. In this church of more than four hundred people, less than a dozen were regularly involved in community ministries outside the congregation. Most members were intensely focused on worship and family-like intimacy within the church.

Highpoint Baptist

Highpoint Baptist is affiliated with the Fellowship of Evangelical Baptist Churches in Canada (the "F.E.B."). With a membership of more than eight hundred, Highpoint is considered one of the flagship churches of the F.E.B. in Ontario. The Fellowship of Evangelical Baptists emerged from the Fundamentalist/Modernist controversy within the Baptist Convention of Ontario and Quebec in 1928.[21] In 2000, the Fellowship included 496 churches with 65,605 members, and claims to be one of the largest evangelical denominations in Canada. Like the Southern Baptist Convention, the F.E.B. does not allow female pastors and tends to be wary of cooperating with Canada's moderate Baptist groups, who tolerate "lax" views of the authority of Scripture. Most of the church's leadership grew up in this distinctive F.E.B. denominational culture, although many members grew up in other Protestant denominations like the Plymouth Brethren—a group which they jokingly referred to as "Practically Baptist."

In Edgell's typology, Highpoint could be categorized as a "leader" congregation: they focused on presenting a strong witness to the outside world. As one of the largest congregations in their denomination, they felt a special responsibility to hold the torch for their particular brand of conservative evangelicalism. In previous summers, they had hosted a speaker series on "Hot-button" issues, which examined what the Bible had to say about diverse topics like abortion, divorce, homosexuality, and unions.

For the last five years, the congregation had been wrestling with uncertainty about their identity and mission, exploring what it meant to be a "leading" evangelical church in a post-Christian society. A set of young laity were concerned that the congregation might age rapidly if it did not attract more young families. A few of these young "movers and shakers" wanted to move beyond holding the torch for conservative evangelicalism, and to start engaging the culture in a more "missional" way.[22] Their explicit priority was to move the worship in a more contemporary direction, although a few also expressed to me that they wanted to rethink the role of women in leadership as well. But the balance of power lay with an older crowd of lifelong members, who favored a conservative style of worship and traditional hymns. For the last ten years, the congregation had compromised on a "blended" worship service that combined hymns with occasional rock songs, accompanied on guitar. During my fieldwork, I observed older and younger members deliberating together about how Canadian culture had become "post-Christian," and concluding that they had to reconsider their approach to evangelism. Highpoint members could no longer evangelize their neighbors by assuming a basic familiarity with the Christian faith—now they would need to be missionaries to a foreign culture, and start by trying to understand the world from their secular neighbors' point of view.

Grace Pentecostal

Grace Pentecostal is affiliated with the Pentecostal Assemblies of Canada (PAOC), a sister denomination of the Assemblies of God. The PAOC is the country's largest Pentecostal denomination, although Canada also hosts many independent Pentecostal and charismatic movements which are rapidly growing in importance. All the pastoral staff and most of the older members grew up in the PAOC, although many of the under-fifty members had been raised in other evangelical traditions. People regularly spoke in tongues at the Sunday worship, but miraculous healing was not as central as at Lifeway Assembly, where praying for healing was almost a weekly occurrence. At Grace Pentecostal, prayer for healing usually took place at periodic "healing" services or special worship events.

Many older members remembered a time when Grace Pentecostal was at the center of a white-hot revival, and these charismatic practices were more common, in their youth and again in the 1980s. As I heard an older woman tell an assistant pastor, "Why can't we worship like we used to? The spirit hasn't changed, and the world hasn't changed!" Later in the conversation, she told me about visiting an independent Pentecostal church, where gold dust fell from the air and the room filled with the scent of roses. Like many Pentecostal churches, Grace had gone through waves of revival over the years, where they experienced greater emotional intensity in worship and more "signs and wonders."

Grace Pentecostal was organized around a "community" model of congregational life. The church created a family-like intimacy, but it was also good at drawing in new people and making decisions that accommodated the needs of many different groups. About fifteen years ago, the church had definitively shifted toward more contemporary worship, which had alienated many of its older members. Many of the older crowd left, but those who stayed had decided to embrace a mission to reach younger generations, even though they preferred the older worship style. The congregation had quickly been replenished with young families and had developed a large youth and young adult program. This successful transition shows that Grace Pentecostal had genuine strengths in making collective decisions and moving forward together, despite disagreement.

TABLE 2.1. MATCHED CONGREGATIONS

	Buffalo, New York	Hamilton, Ontario
Baptist	Northtown Baptist Church	Highpoint Baptist Church
	400 members	900 members
	Southern Baptist Convention	Fellowship of Evangelical Baptist Churches in Canada
Pentecostal	Lifeway Assembly	Grace Pentecostal Church
	400 members	200 members
	Assemblies of God	Pentecostal Assemblies of Canada (PAOC)

RECENT HISTORICAL CONTEXT

In the United States, my fieldwork took place in the aftermath of George W. Bush's re-election and the passage of multiple state-level Defense of Marriage acts during the 2004 election cycle, both made possible through strong evangelical support. In Canada, evangelicals were wrestling with the legalization of same-sex marriage, which had gone unchecked by Stephen Harper and his Conservative government since 2006. In the United States, churches were constantly reminded of their country's military involvements in Iraq and Afghanistan, wars that had grown increasingly unpopular as they dragged on. In Canada, churches were likewise aware of their country's involvement in Afghanistan, as allies to the United States in the so-called War on Terror.

These churches also looked back on local histories of school board politics and pro-life mobilization that occurred in the 1980s and 1990s. In 1993, conservative Protestant activists in one Buffalo suburb had unsuccessfully attempted to elect a majority to area school boards.[23] During this period in Hamilton, a network of pro-family activists emerged in local school board politics, still operating during my fieldwork as the Hamilton-Wentworth Family Action Coalition. In 1992, the "Spring of Life" pro-life movement came to Buffalo, inspired by Operation Rescue and its charismatic leader, Randall Terry. Frustrated by the political process, Operation Rescue adopted the novel tactic of blocking access to clinics that performed abortions. During the period 1988 to 1989, pro-life activists in Canada joined Operation Rescue and blocked abortion access in Toronto and Kitchener, two cities within an hour's drive of Hamilton.[24] This direct rescue tactic was largely abandoned in Canada by the 1990s, because of more vigorous government prosecution of activists.[25] But from 1986 to 1998, pro-life activists in Hamilton regularly marched in protest outside of Henderson Hospital, the area's main abortion provider.[26] In 1998, an extremist pro-life activist assassinated Barnett Slepian, one of the doctors in Buffalo who performed abortions. The same year, there was a similar attempt to kill a Hamilton area doctor who performed abortions.[27] This extremist violence demoralized and divided pro-life activists in both the United States and Canada.

Lifeway had been a hotbed of pro-life activism from the late 1980s to the mid-1990s, and the group's former pastor had helped lead nonviolent protests at abortion clinics. In the late 1990s, the original activist pastor left, and his two successors embroiled the congregation in financial and sexual scandals that turned the congregation's attention inward. During the period of my fieldwork, I found that this history of activism was remembered ambivalently by the congregation. On the one hand, people were still proud of the pro-life cause, but on the other, they felt that the movement had lost its spiritual center, and become too driven by media attention and big egos. After this "season" of activism ended, the congregation moved toward more practical expressions of their pro-life values. One of these practical expressions was to encourage adoption. The lead pastor's family had adopted two children, and one white couple filled an entire pew with their ten children, with the youngest five adopted from different African countries. Another practical expression was getting involved with "crisis pregnancy" ministries in the Buffalo area.

My fieldwork also took place in the context of historical trends related to race and immigration. Given the distinctive political history of white evangelicals in the United States, it was important that all four churches were majority-white with overwhelmingly white leadership. But to make the U.S.-Canada comparison work, it was necessary to find American churches that were taking some steps toward greater racial and ethnic diversity. I quickly found that it was impossible to study Canadian evangelicalism without considering how this subculture was evolving in response to ethnic diversity. It is often assumed that immigrants to Canada bring increased religious diversity and undercut the cultural dominance of white Christians. But surprisingly, the majority of immigrants arriving to Canada are coming as Christians already, and they tend to be more religiously devout than native-born Canadians.[28] Immigration has increased the share of Canadian residents who identify with non-Christian religions, relative to residents who identify with Christianity.[29] But from an evangelical perspective, the latter category was largely composed of unsaved "nominal" Christians, who were just as "lost" as a Muslim, Hindu, or Buddhist. Hence, immigration presented an opportunity, rather than a threat to Canada's Christian identity. In surveying majority-white evangelical churches in Hamilton, I quickly found that all of the healthy congregations were focused on accommodating ethnic diversity within their religious subculture.

To match churches as closely as possible across the border, I identified American churches in which a white majority was wrestling with racial or ethnic diversity to some degree, rather than matching exclusively white churches. Yet in both American churches, white evangelicals set the political tone in public church interactions. Even in private, black and immigrant members did not express alternative perspectives on politics that drew on black Protestant or ethnic church traditions. This sampling strategy allowed me to make meaningful cross-border comparisons, while also shedding light on the distinctive characteristics of white evangelicalism in the United States.

EVANGELICAL IDENTITY: THEOLOGY, MORALITY, AND CULTURAL TENSION

Christian Smith and his collaborators have argued that evangelicals are "embattled and thriving": they strengthen group commitment by generating *cultural tension* with the society around them.[30] According to their subcultural identity theory, cultural tension is a recipe for religious vitality within culturally diverse, modern societies like the United States. Indeed, I found that all four evangelical churches drew strong boundaries between "us" and "the world," but also equipped the faithful to engage with people across those boundaries. They provided members with a vital, morally orienting identity, based on shared theology, traditional morality, and cultural tension with the broader society.

Both Baptist and Pentecostal churches stressed the same three components of conservative Protestant theology: that the Bible was the inspired word of God, that human beings were pervasively sinful, and that salvation was only possible through a commitment to Jesus Christ. Most laypeople practiced a typical form of evangelical biblicism, confident that they could directly interpret the Bible as a guidebook for living without reference to a passage's social or historical context.[31] End-time prophecy was rarely mentioned in sermons and small group discussion, although all four churches privileged the premillennialist perspective described in chapter 1. In both Baptist churches, a minority of more educated laypeople held to an amillennial view that the return of Christ will coincide with the last judgment and the end of history.[32] Both Pentecostal churches also made reference to the notion of the "Latter Rain," the belief that historical dispensations open in the same way that they close. The idea of the Latter Rain was used to encourage believers that God would pour out his spirit and the church would move powerfully and grow in numbers as they approached the end-times.[33]

All four churches promoted the same traditional model of religious familism, stressing sexual purity, gender complementarity, and clear parental authority over children.[34] Teenagers and single adults were expected to avoid sexual intimacy outside of marriage, a strict behavioral norm that put these churches in tension with the broader culture.[35] The church's family discourse stressed the complementarian ideal that a husband should lead the home and a wife should nurture children. Men and women were encouraged to conform to clear gender roles, following separate spiritual paths of "godly manhood" and "godly womanhood." But in practice, gender roles were lived out in surprisingly egalitarian ways, with a great deal of acceptance for women who worked outside of the home and flexibility in household tasks.[36] Like Sally Gallagher and John Barkowski, I found that the patriarchal "headship" model was important as a symbolic boundary-marker, even though it was flexibly applied in practice.

In both the United States and Canada, evangelical churches put great emphasis on clear parental authority over children as being critical for reproducing their religious subculture in the next generation. It is impossible to overstate the value that these churches placed on socializing children. The primary goal of marriage and family life was to raise children in the "knowledge of the Lord," so that they would build their own strong families and elevate the needs of their family above selfish desires. These churches taught an authority-minded approach to parenting, which contrasted with the more democratic or egalitarian models of mainstream parenting experts. Parents were encouraged to prize obedience in children over therapeutic self-realization. Since children's nature was inherently sinful, they could only learn respect for God's authority if they first learned it from their parents.[37] At the same time, these churches placed an equally strong emphasis on positive emotion work: praise, encouragement, and physical affection to children. Even though these churches emphasized authority, strict discipline, and the judicious use of corporal punishment, this parenting style was not truly *authoritarian*. This combination of high standards and high support resembled an *authoritative* parenting style, generally associated with positive social outcomes for children.[38] All four churches placed far more emphasis on the proper socialization of children than on proper gender roles among adult men and women.

In both countries, evangelical churches practiced an "engaged orthodoxy": they sustained a dynamic tension with their sociocultural environment, while avoiding separatism. They defended objective moral truths that applied to their society as a whole, and refused to privatize their moral beliefs. Yet none of these churches encouraged an authoritarian agenda to impose these values coercively on society. Neither did they promote a sectarian agenda, to withdraw from society to protect themselves from corroding influences. Instead, they described their society as an aggregation of individuals, who could be influenced for good or for ill through relationships. Christian morality was universally authoritative, yet practically limited in scope, so Christians must be prepared to engage constructively with people who do not share their morality. When evangelicals in these churches talked about "changing the nation" or "defending traditional values," they aspired to change individuals through personal witness and relationships, not necessarily law and social policy.

Both U.S. and Canadian churches emphasized their responsibility to promote a shared sense of moral truth in the wider society by drawing on narratives of Christian nationalism. Likewise, all four evangelical churches defined their subcultural boundaries through opposition to abortion and same-sex marriage, as "moral issues" that symbolized their nation's moral decline from Christian values. These uses of Christian nationalism were not authoritarian, since all four churches encouraged members to respect democratic norms and transform their nation through individual conversion and personal influence. But they were authority-*minded*, because they defended objective moral truths that applied to the nation as a whole.

CONSTRAINTS ON "POLITICAL" TALK

In both the United States and Canada, evangelical churches enforced a strong sense of consensus on the "moral issues" of abortion and homosexuality. This sense of consensus was more than the sum of the member's private views; one had to affirm the "right" stances on moral issues to be a good member within local church settings. Yet it was not appropriate to talk about abortion and homosexuality in "political" ways. Public, political, or civic-minded talk was patterned by each church's group style, or local customs of group interaction, just as Nina Eliasoph and Paul Lichterman have found in other civic organizations. I observed this group style within face-to-face interaction, as church members drew *group boundaries*, formed *group bonds*, and practiced *speech norms*.[39]

All four churches used abortion and homosexuality to draw group boundaries between "us" and "them," to define the relationship between evangelicals and the wider world. Challenging this surface consensus would brand one as a cultural outsider.[40] To dissent from these moral stances would have violated group bonds, or mutual responsibilities in a church setting. Members were expected to encourage one another to hold fast to evangelical orthodoxy, not to throw these essentials into doubt.[41] Members observed speech norms about how to broach the moral issues, which proscribed "spiritual" talk that focused on personal ministry and individual transformation. Thus, public interaction in these churches reinforced an official consensus on abortion and homosexuality, but also limited "political" talk about these issues.

In both the United States and Canada, pastoral leadership expressed concern that the logic of congregational ministry often clashed with the logic of political mobilization. In private interviews, all four head pastors expressed a personal desire to see Christians involved in politics, particularly to oppose abortion and defend traditional family values. But it was their perception that most people attended church to sing, pray, and receive encouragement in their daily lives, not to be drafted into political conflict.[42] Political engagement also drained limited resources and time away from organizational maintenance, ministry, and evangelism. As a result, ordained pastors followed the initiative and passion of their laypeople when it came to "moral issues" and political engagement.

All four churches placed symbolic emphasis on the authority of the pastor, but their pastors hardly exercised autonomous leadership over laypeople. In personal interviews, laypeople often expressed a desire to be "challenged" or "confronted" by their pastor, speaking with scriptural authority. At the same time, they felt empowered to challenge a pastor who deviated from their understanding of "biblical" teaching. Previous research has focused on how networks of politically conservative pastors have aided Christian Right political mobilization efforts.[43] Yet evangelical congregations are laity-governed organizations, and in most "free church" traditions, the congregation can fire the pastor at will.[44] Unsurprisingly, survey research finds that evangelical pastors are more likely to preach on political topics if they perceive that their congregation already agrees with them.[45] In the chapters that follow, I show that church-based political engagement is actually produced by a more complex interaction between pastors and laity. When evangelical pastors exercise "strong" political leadership, it is because they have a strong base of support from politically engaged and unified lay leaders.

Traditional Morality Does Not Determine Conservative Politics

Throughout the book, I debunk the idea that evangelical congregations enforce an internally coherent "orthodox" worldview. While culture war elites defend "family values" in structured ideological terms, local congregations draw on a varied cultural toolkit to address the practical needs of real families.[46] For example, while all four churches in this study touted their "biblical" model of the family, I found a great deal of variation in how the Bible was brought to bear on gender roles and childrearing.[47] It misrepresents evangelicalism to boil this rich cultural toolkit down to a single underlying dimension: an "authoritarian" disposition, an underlying model of the "strict father" family, or an "orthodox" view of moral authority.[48]

James Davison Hunter is right that the evangelical tradition fosters distinctive patterns of moral judgment that are foreign to many theologically liberal Christians and political liberals. In both the United States and Canada, evangelical churches promoted a particular set of moral intuitions associated with traditional societies: *respect for authority, purity*, and *in-group loyalty*.[49] By contrast, liberal political philosophy has generally assumed that modern societies should reject such backwards concerns, and that morality should be guided by concerns about *harm* and *fairness*. Social scientists have treated harm and fairness as the only two considerations within moral reasoning and development. When social scientists have examined other kinds of moral concerns, they often dismissed them as irrational, pre-modern, or authoritarian.[50]

By contrast, anthropologists find that most of the world's people have historically relied on a broader range of moral intuitions, which go beyond considerations of harm and fairness. While these so-called traditional cultures are internally diverse and complex, they share an emphasis on *authority*, *purity*, and *loyalty*, alongside concerns about *harm* and *fairness*.[51] Moral intuitions about authority motivate people to respond when someone has violated norms of hierarchy or proper respect. Violations of purity motivate people to guard a higher, spiritual domain from a lower, carnal domain of death, disgust, and decay. Intuitions about loyalty motivate people to valorize their in-group and guard group boundaries against the out-group. "Traditional" cultures also care about harm and fairness, but these two concerns can sometimes be trumped by three alternative bases of moral judgment.[52]

In modern North America, traditional moral intuitions are still emphasized by the religious subcultures that Hunter describes as "orthodox," most notably evangelical Christianity. For example, evangelicals draw on modern, therapeutic discourse about "meeting each other's needs" in a marriage, but weave this discourse together with references to biblical authority, sexual purity, or separation from "the world."[53] Even though evangelicals share an overlapping cultural repertoire with other North Americans, they are socialized to value a broader set of moral intuitions that goes beyond harm and fairness. These particular concerns with authority, purity, and loyalty allow culture war rhetoric to resonate with evangelicals in ways that mystify political liberals.

Thus, there is a very real divide between evangelicals and many other North Americans when it comes to moral perception and judgment. Rank-and-file evangelicals do not talk about politics in the same rigid, ideological terms as political elites, and their cultural toolkit includes many of the same tools as political liberals. But when culture war elites strike the tuning fork, their strings are tuned to pick up the vibration. For example, gay rights advocates are often mystified by evangelical opposition to same-sex marriage, asking rhetorically, "Why would people oppose basic *fairness*? How does gay marriage hurt *them*?" The answer is that evangelicals inhabit a broader set of moral intuitions that many political liberals do not feel.[54]

But Hunter is wrong to claim that these moral differences are uniquely polarizing and irreconcilable through democratic politics. Local evangelical congregations do not enforce an internally coherent "orthodox" worldview, based solely on traditional concerns for authority, purity, or ingroup loyalty. Evangelicals inhabit an expanded moral universe, but one that substantially overlaps with that of cultural progressives and political liberals. For example, when polled about gay rights, evangelicals express high levels of support for basic civil rights and freedoms within a democratic society, and respond to arguments based on the principles of fairness and care for others.[55] When I describe evangelicals as morally traditional, I simply mean that they cultivate "traditional" moral intuitions about authority, purity, and loyalty, alongside intuitions about harm and fairness. These traditional moral intuitions are important to recognize, but they also have a contingent relationship to conservative politics.

How Partisanship Becomes Linked to Evangelical Morality

In this chapter, I show that both U.S. and Canadian congregations exhibited the characteristic features of evangelical theology, family life, and identity that have been documented by previous research on evangelicalism. Building on the work of others, I draw attention to internal complexity within evangelical lived religion. But analyzing this internal complexity is not the book's main contribution. Instead, my contribution is to analyze how American evangelicalism has become so closely tied to political conservatism in *spite* of this internal complexity. The United States is not polarized because the two sides of the culture wars lack shared values or moral concerns. Rather, America is polarized because these overlapping concerns and identities are systematically silenced as a basis for public action. By comparing evangelicals in the United States and Canada, I uncover the social mechanisms that contribute to political polarization within this religious subculture.

Comparing churches across the U.S.-Canada border, I found that partisanship served as a critical link between traditional morality and conservative politics. In the chapters that follow, I identify three practices that linked religious identity and partisanship more strongly in American churches than Canadian churches: public narrative, identity-mapping, and lay leadership.[56]

In chapters 3 and 4, I describe how religion and partisanship became fused in the *narratives of Christian nationalism* that church members used to make sense of their responsibilities to a broader society. Partisanship also became linked to religious identity within everyday practices of *identity-mapping*, when liberal politicians and political groups were frequently mapped as salient adversaries to "our" influence in society as Christians. Though political diversity existed within both U.S. and Canadian churches, it was not equally distributed in social space. The most explicit partisan cues did not come from ordained clergy, but rather from a broad base of volunteer *lay leaders*. Through local religious practice, culture war polarization took on a sacred quality for rank-and-file American evangelicals.

CHAPTER 3

· · · · · · · ·

TWO AMERICAN CHURCHES: PARTISANSHIP WITHOUT POLITICS

In this chapter, I compare how political influence operated in two American evangelical congregations, which I call Northtown Baptist and Lifeway Pentecostal. Both congregations reinforced a conservative political orientation, but not in the explicit, militant ways that outsiders might imagine. For church members, political talk didn't fit their church's *group style*, or customs about how to be a good member.[1] But even though both churches avoided "politics," they enforced an informal understanding that good Christians voted Republican. Political influence did not work through explicit *persuasion* or *deliberation*, but rather through implicit *cues* about what political affiliations were for "people like us." These political cues were so powerful precisely because they were distanced from the dirty business of "politics"; instead, they were woven into the fabric of everyday religious life.

Evangelicals Are Not Culture Warriors, But . . .

Previous scholarship has forcefully debunked the stereotype that evangelicals are a disciplined, charging army of culture warriors, bent on imposing their morality through political force. In *Christian America: What Evangelicals Really Want*, Christian Smith concluded:

> When vocal evangelical political activists stand up and preach about the loss of or need for a "Christian America," they often do strike a chord in many ordinary evangelicals. But . . . the chord that this rhetoric does strike with ordinary evangelicals is not necessarily the same chord that the political activists intend to strike. The activists are thinking about sustained Christian political mobilization. But most evangelicals are thinking about basic morality and faithful witness in their personal lives.[2]

In this classic study, Smith and his collaborators found that rank-and-file evangelicals and Christian Right elites often use the same schemas in very different ways. In a national survey, a wide range of evangelicals constructed their identity using language that sounds very much like Christian Right ideology: they affirmed America's historic identity as a Christian nation, took conservative positions on abortion and homosexuality, and believed that Christians should get involved in American public life. Yet this shared narrative concealed considerable political diversity, because rank-and-file evangelicals disagreed about *how* to change American society to fit this moral vision.

Using surveys and interviews, Smith and colleagues found that most evangelicals believed in transforming society through "strategic relationalism." They saw their society as an aggregation of individuals, who can be influenced for good or for ill through relationships. When local churches called on their members to defend family values and restore America's heritage as a "Christian nation," they used this language to strengthen their subcultural identity and mobilize the faithful for *religious* action, not necessarily *political* action. Thus, evangelicals practiced a public faith, without necessarily supporting a Christian Right agenda.

But using ethnographic methods, I found that Smith and his collaborators were only partly right. On the one hand, both American churches cultivated cultural tension with their environment in the very ways that subcultural identity theory predicts. When church leaders in both churches appealed to themes of cultural conflict, Christian nationalism, and "moral issues," it was not to achieve immediately political goals. Instead, they used cultural tension to rally the faithful for religious goals: evangelism, community service, lay leadership. In both U.S. churches, evangelicals talked about the "moral issues" of abortion and homosexuality, but focused on personal ministry and behavioral standards within the church, not political action. Local churches used "culture war" language for distinctively religious purposes that were very different than those of political elites. On the other hand, both churches sent strong signals that real Christians voted Republican.

Even as church members avoided explicitly "political" talk, they enforced an implicit consensus that voting Republican on "moral issues" was an essential part of evangelical identity. Evangelical identity became conflated with partisanship in two ways: First, members of both churches drew symbolic boundaries between "us" and "liberals," with a great deal of slippage between the religious and political meanings of this label. Second, both churches drew on narratives of Christian nationalism that blamed "liberals" for America's moral decline. By mapping evangelical identity in such partisan terms, these churches made it difficult for individuals to publicly identify as both a Christian and a Democrat. American evangelicals are not a mighty army of culture warriors, but they vote like one. This chapter explains how these two American churches became charged with partisanship—without considering themselves "political."

SUSTAINING CULTURAL TENSION IN LOCAL CHURCH LIFE

I extend subcultural identity theory by comparing how Northtown Baptist and Lifeway Assembly draw on culture war themes in church settings. According to subcultural identity theory, evangelical churches and Christian Right elites often use the same schemas, but in very different ways. When rank-and-file evangelicals use the language of cultural conflict, Christian nationalism, and "moral issues," they are not necessarily advocating a Christian Right agenda. Rather, they are performing identity-work to create tension with their sociocultural environment. To sustain this cultural tension, leaders and members work to rally a constant sense of *external threat*, but also the *urgency to engage* the outside world. Here, I extend subcultural identity theory by studying how groups use culture in everyday interaction.[3] I go beyond describing the stories, symbols, and ideas that circulate within the evangelical subculture by asking how evangelicals actually put these cultural tools to use in everyday life to create a strong subcultural identity. I describe how evangelicals performed identity-work in local church settings to produce this sense of cultural tension.[4]

Both churches used abortion and homosexuality to draw *group boundaries* between "us" and "them," to define the relationship between evangelicals and the wider world. But at Northtown and Lifeway, it was not appropriate to talk about abortion and homosexuality in "political" ways. Instead, these churches talked about these issues in "spiritual" ways that focused on personal ministry and individual transformation. Observing local interactions, I found that these two American evangelical churches in this study were not as political as they seemed—at least not in the ways that outsiders might imagine.

Northtown Baptist

Northtown Baptist is allied with the Southern Baptist Convention, the U.S. denomination that is most closely associated with culture war politics. In the 1980s, the Southern Baptist Convention was taken over by a fundamentalist movement that rallied to purge theological liberals from the denomination, combat abortion and homosexuality, defend the patriarchal family, and restore Protestant civil religion within American public life.[5] Yet I never heard these themes invoked for explicitly political purposes at Northtown Baptist. Instead, the language of tension and threat was used to rally members for distinctively *religious* service and leadership.

One spring morning, I observed a lively adult Sunday school lesson on the topic of Persecution. The teacher, Mark, asked a roomful of thirty- to seventy-year-old adults if they had ever experienced persecution for their faith. Each member of the class shared stories about how their faith had created awkwardness or tension in different settings, although most students argued that this hardly amounted to persecution for American Christians. Mark related their personal experiences to a larger struggle over American national identity:

> It's funny because radical Islam calls the United States a Christian country, but the Christians in the Christian country know it's not a Christian country. There's antagonism—not persecution, but antagonism. We have as much a right to share as an atheist does. It's more subtle, that antagonism to our message. The most important thing is our response to it.

Next, Mark invited the class to read John 15:18[6] and asked, "What does it mean that the world hates you?" This question might have opened the door to a discussion of political conflict over America's identity as a "Christian nation." But the class only generated examples of cultural tension in personal relationships. For example, a nurse in her forties named Joanna said, "Your good behavior puts people on edge, because they want to do the right thing, but it makes them jealous." An older, working-class man said, "Our confidence, we don't have fear or anxiety, and that makes them uncomfortable." Another man offered, "We stick out, act different, think different." Though Mark framed this discussion in terms of America's lost Christian heritage, class members defined embattlement in personal, relational terms. The class drew on themes of cultural tension to sustain a vital subcultural identity, rather than rally for political action.

While this discussion reinforced strong boundaries between "us" and "the world," Mark also motivated the class to engage across subcultural boundaries. To dramatize this urgency to engage the world, Mark walked to the chalkboard and wrote down the word: "TRUTH." He observed, "We live in a society that, in the last 200 years, believes there is no such thing . . . that everyone has their own truth." Mark explained that, by contrast, Christians believed that all people are separated from God by sin, which motivated them to engage in evangelism. "That puts us at odds with the world," he concluded, since Christians refuse to "stay in the box" of privatized faith.

Mark asked the class how Christians should respond to this resistance. Hannah, a woman in her late sixties, suggested, "Jesus said to be wise as serpents. It's sometimes okay to be in the box. . . . work within their comfort zone.'" Nancy, a nurse in her forties, advocated a more confrontational stance: "Right now, our governor is talking about same-sex marriage. I'm not as active as I used to be, like Joanna with the pro-life. But I feel like something's going to break if we don't get involved." Here, Nancy explicitly called for Christian political engagement, pointing to the threats of abortion and same-sex marriage. But no one in the class responded to Nancy's call to action: she had violated the group's speech norms. Mark quickly changed the topic, by observing that Jesus had challenged the power structures of his time by embracing outcasts. Then the class resumed brainstorming how they could influence individuals through personal relationships. Northtown's group style curtailed public discussion of "political" topics, even when individuals like Nancy wanted to rally Christians for political action.

As the Sunday school hour drew to a close, class members brainstormed strategies to overcome the culture's resistance to Christian Truth. Hannah talked about how she witnessed through her relationships with international students at the local university: "Through love." Mark emphasized authenticity: "True living . . . Your nonverbal testimony." Nancy suggested, "Holding onto truth and not capitulating, not a peace at any cost. People want to have strong opinions. You have to say, 'This is what the Bible says and me, I'm not going to compromise.'" Mark ended the class with a prayer for the persecuted church, adding: "We thank you we are in a country where we are free to worship you and share our faith . . . we pray it would stay that way." In this context, the language of cultural tension became a resource for Northtown members to share their faith with non-Christians even when it wasn't "nice"—even when it violated the norms of conflict avoidance that prevailed in their workplaces and personal friendships.[7] As discussion leader, Mark encouraged them to overcome their own apathy and fear, by framing their experiences within a larger narrative about the battle for America's soul between Christianity and the forces of moral relativism.[8]

This discussion illustrates how "political" talk was curtailed by Northtown's group style, or unspoken customs about how to be a good member in official church settings. In a year of fieldwork, this was the only time that I observed anyone at Northtown calling for collective action to change policy. Nancy had referred to politics in only the most general terms, stating her opinion that "something's going to break if we don't get involved." Yet even this general comment violated the group style, and required a quick change of subject. From these social cues, individuals like Nancy learned not to speak about their pro-life activism in "political" ways, even though their church expressed a commitment to pro-life values, and even though they were surrounded by like-minded people.

At Northtown Baptist, nationalistic rhetoric conveyed a civic moral: that these "oppressive" forces of moral relativism created a challenge for sharing the Gospel, but one that Christians could overcome with love, relational influence, and resourcefulness. Though the class agreed that Christians should stand up for Truth, all of their ideas for changing society were based on strategic relationalism. Ultimately, Christians should reverse America's moral decline by influencing individuals through their personal relationships.

This group style also shaped how people talked about the "moral issues" at Northtown Baptist. Church members were clearly expected to take conservative stances on abortion and homosexuality. But this sense of consensus was enforced in a quiet way, which members saw as "loving" rather than "political." For example, the church's mission statement included an explicit pro-life stance: "All children, from the moment of conception, are a blessing from God." Yet during my fieldwork, this collective opposition to abortion was only expressed once during official church programming, on Mother's Day of 2007. When I entered the sanctuary that morning, I found a yellow card tucked into my bulletin:

Happy Mother's Day

Wishing All a Very Blessed Mother's Day
In lieu of a gift from the church, a donation in the name of
Northtown Baptist's women has been made to:
SonRays Ministries: "A Ministry For Life"
SonRays Ministries was born out of a deep desire
to uphold respect for life at all stages, from the womb to eternity

As I read the card, I wondered if worship leaders might use the occasion of Mother's Day to rally the congregation behind the pro-life political cause. But I quickly learned that Northtown had a different way of showing their "respect for life": through practical ministry to mothers and babies with special needs. Although James, the lead pastor, announced that a Mother's Day donation had been made to SonRays ministry, he did not explain their pro-life mission. Instead, Pastor James simply asked all the mothers in the church to stand and be recognized. Then a deacon came forward and prayed for Cathy, a young mother whose premature baby had been born with severe health problems:

Lord, we ask that your blessing and peace and joy would be upon them. The doctor says she only had a month, but you have given her five. Lord, I ask that you would multiply the days of her life, so that everyone would know how powerful you are.

During the offering, we watched a slideshow about the church's Disability ministry, which showed pictures of mentally challenged children and their families. The pastor closed by praying for mothers, particularly "mothers who have lost children" and "children who have been born with special needs." I learned that in public church settings, Northtown Baptist only affirmed their pro-life stance implicitly, through ministry to pregnant women and special needs children.

This Mother's Day service illustrated what it meant to talk about abortion in a "spiritual" way at Northtown Baptist. Leaders used a pro-life stance to define group boundaries, or imagine how their group contrasted with, and related to, other groups in American society.[9] Members were encouraged to affirm this pro-life commitment through personal relationships with women, families, and children, rather than direct political action. The pro-life stance also informed the church's group bonds, or assumptions about members' mutual responsibilities in a church context. For example, Northtown's ministers and laypeople had encouraged Cathy as she carried a high-risk pregnancy to term, in spite of the doctor's warnings that the child would live less than a month. But heated anti-abortion rhetoric would have violated Northtown's speech norms: it was appropriate to support SonRays as a pro-life ministry, but not to rally the church against abortion as a "political" issue.

While this pro-life stance set "us" apart from "them," Northtown prepared its members to engage across this boundary in a compassionate way. John, a lay leader in his forties, explained to me that the church did not discuss abortion as a "political issue," but rather as an "area of sin and weakness in our country":

> It's come up in Sunday school classes, somebody has been talking about somebody who was pregnant and decided not to give into abortion. . . . I think is the only case I know about that, probably was last year.

In situations like this, John expected Northtown members to explain the church's position:

> the child is a gift of God, you know that is life, and we are not to . . . extinguish a life, so encouraging the person to follow through and not fall again.

John emphasized that Christians should help individuals as they wrestle with individual decisions. While Northtown Baptist used the issue of abortion to draw boundaries between "us" and "them," they most often talked about "them" as uncertain, morally adrift teenagers who might consider abortion. The clientele of Sonrays' ministry were similarly described as spiritually lost: unmarried, poor, young, undereducated, and in need of moral reformation.[10] Northtown Baptist publicly mapped their relationship to outsiders in terms of loving service, rather than angry condemnation of their pro-choice "enemies." As friends and Sonrays volunteers, Northtown members prepared to minister to "fallen" people facing unplanned pregnancies.

However, Northtown's pro-life efforts were not directed only outside the church, toward misguided outsiders who might have an abortion. Couples within the church also needed encouragement to choose life in challenging circumstances. Northtown had gathered a sizeable population of families with special needs children, and the pastor repeatedly stressed the relationship between their pro-life commitments and their welcoming attitudes toward children with special needs.[11] This pro-life stance informed their group bonds, the ways that members carried out mutual responsibilities to each other. Women like Cathy needed to be encouraged to carry high-risk pregnancies to term, even when doctors advised that the child's life would be difficult and short. As a newcomer at Northtown, I was immediately struck by how openly members shared their intimate experiences with fertility and reproductive loss. For example, when I visited the "30-Something" Sunday school class for the first time, I was warmly greeted by a handful of young people. Within five minutes, a young professional woman named Silvia told me her personal story of reproductive loss: she had recently lost two twins born prematurely. At the time, Silvia and her husband were only casual attendees, but soon after became born-again, moved by how the church ministered to them in their grief. Now, Silvia was helping start Northtown's adoption ministry, which she described as an expression of the church's pro-life stance. In Silvia's experience, being a pro-life church meant that members were obligated to accompany one another through the challenges of fertility, reproductive loss, and adoption.

This avoidance of overtly political talk was even more noticeable in the case of homosexuality. Although the church assumed a shared opposition to gay marriage, there were clear speech norms about how to express this stance in church. As a newcomer, I quickly learned that Northtown Baptist defined its identity as a church in terms of a conservative stance on homosexuality. This moral consensus against homosexuality was not reinforced by fire-and-brimstone rhetoric against the "gay agenda," but rather by the implicit ways that Northtown mapped their identity. For example, I attended a Welcome Dinner for newcomers in spring 2007, organized by the deacons for people who were considering joining their church. After a hearty potluck meal, we went around in a circle and introduced ourselves, sharing our favorite memories from church. In a charming Southern drawl, Patricia told us how much she loved Northtown's free worship, which contrasted with the rigid Fundamentalist church of her childhood. She turned to her husband, Ted, a quiet man who had just gotten baptized this year. Ted shyly introduced himself, "Hi, I'm Ted, and I'm Patricia's wife." The room erupted with laughter. Ted corrected himself, "I mean, I'm Patricia's *husband*." Patricia leaned her mouth to his ear and said in a stage whisper, "We don't do that in *this* church!" Everyone laughed again. This was the only time that I heard Northtown members affirm an anti-gay-marriage stance during an official church activity.

Within Northtown's group style, the group consensus on homosexuality was affirmed in "loving" speech, not angry rhetoric. Patricia had defined Northtown's identity by drawing a boundary between *their* church and other communities that *did* sanction gay marriage. The rest of the group affirmed this surface consensus through friendly laughter. At Northtown, Christian Right rhetoric against homosexuality was suppressed by the church's practical concerns for ministry.[12] As with abortion, leaders and members expressed concern that anti-gay rhetoric would drive away two groups who needed the church: Christians who faced this closeted "struggle" in their own lives, and openly gay people who needed "transformation." Behind closed doors, the church's leadership was struggling to engage this issue in ways that fit their *style*—ways they could consider both compassionate and biblical. This struggle was not over the church's *beliefs*: their fundamental opposition to homosexuality was treated as an unquestionable biblical standard. Rather, this struggle was over how to speak about homosexuality publicly, in ways that drew moral boundaries against homosexuality yet expressed loving concern across those boundaries.

I discovered this ambivalence while I was chatting with Ron, the church's oldest deacon, as we waited in the lobby for a meeting to start. Ronald leaned over and pointed to Sunday school classroom nearby. "They're having a discussion in there about *homosexuality*!" he said in a playful stage whisper, raising his eyebrows for emphasis. Like Patricia, Ronald used humor to talk publicly about homosexuality in a religious setting. As one of the church's oldest members, Ronald remembered a time when homosexuality was such a taboo that it could not even be mentioned publicly in Baptist churches, even to condemn it. But as this taboo was dismantled in the broader culture, churches like Northtown had to find ways to broach the topic. Their response was to sponsor Breaking Free, a support group for people who experienced what they referred to as "same-sex attraction."

This support group was run by a laywoman in her early forties named Ann, who was raised Catholic and was active in evangelical college ministries, until she fell in love with another woman shortly after college. Throughout her twenties, Ann lived a double life: in a closeted lesbian relationship, yet actively involved at a conservative evangelical church. Feeling "convicted," she confessed to her pastor, who showed her understanding and helped her begin a long journey toward celibacy. Since the 1980s, Ann noticed that evangelical churches became more willing to speak openly about this once-taboo topic, a change that she attributes to the gay rights movement and the greater visibility of gays and lesbians in popular culture. For Ann, the "homosexual revolution" has produced one positive by-product: "because it is so 'out there' in society, I have a greater freedom to speak about it in the church."

Ann felt that too many churches rejected Christians like her, which only drove them into the arms of the "gay community":

> There's a lot of people who used to go to church and they abandoned the church because they were dealing with same-sex attraction, they were maybe dealing with active homosexuality. And the church didn't help. Either they were condemning, or they went, "Well, just stop!" . . . there was a lack of understanding and there was a big lack of compassion.

For Ann, it was ironic that the evangelical subculture could offer "grace" to people who struggled with adultery or pornography, but "if you struggled with homosexuality, you better clean it out quick or out." As a result, individuals walked away from the church, and ran into the arms of a gay community that said, "The church doesn't love you and maybe God doesn't love you, but we do!" The church "could've been the agent of love and of healing, but instead pushed people away."

Ann's ministry did not attempt to "convert" gay people into straight people. Ann hoped that someday she might marry a man and have children, but she did not describe herself as "straight." Based on her own experience, she rejected the idea that homosexuality was simply a choice. Yet she also disagreed that homosexuality was an immutable part of one's personhood to be embraced. Instead, she encouraged the church to adopt a third position: that same-sex attraction is a durable disposition for some people, but it is still possible for them to live "faithful" lives where they do not act on these feelings.

> People have been learning that . . . same-sex attraction is a complex issue, it's not black and white . . . that this is a gradual thing and it's not an easy thing to walk away from homosexuality. It's very difficult. So there's lots of grace required.

Ann was particularly critical of Christians who claimed that getting saved would instantly deliver a person from homosexual feelings. By contrast, Ann's primary goal was not to convert gay people into straight people, but rather to transform the way that the church related to individuals who "struggle with" same-sex attraction. Northtown was helping her create a space within evangelical churches that support people like herself in their efforts to "walk away" from homosexuality and live "faithful" lives. Ann felt that the church as a whole was moving in the right direction, even though some churches "just don't get it," and some "bigoted people walk around with signs at the gay pride parade that say 'Fags are going to hell'."

Here, I found a stark contrast between Christian Right rhetoric and the more nuanced approach found within this congregational ministry. Breaking Free made sense of homosexuality within a narrative of life-long "struggle," similar to the narratives that Tanya Erzen heard within another residential ministry to gay Christian men.[13] Ann encouraged participants to hope that someday they might be "freed" from same-sex attraction, and perhaps even be able to enter into marriage with a member of the opposite sex. But even if this never happened, one could enjoy a relationship with God and fellowship with others on a similar path. This approach to personal change was primarily focused on *religious* transformation, rather than "curing" homosexuality.[14]

As a result, it was only appropriate to talk about homosexuality in loving ways at Northtown Baptist: as a ministry concern and not a political issue. As a lay leader, Ann helped coach the membership to maintain this compassionate stance within their personal relationships, even while maintaining moral boundaries against homosexual behavior. For example, the youth group conducted a three-week series about homosexuality in their Sunday night Bible study. The youth pastor's goal was to clarify that homosexual relationships were incompatible with Christian teaching, but also to encourage youth to stand up against anti-gay bullying that they observed in schools. Ann shared her experience, and asked the youth to show understanding and compassion toward gay-identified youth, instead of driving them away from the church through condemnation. Northtown members were expected to draw moral boundaries against homosexuality but also were equipped to engage with gay people across those boundaries.

In short, Northtown Baptist used culture war language for local religious purposes that were distinct from the Christian Right agenda. To sustain cultural tension with their environment, leaders and members rallied a constant sense of *external threat*, but also the *urgency to engage* the outside world. Within their group style, it was only appropriate to talk about abortion and homosexuality in "spiritual" ways that focused on personal ministry, not political change.

Lifeway Assembly of God

I found a similar pattern at Lifeway Assembly of God, but with a Pentecostal twist. This Assemblies of God congregation cultivated a sense of cultural tension by telling stories about the nation's moral decline and their cultural embattlement. But, unlike Northtown, Lifeway described this cultural tension as a literal, supernatural battle between godly and demonic forces. Accordingly, Lifeway Assembly practiced "spiritual warfare" to defend the nation against demonic influences through prayer. This spiritual warfare was aided by four large banners that hung year-round in the Lifeway sanctuary. One of these banners urged us to "Pray for Our Leaders," with a picture of the U.S. Capitol building. Another banner invited us to pray for "Revival," with images of flames of fire falling upon the church. A third banner read "Messiah: Pray for the Peace of Jerusalem."[15] In the past, such practices of spiritual warfare had raised serious red flags for Americans concerned about the separation of Church and State.[16] Taken at face value, this combative imagery of Christian nationalism might seem authoritarian and violent. But on closer examination, Lifeway's practices of spiritual warfare also equipped members to engage in civil and loving ways with people outside their religious subculture.

This language of spiritual warfare might sound authoritarian to a cultural outsider, but I heard it used to inspire people to loving service rather than confrontation. Praying for the nation was part of a Pentecostal practice of "interceding" for whole communities, cities, and regions.[17] For example, the youth pastor Jonathan preached about spiritual warfare for the city of Buffalo:

> I heard God saying, "Get in the car and drive to downtown Buffalo." And I thought, "Yeah, I'm going to pray over the city." As I walked down [the main street in Buffalo], I thought, "God, this is a land that you can take." And then I noticed that I was standing right next to a Masonic symbol.

The congregation laughed, because historically, many Pentecostals have viewed the Masons as a source of demonic influence.[18] At the end of his sermon, Jonathan asked people to stand up if they wanted to commit themselves to take this city for God: "I want to be a Joshua."[19]

> I will stop calling Buffalo a place where your spirit doesn't move. That's why I'm excited to be back in Buffalo. Because I don't see it

in the natural.[20] I don't believe this place is in a downslide. Will you stand up when people badmouth the city, and how bad the economy is? Will you see what God says about the city? When people say, "people are moving out," you say, "God is moving in!"

The congregation responded with loud cries of "Amen!" and about thirty people rose to their feet in response. Jonathan gestured toward all the people who were standing: "These are other people who will not accept the status quo . . . This is a city, this is a region, this is a church that will be full of Your [God's] presence. And You will have your way."[21] This spiritual warfare had a territorial logic, invoking the power of God to drive out demonic influences over geographic spaces and institutions.[22]

At Lifeway Assembly, spiritual warfare was often directed toward "reclaiming the nation." For example, two laypeople told me that they had buried crosses around the perimeter of a local public school in order to reclaim America's schools for Jesus. But when leaders at Lifeway Assembly invoked religious nationalism, it wasn't to mobilize their members for politics; rather, they appealed to the nation to rally them for evangelism and service. For example, Pastor John drew on religious nationalism in a sermon that he gave after the death of Christian Right leader Jerry Falwell. He started by acknowledging that people in his congregation had different views about Jerry Falwell: "I agree with some things and I disagree with others." Pastor John quoted "a secular columnist" to argue that "before Jerry Falwell started the Moral Majority, you never saw Christians praying in a restaurant, because they were ashamed. But now you see it all the time." Pastor John praised Falwell's boldness, while reminding his flock of the limits of politics:

> We serve a different king . . . It doesn't matter who wins . . . Jesus is Lord over the United States . . . *God* is our king. . . . You do the simple thing, God will do the complicated thing. You do the small thing, God will do the great thing. You do the possible thing, God will do the impossible thing . . . You can't change a nation, but God can . . . It's like that passage in 2 Chronicles: "If my people who are called by my name." When we obey God, he blesses us . . . It's his good pleasure to give you the kingdom . . . The just shall live by faith. It brought down the Roman Empire, it brought down the Roman Catholic Church, it broke the power, set the people free to seek God and seek his word . . . God is always looking for an intercessor, someone to stand in the gap in this circumstance . . . God flows his power to us and through us to others.[23]

In this sermon, Pastor John was not mobilizing his flock for an authoritarian political movement to literally "conquer" the nation for Christ.

Instead, he presented a Pentecostal vision of strategic relationalism: God's kingdom outpouring through individuals in ways that transform lives, communities, and nations.[24] When John announced that "Jesus is Lord over the United States," he wasn't calling for political action, but rather modest acts of obedience, which God would use to bring about "the kingdom." At Lifeway Assembly, leaders used religious nationalism to call members to engage others outside the church. Here, John was using this combative rhetoric to strengthen the church's subcultural identity, not to rally them behind a Christian Right political agenda. Just like at Northtown Baptist, nationalistic language was used to call members to personal discipleship and service, not to political engagement. This cultural tension helped Lifeway to create a strong evangelical identity, by drawing boundaries between "us" and "them," but also by motivating the faithful to engage across those boundaries.

Lifeway Assembly of God also drew on the combative imagery of spiritual warfare to talk about sin and its consequences. This Pentecostal emphasis affected how Lifeway drew moral boundaries against abortion and homosexuality. While Northtown Baptist signaled their opposition to abortion in quiet, loving ways, Lifeway Assembly took a much more combative approach during their annual Easter Play. On their largest service of the year, a team of dozens of members dramatized Jesus' death and resurrection for their holiday visitors. In 2007, the play began in the Garden of Eden, where Adam and Eve succumbed to the serpent's temptations and sin entered the world. Skipping forward in the biblical story, the play portrayed Jesus weeping in the Garden of Gethsemane. A young layman portrayed Jesus, begging the Father to "take this cup from me": he lifted up his eyes to heaven and prayed, shaking dramatically to the rhythm of a Blues song. Then, as the song continued, an overhead projector flashed a series of images that represented the consequences of sin in the world. I jotted down a list:

A Klu Klux Klan march
Protesters marching with signs that said "Keep Abortion Legal"
Multiple car accident
Environmental destruction
Homeless people on the street
Scientific table with shells displayed
A cemetery
Images from 9/11: collapsing World Trade Center, rescue workers in
    the rubble
A crying child
A porn shop in a run-down neighborhood

Atom bomb explosion; the wreckage of a bombing in a city

A hurricane, people in New Orleans climbing on a roof to escape
the flooding

War trenches, a concentration camp, a "Jude" star, Hitler, a masked
neo-Nazi

Images of poverty in sub-Saharan Africa: a crying child, a dead ox,
a starving child.

As the song ended, the slide show flashed a final image of Jesus on the
cross. On stage, the actor playing Jesus rose to face betrayal, arrest, and
crucifixion.

Here, I noticed that Lifeway had a rather different group style than
Northtown Baptist. This Easter Play juxtaposed the pro-choice movement with the Ku Klux Klan, the Nazi Party, and neo-Nazis. This slide
show clearly expressed Lifeway Assembly's collective opposition to abortion. But the pro-choice movement was not just wrong—it was implicated in radical social evil, analogous to the evil of the Holocaust and the
9/11 attacks.[25] By contrast, I never heard Northtown leaders or members
talk about abortion as radically evil in public church settings. This was a
difference of style, not belief, since both churches taught that abortion
was wrong, but had different ways of talking publicly about abortion.

Lifeway Assembly's good-versus-evil imagery about abortion might
sound dangerous for democracy and civil discourse. But, like Northtown
Baptist, Lifeway also equipped its members to engage with people who
disagreed with them on the issue of abortion. Julie, a lay leader in her
early forties, explained that in a diverse country like America, Christians
should not demonize people that they disagree with. "Our pastor is always saying that we should welcome open dialogue." Her husband Jonah
added that "love and compassion" were essential virtues that Christians
could bring to "such a politically polarized climate." Here, Lifeway's
combative identity-work on the issue of abortion was disconnected from
their practical strategies of social change. While the church defined group
boundaries in the language of spiritual warfare, members were encouraged to change the world through personal relationships and righteous
living.

Like Northtown, Lifeway also maintained speech norms about how to
talk about abortion in a spiritual way. Although the congregation contained a large network of pro-life activists, the church itself only supported these ministries indirectly, by allowing individual members to an-
nounce fundraisers or set up a booth in the foyer. For example, Lutherans
for Life set up a booth to enroll potential participants, receiving a brief
mention in the announcements. As at Northtown, Lifeway also encouraged adoption and support for single mothers within the church as an

expression of their pro-life group bonds. In personal interviews, multiple laypeople told me that this church addressed abortion as a moral concern rather than a political issue.

Lifeway also had a surprisingly nuanced approach to homosexuality, given their highly supernatural, Pentecostal approach to good versus evil. Just as at Northtown Baptist, it was considered inappropriate to engage in combative anti-gay rhetoric at Lifeway Assembly, out of concern for individuals who struggled with this issue. While homosexual acts were clearly identified as sinful, I never heard homosexuality associated with radical evil the way abortion was.[26] For example, Gordon, a retired lay leader, preached a fiery sermon based on 1 Corinthians 6, a passage that is often used as a proof-text against homosexuality. He read from the Bible and then offered his interpretation:

> Or do you not know that wrongdoers will not inherit the kingdom of God? Do not be deceived: Neither the sexually immoral nor idol-aters nor adulterers nor male prostitutes nor practicing homosexu-als nor thieves nor the greedy nor drunkards nor slanderers nor swindlers will inherit the kingdom of God (Corinthians 6: 9–10 NIV). We live in a world where people are fast trying to justify their sin, and claim their sin is a disease. . . . These are not diseases, they are *sin*.

Here, Gordon drew moral boundaries against homosexuality as part of a larger set of "sinful" behaviors, which he associated with a general failure of personal responsibility in today's society. Yet Gordon never discussed homosexuality directly. Instead, his sermon focused on the dangers of adultery and alcoholism, which he saw as the most pressing dangers to people inside and outside of the church.

This was part of a larger pattern: I never saw Lifeway leaders and members condemn homosexuality using combative, good-versus-evil im-agery, even though they used this language to condemn abortion. In indi-vidual interviews, I learned that Lifeway Assembly was in the process of figuring out how to minister to Christians who struggled with homosex-uality. Laypeople and ministers shared with me their stories about be-loved friends and family members who experienced same-sex attraction or who were living a "gay lifestyle" but were alienated from the church. Church leaders were increasingly aware that homosexuality impacted people within the church, not just those outside the church. This limited their political rhetoric against gay rights, even as the church conveyed a clear defense of heterosexual marriage as the only legitimate context for sexual expression.

Maintaining this balance was difficult: how did the church draw a clear boundary against homosexuality without branding gays and lesbians as uniquely sinful? For example, one lay leader had recently spent a year studying the Bible with a friend who considered herself a lesbian. After several months of Bible study, her friend told her that she was ready to become a Christian, and began musing about what that would mean for the rest of her life. Suddenly, her friend exclaimed, "I'm a gay born-again!" This took the Lifeway Assembly member off-guard: she struggled to clarify that her friend's emerging identity as a "gay Christian" was not legitimate.[27] This demonstrates the challenge of talking about homosexuality at Lifeway Assembly. Lifeway Assembly worked hard to make it clear that "gay" and "Christian" identities remained mutually contradictory.[28] On one hand, church leaders wanted to send the message that all Christians were sinners, to avoid drawing exclusive boundaries that drove people away. On the other hand, they wanted to exclude "practicing" homosexuals from entering the fold: certain kinds of "sinful lifestyles" were simply incompatible with church participation. One could be a closeted Christian who "struggled" with same-sex attraction, or one could be openly gay and alienated from the church. But new Christians could simply not be allowed to exclaim, "I'm a gay born-again!"

At Lifeway as well as Northtown, members avoided explicitly partisan rhetoric against gay marriage, but they also avoided any substantive discussion about homosexuality that might challenge the consensus. It was possible to be a Christian who "struggled" with same-sex attraction, but it was impossible to be a Christian in a committed same-sex relationship. In private interviews, individual members at both churches reported knowing of openly gay people involved in local churches—but these realities were never openly discussed during my fieldwork.

In summary, Lifeway Pentecostal drew on culture war themes in surprisingly civil and nonpartisan ways to perform identity-work. Compared to Northtown Baptist, Lifeway described this cultural tension using the imagery of spiritual warfare: a literal, supernatural battle between godly and demonic forces. But both churches used combative language to rally their members for personal acts of ministry and service, not for collective political action. According to Smith, evangelicals favor this strategic relationalism because their individualistic theology lacks the resources to talk about changing institutions through collective action. But this wasn't the only reason why both churches avoided explicit political mobilization. For church members, political talk didn't fit their sense of "how we do things here." Each church cultivated its own customs about how to talk about abortion and homosexuality in a spiritual way: focused on personal ministry and behavioral standards within the church.[29] Avoiding political speech was an important part of each church's group style, or customs about how to be a good member in their local church setting.

Yet even though both churches avoided political talk, they still enforced an informal understanding that good Christians voted Republican. These two American evangelical churches did more than just reinforce traditional moral stances against abortion and homosexuality. They also engaged in identity-work that helped members to link these issues to *partisanship*.

Linking Evangelical Identity to Partisanship

Significantly, both American churches did more than just signal the "right" positions for Christians to hold on the moral issues. They also signaled a right map for political identity: which party "we" support and which party "we" oppose. In this way, both churches signaled that voting Republican on these issues was an important part of being a Christian. I found that the most explicitly partisan cues happened in unofficial, backstage church settings: small group conversations, chatting over Sunday lunch, informal gatherings with church friends.[30] Evangelical identity became conflated with partisanship in two ways: First, members of both churches drew group boundaries between "us" and "liberals," with a great deal of slippage between the religious and political meanings of this label. Second, both churches drew on narratives of Christian nationalism that blamed liberals for America's moral decline. By mapping evangelical identity in such partisan terms, these churches made it difficult for individuals to publicly identify as both a Christian and a Democrat. Next, I describe how these two American churches became charged with partisanship.

In official church settings, these partisan cues were implicit, since political talk didn't fit within each church's group style. For example, Northtown's Sunday school discussion about Persecution was not "about" politics: it was focused on loving ways to share one's faith with family, friends, and co-workers, rather than the need for political mobilization. But while the lesson was not *about* politics, participants were drawing a shared map of American society, which put Christians on one side of the line, and groups associated with the Democratic Party on the other.[31] Throughout the discussion, different participants drew boundaries against various out-groups in American public life: atheists, Muslims, New York's former governor Eliot Spitzer who supported same-sex marriage, the pro-choice movement. The class brainstormed different strategies about how to engage with these out-groups as Christians. But there was surface agreement about who was "us" and who was "them." While no one explicitly mentioned Democrats or Republicans, participants mapped their identity within a larger narrative of partisan struggle, with Christian defined against an out-group that included Governor Spitzer and the pro-choice movement. By drawing this shared map of evangelical identity, participants sent implicit cues about partisanship without engaging in political debate or disrupting the "spiritual" tone.[32]

Similarly, Lifeway Assembly defined their religious identity in opposition to the pro-choice movement. While the church did not engage in explicit, pro-life mobilization, members could pick up implicit cues about who was on "our" side in a larger political struggle. In this way, both Northtown and Lifeway went beyond opposing abortion and homosexuality as a matter of subcultural distinction. Both churches also sent cues about partisanship, or how Christians should affiliate themselves by reference to the major political parties. Rank-and-file evangelicals drew on Christian nationalism and cultural tension to strengthen religious identity, not for explicit political mobilization. But in effect, this identity-work linked religious identity to partisanship.

In official church settings, I never heard either church make explicit references to political parties. Instead, the most explicit partisan cues were found in unofficial, "backstage" church settings. During my first months at Northtown Baptist, a friendly working-class couple named Bob and Nancy invited me to sit with them for a potluck lunch after church. Bob asked me, "What religious background are you from?" I told him that I grew up Baptist. Nancy asked, "What *kind* of Baptist?" "American Baptist," I answered.

"No offense," replied Nancy, "but I hear that American Baptist churches are kind of liberal." I asked her to explain what she meant by liberal, and Nancy hesitated. Bob chimed in, "She means that they aren't very strict, you can do whatever and they don't care. Like if you have an abortion, it's no big deal." Nancy corrected him, "That's not exactly what I mean. I mean, like you're allowed to drink." Bob protested, "Well, I have a beer from time to time, I don't think there's anything wrong with that. Everything in moderation." Nancy specified, "But you know what I mean—liberal, like the Episcopalians. You know, now they're going to have gay bishops." She pursed her lips and waved her hand dismissively.

Bob added, "Now, I don't have anything against gay people, God loves them, I say, the doors should be open, the doors of our church should be open to everyone. It's just the Episcopalians are liberal, you know, like Bill Clinton." I asked, "What do you mean, like Bill Clinton?" Bob raised his eyebrows, "Well, you know what he did? You know, you see him one day, coming out of his church with his Bible, and the next thing you know, it's the blue dress! No standards, anything goes. I think it goes back to when we took prayer out of the schools, you know, because at least then, it's out there for the general public, and there's a higher chance that they'll take it seriously. That's why you have these school shootings, like the shooting in Virginia, and before that the shootings at Columbine. And now they want to pass gun laws, to take away our guns. It's crazy."

In this conversation, Bob and Nancy used the term "liberal" to define the boundaries of their religious community—and figure out whether I was an insider or outsider. But this conversation illustrates the slippery meaning of the word "liberal," which was used here to connote both theological stances on "moral issues" within the church and a partisan, ideological divide between Republicans and Democrats. Bob and Nancy were not just lacking precision in their language usage—they reflected a broader usage within both American churches. When American evangelicals drew boundaries against "liberals," they were referencing a shared public narrative that conflated religious identity, party identification, and a particular story of American national identity. For Nancy, being "conservative" was an identity, more than a description of her worldview or ideology. While she struggled to explain exactly what conservatives or liberals *believed*, she could still draw a boundary between liberal and conservative people, and put herself on the right side of that line.[33]

At Lifeway Assembly, I also observed that these kinds of partisan cues became more explicit in informal settings. For example, I observed a small group of late-forties to early-sixties women who met to knit prayer shawls together in a private home. As the needles clicked, Barbara announced that the National Day of Prayer was coming up—a day when evangelical Christians around the country organized gatherings for intercessory prayer for the nation. Patricia, one of the leaders of the group, reported that New York State governor Eliot Spitzer had been asked to sign a proclamation recognizing the National Day of Prayer, but had refused, citing separation of church and state. When the small group closed in prayer, Patricia prayed:

> Lord, we pray for all these liberal politicians, so liberal that they don't even acknowledge you, and for Eliot Spitzer, who didn't even want to sign the proclamation for the National Day of Prayer. May he be surrounded with Christians, who will witness to him, every time he turns around. May you soften his heart, that he will accept Christ and worship you.

Barbara prayed, "Nationwide revival, Lord. We want nationwide revival. Move powerfully in this nation, so that people are changed and bow the knee to you. Oh Lord, we want revival in this nation, and all over the world." Patricia added, "Lord, we pray for the men and women in our armed forces, over in Iraq and Afghanistan. We are so grateful that they are over there defending us, laying down their lives to protect our country. Thank you for our young men, who are willing to volunteer to defend our country. Lord, we pray for our nation, for any plans in secret to destroy, any terrorism. Lord, we plead the blood over our nation, defend us from all who seek to destroy us."[34]

This prayer exemplifies the subtle ways that evangelical identity and Republican Party identity had become conflated in religious practice at Lifeway Assembly. On one hand, Patricia and Barbara were praying for spiritual transformation that worked through personal relationships and divine intervention, not through political reform or the creation of an authoritarian "Christian nation." On the other hand, they defined America's problems in terms of "liberal politicians," conflating the political and religious usages of the term "liberal." This prayer implied a close relationship between nationwide revival, American military operations, and the defeat of liberal opposition to state-sponsored prayer. Barbara was not engaged in explicit, partisan mobilization—she was inviting her friends to change the nation through prayer, not by voting or political advocacy. But this prayer still sent partisan cues, since Barbara defined Christian identity in opposition to "liberals," with "liberal" used in both a religious and political sense.

Significantly, these women drew boundaries between Christians and liberals without even referencing the moral issues of abortion and homosexuality. Barbara elaborated a narrative of Christian nationalism, interpreting the war in Iraq as part of America's religious mission to the world.[35] "We" were defined as people who want to restore our nation to its glorious past by overcoming liberal influences in politics. The small group prayed against the influence of terrorists who attacked the nation from the outside—and liberals who undermined our country from the inside. Christians were defined as people who wanted to restore a vision of a strong America built on Christian principles, and we are opposed by liberals who disagree with those Christian principles. In short, this woman's group was reinforcing a shared map of partisanship, which bundled together Christian identity, conservative politics, and support for the war in Iraq. The boundary between "us" and "them" was simultaneously a religious boundary and a partisan one.

At first glance, this prayer group seemed to reject the separation of church and state: "Liberals" opposed the National Day of Prayer because they refused to acknowledge God, not because they supported religious neutrality. This kind of reasoning baffles secular Americans. Why did this prayer group interpret Spitzer's religious *neutrality* as opposition to Christianity itself? Because they used every news event as an occasion to rally a sense of external threat and urgency to engage the world. The group was performing identity-work, not articulating a coherent position on church-state relations.

THE POWER OF AVOIDING "POLITICS"

In summary, both churches avoided explicitly "political" talk, yet reinforced the notion that voting Republican on "moral issues" was an essential part of evangelical identity. Political influence did not work through explicit *persuasion* or *deliberation* about political subjects, but rather through implicit *cues* about what political affiliations were for "people like us." These political cues were so powerful precisely because they were woven into everyday religious practice.

This was even true when churches engaged in activities that might seem objectively connected to political mobilization. For example, Ann had helped to organize a public education event in 2006 to inform the congregation about challenges to traditional marriage. Even though this event took place during a campaign season where gay marriage was a hotly debated issue, Ann did not see this event as an effort to mobilize Christians for political action. Rather, the stated goal was to equip church members to explain the biblical view of marriage to people they knew. This public education event fit within Northtown's group style, because it avoided what Ann considered political talk about homosexuality. At the same time, this kind of nonpolitical discussion sent important cues about partisanship, by emphasizing how the political claims of the gay rights movement threatened "our" religious subculture. When I asked Ann if people at Northtown ever discussed public debates over gay marriage as a matter of law and policy, she could only recall one occasion. At a Breaking Free meeting, the group had discussed what it would mean for them if the gay rights movement was able to legalize same-sex marriage. They contemplated the possibility that eventually, "transformative" ministries like theirs would become marginalized and even possibly outlawed. On the one hand, Northtown Baptist was trying to cultivate a more compassionate approach toward gay individuals; on the other hand, they saw themselves locked into a zero-sum game with the gay rights movement.

Thus, avoiding politics at Northtown and Lifeway was not about the *content* of what one said, as much as the *style* in which one said it. It was inappropriate to engage in explicit persuasion or debate, but it was entirely appropriate to perform identity-work that mapped "our" relationship to politically salient out-groups: the gay rights movement, the abortion rights movement, "liberals." Leaders and members were drawing a shared map of American society, where the group boundaries of religious identity coincided with the group boundaries of partisanship.

LEADERSHIP AND CONGREGATIONAL CULTURE

Previous research focused on the power of ordained pastors to shape political talk in local churches.[36] But in both American churches, the most explicitly partisan cues came from laypeople, not from ordained ministers. For example, Betty, a retired nurse, recalled that she had prayed about the 2000 election with her women's Bible study. During the group prayer, Betty asked for "the Lord to make a way for godly men to get in."

Afterwards, the women talked about the differences between candidates George W. Bush and Al Gore. Betty clarified for the group that "Bush stood for family and good values . . . and I just felt he would uphold the basic Christian tenets of our nation," while Gore "was for abortion."

In both of these American churches, lay leaders initiated most talk about moral issues. Ordained pastors simply blessed their efforts: signing off on their biblical orthodoxy and giving them institutional space. For example, at Northtown Baptist, a lay leader had organized the educational event on same-sex marriage in 2004. Another group of lay leaders had organized to ask Pastor William to recognize a pro-life ministry on Mother's Day. At Lifeway Assembly, Pastor John allowed a member to set up a table in the foyer for "Lutherans for Life" and hand out flyers before church. In previous years, other members had recognized the National Sanctity of Human Life Day during worship, and invited members to take part in regional pro-life activities during the Sunday morning announcements.[37]

Both Northtown Baptist and Lifeway fit a national pattern found in survey research: that political preaching is relatively rare in evangelical churches. In both churches, members recalled their head pastors had simply reminded them of their Christian duty to vote before the 2004 election. At Lifeway Assembly, several members recalled that pastors had made more specific calls to support pro-life candidates. But aside from these instances, pastors talked about moral issues in less explicitly partisan terms, usually by reference to the church's practical ministries. Like other U.S. evangelical congregations, both churches engaged in a fairly limited repertoire of political activism compared to other religious traditions.[38]

At Lifeway Assembly, political cues were legitimately spiritual if they did not involve explicit persuasion or deliberation about public issues. Rather, these cues were communicated through identity-work about who people like "us" should support. For example, a working-class lay leader named Mary explained that Lifeway did not "preach politics." But around elections, "we're urged to read what the people that are running stand for, what they're opposing, what their platform is. Pastor John says read that stuff, just to see which candidates are the best." I asked if members were encouraged to consider any issues in particular. May answered, "I know that Pastor John doesn't want us to vote for anybody that agrees with abortion, that agrees with casinos. Just stuff that isn't morally right, we're not supposed to vote for them." Mary did not consider this to be "preaching politics," because it did not involve explicit persuasion or deliberation—Pastor John was simply engaging in identity-work that fit within the boundaries of legitimately spiritual talk. At Lifeway, moral issues were defined as the issues that all good Christians agreed on—and that good Christians voted on the basis of those issues. There was no public discussion that acknowledged disagreement among Christians about the moral issues themselves, or about which moral issues were most important.

CONGREGATIONS IN INSTITUTIONAL CONTEXT

It is important to consider how larger institutional context shapes the way these churches talk about politics. One possibility is that both churches just talked this way to protect their tax-exempt status. Under U.S. tax law, churches are prohibited from engaging in "political activities" to remain tax-exempt as 501(c)3 organizations. Since the interpretation of political activities is ambiguous,[39] many church leaders choose to avoid naming specific candidates or political parties, and instead talk about issues. Christian Right interest groups play along with this myth of nonpartisan voter education, even when their leaders have explicitly endorsed Republican candidates. For example, James Dobson endorsed George W. Bush's run for president, even as Focus on the Family organized "nonpartisan" voter education events on the dangers of same-sex marriage. Christian Right interest groups insist that it is not "political" to encourage Christians to vote their values—as long as no one names specific candidates or political parties in public gatherings. For example, Christian Right interest groups have coached pastors to use terms like "liberal" and "conservative" rather than naming the political parties directly.[40] These word-games are played by interest groups on both the Right and the Left, as they attempt to mobilize churches for partisan goals without jeopardizing their tax-exempt status.

However, there is more to this story than an instrumental concern for the church's tax-exempt status. First, I found that only the church's paid staff was generally aware of tax-exempt rules, and other lay leaders and members were largely ignorant of such considerations. Second, these cues about the moral issues took on sacred meaning because they were addressed in a properly spiritual way—and that meant keeping politics at arms' length. Avoiding explicit political talk was part of each church's *group style*: the everyday ways that members reinforced their group's boundaries, bonds, and speech norms. Partisan cues were powerful because they were distanced from the dirty business of politics, because they seemed to flow organically from the church's fundamental identity.

As Penny Edgell and others have pointed out, local congregations have an organizational logic that distinguishes them from the worlds of political elites.[41] While political elites are driven by coherent ideologies, local congregations favor a greater sense of pragmatism, therapeutic pursuits, and local concern. Hence, Christian Right elites cannot just storm into local churches and mobilize the faithful any way they please. Interest groups must adapt their message and tactics to fit into the life of local evangelical churches.

Ironically, this divide between local church customs and political rhetoric can actually heighten evangelicals' sense of political victimization. In both churches, members had trouble understanding why gay rights and abortion rights activists felt threatened by Christian political power. In particular, they did not interpret Christian opposition to gay marriage as anti-gay or even political: from their perspective, the church only talked about homosexuality in loving and spiritual ways. As a result, they saw the gay rights movement as an unprovoked, unilateral assault on Christians. For example, a college-educated Northtown member named Alice told me that the gay rights movement's strategy was to "paint the Christian who disagrees with the homosexual lifestyle as someone who is hateful towards those people. Like, 'you must be someone who really is just not compassionate.' . . . That picture is being painted very clearly and that's a way of attacking Christianity." I asked Alice where this perception came from. She responded, "I don't know. But I know it's not coming from conservative Christians. It's not coming from Christians who are doing that." For Alice, it all had "spiritual undertones": Satan was working through the gay rights movement to undermine the Word of God.

Alice's sense of victimization may be surprising, since anti-gay rhetoric abounds in U.S. political discourse. For example, Christian Right figures have compared gays and lesbians to child molesters, and described same-sex marriage as a slippery slope to polygamy and incest.[42] But Alice did not recognize herself in media portrayals of Christian Right activism. The image of the angry, anti-gay Christian bigot did not fit her local church experience. Instead, Alice saw evangelical Christians as simply defending their religious subculture from outside attack. It was the *other* side who was angry and coercive, motivated by their hostility toward Christians. Ironically, this is how gay rights activists feel about the Christian Right, according to social movement scholar Tina Fetner: that they are only defending themselves from militant conservative Christians, who will not let them live in peace.[43] On both sides, gay rights activists and evangelicals feel that the other group is initiating the conflict, and that they are forced into politics to counter the movements of the other side.

This also explains why it has become obligatory for conservative political candidates and spokespeople to emphasize that they love and respect gay people, despite their opposition to same-sex marriage. To many liberals, it seems like the height of hypocrisy to claim to "hate the sin but love the sinner," since the Christian Right seems to mobilize its base by generating fear and hatred toward gays and lesbians.[44] Liberals might assume that this kind of language is directed toward more moderate

Americans and people outside of the evangelical subculture, who would be turned off by hateful rhetoric. But many rank-and-file evangelicals are also upset by an overtly anti-gay tone. Opponents to same-sex marriage must also tread carefully in rallying *their own base*, since many rank-and-file evangelicals want to take a "loving" approach toward gays and lesbians. When candidates and Christian Right elites nuance their language on homosexuality, they are trying to stay relevant to the worlds of local evangelical congregations where demonizing gay individuals is seen as un-Christian. Given the realities of local church culture, it becomes necessary for Christian Right elites to cast *evangelicals* as the victims, so that opposing same-sex marriage becomes an act of self-defense.

CONCLUSION

In both American churches, political cues were powerful because they were not perceived as political at all. Both churches practiced a group style that limited direct political mobilization and deliberation about abortion and homosexuality as political issues. Instead, opposition to homosexuality and abortion was reinforced within lived religion, as members performed the bonds, boundaries, and speech norms that made up their church's group style. To be a good member of the group, one had to acknowledge "our" shared stances on the "moral issues." These moral stances were impossible to challenge without violating these customs of group interaction—and branding oneself as a cultural outsider.

Yet both American churches did more than just signal the "right" positions for Christians to hold on the moral issues. Both Baptist and Pentecostal churches drew on narratives of Christian nationalism that conflated religious identity with opposition to liberal politics. In informal social settings, members sent clear cues about the "right" party identification: which party "we" support and which party "we" oppose.[45] Christian identity was defined in opposition to liberals, understood as both a religious and a political category. Within local religious practice, it was difficult to separate religious identity from affiliation with the Republican Party and conservative ideology.[46]

In the next chapter, I contrast these two American evangelical congregations to two matched Canadian congregations. In both the Canadian churches, evangelicals drew on Christian nationalism in more broadly civic and nonpartisan ways: to draw strong subcultural boundaries, but also to express solidarity with Canadians across cultural, religious, and partisan divides. In official church programs and informal interaction, religious identity was kept separate from the cultural meanings of partisanship.

CHAPTER 4

· · · · · · · · ·

TWO CANADIAN CHURCHES:
CIVIL RELIGION IN EXILE

It was a Wednesday night, and choir practice was about to start at High-point Baptist Church in Hamilton, Ontario. I joined the soprano section, and sang along as the choir rehearsed their annual Easter Cantata to reach out to the Hamilton community. After an hour of singing, Ben, the energetic young choir director, stopped us for a time of prayer. Ben announced that he was going to preach a sermon this Sunday evening, and read his preaching text to us:

> If my people, which are called by my name, shall humble themselves, and pray, and seek my face, and turn from their wicked ways, then will I (God) hear from heaven, and will forgive their sin, and will heal their land. (2 Chronicles 7:14)

Ben commented, "We don't usually think of 'our land' needing healing. But Canada needs the work of God, doesn't it? God will hear from heaven, and forgive our sin, and heal our land. It's not that God wants Canada to be a Christian nation, but he wants the people in Canada to be believers."

An older man in the center spoke up, "I heard an Anglican minister talking on the radio about how Christians need to wake up and change on the gay issue, because Canadian society is changing. And a Jewish guy disagreed with him and said, 'That's not what the Bible says!'" There was a murmur. One woman muttered, "Can you believe that?" Another woman replied, "And it was the Jewish man who stood up."

Leah, a woman in her mid-thirties, spoke up, "Even in the former communist countries . . . I read that the mayor of Moscow said no to the gay rights parade that they wanted to have in that city. And the church was banned there under communism. . . . And I know that the Muslims believe the same as we do on that issue."

An older man reported, "There's a United Church pastor in this area who used to speak out against homosexuality and gay marriage, but then

his son told him that he was that way . . . that his son was homosexual . . . and so now he's changed. And when they ask him why, he says
that the Bible is not relevant for today." The first older man added, "And
the United Church can't figure out why they're losing people! It all started
with the New Curriculum,[1] when they said that you could pick and
choose which parts of the Bible to believe. And now they're performing
gay marriages."

Ben summed it up, "You have to love the people, though. But that
doesn't mean that we agree with everything people do. We have to tell
people what the Bible teaches . . . Let's break up and pray."[2]

Canadian Evangelicals: Differences That Matter

This choir practice took place in Hamilton, Ontario, just a ninety-minute
drive north of Buffalo, New York. In many ways, this Canadian church
group sounded much like the two American churches in my study. Highpoint members lamented "moral decline" in their nation, and mourned
the loss of Christian values in the culture. They drew moral boundaries
against homosexuality, to build a sense of cultural tension with their sociocultural environment. Comparing across the border, I found that U.S.
and Canadian churches shared theological beliefs, and strengthened their
subcultural identity by enforcing distinctive stances on abortion and homosexuality. All four churches even talked about these moral issues in the
same style, avoiding what they considered political talk while encouraging Christians to take action on these issues. But, unlike their American
counterparts, these two Canadian churches did not link religious identity
to partisanship in public church interactions. In Hamilton, both churches
enforced a strong moral consensus on abortion and homosexuality, but
did not draw a shared "cognitive and affective map"[3] of Canada's political terrain that linked Christian identity to a particular party identification. These two Canadian churches kept evangelical identity separate
from political identity in two ways.

First, these Canadian evangelicals saw themselves as embattled, but
not as conservatives in a culture war with liberals. Rather, they were embattled as a *religious minority*, in tension with Canadian society as a
whole. They drew subcultural boundaries against theologically liberal
Christians, but they did not define liberals or other political out-groups
as their adversary. For example, an older choir member at Highpoint
lamented the United Church of Canada's slide into theological liberalism.
He did not blame Canada's moral decline on political actors, but rather
on the church's internal drift from orthodoxy. Both Canadian churches
also wrestled more deeply with what it meant to be a cultural minority,
often describing themselves as missionaries seeking to engage Canada as
a foreign mission field.

Second, the Canadian churches drew on different narratives of *religious nationalism* to make sense of their relationship to their sociocultural environment. Just as in the American churches, leaders often used religious nationalism to rally members for evangelism and leadership. For example, Music Minister Ben appealed to religious nationalism, asking his choir to pray for Canada to motivate them for evangelism and service. But the content of this religious nationalism was different in the two countries. Both Canadian churches identified themselves as a *cultural minority* within a *multicultural* nation, where being a true Canadian and a true Christian were both defined in nonpartisan terms. By contrast, both American churches infused national identity with partisan meaning, where evangelical Christianity and political conservatism were part of being a true American. As a result, both Canadian churches drew subcultural boundaries in ways that did not map directly onto a partisan or ideological divide in politics.

This chapter starts by describing how each of the Canadian churches mapped their subcultural identity, particularly how they talked about moral issues, politics, and national identity. Second, I contrast the *content* of religious nationalism that I observed in American and Canadian churches. In both American churches, religious nationalism was charged with partisan meaning, while in the two Canadian churches, religious nationalism did not have the same partisan overtones. Rather, Canadian churches drew on religious nationalism to bridge religious and partisan boundaries, by sacralizing Canadian multiculturalism in evangelical language. This nonpartisan construction of religious nationalism was closer to what Robert Bellah has called "civil religion." The differences are striking, because these Canadian and American churches were otherwise so similar in their theology and their defense of traditional sexual morality. Finally, I discuss efforts to mobilize Canadian churches around an American-style Christian Right agenda, and how they played out in these congregations during my fieldwork. In both churches, I found a disconnect between Christian Right interest groups and the ways that evangelicals constructed their subcultural identity in local congregations. On multiple occasions, these appeals fell flat because they did not resonate with the everyday uses of religious nationalism that individuals encountered in local Canadian churches.

Highpoint Baptist Church: Hamilton, Ontario, Canada

Highpoint Baptist considered itself a leading evangelical church in the region, with a responsibility to represent a Christian worldview to the larger society. Highpoint sustained cultural tension with Canadian society, using the language of conflict and threat to motivate members to engage the larger society. But, unlike the two American churches, Highpoint drew its subcultural boundaries in exclusively religious terms: against theologically liberal Christians, and against Canadian society as a whole. Highpoint Baptist defined itself as embattled, but as a cultural minority in tension with Canadian society as a whole, not with "liberals" as a political movement.

Highpoint Baptist also wrestled more deeply with what it meant to be a cultural minority. In the two American churches, evangelicals saw themselves as an embattled minority, but also as the rightful owners of American culture, who had been wrongfully pushed aside by "liberals." But at Highpoint, members often went beyond this backward-looking narrative of cultural defense and embraced a forward-looking narrative about living as missionaries to a post-Christian culture. I observed one such episode of identity-work at one of Highpoint's Wednesday night prayer meetings. It was a beautiful summer evening in Hamilton, Ontario, and so we were going to do things differently. "We're going to do a prayer walk," announced Janice, a forty-year-old lay leader. Usually, we met in the church basement for a well-oiled routine: announcements, an opening set of hymns, corporate prayer, and then prayer in small groups. But today, we were going to walk around the neighborhood and pray for all of the church's ministries that reached out to the community. We started by walking around the church perimeter and praying for each of the church's outreach ministries. The group surveyed the community garden and prayed for the families who would receive its bounty. Then, we walked to an open field that would host a soccer camp, and the group prayed that the immigrant children and parents who participated would come to know Christ. I watched as the group mapped their relationship to their community—quite literally moving through geographic space and marking it with social meaning.

For the last prayer site, we took a ten-minute hike to a local public school. Janice informed us that the public schools needed our prayers, because they were about to introduce a new anti-bullying curriculum that encouraged kids to accept homosexuality. "We're going to pray against the system?" said a man, who looked like he was in his seventies. "No, we're going to pray *for* them," said Janice. "That their eyes will be opened." "But we're against the system, we want a new one," he insisted. Janice explained:

> Well, we'd like them to use a different *curriculum* . . . The gay and lesbian groups want them to use a curriculum that teaches them that homosexuality is a good choice to make. And that's not the truth, we want our children to learn the truth. On the other hand, I would never teach my children to be a bigot or to be cruel to an-

other child. We have to teach our children to love everyone, but still teach them that some choices are wrong.

A recently retired woman spoke up: "When I was growing up, I never heard such a thing. People would never even speak of these things in public! And now they're teaching it in the public schools!" Janice explained:

> Yes, children in our day have harder choices to make than we did growing up. They live in a more complicated world, they have more choices that are open to them. And we have to prepare them to make good choices, and at the same time to be loving to everyone around them. . . . There's a teacher in my kid's school who is a homosexual, I believe, but he doesn't teach that, he doesn't make it an issue, and he's a very good teacher. It's just as if there was a teacher who was getting a divorce or committing adultery—you don't fire them for that, that's their life. But you don't teach kids that divorce and adultery are good choices.

Another older man, an immigrant from Germany, turned to me and remarked, "I can't believe how much Canada has changed since I came here fifteen years ago. The moral decline, the lawlessness! In just thirty or forty years! When I was a young man, it was understood that these things were wrong!"

Another middle-aged woman asked, "I'm a teacher, why haven't I heard about this before?" Janice said, "They just sent out a letter at the last minute, I think they want to get it through before parents can speak up. It's hard for us to speak up, because in our culture, people are ridiculed if they take a stand. That's where our culture is now."

Just as in the two American churches, the group avoided explicitly political talk. For example, one woman asked Janice when the next School Board meeting would occur, and Janice wasn't sure, although she thought it might be tonight. Then Janice moved straight to prayer, cutting off any further discussion about political engagement: "Why don't people pray as they feel led, and then when there's an awkward silence, I'll wrap it up and we'll walk back to the church?" Here, Janice was performing identity-work: using the issue of sex education to motivate her prayer group to engage with people outside the evangelical subculture.

In this conversation, Highpoint members expressed the same moral conservatism as both American churches, yet I observed critical differences in how they made sense of their relationship to the larger culture. As in the two American churches, the group drew subcultural boundaries against "the culture" on the basis of their moral opposition to homosexuality, and bemoaned Canada's moral decline. The key difference was that Janice encouraged the group to accept their loss of cultural privilege in Canadian society.[4] When the older members rehashed a backward-looking narrative of cultural defense, Janice countered with a forward-looking narrative, based in her recognition that Christians were now outsiders to Canadian culture. Janice called on Christians to find new ways to engage the majority culture in a post-Christian era, what she called "a more complicated world." Furthermore, the American language of liberal versus conservative was entirely absent from the conversation. For all participants, the most important boundary was between Christians and Canadian society as a whole, not between Christians and political out-groups.

At Highpoint Baptist, I often heard backward-looking talk about the loss of a Christian nation, as in the two American churches. But the *content* of this religious nationalism was dramatically different than in the two American churches. While churches in both countries drew on religious nationalism, the two Canadian churches expressed a stronger awareness of being a *cultural minority* within a *multicultural* nation. The Canada Day celebration at Highpoint Baptist Church provides a vivid illustration. At this Sunday worship service, the congregation celebrated Canada and rededicated itself to transforming the nation. To start the service, the head pastor Mike got up and announced, "Of all the nations of the world . . . God has chosen us to be placed here strategically in this country. I don't know about you, but I love Canada, and I trust that you love Canada too." The congregation applauded loudly. "So today, let's focus on our God, let's focus on our nation and allow God to move in and do a work within us that will change our hearts."

Ben, the music minister, reminded us that Christianity used to be central to national identity. He quoted a verse from Psalm 72, "which our nation was founded on many years ago": which stated that God "shall have dominion from sea to sea, and the river until the ends of the earth." Then he mused:

> You know what, Canada Day used to be called Dominion Day. Not anymore, but that's what it was. And he shall have dominion from sea to sea. He doesn't yet, but someday he will, right? And . . . someday, every knee will bow, and all the nations will gather before the throne and worship the king. And that's why we're here, to celebrate our great God in this great land today.

After a praise song, Ben invited up a laywoman to read an account of the birthday of the Confederation on July 1, 1867. Then the congregation sang the Canadian national anthem.

Finally, six people came up to pray for each region of Canada, standing in front of a row of flags representing the ten provinces, the Yukon,

Northwest Territories, and Nunavat. J.P., a middle-aged Francophone man, prayed for the evangelical churches in Quebec:

> Heavenly father, we want to bring Quebec to you . . . this darkness, oh, Lord God. We thank you that you have sent [Protestant] missionaries over fifty years ago . . . the word being established in Quebec. We pray, oh father, for the churches, that you will strengthen them to face the opposition . . . because of the darkness, the people wandering away from your word and mingling with all kinds of immorality. And father, I pray that many will come to know Christ. Father, mend the family, there's a lot of broken families in Quebec, and we pray that you bring reconciliation.

Here, J.P. was praying about the particular challenges of Protestant evangelists in Quebec, a formerly Catholic society that had turned rapidly secular after the Quiet Revolution of the 1960s.[5] J.P. also prayed about Quebec's troubled relationship with Ottawa: "If there is any bitterness . . . I pray that there will be reconciliation. Heal the land oh father, and bring great revival in Quebec so we may see a great harvest. . . . And father, I pray that we'll stay united in this beautiful country. And I ask in Jesus' name. Amen."

After the team of women and men prayed for each province, Mike, the head pastor, closed with a prayer:

> You are sovereign from coast to coast, oh God, and you rule well. You see the hearts and lives of everyone on this planet. And in your sovereign purpose and will, you established a country known as Canada. And we thank you for Canada; we thank you for every boy and girl, every young adult, every adult that belongs to this country. Every nationality group, every ethnic group, every language that is spoken here. We thank you for the unity and the diversity that Canada is.

Though Canada Day was a special occasion, this service brought together many themes that often appeared in other contexts. Ben, the music minister, invoked the theme of moral decline: Canada had been founded on Christian values but had since departed from them. But this didn't mean that the congregation was being rallied for a cultural backlash against Canada's rising diversity and secularism. Rather, Pastor Mike went on to tell us that Canada's cultural diversity was part of God's sovereign plan. This was a recurring theme in both of the Canadian churches—that Canada's multicultural identity was providential, because it allowed Canadian Christians to reach "people groups" from all over the world.

In both Canadian churches, I often heard the refrain, "God is bringing the nations to us!" This had two meanings in church life. First, it meant that Canadian churches could now reach out to immigrants in their own community, and not just send missionaries to other countries. Second, it meant that internal diversity within Canadian Christianity made global missions work more effective. Naturalized Canadian citizens who retained their parents' language and cultural traditions could return as missionaries to their native "people groups." For example, I attended a fundraiser for Highpoint's short-term mission trip to the West African country of Togo. Each table had a white tablecloth, and red and green paper in the center, with a little basket full of one of Togo's agricultural products, with a Togolese flag coming out of the basket. The church had invited a group of African immigrant women to help them prepare traditional West African food. A layperson named Jay stood up in full African attire, to talk about the goals of the mission trip. Speaking as a white, old-stock Canadian, he gestured toward the food and the table decorations: "This shows you as a church, we reach out to the world. But you know, the world has come to us, and we intermingle with them." This was only one of many occasions at which Highpoint leaders celebrated Canadian multiculturalism and immigration policy, as an opportunity for Canadian churches to deploy missionaries and link local churches across the world.

This openness to multiculturalism may seem surprising, since Canadian Protestants have historically reacted to immigration as a threat to Canada's "Christian" culture.[6] By contrast, Highpoint leaders framed Canadian multiculturalism as part of God's plan for the nations to gather and worship God. Canada's growing ethnic diversity was not primarily framed as a threat, but rather as an opportunity for ministry and evangelism. For example, Highpoint leaders praised Canada's role in refugee resettlement, which opened the country's doors to people fleeing religious or political persecution in their homeland. During my fieldwork, Highpoint actively recruited host families to help Burmese refugees adjust to life in Hamilton, in a partnership with the Immigration Settlement Agency downtown. Coretta, the lay leader who helped organize this matching, told me that she was motivated by both Christian charity and evangelism:

> [I]t's an opportunity to show Christian kindness to vulnerable people who are newcomers, as commanded in the Bible. And there's another reason why we should get involved. It happens that most of the Karen people here in Hamilton are very strong Christians—actually, they're even Baptists! They are very committed to the faith, their religious leader was actually killed in Burma, and they've remained strong through that. But now, the Mormons are very active downtown with the immigrant population, and there's a risk that if we just stand by and let the Mormons take care of it . . . well . . . we

can either watch that happen, or we can reach out to them as fellow Christians.

Within this evangelical framing of immigration, Canada's efforts in refugee resettlement were not just a source of national pride, but also a chance for Christians to support the "persecuted church" from other countries. Instead of bemoaning immigration as a threat to Canada's Christian heritage, the church framed Canada's changing demographics as a race to welcome new Christians and establish them in the "right" kind of Christian church. In a variety of ways, Highpoint Baptist celebrated Canadian multiculturalism as part of a forward-looking narrative of subcultural identity. This forward-looking narrative did not highlight partisan boundaries between liberals and conservatives, but rather celebrated underlying values that evangelicals shared with other Canadians.

This use of religious nationalism was more akin to Bellah's classic concept of *civil religion*, revering consensual symbols that united Canadians across partisan, ethnic, and religious boundaries. But at the same time, Highpoint Baptist constantly defended the strong subcultural boundaries that separated their group from other Canadians. If this was civil religion, it was civil religion in exile. In one breath, Highpoint members used religious nationalism to express their unity with Canadians of all faiths, ethnicities, and political stripes; in the next breath, they used religious nationalism to draw strong subcultural boundaries. Like American evangelicals, these Canadian evangelicals cultivated a sense of embattlement. Religious nationalism allowed Highpoint Baptist to sustain a constant sense of tension with their societal context: to rally their members for action, yet sustain their motivation to engage with people outside of their subculture.

Highpoint Baptist also defined the church's subcultural boundaries by taking "orthodox" stands on issues like abortion and homosexuality. Compared to both American churches, Highpoint even talked about these moral issues in a similar style, avoiding what they considered to be political talk, while still encouraging individual Christians to make their voice heard in the public sphere. But unlike the American churches, Highpoint enforced this moral conformity while still recognizing a diversity of legitimate political identities that existed within the church. For example, the issue of abortion came up during a Sunday night service, when the Head Pastor preached a sermon series on the Ten Commandments: "Right Side Up in an Upside Down World."[7] This was a more casual service in the church's gymnasium, with congregants seated around tables so we could discuss the sermon together. That night, Pastor Robert preached on the Sixth Commandment against murder, arguing that this commandment flows from the fact that humans are "made in the image of God."

Pastor Robert argued that as Canada had departed from biblical values, the value of human life had been lost in the wider culture.

> Each commandment is a whole area of moral value in our culture. The law of respect, a child learns respect in the home, a core command. Without that, everything goes away. Disrespect works its way out into the culture, places of employment, and of course, eventually to God.

Then Pastor Robert listed the social consequences that flowed from Canada's increasingly "amoral culture": increased suicide rates, the practice of abortion, the acceptance of "mercy killing," increased rates of murder and violent crime, and more general problems of uncontrolled anger and hatred. He particularly emphasized the scale of abortion as a problem in Canadian life: "In 2004, there were 170,763 abortions in Canada. Since 1970, there have been 2,792,355. That's 30 abortions for every 100 live births." Then, he broke up the congregation into small groups around their tables, and asked each table to discuss different problems related to the Sixth Commandment: war, capital punishment, abortion, euthanasia, and anger. Pastor Robert encouraged us to consider the challenges of applying this biblical standard to contemporary problems:

> Now, in the evangelical church, we like to paint that wall black, that wall white. But there is a lot of grey—you've read the scriptures. You've got to weigh it through, guided by the spirit of God. Now there are areas that are black and white, but there's grey too.

My table was assigned to talk about abortion. I turned to face a small group of two young couples and two singles in their late twenties, curious to see if they would take up Pastor Robert on his offer to consider abortion's "grey areas." But despite the open-ended format, I quickly learned that there was only one acceptable answer in this discussion: to be opposed to abortion in all circumstances.

Our discussion quickly took the form of coaching each other to give the "right" answers, in an imagined debate with a non-Christian. Phillip started us off, "Well, there's the obvious hard case: the issue of the life of the mother, or a woman who is raped." Jean offered the correct response to this hard case, "Yes, but maybe we shouldn't decide who should die and who should live. It's in God's hands." I was curious to see if the discussion could accommodate diverse views, so I pushed the group: "If it were my friend, I think I would want to save her life!" Jean acknowledged, "Yes, it's hard." Phillip added, "And isn't it rare for rape to end in pregnancy?" I pushed further, "What about the morning-after pill? That's a standard part of rape treatment nowadays." Corey, Jean's husband said, "Yes, that's the question about when life begins."

Then the group agreed on the correct "Christian" stance on the question: life began at conception, which ruled out emergency contraception in case of rape. Throughout this discussion, an unspoken group style limited what opinions could be legitimately expressed about abortion. Supporting a pro-life stance was central to being a good church member and a true evangelical Christian. Pastors were not the only ones enforcing this pro-life consensus; laypeople also enforced the understanding that good Christians were necessarily pro-life. Members enforced this moral consensus by affirming their group bonds, drawing boundaries, and practicing implicit speech norms in small group settings like this one.

While this Sunday night discussion enforced moral conformity on abortion, it did not send partisan cues about what political identities were appropriate for a true Christian. Instead, the broader discussion drew boundaries between Christians and "the world" in ways that did not coincide with the boundaries of partisanship. When Pastor Robert called us back to order, each table shared their conclusions with the rest of the congregation. A middle-aged man reported, "We talked about capital punishment. We decided that it's utopian, with all the corruption in the system." Pastor Robert nodded, "Yes, you can release someone from prison if you make a mistake, but the death penalty is final." The man replied, "Jennifer even said, 'Those without sin, cast the first stone'." The Pastor agreed, "Yes, like the woman caught in adultery. We as evangelicals, we want to stand for truth, but we need to behave more gently." From another table, a woman reported that her group also talked about punishment, but they were concerned that "this principle makes us guilty if we let them out." Pastor Robert said, "Yes, secondary murders, if we let a murderer out and they kill again, we're responsible." Wrapping up the discussion, Pastor Robert prayed, "Lord, we want to act consistently with your character, which includes justice, mercy, and love."

These diverse views on capital punishment were significant, because this issue has increasingly become a partisan flashpoint between Conservatives and Liberals. In 2007, the same year I was in the field, I also watched a shift in the political dynamics of Canadian criminal justice policy. While Canada abolished the death penalty in 1976, Conservative Party leaders have increasingly attempted to rally the public around an American-style "tough on crime" message. In November 2007, Canadian Public Safety minister Stockwell Day announced that Canada would no longer request clemency for Canadian citizens sentenced to capital punishment abroad, a long-standing automatic policy. In response, Liberals passed a motion declaring that the government "should stand consistently against the death penalty, as a matter of principle, both in Canada and around the world."[8] During my fieldwork, Stockwell Day was one of Canada's most high-profile evangelical politicians, and many of the Conservative leaders behind this "tough on crime" shift were also prominent evangelicals.[9] But at the congregational level, laypeople and pastors did not link evangelical identity to this partisan tough on crime message. Rather, their discussion linked both Conservative and Liberal Party stances to "our" theology and identity as evangelical Christians.

This fit a broader pattern. When leaders and members talked about the moral issues at Highpoint Baptist, I did not hear the same slippage between religious identity and partisanship that I heard in both American churches. Across a variety of contexts and settings, Highpoint leaders and members avoided defining "Christian" in opposition to political outgroups: the pro-choice movement, the gay rights movement, or liberals. Rather, they defined their subcultural identity in more narrowly religious terms, using moral issues to draw boundaries between evangelicals and the world. This absence of partisan cues was the most important difference between Highpoint Baptist and Northtown Baptist, an otherwise similar American evangelical church.

On the contrary, I repeatedly heard public acknowledgment of the legitimate political diversity that existed among evangelical Christians, despite their shared opposition to gay marriage and abortion. For example, a deacon named Morton told a Sunday school class for new members that the church was defined by their shared theological beliefs, not by shared politics:

> We want to tell you our story, the story of who we are as a church. This story is not going to be told by our nationality. This story won't be told by our occupations . . . We have all different occupations. This story won't be told by our income . . . This story won't be told by our political views. So what holds us together? We are held together by what we believe, that's what draws us together every week. That's how we tell our story: the things that we hold in common together.

I found that party identification was a closely guarded secret at Highpoint Baptist, a private matter of conscience that members did not even signal in informal, social settings. This recognition of political diversity was even built into Highpoint Baptist's programming that promoted a "Christian witness" on public issues. For example, the church had organized a series of sermons and discussions on "hot-button" issues in 2006, which included a discussion on Christians and Labor Unions. Recalling this event, informants could not remember any particular stance that was taken on the labor movement, for or against; rather, the event was a general discussion of how Christians should relate to unions.

Instead of defining themselves as conservatives by opposition to liberals, Highpoint Baptist drew boundaries between "true Christians" and

Canadian secular culture in general. These moral issues marked the theological boundary that separated authentic, evangelical Christians from mere "cultural Christians" who went along with Canada's secular trends. Though Highpoint Baptist defended the same conservative moral stances as the two American churches, they drew on a different narrative of religious nationalism to make sense of their subcultural identity.

Canada: Grace Pentecostal

I found the same pattern at Grace Pentecostal: the church practiced a vivid form of Christian nationalism, and enforced a moral consensus on abortion and homosexuality, but did not construct Christian identity in partisan terms. Like Highpoint Baptist, Grace Pentecostal also contended for the soul of Canada, but using the distinctive charismatic language of spiritual warfare. The absence of partisan cues was surprising, because the church mixed Christian nationalism and end-times theology in ways that might sound authoritarian, or at best uncivil, to a cultural outsider. For example, a visiting evangelist named Tom used this combative, nationalistic language to motivate Grace Pentecostal members to share the gospel with the "forcefulness of Kingdom authority."

> I'm glad I'm a servant in 2007. I think it's a privilege to live in these closing moments, and I don't care how hackneyed that gets over the years. I know that God wins, I know that the church thrives. I think He's positioning us for a phenomenal move in these End Times . . . But there are assignments of darkness that try to lead the people of God into deception. . . . There are idols in Canada, and not just found in Buddhist temples. The truth, the whole truth, is Jesus Christ and he will set you free. . . . Elijah was so committed to the move of God in his generation, that he was ready to lay down his life for it. . . . And he rebuilt the altar of the Lord that had been in ruins. . . . Oh that this altar would be rebuilt in Canada, so that Canada would see, and this nation would be turned back. We need the fire of God. . . . We confess that Canada is a nation that needs to see the power of God. We confess that Hamilton is a city that needs to see the power of God.[10]

Finishing his sermon, Tom invited everyone to come forward to commit themselves to reclaiming Canada for God, and about forty people surged forward. Tom and a team of prayer counselors laid hands on people and prayed with them. A few worshippers began to speak in tongues. As the band began to play, a man was slain in the spirit, and Tom deftly lowered him to the ground. After an extended period of intense worship and intercessory prayer, a worship leader dismissed the congregation, but invited people to stay behind for prayer.

Like the American Pentecostal church in this study, Grace Pentecostal strengthened their subcultural identity by drawing on the distinctive charismatic practice of "spiritual warfare." Tom drew on a militant, backward-looking narrative of religious nationalism: Christians must reclaim Canada's lost Christian heritage, and "rebuild the altar" so that their "nation would be turned back." Tom seemed to express a dim view of religious diversity, denigrating the "idols" found in Buddhist temples as well as the idolatry of Canada's secular culture. This message might sound dangerously authoritarian: since Canadian Christians were living in the "End-Times," they must position themselves to shower the power of God in Canada in these "closing moments" before the Second Coming. Certain strains of end-times theology have fueled Dominionist political movements in the United States, movements that call for an authoritarian "Biblical" regime to prepare the country for Christ's return.[11] In her 2010 book *The Armageddon Factor*, journalist Marcy McDonald warned that Canadian evangelicals may be advancing a similar Dominionist agenda north of the border.[12] Was this happening at Grace Pentecostal?

After spending a year with Grace Pentecostal, it was clear that their militant rhetoric of spiritual warfare and Christian nationalism did not advance authoritarian political goals. Like the American Pentecostal church in this study, Grace Pentecostal uses Christian nationalism to mobilize laypeople for religious service, by heightening their sense of threat and tension with the surrounding culture. This rhetoric dramatized the urgent need for Christians to engage with others outside their subculture, and look toward a larger national community. When leaders like Tom spoke about showing their nation "the power of God," he was referring to personal witnessing, rather than political domination. Furthermore, the content of this Christian nationalism was more thoroughly nonpartisan in this Canadian Pentecostal church. In the U.S. Pentecostal church, religious nationalism often carried strong partisan overtones, even though it did not advance authoritarian goals or even explicit political mobilization. By contrast, Grace Pentecostal defined their subculture as a *cultural minority* in a multicultural nation, in tension with Canadian culture as a whole rather than specific political outgroups.

Like Highpoint Baptist, Grace Pentecostal celebrated Canadian multiculturalism, yet had an uneasy relationship to religious pluralism. For example, the Head Pastor Jerald drew on Christian nationalism to argue that Canadian Christians had a special role to play in these last days of the end-times. In a fiery "Missions Sunday" sermon, Pastor Jerald pointed to Canada's growing ethnic diversity and argued, "God has positioned us as a church and as a people for such a time as this. . . . Our vision is local, is Canadian, and is global." Pastor Jerald ended by praying ecstatically, as a handful of church members began to speak in tongues:

> Pray faithfully, that God's plan will not be thwarted. . . . Come and set people free, oh God, in our world! The days are short! The rapture of the church, the days are short! Help us to go out in power while we can. We cry out in power. . . . There is one name over every name. We proclaim it over the Muslim world, over the Hindu world, over the religious world, over our nation, over our world.

Within their theology, Grace Pentecostal rejected all other religions and philosophies as part of Satan's work to lead people into deception. Yet paradoxically, Grace Pentecostal celebrated Canadian multiculturalism to define their distinctive mission as Canadian Christians, evangelizing the nations in these "last days" before the rapture.

At Grace Pentecostal, I occasionally heard backward-looking rhetoric about defending Canada's Christian heritage. But such talk was counterbalanced with a strong forward-looking narrative about engaging Canada as a cultural minority. At one church business meeting, Pastor Jerald encouraged Canadian Christians to accept their status as a tiny cultural minority, and to rethink their strategies accordingly. For example, he described a church plant that met at a bar on a local university campus, "And that's an unreached people group in our mind, because there's a whole generation that doesn't know much about Jesus." By describing young college students as an "unreached people group," Pastor Jerald was reframing Canada as a foreign mission field that Christians must engage as outsiders. To back up his point, he described another church plant that Grace Pentecostal was supporting in Nova Scotia: "When you hear the percentage of people on Cape Breton Island who are not church goers, it is shocking and disturbing . . . There are more Christians per capita in Kenya than in Cape Breton Island . . . They've purchased an old United Church and they're renovating it." Here, Pastor Jerald heightened a sense of cultural tension by emphasizing that evangelicals were a tiny minority in places like Nova Scotia.

In both Canadian churches, I found that members and leaders frequently acknowledged that a strategy of cultural defense no longer made sense. Rather, it was important to accept their starting point as a cultural minority, and engage the culture as "foreign" missionaries rather than "native" defenders. This was a very different narrative of cultural embattlement than I heard in the two American churches. Evangelicals looked back to Canada's imagined past as a Christian nation, but envisioned their future through this missionary metaphor. Pastor Jerald invoked this forward-looking narrative when he described a team of evangelicals fixing up an old United Church building. Rhetorically, Pastor Jerald used this image to stand in for a larger historical narrative that Canadian evangelicals told about the rapid loss of Protestant hegemony in Canada.[13] Since the 1960s, Canada's mainline Protestant denominations suffered even more precipitous decline than the American mainline, while only evangelical groups had sustained their numbers. This collective memory set the context for Canadian evangelicals, as they sought to "turn their nation back," and "rebuild the altar that sat in ruins."[14]

While this Canadian Pentecostal church drew on narratives of religious nationalism, they did not define a political adversary as the American Pentecostal church did. To move people to action, social movements must engage in *adversarial framing*, or identify an antagonistic person or group that is responsible for their situation.[15] At Lifeway Pentecostal in Buffalo, leaders and members frequently defined the pro-choice movement and liberals as their adversaries, or out-groups responsible for America's moral decline. But this kind of adversarial framing was missing from Grace Pentecostal Church in Hamilton. Instead, Canada's secularism was blamed on the church itself, particularly the old mainline Protestant denominations that had abandoned theological orthodoxy and failed in their task to evangelize the nation. Grace Pentecostal drew strong subcultural boundaries to separate evangelicals from diverse out-groups, but none of these were singled out as their *antagonists* responsible for Canada's adverse situation.

This difference was apparent when Grace Pentecostal members engaged in spiritual warfare to influence public life through supernatural means. For example, Dolores, a lay prayer minister at Grace Pentecostal, described a small group that met regularly to pray for the city and the nation:

> We pray for a spiritual awakening, we pray for the schools, for our youth, they're having a tough time, so we pray that God continue to draw them, to make avenues for them to be able to be reached. We pray for the city as a whole. We pray for the leaders of our city. That they would be guided by wisdom and that they make right choices for our city . . . That as a nation there would be a spiritual turning back to God and the basic roots of Christianity, a revival that our leaders would be influenced by Godly people and make Godly decisions for the nation.

When I pressed Dolores to explain what kinds of policy changes they prayed for, she told me they never got very specific, besides praying for greater "Godly influence" in the public schools:

Once prayer has been taken out of the schools, we've seen a decline in the school system. There were problems before but now I see it has escalated into a lot of things. They removed any type of Godly influence. I'd like to see that return.

Given the militant language of spiritual warfare, I was particularly interested to see if "they" carried particular partisan or political associations. I pushed Dolores to explain how this "Godly" influence had been removed. But Dolores lacked a clear picture of who "they" were; she could not identify a particular political adversary who was to blame for Canada's moral decline.

Dolores pointed to the removal of the Lord's Prayer, which was recited in Ontario public schools until it was struck down by a court decision in 1988. She explained,

[Y]ou can't go wrong with the Lord's Prayer. It's basic and if kids understand it to a certain degree, it would impact their life at a young age . . . Just Godly teachers that would influence them. I know they can't come out and preach the gospel, but just sharing the goodness in things . . . We pray for the Holy Spirit to move on kids and stand against the plans of the enemy, the enemy's plan is to get kids at a young age, to turn them against God at a young age. We pray that God will protect them. That we'll see them behave the way they're supposed to behave. . . . [We pray] that there will be a more wholesome atmosphere in the city, more of a family unit. That people go back to the family values that we kind of slipped away from.

Here, Dolores had a clear understanding of an adverse situation: the loss of family values in Canada. But she lacked an adversarial framing of the problem: no one in particular was to blame; rather, Canada had simply "slipped away from" these Christian values. This narrative of religious nationalism was different than the narratives that I heard in the two American churches. Like American evangelicals, Dolores drew on a collective memory about Canada's lost heritage as a "Christian nation." But, unlike in the two American evangelical churches, she could not identify a political adversary that was to blame for this moral decline.

In both Canadian churches, the only out-group that I heard publicly blamed was the Protestant mainline, who had failed in their duties to evangelize the nation. The loss of Protestant hegemony was blamed on Protestants themselves, not on politically identified out-groups like liberals, the gay rights movement, or the pro-choice movement. While Grace Pentecostal practiced spiritual warfare to sustain cultural tension with their environment, they defined the enemy in exclusively spiritual terms.

Within Dolores's distinctively Pentecostal outlook, her prayers were expected to influence the city and the nation by "binding up the enemy, the demonic forces in the name of Jesus and asking God to release his anointing, his power and goodness. It's coming against the enemy, against rebellion, pride, self-indulgence, self-centeredness." By contrast, at the American Pentecostal church, this enemy was associated with particular political out-groups, as when a small group prayed for "liberal politicians" who refused to acknowledge God.

In short, the most notable difference between the American and Canadian Pentecostal churches was in how they mapped their religious identity onto the boundaries of partisanship. Like both American churches, Grace Pentecostal enforced distinctive stances on the moral issues of abortion and homosexuality, and encouraged members to publicly defend these values. But unlike in the two American churches, I did not hear the same steady drumbeat of partisan cues at Grace Pentecostal. The church enforced a strong moral consensus on abortion and homosexuality, without drawing a shared "cognitive and affective map"[16] of Canada's political terrain that linked Christian identity to a particular party identification.

This difference was particularly apparent when Grace Pentecostal members observed U.S. politics across the border. On multiple occasions, I watched Grace members puzzle through the Culture War language that they heard from U.S.-based television and evangelical organizations. For example, an informal group went out for lunch after Sunday worship, when they started chatting about how Fox News had become available on Canadian cable.[17] Several members of the group had recently started watching Glenn Beck, so I asked the group to explain who he was. A stay-at-home mother named Jennifer said, "He has a show on CNN, before Nancy Grace." Ryan, a young assistant pastor, added, "He's a real conservative Mormon." Jennifer said, "Yes, he says he's not a Republican, he's 'conservative'." She made quotation marks with her fingers, to explain a distinction that was less familiar for Canadians. "I really like his show," said Ryan, "because he takes positions that Christians take." But in his next breath, Ryan qualified his support for Glenn Beck:

> But you have to watch out with that stuff. You know, because Jesus isn't a Republican or a Democrat. Some Christians are all about just two issues, and that's abortion and homosexuality. But when you look at the Bible, you see that it talks about social justice, and defending widows and orphans. Someone said, "What if a politician promised that he was going to destroy pornography, and lower taxes, and give us full employment, and fight crime, and defend the family?" You'd say, "That's great, I'll vote for you." But that's what

Hitler promised. And people fell for it. Anyone can say they stand for Christian values, so you have to be careful.

As this conversation shows, Canadian evangelicals were increasingly exposed to the polarized political rhetoric of American media. But this does not mean that individuals were being passively indoctrinated into an American-style Christian Right identity. Rather, Grace members were actively puzzling through this unfamiliar culture war language in group settings like this one.

For this group, it was refreshing to hear a commentator opposing abortion and same-sex marriage on religious grounds, a viewpoint that they rarely heard on Canadian outlets. But Jennifer was also puzzled that a Mormon was speaking for the Christian viewpoint, since the Church of Latter-Day Saints was historically disparaged as a cult within North American evangelicalism.[18] She recognized that Glenn Beck identified himself as a "conservative," and that he advocated morally conservative positions that evangelical Christians also shared. But in our personal interview, Jennifer was careful to point out that Glenn Beck was "actually" a Mormon, and that she considered his political views in spite of, not because of, his religious convictions. It was not obvious why being conservative qualified Glenn Beck to speak for evangelical Christians. This conflation of partisanship and religious identity still struck them as foreign; this was not how they mapped their identity as Canadian evangelicals in church life.

In summary, both Canadian evangelical churches defined a subcultural identity by taking shared stances on the moral issues of abortion and homosexuality. Yet neither congregation reinforced a shared map of Canada's political terrain that linked Christian identity to a particular party identification. In the next section, I argue that this was the most important difference between the two U.S. and two Canadian congregations: not their stances on the moral issues, or their attempts to influence public debate on these issues, but the way that evangelical identity was linked to *partisanship* in everyday church life.

COMPARING CHURCHES IN THE UNITED STATES AND CANADA

Both U.S. and Canadian churches were quite similar in how they talked about political engagement. While all four churches reinforced shared stances on the "moral issues" of abortion and homosexuality, it was considered inappropriate to talk about these issues at church in ways that were perceived as political. All four churches had engaged in brief, sporadic efforts to rally the congregation for action on these issues, but such efforts were rare, initiated primarily by laity, and kept to the periphery of official church activities. Comparing churches across the border, the more important differences lay in the *narratives of Christian nationalism* that members used to make sense of their responsibilities to a broader society. While both Canadian churches used vivid religious nationalism to strengthen their subcultural identity, they drew on a different set of narratives that kept religious identity separate from partisanship. By contrast, both American churches reinforced a strong implicit connection between religious identity and partisanship in their everyday uses of Christian nationalism.

On the rare occasions that churches talked directly about political engagement, I found that U.S. and Canadian churches engaged in the same limited political repertoire. For example, in 2006, a female layperson had brought a petition to Highpoint Baptist after Canada's Supreme Court ruled on gay marriage. During the announcement time in worship, she asked Highpoint members to call their Member of Parliament to express their support for traditional marriage. While this laywoman had gained the pastor's permission to make this appeal, she did so as an individual, during the worship time that was dedicated to open announcements from laypeople. This format was strikingly similar to how the American Baptist church responded to the same-sex marriage debate: a laywoman had organized an informational session, which she framed as a nonpartisan effort to equip members to share their beliefs about traditional marriage in a loving way. Churches on both sides of the border had made sporadic efforts to influence public life on abortion and homosexuality, but these efforts were limited by the congregation's group style. Instead, political influence worked primarily through implicit cues about what political affiliations were for "people like us."

In both American churches, the link between evangelical identity and conservative politics went beyond abortion and homosexuality. Religious nationalism was also closely tied to militarism and support for the war in Iraq, in ways that I did not observe in the two Canadian churches. In both churches, I found that military service and war were often interpreted in sacred terms.[19] In the fall of 2007, Northtown Baptist's lobby was graced with a prominent nationalistic display dedicated to the church's young people who were serving in Iraq and elsewhere. There were quilt squares dedicated to each of the divisions of the Armed Forces, and two symmetrical squares featuring an American flag with the profile of a soldier kneeling, a black profile of humble prayer against the backdrop of the American flag.[20] During the same period, Lifeway Assembly had a similar display that mixed religious and patriotic symbolism to honor the American military. By combining the symbolism of Christianity and militarism, these displays evoked a Christian nationalist narrative: the War in Iraq was part of America's God-given role in the world.

War was not always discussed in a partisan way in these churches. For example, in a Sunday school class at Northtown Baptist, a woman in her thirties named Donna prayed, "We want to lift up our president, may he be guided by you. People are saying 'Should we be there?' 'Is this another Vietnam?' I just pray that the House and the Senate would back him up and give him the troop support he needs. And that you would give him guidance. It's gotten to where we don't know what to believe, and church members, and laypeople, are divided about whether we should even be there. I just pray that our president would look to you for guidance, and that he would know what to do." Here, Donna seemed to be assuming that the war was part of God's plan, when she prayed that the House and Senate would give President Bush "the troop support he needs." But in her prayer, Donna also acknowledged that Christians were internally divided on the war, and refrained from implying that Christians were only one side of this political debate.

However, there were other times at Northtown when it was clearly implied that Christians should support the war as a sacred cause. On Memorial Day, an Air Force captain preached about the war in Iraq as an expression of the truth of Christianity, and how his military career intersected with his walk with God. A middle-aged man recounted this sermon in an interview:

> He just talked about a two-sided message, a spiritual message . . . the right and wrong and our guys are serving in Iraq, out there, hoping that we can rebuild the school. He was in the Air Force, and the army guys are standing there, making sure nobody blows up the school. Meanwhile there's someone strapping on a vest full of nails and explosives trying to kill us. And there are absolute rights and absolute wrongs. Rebuilding and protecting schools so people can get an education is an absolute right. And blowing a person up is an absolute wrong.

This "two-sided message" was simultaneously spiritual and partisan, since this Air Force captain legitimated the war in Iraq as a religious struggle between right and wrong. Christians should support the war because "we" believe in absolute right and wrong. Here, the speaker drew a symbolic boundary between "Christians" and people who do *not* believe in absolute right and wrong—by implication, terrorists, but also Americans who criticize the war effort. In defending militarism, this Air Force captain echoed the language that Northtown members used to draw moral boundaries on the moral issues. In this public worship service, partisan cues worked at the implicit level, with no specific reference to Democrats or Republicans, liberals or conservatives. But this message reinforced a shared map of Christian identity, which defined "us" in opposition to "liberals": those people who rejected God's plan for America, who did not believe in absolute right and wrong, and who did not support the president. In this way, Christian identity became powerfully conflated with partisanship in everyday church life.

By comparison, I never encountered Canadians praying for Christian leaders in a way that explicitly spiritualized warfare. At both Canadian churches, members with loved ones serving in Afghanistan would ask for prayer for Canadian soldiers there, but Canada's military operations were never publicly justified using religious language. At the same time, people at both churches expressed pride in Canada's armed forces.[21] For example, Highpoint Baptist showed a slide show on Canada Day about the church's loved ones who were serving in the military. But I never heard Canada's military role in the world being framed in religious terms in public church interaction. In short, the U.S. evangelical churches did not just link religious identity to conservative politics by teaching "orthodox" positions on the "moral issues." Both of these churches continually reinforced a partisan narrative of religious nationalism that went beyond abortion and homosexuality. In future chapters, I show that these different narratives of religious nationalism played an important role in the construction of political identities. In both countries, churches appealed to "the nation" for similar religious purposes: to shore up subcultural boundaries and rally commitment for religious leadership and service. But in the two American churches, religious nationalism resonated with Republican Party ideology, while in the two Canadian churches, religious nationalism did not have these partisan overtones.

Conversely, I never heard American evangelicals talk about multiculturalism as a positive element of U.S. national identity. While both U.S. evangelical congregations aspired to "diversity," this theme was not central to their narratives of religious nationalism. Instead, both American evangelical churches talked about diversity in the language of *personalism*, cultivating close interpersonal relationships that bridged ethnic boundaries.[22] Both churches aspired to be a "New Testament church," by modeling loving relationships across cultural and racial boundaries. But I never saw multiculturalism being celebrated by native-born white evangelicals as a central feature of *national identity*, as part of God's plan for America. Rather, they understood diversity in the language of personalism, in terms of loving relationships between individuals to create a united church "family." This difference is important, since nationalism has historically played a critical role within American evangelical political engagement.[23]

This multicultural nationalist discourse was striking because it was well-established among the *white, native-born* majority in both Canadian churches. In an American context, scholars have documented a growing number of evangelical churches that cultivate an intentionally multiracial identity or serve a majority-immigrant population. These immigrant and multiethnic churches explore new ways of being a "good American" that look very different from these two American churches.[24] But in an American context, multicultural churches like *Mosaic* in Los Angeles operate within a particular niche—their counter-narrative of American identity has not yet become mainstream for white evangelicals.[25]

In a Canadian context, this multicultural discourse was not limited to particular niches within evangelicalism; it had become a mainstream part of the evangelical subculture for white, native-born Christians. While Grace Pentecostal had developed a strong minority of recent immigrants, Highpoint Baptist was overwhelmingly composed of what they referred to as "old stock Canadians." For these white Canadian evangelicals, it was simply common sense that multiculturalism was part of God's plan for their nation. In both Canadian churches, this multicultural narrative was the *dominant* narrative of Christian nationalism that white evangelicals drew from the wider field of Canadian evangelicalism. This makes sense, when we consider that Canadian Protestants were already practicing a multicultural civil religion in the 1960s as a response to the challenge of Catholic Quebec.[26] For American Protestants, multiculturalism is instead tied to the cultural trauma of the 1960s, when white evangelicals rejected the civil rights movement.

In comparative perspective, we gain greater perspective on how the American tradition of civil religion has fractured since the 1960s. Robert Wuthnow has argued that American "civil religion" has become split along liberal-conservative lines, so that evangelical Christians defend a very different construction of national identity than liberal Christians or secular people. While displays of civil religion have diminished in public life, American evangelicals continue to assert that Christianity is the rightful foundation for national identity and a moral code for public life. What is interesting is that these Canadian evangelical churches also defend their country's tradition of civil religion, but in a civic, nonpartisan way.[27] Since some form of multiculturalism is celebrated by all three of Canada's major political parties, these symbols were not associated with any particular party, but rather invoked an "imagined community" that included all Canadians.[28]

Both Canadian churches also wrestled more deeply with what it meant to be a cultural minority, often describing themselves as missionaries seeking to engage Canada as a "foreign" mission field. Both churches drew subcultural boundaries against theologically liberal Christians, yet I did not hear liberals or other political out-groups identified publicly as their adversary. While they were embattled, they were embattled as a *religious minority*, in tension with Canadian society as a whole. This narrative of subcultural identity was not idiosyncratic to these two churches; it reflected broader trends within Canadian evangelicalism. In a random sample of 478 Canadian evangelical churches, Michael Wilkinson and Sam Reimer found that "missional" was the second-most common identifier claimed by pastors, second only to "evangelical." More than one-third of Canadian Baptist churches and more than 75 percent of Canadian Pentecostal pastors claimed this label for their church. The missional movement, associated with theologians like Darrel Gruder, is not a marginal or countercultural emphasis within Canadian evangelicalism like the emerging church. Rather, this label is disproportionately embraced by Canada's largest and most demographically vibrant evangelical churches.[29]

These ethnographic findings help us interpret puzzling differences between U.S. and Canadian evangelicalism that are found in survey research. For example, Canada's theologically conservative Protestants report less antipathy toward gays and lesbians than their American counterparts, even though they are just as morally opposed to homosexuality. In 2005, only 12 percent of Canada's regularly attending conservative Protestants felt "very uneasy" about meeting a male homosexual, while 33 percent of their American counterparts rated their feelings toward gays and lesbians as *zero* on a 0–100 feeling thermometer. From 1984 to 2000, negative affect toward homosexuals declined steadily among both Canadian and American evangelicals, as in the general population. From 2000 to 2005, feelings of unease around lesbians and gay men continued to decline among Canadian evangelicals. But from 2000 and 2005, zero-degree coldness toward gays and lesbians actually *increased* among American regularly attending evangelicals, from 26.7 percent to 33.6 percent.[30] U.S. and Canadian evangelicals seem to have responded to the gay marriage debates of the early 2000s in diverging ways, despite their shared moral conservatism. Canadian evangelical churches may be less likely to cultivate an adversarial relationship with gays and lesbians, because they see themselves as embattled by Canadian culture in general, not the gay rights movement or liberals in particular.

American evangelicals are not just bound to conservative politics by the moral issues of abortion and homosexuality. In the next chapter, I describe how both American churches reinforced a "natural" connection between faith and conservative, laissez-faire economic policies, while Canadian churches did not. Comparing across the border, I found that American narratives of Christian nationalism anchored this commonsense connection between evangelical theology and conservative economics.

CHAPTER 5
. . . .

EVANGELICALS, ECONOMIC CONSERVATISM, AND NATIONAL IDENTITY

In 2001, the Bush administration established the White House Office of Faith-based and Community Initiatives, and generated a public controversy about the role of religion in providing public services. Prominent American evangelical leaders advocate a "Compassionate Conservative" approach to poverty, claiming that decentralized, voluntary caring is a superior alternative to state-initiated, structural solutions.[1] Many scholars argue that evangelical Christians are particularly resistant to redistributionist social policy and more supportive of economic laissez-faire. Pundits have characterized rank-and-file evangelicals as Compassionate Conservatives: personally generous toward the poor, but critical of the welfare state as a means to address poverty.[2]

But in cross-national perspective, this link between evangelicalism and economic conservatism is hardly universal.[3] This becomes clear when one compares the United States with Canada, where about 10 percent of the population is evangelical Protestant, compared to 25 percent in the United States. In both countries, evangelicals maintain strong subcultural boundaries based on a shared set of theological beliefs and "strict" moral standards, and are similarly opposed to abortion and homosexuality. Yet U.S. and Canadian evangelicals diverge dramatically in their attitudes toward income inequality, the government's role in society, and the welfare state. Both evangelical and non-evangelical Canadians are more concerned about economic inequalities and more supportive of government's role in alleviating them than are their American counterparts.[4] This leaves us with a puzzle: Why is the evangelical subculture linked to economic conservatism in the United States but not Canada?

This is an important question, since scholars often assume that evangelicals' individualistic theology makes them economically conservative. Christian Smith and Michael Emerson argue that most Americans are individualists, but white American evangelicals subscribe to "accountable individualism," which emphasizes moral accountability before God, and tends to reject any attempts to evade responsibility for one's situation by pointing to structural forces. This "anti-structuralism" makes white evangelicals resist structural explanations of inequality and government attempts to remedy them. Instead, evangelicals prefer to transform unaccountable individuals using the "relational strategy," by addressing the good and bad influences of personal relationships like family and friends. Because of this theological emphasis on accountable individualism, evangelicals are even more intensely committed to the values of individualism than other Americans.[5] By contrast, Black Protestants have an alternative tradition of collective struggle for racial equality, which counterbalances their theological concern with individual accountability. Mainline Protestantism sustains a Social Gospel tradition, which advocates policy reforms that fight structural sin and achieve social progress.[6]

Multiple studies find that theological conservatism and economic conservatism are correlated among white, middle-class evangelicals in the United States. Theological conservatism and membership in evangelical denominations are strong predictors of anti-welfare and small-government attitudes. White evangelicals are divided along socioeconomic lines, with middle-class evangelicals more inclined toward economic laissez-faire than poorer ones.[7] But controlling for socioeconomic status, religious commitment leads to strong, significant increases in anti-egalitarian and small-government attitudes among evangelical Protestants, but not mainline Protestants or Catholics.[8] White American evangelicals are also sensitive to framing effects related to personal responsibility. While all Americans tend to be more generous to "people in need" rather than "people on welfare," white evangelicals are particularly punitive toward "undeserving" target populations.[9] This fits the argument that redistributive social policy clashes with accountable individualism.

But why do white American evangelicals draw on this *particular* tool to evaluate welfare policy, from their broader theological toolkit? Conservative Protestant theology is a mix of ideas about scripture, sin, and salvation, which contains a logic of compassion as well as a logic of judgment.[10] In their personal charity to the poor, white evangelicals are more likely to draw on theological tools about compassion, rather than judgment. Theological conservatives give more generously to the poor than other Americans, if generosity is measured in terms of charitable giving, rather than social policy attitudes. While religiosity increases charitable giving for liberal Protestants and Catholics, it increases giving the most for conservative Protestants.[11] Why don't American evangelicals draw on the logic of compassion to affirm the welfare state? Conversely, why don't

Canadian evangelicals draw on accountable individualism to reject the welfare state? This raises an unanswered problem in the sociology of culture: whether and how some cultural elements control, anchor, or organize others.[12]

To solve this puzzle, I compared how evangelical churches in the United States and Canada talked about poverty and the role of government. Though all four churches drew on the same repertoire of conservative theology, their religious discourse about poverty was very different. In both American churches, the growth of the welfare state was associated with America's decline as a Christian nation. American evangelicals defined "pure" compassion by opposition to government programs, which were seen as degrading and morally corrupting. Compassion toward poor people was not interpreted in terms of national solidarity, but as "grace" to people assumed to be undeserving. By contrast, both Canadian churches talked about compassion toward the poor by reference to *positive* collective memories about the welfare state. Acts of religious charity toward domestic poor people were interpreted as expressions of national solidarity and social inclusion. Canadian churches did not rely as extensively on the language of grace to talk about poverty, because they extended cultural membership to "our" poor as fellow Canadians. Comparing across sites, I found that constructions of national identity worked an *anchoring mechanism* for religious talk about poverty, leading U.S. and Canadian evangelicals to use their shared theological tools in very different ways.[13]

Based on this analysis, I argue that *visions of national solidarity* play a critical role in linking religious practice to political attitudes and civic engagement. In the sociology of religion, there is growing recognition that religious subcultures imagine their broader national context in varying ways. This sense of national community can motivate the faithful to bridge social inequality and group boundaries, in a way that parallels the notion of religion as social capital. Alternately, religious groups can define cultural membership in ways that exacerbate social inequality, enforce exclusionary social boundaries, or weaken the links between religion and civic engagement.[14] Yet this critical relationship between religion, cultural membership, and national identity is often treated as a separate topic, relegated to specialized debates about civil religion or religious nationalism.[15] When scholars examine the political and civic effects of religion, they do not regularly consider how religious groups draw boundaries of cultural membership, or draw on "the nation" as a schema within religious practice.[16] In this chapter, I show that economic conservatism among American evangelicals is anchored by religious constructions of national identity, in ways that previous scholarship attributed to theology alone.

A "THIN COHERENCE" APPROACH TO POLITICAL CULTURE

This chapter compares evangelicals in the United States and Canada, to understand how American evangelicals have become so closely tied to economic conservatism. This comparative approach to political culture is indebted to the work of Seymour Martin Lipset. But I reject Lipset's assumption that political culture is internally coherent, consensual, integrated, and stable over time. Below, I lay out an alternative approach to cross-national comparison, which assumes a relatively "thin" coherence between elements of political culture.[17]

In a classic comparative study, Lipset argued that the United States was more like Canada than any other country, yet each society was organized according to different "national values." As former British colonies, Canada and the United States had shared roots in a broad liberal tradition.[18] But through its revolutionary founding, the United States developed a more individualistic political culture, while Canada sustained a stronger collectivist and social-democratic tradition that deferred to state authority.[19] Lipset defined political culture in Parsonian terms, as latent variables that characterized whole nations. Within this research tradition, national values shaped the development of individual personalities and the evolution of social institutions.[20]

But in the 1980s, many scholars began to reject the idea that societies are organized around a coherent set of national values.[21] The "strong program" in cultural sociology replaced Talcott Parsons's thin analysis of values with thick descriptions of culture's internal structures.[22] Denying that values motivated behavior, Ann Swidler redefined culture as a "repertoire" of symbols and strategies that people draw on to guide practical lines of action.[23] New comparative-historical research showed that "essential" U.S.-Canada differences were actually shaped by power struggles and pathways of institutional development, not different national values.[24] Other scholars debunked Lipset's assumption that a nation's "founding moments" permanently imprinted its national character. Indeed, collective memories about a nation's founding moments changed over time, as elites constructed the past to meet the needs of the present.[25] Working in diverse fields, scholars converged on a critique of national values and its associated cultural paradigm.

Political culture was subsequently re-conceptualized as a *repertoire* of internally heterogeneous elements, contested by members of different subgroups and susceptible to change. Comparative scholars argued that different national contexts made some tools more available than others, through historical and institutional channels.[26] Drawing on this new paradigm, survey researchers have found that cross-national differences in public opinion cannot be reduced to American individualism versus Canadian collectivism. On a variety of measures, Canadians are as committed to the values of individual self-reliance and personal responsibility as are Americans.[27] Americans and Canadians are equally likely to say that there should be more incentives for individual effort rather than an equalization of people's incomes; that unemployed people should be obliged to take any available job rather than remain idle; and that individual freedom from government is good for the economy.[28] Yet Canadians also report higher levels of support for the idea that "government should take more responsibility to ensure that everyone is provided for."[29] These survey findings are consistent with the idea that political culture is internally heterogeneous.

At the same time, scholars should not overstate the internal incoherence and strategic malleability of political culture. Social policy attitudes vary cross-nationally in patterned ways that endure over time.[30] These national differences in public opinion cannot be dismissed as policy feedback effects, because they contribute to different trajectories of policy change and stability between countries.[31] To make sense of these cross-national differences, analysts must consider that political culture can be internally heterogeneous, but also identify sources of limited or thin coherence that run along national borders. For example, Amin Ghaziani and Delia Baldassarri find that internally diverse social movements are held together by "cultural anchors" that organize internal differences and provide sufficient coherence for collective action.[32] Similarly, Lyn Spillman shows that particular objects and events are more likely to endure as symbols of national identity if they afford meaningful ground to organize *contention* as well as consensus. Comparing how elites commemorated founding moments in the United States and Australia, Spillman shows that symbols and collective memories endure within national identity when competing groups can appeal to them for different purposes.[33]

In this chapter, I consider how constructions of national identity inform these Canada-U.S. differences in social policy attitudes. National identity can bolster or undermine public support for the welfare state, depending on the *collective memories* and *categories of cultural membership* that are associated with social policy. Different collective memories about national origin and state-building enshrine different roles for government as essential to national identity.[34] In countries where redistributive social policy is more popular, these programs are linked to collective memories of national pride.[35] Unpopular social policies lack this association with national pride and solidarity. Universal policies are more easily linked to nationalism because eligibility is defined in terms of shared citizenship: recipients are categorized as deserving members of a national community.[36] Targeted social policies are more vulnerable to popular backlash; by stigmatizing recipients as members of a morally inferior or racialized category, they can trigger backlash against "undeserving" policy recipients.[37] National identity drives welfare backlash when the public draws symbolic boundaries that exclude welfare recipients from the imagined community of the nation. Conversely, redistributive social policy is legitimated when constructions of cultural membership include "the poor" as part of "us."[38]

By considering the construction of national identity, we can gain a more complex understanding of Canada-U.S. differences. In comparative perspective, the United States and Canada are both considered liberal welfare states with individualistic, market-based approaches to inequality, as opposed to conservative or social-democratic regimes.[39] But there are small differences with big consequences for public discourse about poverty.[40] Both government and charitable aid to the poor are structured by cultural categories of worth, within a moral order of who deserves what kind of assistance.[41] Historically, American welfare debates have been structured by durable distinctions between the "deserving poor" (who were not expected to work because of age, gender, family status, or physical limitations) and the "undeserving poor" (who were expected to work and thus merited only limited government assistance).[42] These categories laid the groundwork for a contemporary anti-welfare backlash, which culminated in the Personal Responsibility and Work Reconciliation Act, or PRWORA.[43] By making welfare benefits conditional upon work, this reform only reinforced popular animosity toward "the poor," and failed to raise public awareness of the invisible "working poor."[44] The law was passed with bipartisan support, with both parties invoking a narrative that blamed poverty on "welfare dependency" and its corrosive effects on the moral discipline of poor people. This Jeremiad constructed national identity in ways that excluded "the poor" from cultural membership in the imagined community of good Americans.[45]

By comparison, the Canadian liberal welfare state still partly institutionalizes an ideal of social citizenship, or non-stigmatized welfare provision.[46] In Canada, this ideal is embodied most visibly through the popular universal health care program known as Medicare. Canada's provincially administered health insurance has become a symbol of national pride—indeed, the founding of Medicare has become part of Canada's collective memories of nation-building.[47] This program has no American counterpart besides Medicaid, which targets only the indigent poor, and the U.S. Medicare program, which enrolls the elderly.[48] American Social Security remains a popular universal benefit to seniors, but is not publicly recognized as a symbol of national pride or solidarity in response to poverty.[49] Like the United States, Canada has experienced anti-welfare backlash and a shift toward "workfare" models of social assistance.[50] But at the same time, Canada has continued to support more generous benefits for the working poor, creating greater public recognition of this "worthy" category of fellow citizens.[51] The rhetoric of retrenchment is still punctuated by the message that taking care of "our" poor is central to who "we" are as a nation. This social citizenship framing of national identity has never gained the same traction within American politics.[52]

In summary, U.S. and Canadian cultural repertoires share elements of individualism, but provide different resources to construct national identity. National identity affects public support for redistributive social policy, through collective memories about the welfare state and categories of cultural membership.

EVANGELICALS AND NATIONAL IDENTITY

Within this approach to political culture, scholars expect that different groups within the same society will elaborate collective memories about "the nation" from distinctive vantage points, and draw boundaries of cultural membership in different ways.[53] Visions of national identity may foster consensus between groups, but they also can serve as *cultural anchors* that organize differences. Indeed, national identity plays an important role within the distinctive civic and political attributes of American evangelicals. For U.S. evangelicals, American national identity has a distinctive religious meaning that goes beyond a generic civil religion. While civil religion has diminished in American public life, American evangelicals continue to practice a potent form of religious nationalism.[54]

As discussed in chapter 3, American evangelicals assert that Christianity is the rightful foundation for national identity and a moral code for public life. While nationalism often draws on mythic or religious forms, the term "religious nationalism" refers to stories and symbols that sacralize American national identity in terms of a supra-empirical reality.[55] Because American evangelicals imagine national community as inextricably tied to a Judeo-Christian core of values, they tend to draw the boundaries of national solidarity more exclusively. When asked about abstract *values*, American evangelicals seem to share a broad set of national ideals with other Americans, valuing a balance of equality and freedom, moral standards, and respect for diversity.[56] But when evangelicals are asked to draw the symbolic boundaries of "their" America, they are more inclined to exclude people from cultural membership in the nation if they are perceived as symbolic threats to this vision. For example, religious nationalism is a strong predictor of evangelical opposition to immigration.[57] Yet previous work on religion and economic attitudes has ignored *religious constructions of national identity* as a possible mechanism.[58]

SAME PRACTICES OF CHARITY, DIFFERENT DISCOURSES ABOUT POVERTY

Comparing the two American and two Canadian churches, I found that all four engaged in a similar repertoire of poverty-related activities, fitting a well-documented pattern among evangelicals in the United States.[59] In both countries, church activities were oriented toward charity rather than structural change, using the relational strategy of changing individuals through relationship-building and direct service. All four churches justified these activities in the theological language of evangelism and compassion, not the Social Gospel theology of improving society through structural reforms.[60] In each of these churches, I heard the Social Gospel regularly disparaged as a departure from evangelical orthodoxy.

Despite sharing similar activities and theology, the American and Canadian churches drew differently on the language of national identity to talk about poverty. In Canada, religious charity and outreach to the poor was framed as an expression of national solidarity, in ways that extended cultural membership to poor people. Both Canadian churches publicly articulated positive collective memories of welfare state formation, which legitimated redistributive social programs. In the United States, neither church used a public language of solidarity and national membership to describe domestic poverty. Instead, these church outreach efforts emphasized individual expressions of "grace" toward morally unworthy people.[61] Both American churches framed their activities using negative collective memories about welfare state formation, narratives that linked the growth of government to moral decline. In short, the differences between the U.S. and Canadian churches lay not in their theology, but in the way that they mapped their relationship as Christians to poor people in the context of a broader national community.[62] In the following sections, I analyze these religious uses of national identity in two American churches, and then compare them to two Canadian churches.

United States: Northtown Baptist Church

A recurring theme within Northtown Baptist Church was that caring for the poor and service to the community were the fruits of transformation—not good works necessary for salvation, but certainly signs of genuine transformation. However, at Northtown Baptist, religious responsibilities to the poor were often contrasted negatively with structural efforts to remedy poverty. Rejecting Social Gospel theology, church leaders framed this relational strategy of individual change as the Christian approach to poverty. For example, Charles, the youth pastor, regularly brought up issues of poverty in church. In a sermon, he urged the congregation to "look to God's heart" for "the poor" and "the down and out":

> Reading the Bible, there are few things that stick out more than God's heart for the poor. . . . We are so blinded by our own prosperity. God has blessed this nation, but what have we done with the prosperity that was given us? Are we not showing favoritism when we're not willing to give? . . . Has not God chosen the poor to be rich in faith? . . . We are broken by needs of people living in a trash dump. Now, people have all these utopian ideas: . . . "if the US would give this much, we could end poverty." But that's completely against what Jesus says. He says, "The poor you will always have with you." Jesus said, "There will never come a time when there will not be poor." I don't think poverty will ever be alleviated—that's never going to happen.

In rejecting structural reform, Charles was drawing important theological boundaries between "spiritual" and "secular" efforts to address poverty. But he was also defending a narrative of America as a blessed but ungrateful nation—ungratefulness that he particularly associated with domestic poor people.

While Charles recognized that God favored the poor to be "rich in faith," he did not see this spiritual blessing to fall on American poor. In an interview after the sermon, Charles told me that he felt ambivalent about addressing poverty as an American social problem. Charles saw this work as an expression of grace or compassion, but he was unwilling to extend solidarity or cultural membership to American poor people. Last year, he had sponsored a church trip to do house repairs in poor neighborhoods; this fall, he was planning outreach activities in the inner city and organizing a youth event to raise awareness of homelessness. But when I asked Charles how he wanted these activities to change the way his youth participated in their own country, he answered:

> I would say there is no true poverty in America and so my inclination is not really . . . to focus on that. We don't disqualify it altogether; obviously through Mission Blitz and World Changers and things like the Great Sleep-out we address those things.

I asked Charles to explain what he meant by "true poverty":

> If you look at the poverty line in America, you give that allowance to anybody in any other country . . . you are going to be a king . . . I have done many houses, and you are talking about people that, more than anything, have an issue prioritizing necessities. They have the satellite cable hooked-up to the back of their house and they are having us do their roof . . . I don't have cable and that's

because I made a choice . . . I prioritize other things, and mostly it's putting food on the table . . . It's a question of how *truly* impoverished you are, it's a relative term.

Charles was highly invested in mobilizing the congregation to show compassion for the poor, in the United States and across the world. But he was also highly ambivalent toward the domestic poor: he saw this category of people as undeserving of cultural membership, and so he viewed his charity work as an expression of grace to generally undeserving people.[63] Indeed, Charles's definition of the deserving poor was even more stringent than the institutionalized categories of the 1996 Welfare Reform, since *no* Americans seemed to qualify as morally worthy.

Analyzing a year of fieldnotes, I could not find any cases at Northtown Baptist where members talked publicly about American poor people as deserving of solidarity as fellow citizens. Welfare state research has found that national boundaries affect the construction of reciprocity and solidarity, creating a tendency to privilege the needs of "our poor" over the needs of "outsiders."[64] But at Northpoint, the suffering of the global poor repeatedly served as a foil for the undeserving American poor. For example, when a mission group came back from Mexico, several returning mission team members exclaimed in the worship service that they had never seen such poverty, and the trip taught them to be grateful for how much "we" had in the United States. The next week in Sunday school, the Southern Baptist denominational curriculum prompted the class to talk about being grateful for our wealth, talking about how "even the poorest Americans are wealthy by global standards." This trope was often repeated in church life and in interviews, as part of a larger narrative about how American wealth had made us ungrateful and materialistic, unlike poor people in other countries, who were truly grateful for what they had. While this narrative about American wealth motivated concern for global poverty, it also negatively contrasted the U.S. poor with the deserving poor of other countries.

Listening to the bundle of narratives that constituted Northtown Baptist's subcultural identity, I found that denigrating the government was a recurring theme.[65] For example, a team of Northtown men returned from helping rebuild houses in the Gulf Coast after Hurricane Katrina. At a church reception for new members, a middle-aged businessman told me how impressed he was with the Southern Baptists' mobile kitchens, and their ability to efficiently mobilize volunteers on such a large scale. At another church potluck, church members marveled at the capacity of the Southern Baptist denomination to respond to natural disasters like Katrina. Ann, a soft-spoken deacon's wife, shared about the church's disaster relief effort in Alabama and New Orleans:

We do a lot of disaster relief. You know, I heard after Hurricane Katrina, the churches all around were so prepared to go in and help out. And it seems like they were even better prepared than the government. It seemed like the government really made a mess of it, they weren't prepared to respond like the churches were.

For Ann, this story carried a clear moral: churches must reclaim their rightful place in the public square, which has been wrongfully taken by government. In rejecting government programs, Ann drew on the accountable individualist theme of anti-structuralism. But she also invoked a negative collective memory about the welfare state, which associated the growth of social policy with the decline of religion's public role.

This was a recurring pattern: American evangelicals used accountable individualist language, but by reference to this evangelical narrative of national identity. For example, Don, the director of a parachurch ministry, explained how the church should equip young people to be good citizens:

Well, I think teaching them what the Bible tells us about how to love our neighbors is a big part of that . . . and so as a good citizen, as a good Christian, you are going to be a good citizen because you'll love them. You'll care for your neighbors, and their family and their friends; and the church should be the best institution for taking care of people. That's how it used to be. Although we subjugated that by giving that over to the government to take care of, but we're seeing our young people rise up and take responsibility.

Using the language of accountable individualism, Don defined the problem as a breakdown in personal responsibility among Christians. According to Emerson's and Smith's framework, Don's anti-government attitudes were driven by the theological language of anti-structuralism: Christians had yielded to a sinful tendency to look to structural forces, to escape their personal obligations to "care for neighbors." But Don was also drawing on a particular collective memory which blamed a decline in the public role of Christianity on the growth of the welfare state. Redistributive social policy threatened his religious identity, because it represented moral decline from "how it used to be" in America. Thus, Don drew on accountable individualism in ways that were anchored by his narrative of Christian nationalism.

United States: Lifeway Assembly of God

I found a similar pattern at Lifeway Assembly, which had an even stronger history of outreach to poor communities, particularly a public housing development located in their suburb. Through evangelism, a biweekly food pantry, and a bus ministry to poor children, Lifeway aggressively recruited "the poor" as church participants, and not just distant objects of charity. Both the pastoral team and the lay leadership were united in this active outreach to poor people, not just solidly working-class and middle-class families that resembled their current membership. Yet at Lifeway Assembly, public expressions of anti-welfare state sentiment were a way of affirming religious identity.

Audrey, a college-educated homeschooling mother in her early forties, described her experiences of service at the church's food bank:

> The people that come to them for help know that they are appreciated, and loved and valued and encouraged. For one thing, they are way more efficient than anything government. I mean that's the other thing, there, none of them are paid. They are all volunteers and it doesn't become this bureaucratic handout program, it becomes personal, they want to express the love of God to people.

Audrey defined Christian compassion by denigrating government programs as "bureaucratic handouts." Thus, her use of theological tools was anchored by a distinctively evangelical narrative of national identity, which associated the growth of "handout programs" with America's slide from "Christian values." I frequently heard this narrative as a reference point for public interaction at Lifeway Assembly. For example, Audrey articulated this narrative explicitly during a casual conversation after church, paraphrased in my fieldnotes. Her son had just written a college paper that compared the practice of Jubilee in the Old Testament, with U.S. programs that deal with poverty today. For Audrey, his paper proved that "God did a better job of taking care of the poor in ancient Israel than in our War on Poverty that Johnson launched." Within this collective memory about the welfare state, Johnson's War on Poverty failed because it took America away from biblical principles of personal compassion.

However, these practices of personal compassion were fraught with considerable ambivalence toward "the poor" as a cultural category. On one hand, church volunteers like Audrey desired to "appreciate, love, value, and encourage" poor people as individuals. On the other hand, I heard considerable unwillingness to extend *cultural membership* to Americans in poverty: to relate to poor people not just as individuals but as worthy members of a national community. Service to the poor was frequently described as an expression of grace to people who may or may not deserve help. For example, Matt became a Food Bank volunteer after he was laid off from his blue-collar job. Matt told me that he tried not to judge people who used the food bank, he would just "love them up" and "let God sort it out." Ironically, Matt's recent unemployment did not make him identify with the poor as a group; in Matt's usage, poor people were by definition chronically unemployed. Matt used the language of grace to map his relationship to the poor, but he had no religious language to express solidarity with poor people as fellow citizens. Indeed, "loving people" as individuals meant deliberately ignoring the larger structural and political context of poverty.

In summary, both American churches were motivated by more than just accountable individualism when they reject redistributive social policy. They were also defending a particular narrative of Christian nationalism. Evangelicals used the theological tool of accountable individualism in ways that were anchored by collective memories about the welfare state and constructions of cultural membership. The role of national identity becomes even clearer when we compare evangelical congregations in the United States and Canada. Both Canadian congregations talked about poverty in ways that linked the welfare state to symbols of national pride, and constructed the poor as deserving cultural membership in that national community. Like their American counterparts, Canadian evangelicals expressed concern for Canada's "Christian" heritage. But unlike American evangelicals, they elaborated these concerns about national identity in ways that *legitimated* redistributive social policy. This sheds light on why Canadian evangelicals are not more economically conservative than other Canadians, even though they share individualistic theology with their American counterparts.

Canada: Highpoint Baptist Church

Just as at Northtown Baptist in suburban Buffalo, Highpoint Baptist made sense of poverty through their partnerships with international missions, domestic parachurch ministries, and sister churches in poor neighborhoods. In particular, Highpoint maintained a close relationship with City Centre Church, a Baptist church plant in downtown Hamilton that performed extensive outreach to poor people and immigrants. The pastor and lay leadership at City Centre frequently visited Highpoint to tell them about their work in the "urban core," and mobilized volunteers to help with their soccer camps, holiday outreach, and other ministries to their low-income neighborhood. The church was often visited both by representatives from parachurch ministries that worked with poor Canadians, and by missionaries who talked about global poverty. But in contrast to Northtown Baptist, clergy and laity at Highpoint Baptist were much more likely to talk about poverty and poor people in ways that invoked themes of national solidarity and citizenship.

These differences are puzzling, since Highpoint Baptist emphasized an individualistic theology of salvation that prioritized evangelism over all other goals. In an interview, an assistant pastor explained to me that he was wary of any kind of "social ministry" that might blur the fundamental boundary between born-again Christians and people who hadn't been saved. I repeatedly heard church leaders denouncing the Social Gospel, because it de-emphasized the need for personal salvation. For example, Head Pastor John emphasized this point after a visit from the pastor of City Centre Church:

> Do you realize that across this nation and world, churches that say the Gospel teaches works and you do not need the cross of Christ? You cannot point someone to redemption of Jesus Christ unless they recognize their need for a savior. . . . This is where sociologists can't get it right. The guys this morning from the City Centre church plant told us that they get to a point where they can't do it. . . . Christ not only forgives, but he changes lives.

Pastor John's sermon brought home a central theme within evangelicalism: the incapacity of human beings to please God through their own striving, whether through secular social change or through the much-disparaged Social Gospel. Like American evangelicals, Pastor John argued that the cross of Christ empowered believers to minister to the poor in personal ways that social-scientific knowledge couldn't comprehend. As in the two American churches, I often heard this kind of boundary-work around how "we" as evangelical Christians did social ministry, as opposed to secular governments and nonprofits. The main difference was Highpoint Baptist did not map its identity by denigrating government efforts to help the poor.

To the contrary, I found that Highpoint leadership and members constructed poverty in ways that linked the welfare state to symbols of national pride. Like Northpoint Baptist in the United States, Highpoint Baptist contrasted their nation's "godless" prosperity to the grateful dependence on God that they associated with poor people in the Third World. But when Highpoint Baptist elaborated their identity as wealthy Canadian Christians, they often invoked Canada's welfare state and "good government" as sources of national pride, part of what "we" had to be thankful for as Canadians. This theme emerged during a special Sunday worship service, which the church's music minister planned around a theme of prayer for Canada. The music minister invited individuals in the congregation to stand and share their blessings and prayer concerns about the spiritual condition of the nation. Todd, a businessman in his thirties with two young children, stood up at the front and expressed his gratefulness for God's blessing—his comfortable house, his personal safety—in a world where many people did not have enough to eat. Next the music minister instructed us to gather in small groups for intercessory prayer. Huddled with a small group for prayer, the young man next to me prayed that Canada would be "good stewards of our prosperity."

In settings like this, Highpoint Baptist mapped their identity as rich Canadians without creating a negative contrast between the deserving, truly needy Third World poor and the undeserving, ungrateful Canadian poor. For example, I attended a presentation by a team of Highpoint members who were going to Bosnia for a mission trip, to work with young orphans and at-risk youth in a hockey camp. This hockey camp was a vehicle to "build relationships" with local youth in a majority Muslim area, with the ultimate goal of converting them to Christianity. Showing compassion was also part of the mission of the hockey camp, by providing routine medical care and regular meals to these youth. But the leader of the mission team explained this need for compassion by reference to Canada's welfare state: "Their health care system was destroyed by the war, so there's a real need for us to provide medical care." This appeal implied a particular construction of national identity: that "we" as Christians were part of a national community defined by universal health care, and so we should consider poor people in other countries whose national institutions had failed them. By contrast, both U.S. churches constructed global compassion in ways that denied solidarity with poor Americans.

Furthermore, I also heard public talk about poverty at Highpoint that recognized the cultural membership of poor people as worthy Canadians, and sometimes fellow Christians. I regularly heard Christians publicly identify themselves as low-income, or describe how they benefited from programs that targeted the working poor. For example, we heard a guest sermon from the director of an outreach to low-income First Nation youth. Describing his ministry, the guest speaker told us that he and his wife were about to buy a new home, with an extra guest room for youth who needed a safe place to sleep. Without a hint of embarrassment, he informed us that his new home was made possible by a subsidized loan from a provincial initiative to encourage home ownership among low-income people. Then he publicly thanked God for providing for his needs in this way, overlaying this news of secular assistance from the government with religious meaning.[66] His public presentation blurred the boundaries between the "poor people" being helped by his ministry, and his own status as head of a respectable, lower-middle-class family whose ministry was enabled by government assistance. By contrast, my fieldwork in both American churches did not yield similar examples of lower-income Christians who openly shared their reliance on any government program as a "blessing."

In mapping "the poor" as part of "us," church members framed poverty as a problem of social inclusion and national solidarity. This basic assumption was held even by respondents like Amanda, who was critical of unemployment "handouts" that did not require people to work. When I asked Amanda what growing inequality would mean for Canada, she framed poverty as a problem of social exclusion:

> Probably that poor people would get lost in the shuffle, cause I think a lot of times, it's the middle class that looks after the lower, because they're closer to that class than the upper—sometimes they are willing to share in their finances but not always their time, which is sometimes more important. . . . [The middle class is more] willing to work in some areas, to help integrate them into communities. Well, I think that's more in the middle class to do than the upper class, they can't be bothered to: "Here's my money and just do whatever you want with it."

Amanda was looking forward to volunteering at a homeless shelter in the fall with her church choir, which they had scheduled to do one evening a month during their regular practice time. She believed that it wasn't just up to the government to reduce differences between the rich and the poor: "people have to come together and work together to do that." But Amanda saw this kind of church outreach as an extension of the government's responsibilities to be a support to low-income people. Amanda stated, "the church certainly can get involved in that. You know, running after school programs for kids. . . . We don't have to be that organization, but we can certainly come alongside and help them." Unlike American evangelicals, Amanda saw church-based efforts as an extension of governmental efforts, not as a superior alternative. Religious compassion was an expression of solidarity, not an expression of grace to undeserving people.

Surveying fieldwork and interviews, I could not find any cases where the growth of welfare programs was linked to Canada's moral decline as a nation. Instead, Highpoint members mapped their relationship to poor people by invoking *positive* collective memories about the welfare state, referring to inclusive social programs as symbols of national pride and solidarity. Joan, who coordinated community volunteer work, articulated her religious narrative of Canadian national identity:

> So many of the principles that affect our way of life in North America, came directly from a biblical perspective . . . It was basically the same progression in Canada . . . The fact that the church felt like it was their responsibility to care for people. Way before there was all

the government funding and regulations . . . and the expectations of health care in Canada . . . at their roots, at their core, it was church denominations feeling like people should be educated and should have medical care. But if you just pulled some Joe person off the street . . . they wouldn't know that.

Here, Joan was not simply drawing on the larger Canadian cultural repertoire, made available from *outside* the evangelical subculture. She was also articulating her distinctively evangelical concerns about defending a shared Christian heritage within an increasingly secular, multicultural Canada. Like American evangelicals, Highpoint Baptist defended the idea that national solidarity and social norms should be based on a common Christian heritage. But unlike American evangelicals, their religious uses of national identity worked to legitimate redistributive social policy and extend cultural membership to Canadians in poverty.

Canada: Grace Pentecostal Church

At Grace Pentecostal, talk about poverty often emerged in relationship to the church's active involvement with international missions. During my fieldwork, Grace Pentecostal conducted a major mission trip to Kenya, to partner with an urban Kenyan Pentecostal church that was opening up a medical mission to a traditionally Muslim ethnic group in the rural areas outside their city. In a Sunday worship leading up to the mission trip, Pastor David encouraged the congregation to keep contributing generously with their time and money, by reminding them of Jesus' words about the "least of these my brethren":

> You see what doors God has opened . . . I really feel that God believes in us, and God trusts us that what he gives to us, we're not seeking to hoard, but we're just a conduit. . . . This is part of our mission, helping the widows and the orphans . . . "I was in prison, I was sick, I was . . . and when did we see you?" In as much as you did it unto the least of these my brethren, you have done it unto me.

In the months before the mission trip, the music minister encouraged the congregation to tell others about the medical mission, as an opening to share the gospel with them. In a church announcement, he said, "We've given you this flier about the Medical Mission, so that you can tell your family and friends about it. We're not asking you to go door-to-door asking for money or anything. But it's a great opportunity to witness to friends and family, and say, 'This is what Christianity is all about, this is what our church is all about, this is what I'm all about'." The flier reported that this ethnic group was devastated by severe flooding and needed basic medical care, and appealed to Canadian generosity with the reminder: "Access to a Doctor and medicines/vaccinations are things we take for granted here in Canada."

As in the two American churches, Grace Pentecostal's mission trips elaborated national identity in religious ways: by mapping "our" place as prosperous Canadians in a world of poverty, church members cultivated greater appreciation for their relative prosperity. But as at Highpoint, being a wealthy Canadian Christian also meant expressing grateful pride in the nation's healthcare system, and showing compassion to those who did not live in such a well-governed country. Since Canadians at both churches measured their country's wealth in terms of national institutions as well as income, they could talk about absolute deprivation in Kenya without making a negative contrast between the "deserving, needy" global poor and the "undeserving, not truly needy" domestic poor.

Like most Protestant churches in the United States, Grace Pentecostal's outreach to domestic poor people was more oriented to intermittent service, like sending the youth group to participate in a citywide Christian public service day.[67] The church's most sustained, collective outreach to the local poor was their semi-annual Thanksgiving assistance, where the church gathered donated food and went door-to-door in low-income neighborhoods to offer holiday baskets. Grace Pentecostal did not partner with any social service providers as a church, although individuals from the church had ongoing ties to different social agencies as volunteers. Nonetheless, the problem of domestic poverty was periodically lifted up in the spiritual life of the church, even in charismatic practices of "spiritual warfare."

Pastor David explained that one of their themes for a recent prayer emphasis was interceding on behalf of Hamilton's inner city core, which was wracked by high rates of poverty, unemployment, and violence. The congregation had been praying for job creation, poverty alleviation, crime reduction, and spiritual revival. In the language of spiritual warfare, poverty was an affliction that affected the city of Hamilton as a whole, not just individuals. Small teams from the congregation interceded for Hamilton by praying over places that symbolized the city's common life—the city hall, the public schools, a pedestrian bridge on a major road that connected the wealthier mountain neighborhoods to the urban core. Other small groups organized regular "prayer walks" through neighborhoods recently struck by violence.

Like their American counterparts, Grace Pentecostal sought to transform their city through a strategy of personal influence, consistent with their accountable individualist theology. These Pentecostal practices of spiritual warfare also drew on religious nationalism, by contending that national solidarity and social norms should be based on a common Christian heritage. But, unlike American evangelicals, they elaborated these concerns about national identity in ways that legitimated redistributive social policy. For example, Cindy explained to me why Canada's welfare state ultimately required Christian principles to succeed.

> [W]hen you have moral character, leaders in the country would have a total different outcome in society than individuals driven by selfishness. . . . [A]s a country you have to govern both [the rich and the poor.] You have to have things that help the poor, and you have to give the rich opportunity to conduct business. I think the problem is when you don't have moral guidance in it, these plans get out of whack . . . and there's nothing to build character into those programs . . . When you have a leader with moral character, that says: "This program is to help you during this period of time, and then it's going to move you into being self-sufficient again." . . . There has to be something to get them back on their feet . . . When you're governed that way as a person, then you would understand to do that as a country. Because you almost have to have a morally guided leadership in order to have it work for the country. And when you remove that everything gets out of balance.

Here, Cindy drew on her theological language of accountable individualism to frame the problem of welfare dependency, which violated her ideas of personal responsibility. But her focus was not on the moral failings of the poor; it was on the need for morally guided leadership that overcame selfishness and governed the rich and poor fairly. Here, she was articulating a religious narrative about the growth of Canada's welfare state, but one that was very different from the collective memories that I found in the two American evangelical churches. In Cindy's narrative, the problem started when Canada's leaders stopped sharing the Christian moral character that presumably once guided the nation's welfare state. But unlike many American evangelicals, Cindy passionately believed that the government had a moral responsibility to care for the poor. As her husband Brian explained, "Spiritual mandates apply for us and kings and government as well . . . it's *all* of our responsibility." Compassion for the poor was not simply the private responsibility of believers, but also an expression of cultural membership in Canadian society.

In conclusion, Canadian evangelicals drew on the same tools of accountable individualism as their American counterparts, but drew on different narratives of national identity to define their religious responsibilities toward the poor. Accountable individualism did not motivate them to reject structural solutions to inequality, when used in reference to different constructions of religious nationalism.

CONCLUSION

Comparing across the border, I found that economic conservatism among American evangelicals was anchored by religious constructions of national identity, in ways that previous scholarship had attributed to theology alone. American evangelicals drew on theological tools like accountable individualism, grace, and compassion in ways that were anchored by a subcultural narrative of religious nationalism. While many Americans share negative collective memories about the welfare state, U.S. evangelicals elaborated these narratives in particular ways that linked the growth of the welfare state to the loss of a Christian America. By contrast, Canadian evangelicals drew on positive collective memories about the welfare state within local religious practice to set their personal acts of charity in a broader narrative context.[68] As a result, evangelical churches in the United States and Canada drew on their shared theological tools very differently to talk about poverty and the role of government.

In both the United States and Canada, evangelicals were certainly drawing on narratives of national identity that were reinforced outside of their religious subculture. Canadians generally support a greater role for government in addressing poverty than Americans do, and these sentiments are reinforced through collective memories that associate the welfare state with national identity. The design of U.S. and Canadian social policy has also institutionalized different categories of who "the poor" are, and these differences shape the public's civic identities, constructions of target populations, and notions of government responsibility.[69] Canada's policy design frames poverty as a problem of social inclusion, likely influencing how evangelicals make sense of their religious responsibilities to the poor. By contrast, the design of U.S. social policy has likely helped render the working poor invisible within the two American churches. The United States and Canada have also institutionalized different relationships between government and faith-based services. In Ontario, churches are more likely to work in coalition with secular and government providers than American churches, who are more likely to have free-standing services. Canadian churches undertake more social opportunities for mothers, homelessness efforts, and refugee resettlement, while American churches provide more charity healthcare, following patterns of government involvement.[70] Independently of religious factors, these institutional channels have made some tools more available than others to talk about poverty in the U.S. and Canadian national contexts.

But the differences between U.S. and Canadian congregations do not simply "reflect" the wider national context. In both countries, evangelicals in both countries drew on discourses about national identity for distinctively religious purposes, to strengthen their subcultural identity as evangelical Christians. For example, Canadian churches interpreted religious practices like prayer-walking and charity work through the language of social inclusion, *sacralizing* this language in ways that lent religious legitimacy to the welfare state. By contrast, American evangelicals drew on broader themes of anti-welfare resentment, but infused them with their distinctive religious concerns about national identity. Such diverse practices of "banal" nationalism arguably contribute to stable, cross-national differences in political attitudes between the United States, Canada, and other countries.[71]

By analyzing these religious visions of national solidarity, scholars can better disentangle the complex relationship between religion, race, and economic conservatism. Compared to other white Americans, white evangelicals are not just more economically conservative, but more likely to reject government efforts to remedy racial inequality.[72] While Emerson and Smith point to accountable individualist theology, other scholars contend that this race-neutral language is actually loaded with racially coded meanings that link whiteness to cultural membership and national identity.[73] Future research might profitably compare how white and black American evangelical congregations construct religious nationalism, to understand how racial boundaries become inscribed within religious visions of the nation.

Finally, this analysis challenges a central claim of Compassionate Conservatism: that the welfare state makes passive citizens who leave caring for the poor to the government. Government bureaucracies allegedly crowd out Christian compassion and force evangelicals to relegate their faith to a realm of private motivations.[74] But as these data show, there is hardly a zero-sum relationship between social welfare programs and voluntary charity.[75] Canadians evangelicals see faith-based compassion as an *extension* of government-led efforts to fight poverty, and overlay secular government programs with religious meaning. Evangelicals are not easily crowded out by government programs, because their subculture thrives by sustaining distinction from—and engagement with—the larger society. In the United States, evangelicals define their identity by denigrating government programs; in Canada, by tackling the spiritual dimensions of social exclusion. In both countries, evangelicals are confident that their distinctive approach to spiritual transformation has no secular substitute.

CHAPTER 6

CAPTAINS IN THE CULTURE WAR

Many political commentators have blamed the culture war on its generals: national elites who exaggerate cultural differences among Americans for political gain. But this conflict is also a captain's war, waged by local religious leaders embedded among the rank and file. While national generals may articulate the formal ideologies behind the conflict, these local captains are critical to rallying rank-and-file evangelicals behind a Christian Right agenda. Pastors are not the only ones who serve as local captains for culture war politics. They share this role with a much broader set of volunteer, lay leaders. These lay leaders are particularly important for shaping small group interaction within local churches, since they lead Bible studies, prayer groups, and small group gatherings.[1] In both American churches in this study, the most explicitly partisan cues actually came from lay leaders, not from ordained pastors. Yet we know very little about the political influence of lay leaders within local church life.[2]

In this chapter, I introduce a group of prominent lay leaders at Northtown Baptist and Lifeway Assembly who served as captains for culture war politics. This group fits James Hunter's ideal-type of the orthodox culture warrior. They defined both religious and political differences as a struggle between two views of authority, which they termed "liberal" and "conservative." For these lay leaders, culture war schemas had become deeply internalized, informing their everyday religious practice and moral judgments as well as their political behavior.[3] Using in-depth interviews, I explore how these leaders came to experience this strong emotional and motivational link between religion and conservative politics.

CULTURE WAR CAPTAINS AT NORTHTOWN BAPTIST

At Northtown Baptist, the strongest partisan cues came from a group of active lay leaders, who were strongly invested in culture war politics. These individuals were not more politically conservative because they were more religiously devout than other members. Rather, they had learned to connect religion to conservative politics from sources *outside* of the local congregation: Christian Right interest groups, parachurch ministries, the pro-life movement, and partisan news sources like Fox News.[4] This partly supports the argument that the culture wars are driven by top-down elite mobilization, rather than by different religious world-views. But top-down framing does not fully explain why these individuals felt a sense of "thick coherence" between religion and politics. I found that Christian Right frames only became "sacred" when laypeople incorporated them into their everyday religious practice. Culture war rhetoric did not simply resonate with their preexisting beliefs or religious identity; rather, it had shaped their religious identity, beliefs, and practices from the ground up.

Converting to a Conservative Identity

During my fieldwork, Richard and Pam were prominent lay leaders at Northtown Baptist: Richard served as a deacon, while Pam helped run the youth group. This middle-class couple in their early fifties exemplified Hunter's ideal-type of an "orthodox" culture warrior identity. But they had been politically moderate Episcopalians until they "got saved" in their early forties. Richard grew up Catholic and Pam grew up Presbyterian, so they compromised by getting married in the Episcopal Church. During their first years of marriage, they attended Episcopal churches and occasionally visited a United Church of Christ congregation (a liberal mainline denomination). Their journey into the evangelical subculture began when Richard attended a Promise Keepers rally in June 1997, at the age of forty-one. Looking back, Richard says that he wasn't really a Christian then; he was just "going through the motions" at their Episcopal church. But then the Lord started reaching out to him through a series of "coincidences" that led him to attend a Promise Keepers rally.[5] First, Richard heard about the Promise Keepers on Christian radio, while he was surfing through the channels in the car. At the time, Richard strongly disliked Christian radio, but on that day, he remembers thinking:

> Wow, this man doesn't sound like the typical Christian on the radio . . . someone who is thumping their Bible . . . and has a Southern accent . . . I heard him speaking about the Lord in a way that I had never heard another man speak about the Lord. And I thought, There is something to this and I don't know what it is.

That Sunday, a man at Richard's church invited him to watch a 20-minute video promoting the Promise Keepers rally. When the video moved him to tears, Richard agreed to go: "The Lord was really working in my heart." Even though his Episcopal church wasn't "Bible-believing," Richard explained that "there was this small group of born-again believers in that church" who brought him to the event at Buffalo Bills Stadium. On his first night at the Promise Keepers event, he found the emotional worship unsettling, because it was so different from what he had known in liturgical churches. But he was intrigued by the preaching: he had never heard anyone explain the story of salvation in a way that called for a personal decision. At the end of the night, he went down for prayer and made a decision for Christ on the football field.

Afterward, Richard started reading his Bible regularly and started listening for the "gospel message" in the preaching in his Episcopal church. Although Richard recognized this message "hidden in the liturgy," he grew frustrated that the pastor never called on the congregation to make a personal decision for Christ. After a year, he told Pam that he didn't think their church preached the truth, and he wanted to look for a new church. They started visiting other Episcopalian churches, and then churches from other Protestant denominations. In the summer of 1998, they decided to visit Northtown Baptist because it was just down the street and their children had attended Vacation Bible School there one summer. Richard talked to people and concluded that Northtown Baptist was what he was looking for: a "Bible-believing" church. Pam became born-again in the course of joining the church: When the pastor realized that she couldn't name a specific time when she became a Christian, he invited her to pray to receive Christ. They were both baptized and became members in September 1998. When I interviewed Richard and Pam, they had attended Northtown Baptist for ten years.

Richard did not convert to evangelical Christianity because he wanted to enlist in a culture war. In fact, Richard held a negative stereotype of ignorant, self-righteous "radio preachers" before he attended the Promise Keepers rally. After Richard was born-again, he didn't become frustrated because his Episcopal church was too "liberal" or because they took the wrong position on moral issues. Rather, Richard explained to me that he just wanted to grow in his new understanding of the Christian faith. But as Richard and Pam developed a new way of mapping their religious identities at Northtown Baptist, they also remapped their political identities. Richard and Pam both report that they were relatively apolitical in their young adulthood, but as they became more involved in the evangelical subculture, they became much more politically conservative.

Within Hunter's culture war framework, we might assume that this shift in political identity was caused by Richard and Pam's conversion to an orthodox worldview. But they actually learned to connect their religious and political identities from sources *outside* their local congregation. Richard became an avid listener of Christian radio, and started hearing about the work of Christian interest groups like Concerned Women of America, which Richard now supports financially. After their conversion, the couple started listening to James Dobson's advice on parenting, and continued to rely on Focus on the Family for information as Dobson's organization moved into political advocacy. Richard was proud to identify himself as a member of the Presidential Prayer Team, a group of Christians who volunteered to pray regularly for President George W. Bush, as a devout Christian who needed his support.

Pam explained that they relied primarily on Fox News to learn about world events and national politics, because other news sources were "liberal." As Pam explained, "It would be nice if you could get the truth on the media but you can't so you don't know . . . and I think the general public unfortunately listens to the media much more than they should." In particular, Richard and Pam felt "the media" emphasized the negative aspects of the wars in Iraq and Afghanistan, and ignored the positive facts on the ground that they heard from their son in the military. Richard trusted Fox News to portray a "balanced" perspective, unlike other media sources that only represented the "liberal" perspective.

> They [Fox News] do give you both sides of the argument, so you can make your decision. And they are also not afraid to represent the conservative point of view, where I think some of the other ones won't even talk about it. You hear one side of the story and that is not good news for me . . . people need to make a decision for themselves.

Despite Richard's insistence that he sought out a "balance" of liberal and conservative perspectives, he was not personally open to liberal arguments. Rather, he interpreted the news as a series of liberal assaults on truth and Christianity, following the narrative that he heard over and over on Fox News and Christian radio. For example, I asked Richard to talk about any news events that could affect him personally. He explained that liberals were trying to prevent Christian groups from meeting in the public schools, unless they included other religions:

> Right now there is some legislation, going on trying to get rid of classroom's free speech pretty much. So this is what the liberals are trying to do: trying to put Muslims into Christian groups. . . . Focus on the Family is a group that we listen to. I listen a lot, James Dobson is someone who we kind of raise our kids on a lot of his philosophies in his teaching, counseling on raising children. There is a lot of talk in his show on what is going on in the political world.

Because the media was liberal, Richard felt he could only trust sources like Focus on the Family, the Family Research Council, or Concerned

Women of America to tell him "what is really happening . . . what Washington is trying to do."

Yet Richard emphasized that he and his wife were "not very politically minded," even though they followed the work of multiple interest groups who engaged in public policy advocacy. This makes sense if we consider that Richard and Pam understood these organizations as "ministries" rather than political interest groups. They engaged with parachurch groups like Focus on the Family to deepen their religious practice and obtain practical guidance, rather than to influence public life. They did not think of themselves as political activists, but rather as Christians who interpreted politics through a spiritual lens. As Richard put it,

> I think many Christians . . . don't see the lines of politics spiritually—they think they are separated. . . . but there are some Christians that are very much into politics and they like that stuff. We don't really . . . like politics all that much to the point where we would want to be active members in a political party because we wouldn't be drawn to politics if we weren't Christians.

Pam added, "I guess it just leaves a bad taste in my mouth all the way around, because I think a lot of politicians are crooked and hypocritical and I just don't like the whole thing that represents." While rejecting "politics," this couple drew the "lines of politics" in "spiritual" terms, as a battle between liberal and conservative worldviews. While this language of liberal versus conservative came from partisan media sources, Pam and Richard experienced this frame as a *spiritual* lens on politics, rather than a *political* lens on religion.

For Richard and Pam, this culture wars discourse informed their everyday lives. In particular, Richard and Pam understood parenting through the lens of a conflict between liberal and conservative worldviews: what would uphold or undermine the conservative values they wanted to instill in their children? For example, during a discussion of their religious identity, I asked Pam, "What does the term liberal convey to you?" She answered, "Permissive to an excess would be the word, taking liberties with interpretation of the Bible, taking liberties into interpretation with the law." I asked her to clarify what she meant, and she answered:

> Twisting [the law] for your own needs, pushing the envelope just as far as possibly you can. And if anything, we are on the conservative side in everything: the way we raise our kids, the way we dress our kids, the way we dress, it's everything . . . I'm proud of it and our kids are too.

Pam described how she promoted conservatism as one of the parent sponsors for the youth group:

There have been times when girls showed up and got handed a T-shirt because they haven't been appropriately dressed and I have been very grateful for that. I think that is very biblical . . . And some of the girls that show up need to be brought up short, and if their mothers are not going to do it, then the youth pastor or his wife will say it . . . "Here, put on this on while you are here, we don't need to see all what we are seeing." And so I have been very grateful that there has been that kind of conservatism.

I asked the couple how being conservative in this religious context was related to being politically conservative. Pam pointed out that their church's casual, expressive worship style was probably considered "liberal" by Southern Baptist standards: "I think we would blow some of the Southern Baptists out of the water. I think they would be appalled if they came to our church and saw some of the things going on here." Richard added:

But if you listen to the message of the sermons, I believe they are right on with the conservative aspect of the Bible . . . As far as how it relates politically, it's very important to me to vote for a conservative-thinking candidate. Because generally their point of view in a lot of things that relate to our faith are mostly alike. Abortion . . . there are a lot of ways, if you are very liberal, very free thinking and very non-conventional way of thinking, which is in opposition to our faith.

Richard defined their politics in terms of a conservative identity, which he associated with the Republican Party:

Conservative-thinking politically tends to be more in line with our faith, thinking spiritually. . . . Generally Republicans are more conservative than Democrats, but you just don't go right down to a box and just vote all Republican, without just knowing or trying at least to figure it out the best you can—which is very difficult these days—some idea of what they believe.

But while the couple emphasized their independence from the Republican Party, voting for Democratic candidates was out of the question, given their culture war map of politics.

Consistent with the political mobilization thesis, Pam and Richard primarily encountered culture war rhetoric through parachurch groups and partisan news sources, which taught them to fear liberals as a political threat to Christianity. But Pam and Richard had also exercised cultural agency in this process, as new converts seeking to apply their new faith to every aspect of their life. Significantly, this couple initially engaged with

Christian Right interest groups to deepen their religious practice, not to express preexisting political commitments. By following James Dobson's advice on parenting, they learned to interpret their own childrearing values in partisan, ideological terms: as a way to reinforce "conservative" values and defend their children from the attack of "liberal" influences. Because Dobson's parenting advice had shaped their religious identity in *constitutive* ways, Richard and Pam felt that conservative politics were a natural part of their faith.

Parachurch groups helped foster this sense of coherence by representing themselves as "ministries" that supplemented the religious guidance that Pam and Richard received in their local congregation. For example, Richard regularly prayed for President George W. Bush as a "Christian leader" with the Presidential Prayer Team, but he did not think of this as a "political" act. From his perspective, he was engaging in a religious practice, but one that deepened the organic connection that he felt between evangelical identity and conservative politics. This was a larger pattern in both American churches: laypeople engaged with parachurch groups to deepen their religious practice, not to achieve preexisting "political" goals. Christian Right interest groups did not simply provide laypeople with a vehicle to express preexisting political commitments; rather, they helped cultivate their religious practices in ways that could *develop* those political commitments.

Furthermore, Richard and Pam thought it was important for parachurch ministries to distance themselves from "politics," as a marker of authentic spiritual leadership. Groups like Focus on the Family were trustworthy sources of political news precisely because they were understood as a "ministry," independent of the dirty world of "politics." This was a recurring theme in individual interviews. Laypeople viewed Christian Right parachurch groups as providers of religious services: resources to develop one's prayer life, parenting, and relationship advice, materials for personal Bible study, and sources of "reliable" Christian news. By engaging laypeople in *religious* practices like "praying for our President," parachurch groups helped them to connect religion and politics much more explicitly than they would in the context of local congregations. Ironically, these groups exercised *political* influence by actively engaging laypeople like Richard and Pam in *spiritual* disciplines like prayer, Bible study, and family devotion.

The Pro-Life Movement as Religious Practice

This was particularly true for laypeople active in the pro-life movement. Social movement scholars have often assumed that evangelical Christians learn to be pro-life in church, and then are recruited by activist groups who offer them the opportunity to express this religious commitment in political action. But I found that pro-life ministries actually *formed* people's religious beliefs and identities, as much as they appealed to preexisting religious beliefs and identities. For Northtown members who were active in the pro-life movement, the movement itself provided them with a *separate* stream of religious practice, quite independent from their congregational participation. This is consistent with Ziad Munson's research on the recruitment of pro-life activists: that this movement actually provides an alternative space for religious practice, rather than simply appealing to the preexisting religious commitments developed by churches.[6]

This phenomenon is illustrated by Betty, a college-educated nurse in her early sixties who regularly attended Northtown Baptist. Though Betty attended church every Sunday, she spent an even greater amount of time each week participating in a pro-life ministry called SonRays Ministries. As a volunteer for SonRays, Betty counseled women experiencing crisis pregnancies and led life skills classes for homeless mothers who were staying in an affiliated shelter. In fact, the majority of Betty's *religious* practice also occurred through this pro-life ministry, rather than her local church. Betty gathered with other SonRays volunteers twice a week for devotional purposes: a weekly Bible study on Wednesday or Thursday morning, and a time of collective prayer on Wednesday night. These devotional activities through SonRays were not strictly focused on ending abortion, but also provided participants with personal support and spiritual growth. Participants often brought their own prayer requests to the group, asking group members to pray for their own private troubles throughout the week. Each week, the group created a list of their collective prayer requests, which they would take home and use to guide their daily prayer as individuals.

For Betty, praying with pro-life Christians was both as a religious practice and a strategy of political change:

> At home, we would pray for people's requests . . . and definitely we were praying for the nation in general, and plus the presidency, and Governor Spitzer, we'd pray for all of that. . . . I prayed for godly people to be placed in positions and that they would be surrounded with godly people also that would influence them. . . . definitely before presidential elections, we pray that God would put men of God in the presidency.

New York Governor Eliot Spitzer was particularly in need of godly influence, because he had ordered an investigation of a pro-life counseling center for allegedly pressuring women away from abortion, confiscating their computers and paperwork and shutting them down.[7] Betty considered prayer to be both a religious practice and a strategy of social change: she prayed that God would either replace misguided leaders like Governor Spitzer, or surround him with Christians who would change his heart. For her, SonRays was a religious community as much as a vehicle to end abortion: a space in which she developed her faith, shared the Gospel with women at risk of abortion, and found fellowship with other Christians.

Betty explained that SonRays recruited their activists primarily from local evangelical churches, as well as some Catholic and mainline Protestant congregations. But while SonRays recruited activists through church networks, the ministry did not rely on congregations to socialize people into a deep religious opposition to abortion. Rather, SonRays drew laypeople into a parallel stream of religious practice, offering a familiar mix of relational support and spiritual growth similar to that provided by evangelical churches. By sponsoring Bible studies and prayer groups that encouraged religious practice and pro-life advocacy, SonRays helped evangelicals and other Christians to develop a new, politicized understanding of their religious identity, centered on their opposition to abortion. Like Focus on the Family, this parachurch ministry was an important agent of religious *socialization,* as much as a vehicle for Christians to act on preexisting religious commitments.

Betty herself followed this trajectory of movement-based religious socialization. She first connected with SonRays by engaging in prayer and religious fellowship with the movement, which helped her develop a strong identity as a pro-life Christian. Only later did she move into direct service to prevent abortion, and years later, into political activism. She first learned about the pro-life cause when SonRays' founder visited her church and showed a film called "Assignment Life," produced in 1980 by James Dobson. After watching the film and talking with SonRays' founder, Betty felt that God was calling her to get involved:

> I just had this sense that I should be a part of this little group, because God really placed it in my heart to do that. And I called them and they were meeting in a home with only about seven people, coming together to pray to see how God would grow them.

Betty's initial motivation was to be part of a new religious community, coming together to pray and look for God's direction. She was also compelled by the personality and depth of conviction of the SonRays founder, who she described as an "awesome lady." Prior to developing a clear set of beliefs about abortion, she responded to a call to seek God's will with a small group of fellow Christians.

By participating in SonRays as a religious community, Betty developed a more elaborate set of beliefs about why abortion was wrong and began to engage in political action. In 1992, Betty participated in several protests through the Spring of Life, and was even arrested once. Betty recounted the experience with some ambivalence:

> But we were all arrested and placed in a gymnasium but no charges came against any of us, so that was the end of that. Thank God . . . I could have lost my license if I ended up getting charged. And what we did was sit in front of the doorway so that people couldn't walk in and that's against the law. So we stopped doing that . . . I stopped being a part of that. Okay?

In retrospect, Betty had concluded that direct action was a misguided strategy, and now focused her efforts on ending abortion by ministering to women as individuals. She followed the example of Jesus, "he was proactive, he showed the right way to do it, but he didn't use force, he really spoke love. And this is the way I chose to live out my walk with God . . . we encourage our girls to grow up in God and to follow the right path and not to choose abortion." But Betty was still committed to making abortion illegal, and she had gone to Albany twice to lobby for the pro-life cause with an organization called New Yorkers for Constitutional Freedom.

For Betty, "Christian" became her primary political identity, with both her religious devotion and political participation defined by reference to abortion. Unlike Richard and Pam, Betty did not describe herself as an ideological "conservative"; rather, she described her political identity simply as a "Christian." Pressed to explain further, Betty told me that she thought of herself as "more Republican," but it was important to her to "look individually at what everyone believes in before I make my vote in the United States Presidency next year." But it would be a mistake to classify Betty as an Independent who merely "leaned" Republican, since she mapped politics as a conflict with Christians on one side, and Democrats and liberals on the other. When I asked Betty if there were any Democratic politicians that she particularly liked, she was surprised that I would even ask:

> If you'll read exactly what Doctor Dobson said? Doctor Dobson gives you a little synopsis of what everybody believes in the Democratic line up and what they said about partial birth abortion. And that, to me, opens my eyes.

Betty explained to me that Democrats had waged an attack on Christians' religious freedom, drafting a bill that would keep pastors from explaining Christian stands on moral issues. After the interview, Betty sent me home with a Focus on the Family newsletter, since my questions revealed a shocking political ignorance. For Betty, the Republican Party represented Christians and family values, and voting Democrat was inconceivable. She was an Independent only in the sense that she used the abortion issue as a litmus test to support Republican candidates.

Like many Independents who say that they "lean" Republican, Betty, Richard, and Pam were actually quite loyal to the Republican Party in their voting behavior.[8] For all three, their primary political identity was Christian, and for this reason, it was important for them to express their independence from the Republican Party and the "dirty" world of partisan politics. However, all three described a map of politics where Christians and Republicans were allied on one side of the line, and "liberals" and Democrats waged war on Christians from the other side of the line.

Significantly, Betty's attitudes were not structured around a consistent conservative ideology. She retained some of the economic perspective that she had learned from her working-class, Democratic parents. Her political identity had simply changed, so that economic issues no longer defined her map of politics. As she explained:

> Mom and Dad were Democrats. They felt that the Democratic Party was for the working man and she stuck with it because of that mentality. And I switched from it because I felt that the Republican Party was more in keeping my values as a Christian. I try to explain it to her, but I think she's in that mode where she thinks the Democrats will help the working man. Which my dad was, you know.

Betty had little to say about the economic dimension of politics. When I pushed Betty further, she associated the Democratic Party with social programs: "the Social Security system and everything, they stand by it. The welfare system, they really agree with. . . . I don't know much more about the Democratic Party." As a recent retiree, Betty agreed with the Democrats' support for Social Security, and stated that welfare reform had addressed her concerns about women getting "dependent" on the system. But economic issues were not salient to her political decisions, partly because she felt that Republicans also cared about poverty and working people.

> I feel that [President Bush] is trying to do the best job he knows . . . help those who need education, help those who need financial help . . . he wants to see our country grow to be . . . what is the term? A gentler society.

Betty admired President George W. Bush as a "caring gentleman" who wanted to improve the quality of life for working people. Since Betty did not see differences between the parties in their concern for working people, economic issues did not inform her map of political identity.

In summary, Betty's individual *attitudes* were not ideologically polarized: her statements on economic issues could be classified as moderate, and she did not identify herself as a strong Republican or a political conservative. But her culture war map of politics reflected political polarization at the group level. As Betty defined her religious identity by reference to a political conflict between Christians and Democrats, economic issues became less salient to her. But for another Northtown lay leader named Ann, her economic attitudes actually changed as her political identity changed, so that economic conservatism now seemed to flow naturally from her religious worldview.

Religious, Sexual, and Political Conversion

Ann had become a culture warrior through a very different pathway: she began her young adult life as a liberal Democrat living in a same-sex relationship. A journalist in her late thirties, Ann organized Northtown Baptist's ministry to people "struggling" with same-sex attraction, as described in chapter 3. Ann grew up Catholic in the Buffalo area, although she sometimes attended evangelical Bible studies in college through a friend of hers. After college, Ann completed a year-long Catholic internship in Chile, where she fell in love with another woman. After the internship, she moved in with this female partner and stayed in Chile another year, photographing the fall of the Pinochet dictatorship as a freelance journalist. In the course of this relationship, Ann reported that she drifted away from the Catholic Church.

After two years in Chile, Ann moved back to Buffalo to find work, hoping that her partner could join her in the United States. But the long-distance relationship did not last, and eventually Ann began an affair with a married woman with young children. Ann felt increasingly guilty about this secret relationship, and tried unsuccessfully to break it off many times. During this time, she began attending an evangelical Protestant church in the area, hoping that religion would give her strength to end the affair. Since Ann had never identified herself publicly as a lesbian, the congregation remained unaware of her circumstances. After she joined the church, she confessed her situation to the pastor, who she felt was surprisingly compassionate. Ann eventually found the strength to end her relationship and practice celibacy, by engaging in intense prayer and Bible reading. She now ran a parachurch ministry for people who struggled with same-sex attraction, as described in chapter 3.[9]

As a young adult, Ann had identified as politically liberal, but her politics changed after she became an evangelical Christian. Ann described this change to me:

> For years I was a Democrat, because . . . my heart was more toward social programs. But then I became a Republican, because . . . I felt

like a society falls apart if you don't stick to the moral issues . . . I changed the closer I got to God. When I was . . . walking in sin . . . I was totally a Democrat. And then as I walked away from my sin, and I started giving in to the word, and getting closer to God, than all of a sudden I started changing my opinion.

Ann's sexual and religious conversion occurred simultaneously with her *political* conversion to a conservative, Republican identity. Ann's political identity changed as she reconstructed her biographical narrative around themes of self-discipline, submission to God's loving authority, and the rejection of her old "liberal" self. In our interview, Ann linked her biographical narrative to a public narrative about America's need for redemption.[10] Ann supported Christian interest groups who opposed gay marriage:

I do believe that as Christians . . . we should not lie down and let a sexualized culture just walk over all the values established in our governmental system. I think we need to stand up and say, "No, that's wrong!"—Oh, what a novel word!

In keeping with Hunter's culture war model, Ann described American politics as a conflict between conservative and liberal views of God's authority in national life:

The liberal point of view is that we don't want to have too much of God in our public life, so we need to quiet down a bit and we need to loosen the moral standards 'cause that is restrictive to people . . . the liberal view has a different perspective of compassion . . . compassion means giving people what they want. And that's not always true compassion. And that's often times why people who say homosexuality is a sin are called bigoted, homophobic, and hateful even. Because the idea is, if people want to be homosexual, they should do anything they want . . . it's a free country.

By contrast, Ann defined conservatives as people who were brave enough to draw moral boundaries against sinful behavior, in spite of liberal hostility:

But I say, it's a loving thing to go, "You know what, that's sin and it's only gonna hurt you and the people around you," . . . I think it's a boundary issue . . . tighter boundaries tend to be more conservative and loose boundaries are more liberal.

Here, Ann was arguably drawing on the rhetoric that she heard from Christian radio, the national Exodus organization, and Focus on the Family, her three primary sources of political information. But she was not just parroting back Christian Right talking points. Rather, Ann had actively elaborated her own personal testimony that linked her individual "turn from sin" to *America's* need to turn from sin. This "confessional" template for political identity has a long history in American social movements, particularly the abolitionist and temperance movements.[11] In these confessional movements, participants shared their own testimony about renouncing personal sin, and resolved to bear witness to the special sins of the nation: slavery or alcohol. Likewise, Ann's personal testimony compelled her to bear witness to America's special sin: abandoning God's standards of sexuality.

Viewed from outside the evangelical subculture, Ann's political transformation might seem puzzling. But by tracing Ann's trajectory of identity change, it is possible to understand how Christian Right frames came to resonate with her personal experience. Even before her religious conversion, Ann reported that her affair with a married mother caused her considerable guilt.[12] When her pastor helped her assert "tighter boundaries" in her own life, she experienced this intervention as compassionate rather than restrictive.[13] As Ann embraced a new identity as a celibate evangelical Christian, she learned to tell her own biographical narrative according to this confessional template, that linked her turn from sexual sin to the special sins of the nation.

As Ann's political identity changed, her attitudes changed on economic issues as well. For her, economic and moral conservatism now seemed organically connected within a coherent, "conservative Christian" worldview. As a young woman, Ann had identified as a political liberal and a Democrat because she was concerned about poverty and believed in generous social policy. But now, Ann had rejected her old attitudes on economic issues:

> I think that our whole welfare system is kind of messed up right now—not that there shouldn't be help for people who are poor, 'cause there should be. But I think it got over into . . . "we just don't wanna see them suffer," so it got to be a huge machine, where money was just piled into it to give to people that are poor. Rather than having some tighter boundaries on it, so that they would be motivated to *press in*, work, get educated, etc. And the liberal idea was, "Well, the system crushes them and there's no way they're gonna be able to do it, so let's just give them some money." And I think the more conservative point of view is, "No, let's deny some of that, *deny it* so that they'll be motivated."

Conservative welfare policies appealed to Ann because they required poor people to "press in"—an evangelical term that refers to the disciplined pursuit of God's will. Through her religious and sexual conversion, Ann reinterpreted her own biographical narrative through the lens of self-denial, submission to God's authority, and the rejection of her old liberal identity. This personal narrative became her lens on social policy: she now framed welfare policy as another domain where self-discipline and authority have broken down because of "liberal" ideas. Ann's policy attitudes on moral and economic issues were woven together by her personal, confessional narrative.

The Political Influence of Lay Leaders at Northtown Baptist

For these four lay leaders, culture war rhetoric had become integral to their personal testimony and religious practice. Within a classic model of political socialization, we might assume that Christian Right frames resonated with these individuals because they had been previously socialized into moral traditionalism. Indeed, all four individuals placed particular emphasis on traditional moral intuitions: respect for authority, sacredness, or purity, and in-group loyalty. Explaining their childrearing values, Richard and Pam emphasized sexual purity and respect for authority, as expressed by modest clothing choices that avoided rebellious, countercultural styles. For Betty, pro-life activism took on sacred meaning, as a way to be obedient to God. Ann's conversion narrative was centered on these traditional moral intuitions: her submission to God's authority, embrace of sexual purity, and standing up for her group's Christian values.

But political elites had done more than appeal to their preexisting moral intuitions or religious identity, as previously formed in evangelical congregations. Rather, parachurch groups and social movements had played key roles in their *religious* socialization, by helping them to define the boundaries of their religious identity and evangelical orthodoxy in opposition to liberals. Culture war frames had shaped their religious identities in *constitutive* ways: they defined their identity as Christians by opposition to liberals and Democrats.

None of these four laypeople identified as a political activist. Instead, their leadership was focused within the evangelical subculture, helping other Christians to link their religious identity to conservative politics. While Richard and Pam did not think of themselves as particularly "political" people, they were well-positioned to send informal partisan cues, speaking from their confidence that faith and conservative politics were generally alike. Before the 2004 election, Ann had organized an informational session on gay marriage, using resources from Focus on the Family to educate fellow church members on threats to the traditional family. During the same time period, Betty had prayed about the election with her Northtown women's group. She asked for prayers that the pro-life candidate would prevail over Al Gore, whom she described as the "pro-abortion" candidate. Betty also worked hard to make sure that pro-life concerns were continually emphasized in the congregation, as an active member of Northtown's women's ministry. In her efforts to raise the profile of "life issues" at church, Betty was assisted by four other Northtown laypeople who served with her on SonRays' advisory board. It was this team of lay leaders that pushed Pastor William to recognize the SonRays ministry and make a pro-life statement on Mother's Day. Together, these prominent lay leaders helped to weave culture war themes into local congregational life.

CULTURE WAR CAPTAINS AT LIFEWAY ASSEMBLY

Lay leadership also played a key role in linking religion and politics at Lifeway Assembly. By understanding the formation of lay leaders, we gain a better perspective on religious practices that mapped political conflict as a spiritual battle between good and evil. For example, it was a team of lay leaders who wrote Lifeway's Easter drama, which juxtaposed an image of pro-choice activists with images of death, genocide, and Nazis. Gathered in a private home, it was two lay leaders named Patricia and Barbara who led their small group in prayer for "liberal politicians" that refused to acknowledge God. In both of these cases, key lay leaders were serving as culture war captains, motivated by a sense of thick coherence between religion and politics. But interviewing these lay leaders, I found that even Lifeway's most politically engaged members drew strong boundaries between their religious practice and the dirty world of partisan politics. To understand this ambivalence toward politics, it is helpful to consider the biographical narratives of lay leaders like Patricia, a retired woman in her sixties, who led her small group in politically charged spiritual warfare.

Pure Worship and Dirty Politics

Hearing Patricia pray in such absolutist language, a cultural outsider might wonder if she supported an authoritarian political agenda to impose Christian morality on the populace. But chatting informally with her group, Patricia expressed ambivalence about Christian engagement in politics: politics was a dirty business, and politicians often tried to manipulate religion for personal gain. Immediately before leading the group in prayer, she announced that she was disgusted with New York's mayor at the time, Rudy Giuliani, for claiming to be pro-life: "That's not true! I know he's pro-choice. That's the stupidest thing I've ever heard! . . . He was probably speaking in front of an audience where he thought that would go over well." For Patricia, religious practice needed to be kept separate from electoral politics, to preserve its sacred quality.

Patricia's ideal of revival reflected America's long tradition of civil religion, rather than a coherent political agenda. For example, from 1993 to 2000, she had helped organize a charismatic revival event called March for Jesus, which brought members from diverse evangelical churches together for a day of public worship. The goal of the event was "honoring the Lord," by marching through the streets with speakers playing out of cars. The March ended with a rally at City Hall, with "food for the poor" and "tents up to witness to people." The march closely resembled a social movement protest in form: Christians projected their presence into a public place, by gathering to pray outside of City Hall, the State Building, and the jailhouse. But for Patricia, this event was not political, because it transformed America through the miraculous means of evangelism and supernatural forces.

In Patricia's experience, politics often corrupted authentic religious experience. On the one hand, she wanted politicians to participate in public religious events like the March for Jesus: her hope was that nationwide revival would drive politicians to their knees, publicly acknowledging God's authority. On the other hand, she wanted to keep public worship separate from electoral politics, to preserve its sacred quality. She acknowledged that this pure form of civil religion was hard to achieve in practice:

> One time at the March for Jesus, I asked the mayor to come. When he stepped up to the microphone, he whispered in my ear, "Kiss me on the cheek." It was all for publicity! So I didn't invite him back. I didn't want him to use it as his deal.

Then, a few years later, the mayor showed up again at the March for Jesus. Although Patricia didn't want him to use the event for his own gain, the worship leader persuaded her to invite him onto the platform. Then, the worship leader started to pray for the mayor, "You have to humble yourself, you are not the king, you may be the mayor, but you must humble yourself before the King of Kings."

When Patricia prayed for a return to a Christian America, she did not envision a particular political platform or the formal establishment of Christianity as a state religion. Rather, she imagined the March for Jesus: voluntary public worship that recognized that politicians and governments are ultimately accountable to God. Patricia's narrative of social change that featured a miracle motif: dramatic personal conversions would solve America's problems, without any need for Christians to address messy institutional realities.[14]

In Christian Smith's classic study of evangelical identity, he found that this kind of ambivalence toward politics is common.[15] Finding that most evangelicals could not articulate a coherent strategy of institutional change, Smith concluded that they were not unified around a coherent political agenda. Ten years later, my fieldwork suggests a different interpretation. Patricia imagined that America would return to God through individual transformation, not institutional change. But Democrats and liberals represented a political obstacle that must be removed to achieve this "voluntary" influence. If many Americans remained persuaded by the Gospel, it was because liberals were preventing Christians from voluntarily sharing the truth. By supporting godly Republicans, Patricia could defeat the political forces that stood in the way of this voluntary, miraculous national revival.

Patricia's ambivalence toward politics should not be misunderstood as ambivalence about her political identity. In Patricia's kitchen, she proudly displayed a signed portrait of George W. Bush that she had received as a thank-you gift for her political donations, and she was unapologetic in her understanding that Christians should be politically conservative. While Patricia wanted to keep politics separate from authentic religious practice, she did not define this boundary in the same way assumed by liberal political theory: she was not referring to the boundary that separated church and state, nor was she arguing that religious authority should only govern private decisions.[16] Rather, Patricia was preserving the boundary between sacred and profane, a fundamental distinction that separated religious rituals and symbols from the mundane business of everyday life.[17] Prayer and worship could only release spiritual power if they were set apart from the dirty world of partisan conflict and electoral ambition.

Patricia did not identify with the Christian Right as a *political* agenda, but rather with this *religious* agenda of national revival. But this revival narrative was charged with partisan meaning: Christians had to remove the political obstacles that stood in their way, like godless liberal politicians who refused to recognize the National Day of Prayer. As the lay leader of a small prayer group, Patricia served as a captain in the culture war: she wove this partisan language into everyday religious practice, and helped other laypeople to connect religion and politics.

Spiritual Warfare and Political Identity

Interviewing other lay leaders at Lifeway Assembly, I found a similar pattern: they drew on Christian nationalism in their religious leadership, but did not think of these practices as part of a "political" agenda. Yet, despite their ambivalence toward politics, they still experienced a thick coherence between their religious and political identities. This was particularly clear in the case of Audrey, another Lifeway lay leader who regularly engaged in spiritual warfare for America. Like Patricia, Audrey drew strong boundaries between her religious practice and electoral politics, but not along the same lines assumed by liberal political theory.

A homeschooling mom in her early forties, Audrey led an intercessory prayer team at Lifeway Assembly, and also prayed for Buffalo and the region as part of a citywide charismatic prayer group. Like Patricia, Audrey engaged in combative practices of spiritual warfare, informed by Christian nationalism. But she understood spiritual warfare to be a personal, religious practice, separate from politics. She used the language of spiritual warfare to make sense of her encounters with cultural diversity, while sustaining strong boundaries against her pluralistic social environment. Audrey described how she relied on her emotional responses, or moral intuitions, to discern invisible spiritual forces around her as she navigated non-Christian social spaces. Attending the University of Buffalo in the late 1970s, Audrey had felt alienated as a newly saved Christian. By comparison, she felt a more "uplifting" atmosphere at her two sons' colleges, since one attended a Catholic university and the other attended an Assemblies of God university.

> I mean when you walk on the campus there, you can feel an uplift, it's in the air almost. But you know, when I go out on the campus in Buffalo state and UB, I just feel a lot of oppression; I think we rule God out and I think they are looking to themselves and the enemy is more . . . He's got open season there, to some degree.

Audrey made sense of her experiences as a religious minority through a charismatic framework, where her emotional experiences of "oppression" and "freedom" revealed the spiritual forces at work in these institutions. When Audrey felt negative emotions on the University of Buffalo campus, she discerned satanic forces at work in that space. When she felt positive emotions at her sons' Christian university campuses, she discerned that these spaces were free from such demonic "oppression." Audrey's everyday use of culture war language did not reflect a coherent political agenda. Rather, Audrey used the language of spiritual warfare to quite literally map her subcultural identity as she moved through geographic and cultural space.

Informed by a Pentecostal narrative of Christian nationalism, Audrey regularly engaged in intercessory prayer for America. Audrey explained to me that when institutions and communities refused to acknowledge God, they opened themselves up to demonic attack. For example, her prayer group started praying for the safety of kids at school about fifteen years ago, after they received a prophetic warning that the nation's schools would begin to see "horrendous atrocities." When the school shootings started happening, they interpreted it as the consequences of taking prayer out of the public schools:

And so we would pray for safety and for righteousness and godliness to be returned to the schools. Because if God is rooted out, it leaves room for the enemy to come in. And when the enemy comes in there's room for destruction, one way or another.

Audrey's narrative of Christian nationalism had a collective, territorial logic: If American schools did not publicly acknowledge God, they would be attacked by demonic forces.[18]

But when I asked Audrey how she wanted to see "godliness returned to the schools," she stressed the importance of working through prayer, personal influence, and trusting in God to "move things in the heavenlies and change people's hearts and minds." Rather than forcing her beliefs on others, Audrey wanted to lead by example: "Because we have the spirit of God in us, so we are walking with the fruit of the spirit, in love. People are very drawn to that." Audrey did not recognize any contradiction between her combative Christian nationalism and her desire to "love" non-Christians. After all, *she* felt free in a faith-saturated environment and oppressed in religiously neutral ones, and so she did not understand why school prayer might infringe on other people's freedom.

In this respect, Audrey sounded much like the national sample of evangelicals in Christian Smith's classic 1999 and 2002 studies. She wanted to make America a "Christian nation," yet she could not articulate a coherent political agenda for institutional change. Instead, she imagined a form of *voluntary* absolutism: Christians could achieve cultural unity by converting Americans to evangelical Christianity. Audrey also distanced herself from the Christian Right, understood as a political agenda. When I asked Audrey if she considered herself evangelical, she told me that she didn't like that term, because it had become "associated with the far right in politics . . . I am evangelical but I don't like to identify with the movement, because of that stigma." Audrey drew on combative Christian nationalism to strengthen her subcultural identity, but she distinguished these practices from a right-wing political agenda.

Yet Audrey still identified strongly with conservatives as a social group. Since her early twenties, Audrey's political identity had evolved in conversation with her husband Joe, who was also active at Lifeway Assembly. Audrey and Joe now described themselves as conservative Republicans, but as newly converted teenagers in 1976, they had both enthusiastically voted for President Jimmy Carter. Audrey explained, "my first election, when I was eighteen, I voted for Jimmy Carter because I heard he was a born-again Christian." By 1980, they had both become dissatisfied with Jimmy Carter, and voted for Ronald Reagan instead. Audrey struggled to explain why: "I saw that his values didn't coincide with mine in some ways, and I don't even remember now what they were. But as I learned these other things, I associated more with the Republican Party."

In part, this shift was driven by the abortion issue, as Audrey noted that there are "more Republicans that are pro-life and very few Democrats that are pro-life, and that became an issue with me." But more fundamentally, their support for Reagan was driven by a narrative of national revival: miraculous social change led by transformed, godly individuals. In the 1980 election, Ronald Reagan became the hero in their Christian nationalist narrative, by casting himself as the godly leader who could turn the tide of America's moral decline.[19] Joe explained that Reagan's appeal went beyond the abortion issue: "Everything impressed me about Ronald Reagan, his moral stance . . . when he talked about an issue, it came from his heart, you could tell . . . And he was the real deal . . . he was a real hero for our country at the time." Despite Jimmy Carter's credentials as an evangelical Christian, he had failed to become the hero in their narrative of Christian nationalism.

Audrey's revival narrative had become charged with partisan meaning, as she came to define conservatives as the kind of transformed people who could lead America back to God. She did not see her vision of national revival as a political agenda, because she hoped to see America change through transformed individuals, not changed institutions. But for Audrey, godly personal character was what distinguished liberals and conservatives on both moral and economic issues. Liberals were people who believed in two things: first, "throwing away morality," and second, in being generous toward the poor. While this generosity was "a good thing," Audrey interpreted this liberal stance as a lack of personal character:

> A lot of times, the way they interpret it, is that the *government* should be liberal towards the poor. And I don't agree with that . . . I think it's us as an *individual*. The people that are the most liberal, they are the least giving. They want the government to do it, but they're not giving themselves . . . it's those who are closest to the Lord, conservatives, that are the most giving of their personal resources.

Conservatives showed their godly character by taking personal responsibility to take care of the poor, while liberals used government as an excuse to avoid this responsibility. For Audrey, liberals were, by definition, people who lacked the kind of transformed character to lead America back to God. She no longer had a place on her political map for Democrats like Jimmy Carter, who were both "godly" and "liberal."

Informed by this narrative of godly leadership, Audrey supported President George W. Bush despite her concerns about the war in Iraq. She praised Bush as a "godly man," although she specified that his godliness did not make him infallible: "Is he doing everything godly? No, not necessarily. Is everything I'm doing godly? No, not necessarily. I think he's sincere." But the president's personal faith allowed God to work through him, and even speak to him through prayer. By this, she did not mean that God spoke audibly to President Bush and dictated his policymaking. In her own experience, hearing from God was more subtle and mysterious: she prayed about situations that troubled her, and God would give her an intuitive sense of peace about a potential solution. For example, when Audrey was feeling doubts about her support for the war, she had prayed about it and received reassurance "that God had a strategy in Iraq." Audrey described what it was like to hear from God:

> I could not explain it to you in terms that even I understand, because it was something like revelation with the spirit. . . . And I'm not against what he's [President Bush]'s doing in Iraq, simply because of what the Lord has showed me, that He has a strategy there.

Through prayer, Audrey received spiritual reassurance that her support for President Bush and the Iraq War was consistent with God's will. Audrey used prayer to help her interpret current events, using her emotional intuitions to discern the unseen spiritual forces at work.

This example shows that top-down political messaging was not sufficient to link Audrey's faith to conservative politics in a deep, experiential way. In part, Audrey's religious interpretation of the Iraq War reflected the Bush administration's efforts to frame the war using Christian nationalist language.[20] But Audrey had also "tested" these political messages through prayer, which she saw as an independent source of political knowledge. Her emotions and intuitions allowed the Lord to "show her" spiritual reality that was invisible to empirical observation. These practices of "spiritual discernment" helped to validate conservative frames as an authentic expression of her personal religious experience.

In a similar way, the pro-life cause became sacred to her because it stood apart from the profane world of politics. In the early 1990s, Audrey and her husband had engaged in pro-life direct action together, but they dropped out after the movement became too political. Initially, they were drawn to participate in the "rescues" as a powerful religious experience. When Audrey prayed outside of abortion clinics with other Christians, she felt a powerful sense of connection to God, "where we would just walk in His love . . . and enjoy Him, you're obedient." Pro-life activism deepened the couple's faith, because they saw God's power to change society, apart from humanity's own projects of institutional reform. Recalling the early days of the movement, Joe saw signs that God was working through them in miraculous ways:

At the beginning it was exciting . . . It was wonderful. Things were happening. Babies were saved because of that, and are alive today because of that. And it started out very prayerful, very humbling, at first—it wasn't the political thing that it became. And the people who were involved with me . . . had the same heart and were willing to lay our lives down and to be arrested if necessary, stand the abuse that we went through.

These experiences of worship and religious community gave Joe confidence that the movement was "of God," not "of man." But as the protests became "less prayerful and more political," Joe felt that the movement reflected "the planning and imagination of man," rather than God's will. Increasingly, Audrey felt that movement leaders were exercising too much instrumental control over the movement, rather than letting the spirit of God move freely. People were being assigned to pray in strategic locations for the benefit of the news cameras, rather than everyone being in a "spirit of prayer." Audrey no longer experienced the protests as authentic worship; her participation had become a "work," instead of flowing naturally from her personal relationship with God.

This couple's experience shows we cannot assume that religious beliefs and identity are causally prior to political behavior. Audrey and Joe did not oppose abortion because of their pre-existing theological beliefs and sense of religious identity. Rather, the abortion issue increasingly became *constitutive* of their religious beliefs and identity. Pro-life activism became sacred as a spiritual battle that stood apart from the profane world of "politics." Audrey and Joe deepened their faith by stepping into this sacred drama between good and evil, to "lay down their lives" for God. When "babies were saved," Audrey and Joe recognized a sign of God's power to work through their humble acts of faithfulness. Pro-life action helped define the boundaries of their religious identity, as much as their preexisting religious identity informed their stance on abortion. By praying with other pro-life activists, the couple experienced an intense feeling of solidarity with fellow Christians. By receiving abuse from political opponents, the couple gained a strong sense of cultural tension between "us" and "them" that defined their religious identity.

This sheds light on how abortion has become a defining issue for rank-and-file evangelicals since the *Roe v. Wade* decision, even though Protestants were initially neutral or supportive of the ruling. Abortion did not simply become a moral issue because it violated the religious beliefs of evangelical orthodoxy, as James Hunter claims. Rather, abortion has become sacred for rank-and-file evangelicals because it strengthens a sense of cultural tension with their environment. Understood as a spiritual drama between good and evil, the pro-life cause helps Christians to define their moral and social boundaries against the world. Even for evangelicals who do not engage personally in pro-life activism, the movement still provides them with a dramatic image of Christian faithfulness, defined against the worldly opposition of hateful political opponents.

Countercultural Conservatives

Framed as a spiritual drama, the abortion issue has come to define the boundaries of evangelical identity. This helps us understand why abortion has become a defining political issue, even for evangelicals who express more liberal attitudes on other issues. For example, Jonah and Julie, a Lifeway Assembly couple in their forties, were oriented toward the artistic community, and attracted to causes like multiculturalism and environmentalism. Julie was a lapsed Catholic as a young woman, until she joined the Peace Corps in Liberia, where she went through a personal crisis that brought her to the Pentecostal church. Jonah was raised in a Catholic Puerto Rican family, and was now a professional jazz percussionist.

Julie was homeschooling their four children, but she rejected many aspects of the conservative Protestant homeschooling culture as too "ethnocentric": she wanted her kids to learn to be global citizens, rather than learn what she perceived as a whitewashed view of American history that didn't talk about Native Americans or the black experience. Julie got angry when she came across a Christian history textbook that talked about South Africa and didn't mention apartheid. To address these shortcomings, she drew on homeschooling resources from more progressive countercultural perspectives, as well as from conservative Protestant perspectives.[21] Jonah and Julie also wanted their children to grow up to be good "stewards" of the earth, and wanted the church to take the lead on environmental issues.

The couple was also active in Buffalo's arts community, which brought them into regular contact with people outside of the evangelical subculture. Jonah had made many gay and lesbian friends through his music, and he was concerned that the church didn't know how to love gay people. At the same time, Jonah and Julie thought that homosexuality was morally wrong. They told me several poignant stories about how they negotiated this tension in their friendships, which had left them with the conviction that churches should not drive gay people away by focusing on homosexuality as a special sin. Jonah and Julie believed that if they could bring their gay and lesbian friends closer to God in a nonjudgmental way, the Holy Spirit would ultimately convict them.[22] On the surface, Jonah and Julie seemed to embody a mix of liberal and conservative sensibilities: while they were morally traditional, they rejected anti-gay stereotypes and valued the environment, multiculturalism, and the arts.

But while Jonah and Julie were not stereotypical culture warriors, they still mapped their political identities in culture war terms. As Jonah put it: "We both have a strong pro-life stance. . . . I'm a conservative person. I'm a registered Republican but I have a lot of libertarian tendencies." Though Julie identified as a political "Independent," she leaned strongly toward the Republican Party. Throughout the interview, she consistently used the pronouns "I" and "we" to describe conservative or Republican ideas, and "they" to describe liberal or Democratic ideas. When I asked the couple to explain why they identified as political conservatives, they described the pro-life cause as a spiritual battle between Christians and hateful, left-wing activists.

For Jonah and Julie, Buffalo's Spring of Life was a powerful image of Christians under attack from hostile forces in the media and left-wing movements. Their memories of this event defined their map of American politics. Jonah recalled how he and his wife drove down to observe the protests for themselves:

And the picture had been painted that all the radical people were in the pro-life side. And when you went down there it was the exact opposite. And I think since the sixties, the left has become progressively more and more radicalized. So like almost every anti-family thing that exists is attracted to that political side.

Julie described a clear contrast between the right and left "sides of the street." On the left side of the street, she saw pro-choice activists, "very angry women . . . they were just hostile . . . militant women." On the right side of the street, she saw the pro-life activists, quietly praying as their pro-choice opponents spit on them and yelled vulgar things. Yet in the national media, she saw the "right side of the street" characterized as aggressive and inconsiderate. Though Jonah and Julie had never been personally involved in pro-life activism, they identified vicariously with pro-life activists as models of Christian witness. As a result, they interpreted negative media portrayals of the pro-life movement as a personal insult to Christians like themselves.

When Jonah and Julie defined their map of politics, they referred back to this dramatic image: Christians quietly praying on one side, hostile pro-choice opponents on the other. Jonah interpreted criticism of the pro-life movement as criticism of Christianity:

One guy said, "You should take this to the proper political channels." What are we doing? This is America, we're demonstrating. This *is* the proper political venue. So your response to that is showing up with pitchforks and torches and swearing at these people. I mean it was a real radicalizing experience to see that, wow, one side is totally right and one side is totally wrong. Do you know what I mean? It was made manifest right in front of us.

The abortion issue was a spiritual drama that defined a strong boundary between good and evil, us and them. On the right side of the street, they saw pro-life Christians, peacefully praying. On the left side of the street, they saw their angry, pro-choice, anti-family opponents, carrying "pitchforks and torches." The abortion conflict served as their map of politics, a powerful metaphor for all the ways that the political left was hostile to Christians in the public sphere.

Furthermore, Julie identified the political left with the crass, oversexualized cultural trends she saw on television. For her, voting Republican was about more than taking a pro-life stance; it was a way of expressing her opposition to these more general trends.

> I think the political engagement is really a moral engagement. And I'm seeing—in just the past ten years—a rapid decline of the moral fabric. I mean, just things that probably have always been around, but now, it's just out there . . . It's in the open. It's assumed to be acceptable.

Julie felt that sexual promiscuity had become pervasive in the media, even in children's movies, through subtle aspects like "the importance of having a boyfriend." She protested that "there's no time allowed for innocence." Jonah and Julie felt that gay marriage was just the latest political assault on the cultural climate in which they raised their children.[23]

Political liberals might protest that they, too, are opposed to violent television and hypersexualized marketing to twelve-year-olds. As Alan Wolfe asked, why didn't they realize that "breast-bearing Super Bowl halftimes have more to do with market share and earnings reports than with left-wing activists trying to impose their unpopular views on the majority"?[24] Jonah and Julie had arguably been influenced by Christian Right rhetoric, which blamed these cultural trends on liberals. Yet Jonah and Julie had gay and lesbian friends, and they prided themselves on being independent-minded and open to diverse perspectives. On other topics, they freely acknowledged that the white American evangelical subculture had blind spots, like ethnocentric history and lack of environmental concern. Why did they still embrace political rhetoric that blamed gay people and liberal elites for the nation's moral decline?

For Jonah and Julie, culture war rhetoric rang true with their personal struggles as parents. As Jonah explained:

> You can't watch TV with your kids anymore . . . there's no time that has been reserved for family . . . almost nothing we can watch with the whole family in the room. And why should that be? If you be-

lieve in choice that's great, but why should I be forced to see that? Maybe someone else should have to make a choice to see that, rather than me have to turn the TV off and never turn it on in a public forum. Do you understand what I'm saying?

For Jonah, conservative frames addressed a practical problem: why couldn't they watch prime time television with their children, without being assaulted by images of sexual promiscuity and violence? Christian Right leaders offered them a simple answer: because left-wing forces have waged an attack on Christian values in our culture. From the political left, they heard only the language of personal choice: if you don't like what you see on TV, just turn it off.

According to philosopher Michael Sandel, this frustration speaks to the impoverishment of American civic discourse. Sandel laments that, since the 1970s, liberals have "embraced the language of neutrality and choice, and ceded moral and religious discourse to the emerging Christian right."[25] Jonah explained that he and Julie wanted to "have our say" in defining "what our values are going to be." They supported conservatives because they were the only ones talking about the broader cultural forces that affected their children, the only voices who validated their concerns about the need for shared values.

But despite this couple's concern for the common good, they both supported laissez-faire economic policies. In one breath, Jonah explained why private choices should not drive the nation's cultural values, and in the next breath, he identified himself as a libertarian on economic issues. Julie appreciated that Democrats took a principled stand on poverty, but she opposed "big government" social programs that helped poor people. Why wasn't this couple more attracted by Democratic economic ideas that prioritized the common good over private choice? Ironically, their populist resentment against "liberals" linked their concerns about shared values to laissez-faire economics. While Julie admired the Democrats' "passion" for social programs, she still did not trust them as stewards of the common good:

> I like [the Democrats'] consideration, although I don't always agree with their policies on how they do it. But I do like that they want to help the person who's downtrodden. . . . I don't think we need a lot of big government. I think the people down in Washington making decisions about how people in New York are going to live is dangerous.

Ironically, Julie did not think it was dangerous for people in Washington to make decisions for New Yorkers when it came to abortion, sexuality, or media content. She did not hold a consistent libertarian stance on the proper scope of government intervention. Rather, her mistrust of big government could be more accurately described as mistrust of the Washington elites who championed social welfare programs.[26] Populist resentment against liberal elites linked the couple's moral and economic attitudes.

Economic Individualism and the Disciplined Self

For the Lifeway laypeople profiled so far, the pro-life cause defined both their religious and political identities. But for Brian, laissez-faire economics played this role as a defining "moral issue." Brian and his wife Cindy were central lay leaders at Lifeway Assembly, who had recently taken charge of the young adult small group. Brian was raised at Lifeway Assembly, in a historically Democratic-leaning military family. But Brian began to identify as a Republican in his teenage years, attracted by the individualistic ideal of economic freedom:

> ... Republicans put more responsibility on individuals and less responsibility on government. You have rights, you have responsibilities to perform a certain way in a society, and you are not entitled to anything but the freedom to go after your dreams. You are not entitled to have a job ... you are not entitled to a huge house or vacations, or whatever.

Brian explained that Republican ideas appealed to him as a young man because they were "pretty much like Christianity":

> God doesn't say, "You have to be a Christian and I am not giving you a choice about it!" God created free will ... so we choose our god and are free to worship. And if you don't want this freedom, if you don't want to be saved, then you don't have to. I think that, for me, is what the Republican Party has to offer: you have freedoms to achieve as much as you want to achieve in life so go for it.

For Brian, his religious beliefs were a natural fit with his small-government economic conservatism. As a small business owner, he was proud of building his fortune from scratch, without help from his parents and just two years of college. He had chosen to live the American dream. Poverty was a choice that some people made, just like some people made the choice to refuse God's free gift of salvation.

Brian explained that Democrats claimed to care about poor people, but their social programs actually made poverty worse, by shielding people from the consequences of their bad choices. Within Brian's metaphor, everyone was offered the "salvation" of the market economy, but not everyone would be saved. Like sinners destined for Hell, poor people could only be urged to repent. But instead, Democrats told them, "It's not your fault, someone did that to you, you are entitled to that, you should have it." If only Republicans could eliminate social programs and regulations, they could push poor people to more responsible choices. By freeing Americans from "political regulations," people in "the lower brackets" would be enabled to "raise themselves to the next level." Brian knew that trickle-down economics would not help everyone, but it would help everyone who was willing to work hard, to claim the market's free gift of salvation.

For Brian, the appeal of laissez-faire economics went deeper than the emphasis on individual choice. Brian also associated the "invisible hand" of the market with the hand of God:

> Where there is a lot of struggle, people are on their knees praying to the Lord, "Lord, help me." Faith is, "are you going to be able to feed your family today?" . . . and you have to believe that the Lord is going to provide for you. . . . there is a lot more need to be seeking for the Lord in an environment like that. In our society . . . even if you are not going to work, you are going to get a check anyways. So why do I need God? I am being taken care of.

In Brian's mind, it was wrong to try to spare people from the stress of economic insecurity. Poverty played a redemptive role, by bringing people to their knees. When people were subjected to the discipline of the market, they were forced to rely on God to help them feed their family. But when people felt financially secure and entitled to a government check, they no longer felt their need for God.

Brian associated America's moral decline with the growth of the welfare state. In his interpretation, the Founding Fathers intended for the United States to be a Christian nation. The Establishment Clause was intended to protect religion, not the government, and so the separation of church and state was not constitutional. Brian prided himself on reading the Constitution literally, just like he read the Bible, although he stressed that the Bible had priority to him as a "perfect document." Like the Bible, the Constitution offered us "black-and-white" answers to contemporary political problems, if only we would read it strictly. The problem was that "different judiciary elements" kept creating "new rights" that weren't necessarily in the Constitution. Unconditional rights were not in keeping with the nation's "founding principles," because the framers believed that "with rights you have responsibilities as well."

For Brian, the welfare state had grown because the nation had abandoned God's plan and the principles laid down by the Founding Fathers. When America was a Christian nation, people took care of each other in local communities, rather than looking to the federal government:

When you look back to the old days, when America was just starting, there was a mentality of mentoring and just nurturing the society from a more local level, which I think was more the norm
throughout the whole country. Versus what it is today where people
are just waiting for the government to come in, or some other
agency to come in and help them out.

Brian believed that the growth of government programs had pushed the
church out of its rightful place as a social service provider. While government programs were impersonal, inefficient, and bureaucratic, the church
provided empowering, holistic service that taught people to provide for
themselves. For Brian, the welfare state was locked in a zero-sum relationship with Christian charity.

Brian associated the growth of the federal government with the mar-
ginalization of Christians in public life, justified by the false doctrine of
"separation of church and state." For Brian, these trends both proved
that the United States had departed from God's plan and the principles
laid down by the nation's founders. He blamed liberals for both trends,
because they had led the nation away from a "black-and-white," conservative reading of the Constitution and the Bible. As an avid reader of
American history, Brian was informed by a parallel world of uncreden-
tialed historians like David Barton, who have forcefully advocated this
Christian nationalist account of American history.[27]

When Brian talked about individual freedom, he was really talking
about submission to authority. A "free" society was one that rewarded
people who submitted to external discipline: the discipline of the market,
the Constitution, and the Bible.[28] Liberals were people who rejected any
higher authority that could hold them responsible for their actions. By
contrast, Conservatives showed their respect for authority, by succeeding
in the free market, defending the Constitution, and honoring God. For
Brian, "economic freedom" was a constitutive part of his religious identity, just as the pro-life cause was for Audrey and Joe.

The Political Influence of Lay Leaders at Lifeway Assembly

For these five Lifeway leaders, conservative politics was a constitutive
part of their religious identity. This made it possible for them to send
strong partisan cues, while avoiding what they considered to be political
talk. For example, both Patricia and Audrey led small groups of women
in intercessory prayer for their city, state, and nation. Both women
thought of this religious practice as separate from politics: they were simply praying for godly leaders, personal conversion, and national revival.
But in practice, godly leaders were understood to be conservative Repub-

licans. To pray for godly leadership was to pray for the defeat of Democratic politicians. To pray for revival was to pray for the rollback of the "liberal" agenda. Christian nationalism was powerful precisely because of this polysemy, or multiple meanings that blurred the lines between "religious" and "political" practice. Because of this polysemy, Patricia and Audrey experienced their prayers as "sacred," or separate from the mundane world of politics, even though they were charged with partisan meaning.[29]

Significantly, none of these lay leaders saw themselves as exercising *political* influence; they were not self-consciously rallying the faithful behind a conservative political agenda. Their goal as lay leaders was to exercise *moral* influence, to help fellow Christians to grow in their spiritual knowledge and their personal integrity. But it happened that part of being a "good Christian" was standing up against the liberal agenda. For example, Brian hoped that if he formed his church's young adults in Christian character, they would go out and transform the nation:

> Basically if you are a Christian, a true Christian, you are going to be of more help on society than you are going to be a burden on society. So if you are a true Christian . . . you are going to take care of your neighbor. And I think from a country standpoint, I think you are conscious of what the Lord is telling you, what is right and wrong to do. And hopefully you are electing people who are like-minded, so that your local sphere of influence becomes more of a national sphere of influence.

When Brian talked about electing "people who are like-minded," he did not mean *any* sincere Christian political candidate—he was referring to conservative Republicans. By defining Christian identity in partisan terms, Brian could send political cues to his small group even without introducing political topics.

Like their Northtown Baptist counterparts, these Lifeway lay leaders were primarily focused inward, on the formation of Christians in their church, rather than outward on political issues. But if we concluded that these lay leaders were only focused on personal, spiritual matters, we would drastically underestimate their political influence. As captains in the culture war, these lay leaders reinforced a particular prototype of the "good" group member: an ideal Christian is politically conservative. They also drew boundaries against out-groups, by identifying liberals, pro-choice activists, LGBT people, and Democrats as the adversaries to Christian influence in society. For example, Jonah and Julie helped script Lifeway's Easter drama, which featured an image of pro-choice protesters as one of the evil consequences of man's Fall from Grace. They did not see this as an effort at political mobilization; rather, they were challenging the faithful to take their place in a spiritual struggle between good and evil.

At Lifeway Assembly, the culture war was not simply a conflict between two abstract worldviews. It was a literal battle between godly and satanic forces, which believers could experience through charismatic practices of worship and prayer. This marked an important difference between Baptist and Pentecostal culture warriors. When Baptist laypeople talked about defending orthodox Christianity, they referred to a set of abstract ideas discovered through the right model of biblical exegesis.[30] By contrast, Pentecostals did not just evaluate political ideas based on abstract theology or biblical proof-texts—they also discerned the underlying "spirit" of ideas through personal religious experience.[31] For example, Audrey knew the pro-life cause was sacred because she felt a "spirit of prayer" among activists that indicated God's presence. Randall Collins has described this "spirit" as emotional entrainment, a state that can only be achieved through face-to-face interaction that builds energy around a shared ritual.[32] Christian Right frames resonated because they were reinforced by this kind of sacred experience.

CONCLUSION

At Northtown Baptist and Lifeway Assembly, an important group of lay leaders saw politics as a struggle between two views of authority: conservative and liberal. These individuals fit Hunter's description of the "orthodox" culture warrior. But they were not more politically conservative because they were the most religiously devout or theologically informed. Nor were they simply following their pastor's interpretation of the tradition. Rather, they had learned to connect religion to conservative politics from sources outside of the local congregation: national figures like James Dobson, parachurch ministries, the pro-life movement, and Christian radio. At the same time, these culture warriors felt that their local church supported their political views. Even though ordained leadership avoided explicitly partisan talk, they were personally sympathetic to conservative politics and supported their stances on the "moral issues." And, as I will discuss in the next chapter, there were no lay leaders who publicly offered a countervailing perspective, by defining Christian identity on a different kind of partisan map.

Unlike Christian Right elites, these lay leaders used culture war language for local, religious purposes, which they saw as separate from electoral politics. For example, Audrey did not identify with the Christian Right as a political agenda, since political conflict merely reflects an underlying spiritual battle. When Audrey led other women in prayer for America, she hoped to change the nation through miraculous revival, not through sustained political mobilization. But her prayers also had a more direct political effect: reinforcing a clear partisan map that defined liberals and Democrats as the adversary to Christian influence in society. As a lay leader, Audrey drew on Christian nationalism for different purposes than national Christian Right elites. Nonetheless, she still served as a "captain" of culture war politics, by helping other Christians link their faith to partisanship.

Lay leaders exercised political influence in ways that national elites could not: by serving as flesh-and-blood prototypes of what it meant to be a good Christian. For example, when Jonah and Julie described their ideal of Christian faithfulness, they described an image of pro-life activists kneeling in prayer outside of an abortion clinic. Within this iconic image of Christian devotion, the pro-life activist became the evangelical equivalent of a Catholic saint. In each church, only a handful of members were active in pro-life activities, but these individuals still influenced their congregations by serving as a prototype of the "true" or "exemplary" Christian. The pro-life cause was not just central to Christian identity because James Dobson said so. Lay leaders like Betty also reinforced this message, speaking from the authenticity of their personal experience.[33] When Betty asked her women's group to pray for pro-life politicians, she was informed by the culture war rhetoric of James Dobson's newsletter. But this message was more powerful coming from Betty, a respected church member for whom the pro-life cause was an integral part of her faith.

In conclusion, both national "generals" and local "captains" play an important role in fostering political homogeneity among white evangelical Protestants. Because the evangelical subculture has no single "cockpit," it is misleading to argue that Christian Right elites have "hijacked" the faith. Instead, it is more helpful to imagine a two-step process of political influence, first identified by the political scholars Elihu Katz and Paul Lazarsfeld. Katz and Lazarsfeld argued that for elites to influence mass publics, they must first reach a broad set of opinion leaders, who are considered trustworthy members within their social networks. Second, these opinion leaders reinforce elite messages within their personal networks, translating these messages into locally relevant terms.[34] This two-step model helps us understand how Christian Right generals have been so successful at building a conservative political consensus among rank-and-file evangelicals. In the next chapter, I trace this two-step process of influence in two American churches.

CHAPTER 7

THE BOUNDARIES OF POLITICAL DIVERSITY IN TWO U.S. CONGREGATIONS

In this chapter, I debunk the stereotype that American evangelicals share the coherent ideology promoted by Christian Right elites. I describe the political diversity that existed in both American churches, by introducing a second group of members who didn't fit the culture war mold. But I offer a different interpretation of this individual-level diversity than many survey researchers and political pundits, who conclude that the influence of the Christian Right is therefore exaggerated, weak, and in decline.

Evangelical Christians do not all subscribe to consistently conservative attitudes on economic, moral, and foreign policy issues.[1] Working-class evangelicals often combine moral conservatism with more progressive attitudes on economic issues.[2] "Culture warrior" stereotypes don't fit more cosmopolitan evangelicals, who live in big cities outside of the South, and work in creative or "new class" professions.[3] In recent years, a new cohort of younger evangelicals have challenged the Christian Right, by advocating a less confrontational stance toward postmodern culture, and advocating for a new set of issues like global poverty, human trafficking, and environmentalism or "creation care."[4] Unlike white evangelicals, black, Latino, and other non-white Christians often combine theologically conservative beliefs with liberal politics.[5] This picture of diversity seems to confirm Morris Fiorina's argument that the United States is "one nation after all."

The problem with this interpretation is that it treats evangelicalism as the aggregate of the individuals who belong to it. But this ignores the powerful mechanisms that link evangelical identity to partisanship at the congregational level. In both American churches, only a minority of evangelicals fit the culture warrior ideal-type. But this minority still had disproportionate influence to set the political tone within their churches. These culture war captains helped link religious and political identity for less politically engaged evangelicals in their church. As a result, this second group still experienced a relatively *thin* coherence between their religion and conservative politics. This sense of coherence was reinforced by partisan cues within their social environment, even when individuals could not personally articulate a coherent political perspective.

THIN COHERENCE BETWEEN RELIGIOUS AND POLITICAL IDENTITY

This thin coherence between religious and political identity is exemplified by Tammy, a stay-at-home mom in her early forties, who had helped found Northtown's ministry to special-needs children and their families. Tammy had been an active Democrat in her twenties, and had even held public office as a Democrat, serving on the zoning board for the city of Niagara Falls. But now, Tammy identified as a Republican. When I asked her to explain why her politics had changed, Tammy had very little to say about the matter:

> Probably that they're more conservative in their values . . . so I was on the zoning board and I was a Democrat . . . but I just think they're probably more conservative, more to . . . my values are now . . . as a Republican.

Unlike Ann, Tammy did not share a biographical narrative about a dramatic political conversion. Nor did Tammy identify with the label "conservative," posed either as a religious or as a political identity. In a series of questions about religious identity, I asked Tammy if she identified herself as a conservative, and she answered, "I definitively don't consider myself conservative, not particularly." Later, when Tammy told me that she identified herself as a Republican, she qualified this statement by adding "I'm not ultra-conservative." She was not on the mailing list for any Christian Right groups like Focus on the family, and she got her news from local broadcasts rather than from any polarized cable networks like Fox. Tammy experienced a thin coherence between religion and politics, rooted only in an intuitive sense that voting Republican "probably" went along with being a Christian and subscribing to "conservative values."

Despite Tammy's statement that her values were now more Republican, her positions on social policy seemed closer to those of the Democratic Party. She felt strongly that the government should support generous social services, based on her own experiences parenting a special needs child. She passionately disagreed with the idea that taxes were too high, pointing to the need to fund valuable programs such as New York State Early Intervention:

> Any child that qualifies that has a disability or delay, they're given free therapy. Up until [my son] went to school, we had a therapist

come to the home. And I have to tell you, people complain about taxes all the time, and I'm telling you New York State is the best for a child's disability hands down. You will not find another state in the whole United States that gives the children what New York State gives them.

Yet Tammy's values about social policy did not seem to inform her politics. A social policy scholar might point out that New York State has more generous special needs programs than other states precisely because of the greater strength of the Democratic Party.[6] Furthermore, Tammy's social policy attitudes were strong, salient to her personal experience, and informed by extensive research that she had done while founding a special needs ministry in her church. Unlike Ann and Betty, she did not offer a reason why moral issues should trump social policy issues, nor did she express a deep, personal commitment to the pro-life cause.

Tammy did not vote based on social policy issues, because these issues were not linked to her cognitive and affective map of politics. When I asked Tammy to describe the differences between the two political parties in her own words, she did not even mention economic or social policy issues. Instead, she defined the differences between the parties as a battle between groups with two competing views toward God's authority. She associated Democrats with a social group that she called the "far left wing," who represented what she described as "anything goes":

> They're for mixed marriages, meaning you know two partners of the same sex. They're really for anything, it's just whatever you feel: "Go for it." Cause . . . you know, they're not under any type of law, not under God's law.

Tammy did not associate Democrats with any positive group of people who shared her values about social policy. Nor did she claim any ideological label that linked her social policy attitudes to her personal identity. In short, Tammy did not develop her political identity by tallying up her individual policy attitudes, or by rationally weighing the relative priority of economic versus moral issues. Rather, she was following political cues around her that good Christians voted Republican.

From spending time in Tammy's social world, it was not difficult to infer how her map of politics had changed. In chapter 3, I described how Northtown members regularly drew symbolic boundaries against "godless" liberals, drawing a cultural map of politics that placed Christians in opposition to Democrats. Tammy could not recall a particular occasion when someone had persuaded her of the rightness of the Republican cause, explained why moral issues should trump economic issues, or explicitly told her why she should no longer be a Democrat. But group members need not influence each another through rational deliberation or the open exchange of political information. Instead, Tammy's political shift illustrates what Elizabeth Suhay has called "conformity without persuasion."[7] Tammy had likely responded to diffuse cues about political identity from her congregational setting, which linked "Christian" stances on the moral issues to a partisan conflict between Christians and liberal Democrats.

WORKING-CLASS EVANGELICALS

This framework can help explain why many working-class evangelicals vote Republican, even though the Democratic Party has traditionally appealed to lower-income voters. In theory, working-class evangelicals are politically cross-pressured: torn between Democratic appeals to their economic self-interest and Republican appeals to their conservative morality.[8] Using open-ended questions, I examined subjective experiences of class among working-class evangelicals, to understand how they perceived the tension between their economic self-interest and their moral values.[9]

Surprisingly, I found that working-class evangelicals did not always *feel* politically cross-pressured, even when one might expect it based on their objective circumstances. Class took on different subjective meanings, so that respondents did not necessarily perceive an obvious link between economic self-interest and support for the Democratic Party. When individuals felt cross-pressured, it was because their social networks reinforced countervailing loyalties to the Democratic Party, in the same way that their churches did for the Republican Party. Voting on economic issues had to be reinforced by personal relationships and group identity, just like voting on moral issues. By examining this social context, we can better understand diversity within the white working class, particularly the divide between men and women.

Thomas Frank famously lamented that the white working class has been tricked into voting against their economic self-interest, through symbolic appeals to religion, racism, authoritarian beliefs, and cultural identity.[10] However, it is working-class *men* who are most politically swayed by Republican cultural appeals. Lower-income white evangelicals are more likely to vote Democratic than their middle-class counterparts, just as lower-income whites vote Democrat in higher numbers than higher-income whites.[11] But on closer inspection, these income differences are driven primarily by women and very poor whites, many of whom are unemployed. If the working class is defined by employment in blue-collar occupations, we find that white working-class men have increasingly abandoned the Democratic Party since 1980.[12]

This raises a question: why do cultural appeals trump economic self-interest for men but not women? In his 1960 classic *Political Man*, Seymour Lipset argued that working-class voters are more inclined to support progressive economic policies, but also more inclined toward authoritarianism.[13] Authoritarian beliefs are motivated by a need for order and an aversion to difference, ambiguity, and non-conformity.[14] Among white working-class men, both religious traditionalism and authoritarian beliefs are important predictors of Republican affiliation. But significantly, authoritarianism does not affect the politics of white working-class women, who tend to support the Democratic Party even when they are religiously traditional.[15] My fieldwork sheds light on how blue-collar and low-income evangelicals perceive this tension between economic and moral issues.

To understand why working-class men respond to authoritarian rhetoric, it is helpful to consider the case of Ronald, a 67-year-old Lifeway member who performed manual labor for a lawn company. When I interviewed Ronald, he was visibly sunburned, and his hands and arms were leathery from years of working outside. Though Ronald was struggling economically, he did not see Democrats as fighting for people like him. In fact, he blamed liberals, big government, and affirmative action for his economic situation. As Ronald explained, he was from the "wrong sex, wrong color, and wrong nationality."

> This is when the government said "We have to give these jobs to minorities, to under privileged people." You know so, give them to women, give them to blacks, give them to Asians, and give them to the minorities. And there's nothing minority about me.

Voting Democratic was not in his economic self-interest, because he believed that Democrats only cared about "the minorities." His perceptions fit a group position theory of the gender gap, which posits that men are more Republican than women due to a desire to maintain their cultural and economic superiority over other groups.[16] Republican cultural appeals tapped into Ronald's sense that socially and morally inferior groups were getting ahead at his expense.

Ronald did not identify personally with poor people, even though he engaged in a great deal of service to the poor. As a church volunteer, he had spent hours knocking on doors in a low-income housing complex, inviting people to church. But he saw poverty as the consequence of individual sin and family breakdown, rather than structural forces. When I asked him why life was so hard for people in that housing complex, he explained that "Satan is working overtime over there":

This is an area that they rely upon their drugs and their alcohol and their worldliness and they just haven't seen the light. It's a sense of evil over there. There's so much worldliness, the drinking, the drugs and the alcohol, that's their way of life, you know. Bottles and trash . . . it's just all over the place. The kids grow up in that environment.

Ronald defined his identity as a working-class man by drawing moral boundaries against poor people, a group defined by their deviant way of life.[17] When Ronald described his response to poverty, he did not talk about compassion or anger at injustice. Instead, he described feelings of *disgust* and moral intuitions about purity and sanctity. Poor people lived a "worldly" lifestyle of drinking, drugs, and "trash." His compassion was limited to innocent children who grew up in that environment through no fault of their own. These moral boundaries were closely tied to racial boundaries. The housing complex that Ronald described was predominantly black and immigrant, and when Ronald talked about poverty, he continually referred to "inner-city" and "black" problems.[18]

Ronald resented liberals, minorities, big government, and poor people because they threatened his patriarchal vision of social order. He believed that society would break down without the discipline of a father-led home, a model that George Lakoff has called "strict father" morality.[19] America was in chaos because liberals had defied God's plan, and allowed people to engage in nontraditional family practices:

Ask me what I hate, I hate liberals. I hate people who think the proof of the pudding is in the tasting . . . I'm very conservative, very strict and voice the Word of God. . . . In a political sense, liberal is tax and spend, big government you see. God . . . didn't mean for government to be as big as it is. He let the families do many of the things that government is doing today. Government has taken the place of the family. Government . . . has destroyed the family. It has destroyed marriages you know. It's liberalism again. I just have little time for it.

In particular, Ronald was concerned about the behavior of poor women and African Americans. He lamented the fact that poor women no longer suffered economic deprivation if they got a divorce or got pregnant out of wedlock.

[G]overnment has said, "If you're not happy in your marriage, get a divorce." If you become pregnant, you don't have to marry the person. The government will take care of it. We'll even set you up. We'll get you an apartment. We'll take care of all your expenses and this kind of thing . . . Government is almost anti-family.

Ronald believed that big government undermined the authority of the father: "It's destroyed the black family in the inter-city. Taken the man out of the family. The government has become the father for many people." Poverty among African Americans was ultimately caused by sinful lifestyles, made possible by amoral, big government programs. His solution was to "stop all these entitlements," and say, "That's tough!" Ronald did not express overtly racist beliefs, but his attitudes reflected symbolic racism, or the idea that racial inequality was caused by African Americans' inferior values.[20] He lacked empathy toward poor people because he defined them as both racially and morally "other."

Ronald's punitive impulse made him different from other morally traditional people in his church. While Lifeway Assembly promoted an absolutist, traditional understanding of morality, the church also fostered loving attitudes toward people who disagreed. By contrast, Ronald expressed open hatred for "liberals"; for example, he told me "I just want to scream" when he saw "liberal preachers" on television.[21] Ronald was not the only Lifeway member to talk about the decline of traditional family values. But other members emphasized their practical concern for parents and children, not their anger toward outsiders.[22]

In a sense, Ronald was an economic populist: he felt ordinary people were under attack from shadowy elites who were undermining the moral order. Even though Ronald wanted "small government," he did not subscribe to a libertarian or laissez-faire economic ideology. He wanted to cut welfare programs to enforce conformity on people who violated his "strict father" morality, not to protect individual freedom. Ronald was also critical of big corporations, and thought they had "too much power" in American life. He blamed corporate America for pushing the selfish values of consumerism: "Somebody's making us too materialistic. . . . There's a lot of power out there. Corporate America's got a lot of power."

In another era, working men like Ronald might have joined a populist movement to hold corporate elites accountable.[23] But his skepticism of big business did not inform his politics, because he did not think of government as a force that could hold corporate power in check. Instead, he focused his political anger on liberal elites, a phenomenon that Thomas Frank has described as "rancid populism."[24] Ronald identified as a political conservative, but distanced himself from the Republican Party. While he voted consistently Republican, he did not "have much faith" in the Republican Party because they were not fervently anti-government enough. It disgusted him that many Republican politicians continued to talk about "government doing this, government doing that." As long as government did *anything*, Ronald's anger could never be appeased.

In summary, Ronald did not feel cross-pressured between his economic self-interest and moral issues, because he blamed liberal elites for both his economic problems and America's moral breakdown. His politics were actually quite consistent with his class position, when we consider that Ronald defined his economic self-interest as a white man. Ronald clung to the most punitive elements of his Pentecostal subculture because they filled an important psychological function. He drew on his religious tool-kit to defend his sense of dignity as a white, working-class man, by drawing moral boundaries against inferior groups.[25] He blamed "liberals" for America's moral decline, because their "big government" programs upset the natural hierarchy of the patriarchal family and rewarded sinful behavior.

Ronald's conservative politics also played an important social function in his predominantly white, male workplace. Since his co-workers were not born-again, Ronald often felt alienated from his lawn company's hard-living culture. But Ronald's boss enjoyed talking about conservative politics, and this topic facilitated sociability between them—as long as Ronald avoided talking about his religion. Ronald's white, male co-worker also liked to listen to Rush Limbaugh on the truck radio while they were out cutting lawns. As a result, Ronald did not feel that his political interests as a worker put him in tension with his boss; instead, hating big government was something that they had in common. On closer inspection, Ronald's political outlook was not at odds with his class position, because it reflected his socialization within a predominantly white, male workplace.

In Ronald's case, we might assume that morality and religion were nothing more than weapons in a struggle for group control over status and resources.[26] Consistent with group position theories, Ronald drew on Christian Right rhetoric to defend his superiority as a white man. But this was not true for Matt, a white, forty-five-year-old, blue-collar worker who got saved at Lifeway Assembly ten years ago. Unlike Ronald, Matt did not wield his moral and religious beliefs as weapons to defend his group dominance. Quite the opposite: he voted on moral issues to reject his former sense of status and "entitlement" as a union man. Matt recognized that he was cross-pressured between Republican appeals to his moral values and Democratic appeals to his economic self-interest. But he voted pro-life as an expressive act of humility, putting moral beliefs above his own selfish pride. For Matt, religious beliefs served as transcendent standards that stood apart from his perceived group self-interest.

For most of his career, Matt had worked as a unionized machinist and autoworker, but he had been unemployed and underemployed for the last year. Despite his union history and recent economic troubles, Matt now voted Republican. When I interviewed Matt after a church picnic, he told me that his politics changed after he became a Christian: "that's when I started looking more at what the candidates believed in, some of the biblical perspective." The abortion issue became a political litmus test for Matt, trumping all other issues: "If a candidate came out and said 'I am going to fight to make abortion legal,' you know, I hate to pick a reason why I am not going to vote for you, but that would be it." Matt did not describe himself as an ideological conservative or a strong Republican, but he felt that as a Christian, he saw more "Christian values in the Republican Party."

Unlike Ronald, Matt freely acknowledged that he voted against his self-interest, "because I was a union guy and involved with the union." When Matt described his map of politics, he defined Democrats as the party that stood up for "working people" and "the union guys." By contrast, "the Republicans have more of a moral base than the Democrats, as far as biblical morals." Matt recognized that Democrats also talked about morality, but their appeals struck him as inauthentic: "Unfortunately, I see it is more selfishly motivated to change some of their views or to be wishy-washy on some of them depending on who they are talking to." This raises a question: why did Republican cultural appeals resonate with Matt's religious identity, while Democratic appeals rang false? Matt did not just privilege abortion over economic self-interest because of top-down political appeals. To solve this puzzle, we must also consider how Matt's biographical identity had changed from the bottom-up, as he joined a local religious subculture and weakened ties with his union workplace.

For Matt, voting Republican on moral issues flowed naturally from his own, personal conversion narrative. When Matt shared his personal testimony, two themes emerged: First, he and his wife repented of their decision to get an abortion as teenagers, before they were saved. Second, God had used economic hardship to break his pride as an "entitled" union man, and to teach him to depend on God. The abortion issue was not just central for Matt because national elites or pastors said so. Matt had made abortion central to his personal testimony:

> It still hurts inside thinking that we could have a child that is older than our son, because we thought we were too dumb and too young. And . . . you can't take it back. It is becoming more easy for my wife to speak to other people about it, to encourage other people not to go that route. God has a plan for each person and each baby.

His pro-life commitments were strengthened by his own reproductive story, a genre of storytelling fostered by evangelical churches and the pro-life movement.[27]

Within Matt's confessional schema, voting Republican was a public way to witness to his personal repentance. His church had helped to encourage this interpretation, but not by telling him point-blank to vote Republican. Matt had only heard politics come up in church on a handful of occasions, but never with an explicit partisan message: "They never said 'don't vote Democrat' or 'don't vote this or that,' or 'don't vote this person because of that'." Instead, he was told to "look at the biblical values of the candidate." In Matt's experience, Lifeway had never gotten "on the pulpit for a certain group or a certain party or a certain person." Instead, his church had encouraged him to share his own pro-life testimony, and helped him to link that personal testimony to a map of politics. These implicit partisan cues helped create a thin coherence between Matt's religious identity and voting Republican, even though he did not articulate a coherent culture war ideology.

Matt became a UAW autoworker shortly after his conversion, but his union membership did not exert a countervailing influence on his political identity. Matt associated union membership with negative character traits that he needed to reject in order to become a Christian. Looking back, he explained, "I never pictured myself as a traditional UAW person because my mind set a UAW person as an arrogant, me-first, 'get out of my way, I am an autoworker' person." As a young Christian, Matt had rejected his former hard-living persona, wrestling with his love of rock music, heavy drinking, marijuana smoking, and aggressive motorcycle riding. He didn't want to develop a pushy, selfish "I am an autoworker" attitude. When I asked Matt what that attitude looked like, he described "the person you meet at a grocery store that would bump you to get past you, with their shoulders broad." Matt never fully identified with his fellow autoworkers, because he had thought of his job as a "mission field." As he developed work relationships, he realized that he shouldn't "judge a book by its cover." But he still distanced himself from a mentality that he described as, "This company owes me because I have worked here for twenty years, I shouldn't have to work now, I just have to be here." This helps us understand why Matt rejected Democratic appeals to his economic self-interest. Matt had defined his religious identity by drawing moral boundaries against the prototypical "union man": macho, selfish, and entitled.

During my fieldwork, Matt underwent a year-long spell of unemployment and underemployment, and he had just found steady work at a small machine shop. Despite his economic hardship, Matt had not become more receptive to Democratic politics. In his mind, it was not legitimate to feel angry about his economic situation. Instead, he framed his hardship as an opportunity to rely more fully on God to provide for his needs. When his prospective employer asked how much he needed to get paid, Matt said, "I truly believe that God was going to bring me to a company that I could pay my bills" and asked for the minimum: "I need to make ten to fifteen dollars an hour." To his surprise, the employer told him, "We are now at twenty dollars an hour." Now Matt felt a new sense of God's presence in his life: "God was putting his finger on my life and going 'here you go,' blessing me and overwhelming me."

Though Matt's new job did not pay as well as the auto industry, he was not angry about his loss of economic security. Instead, Matt interpreted his time of underemployment through a religious narrative: God was refining him through a time of trial, before finally pouring out His blessing at a strategic time so that Matt would be overwhelmed by His power and love.[28] Coming from the auto industry, Matt had once assumed that a job "would last forever." But through his trials, that assumption had been "blown out of the water and I am just enjoying the season that He has me there right now." For Matt, "dependence on God" required cheerful quiescence to the economic status quo.

Matt had relied on unemployment insurance after being laid off, but he still did not see himself as benefitting from government social programs. In his mind, "government programs" only helped "poor people," who he defined as dependent on welfare programs. For example, I asked Matt if the government should reduce differences between rich and poor. He answered:

> Well, I don't know if the government is involved with the producing rich and poor.... I think there are individuals that become poor and it's been a generation thing where, now the kids are poor and it gets into the mindset that, "we can get State aid, we can get grants, we can get free food," and they don't try to get themselves out of that.... I can't see people with lots of money being acceptable to taking my money to pay for someone that doesn't want to work. I don't fall in either of those categories right now, praise God.

As described in chapter 5, Matt defined poverty as a moral category: he wasn't poor because he was hard-working. Instead, he thought of himself as in the middle, neither rich nor poor.

Identifying as a hard-working man in the middle, Matt did not recognize his self-interest in social programs that, in his mind, only helped poor people.[29] Like many lower-income Americans, his political identity was not tied to programs that benefitted so-called working people, like the Earned Income Tax Credit, Unemployment Insurance, and Social Security. Matt did not see wealth as a reward for righteousness, unlike Brian, the wealthier businessman from chapter 6. Unlike Ronald, Matt did not blame liberals for his economic troubles, express a punitive desire to cut welfare benefits, or rant against "big government." Instead, he was simply ambivalent and uncertain about social programs that benefitted low-income people. Matt did not aspire to be rich, only to have God provide for his basic needs. As a result, Democratic appeals to his economic self-interest did not resonate with Matt's subjective class identity.

However, other respondents recognized how these other social programs benefitted them, and also recognized that the Democratic Party favored these policies. For these respondents, the problem was their negative affect toward the social group of "liberals": secular people, gay rights activists, and pro-choice activists. Even when respondents supported the economic positions associated with Democrats, they had trouble stepping across the symbolic boundary that separated them from the "liberal" side of politics.

For example, Penny was a forty-three-year-old Northtown member, now studying for a nursing degree after years of staying home with her four kids. Her husband worked in maintenance at a sandpaper factory, after undergoing several periods of unemployment between precarious sales jobs. Last year, she decided to go back for her college degree, concerned about instability in her husband's work. When she applied for financial aid at the University of Buffalo, she discovered that she was eligible for a large grant that covered almost all of her tuition. Penny was delighted, because she never realized that the government could help people like her; she had thought that social programs were only for people who were "desperate" and "unemployed." She appreciated that this program recognized her hard work, and she thought that the government should be doing more to help families like hers, not just people who were absolutely destitute.

Until a couple of years ago, Penny had defined herself in opposition to liberals and identified with the Republican Party. She once considered herself a strong Republican and even supported the party financially. But now, she felt "in between." I asked Penny how she started feeling more "in between and not as close to the Republican Party." She answered right away:

> Going to school . . . well, schools are liberal. But I think that they have some good point of views. I guess you could just say more awareness. Because when you're home, just raising children, it's just a totally different environment. . . . I just heard a lot of things that maybe I never had thought about much. Like . . . political differences. How do you address issues like gay rights, abortion rights and things like this?

Most important, Penny had developed new social relationships outside of the evangelical subculture, which led her to rethink her stereotypes about liberals.

But as you get into more of a city atmosphere, too, you're going to see all different . . . walks of life. You know, because I was just raising my children, and then going to church, and then doing my little volunteer things. So that's a pretty narrow group of people that I'm going to be associated with.

Now that Penny had developed more relationships with people outside of her church, she had realized, "Well, these are nice people too, they just think differently. . . . they're cool, I like them, you know." She felt that in recent years, she had become "not so shortsighted . . . not so narrow." It wasn't just Penny's perception of self-interest that changed; it was her attitude toward liberals as a social group. Until then, Penny would never have considered voting Democrat, because she and her husband associated that party with "extremists" and "special interests." But now that she knew liberal people who were "nice people too," she was more open to considering how Democratic politics might be compatible with her values. Her experience shows how partisanship and political attitudes are anchored in social group memberships and networks.[30] Penny did not feel *politically* cross-pressured between moral issues and self-interest until she became *socially* cross-pressured by network ties outside of her church.

This was also true for Mary, a semi-retired court reporter introduced in chapter 5, who felt cross-pressured between Democratic economic appeals and Republican moral appeals. She felt strongly that the healthcare should be a right, that the government should do more for working people, and that there should be a social safety net. But she was also pro-life and morally traditional. Mary was not just cross-pressured on the issues; she was also cross-pressured between two different social networks. Her husband was a proud union man and loyal Democrat, who regularly told her that "only Democrats are good people" and that "Democrats are the workers . . . they're the working party." He was not personally swayed by Lifeway's political ethos, because he had attended a local Catholic church since their marriage.

As a result, Mary told me that she just voted for individual candidates. She did not identify with either party, telling me flatly, "I don't like politics." She wished there was a party for people like her:

We need a third political party, and we need people who are poor that can afford to run, because if you don't have a lot of money you can't run for office in this country, and it's not right.

Her ideal political party was one that represented "people who are poor." Although she thought of herself as financially secure, she identified with "poor people" as opposed to those with "a lot of money." This populist, working-class identity was reinforced by partisan cues from her husband, who ran in different circles as a union man and active Catholic.

In summary, these four lower-income evangelicals had different ways of understanding the tension between their economic self-interest and morality politics. Their class identity took on very different moral meanings, depending on their social networks and occupational contexts. Both Peggy and Mary felt politically cross-pressured because they were also *socially* cross-pressured. For both Ronald and Matt, the meaning of class was highly gendered, shedding light on the political divide between white working-class men and women. Ronald defined his identity as a working man by opposition to women, minorities, and poor people, in a gender-segregated workplace where conservative politics bonded him with his white boss and co-workers. Matt's class identity was gendered in a very different way: he defined his identity as a hard-working Christian by opposition to macho, selfish "union guys." The relationship between economic self-interest and voting Democratic was not obvious. This link had to be reinforced within their social networks, by people like Mary's husband, who insisted that "only Democrats are good people." But such countervailing social influences only came from sources outside the church. Both churches lacked strong Democrat opinion leaders like Mary's husband, who could help people like Tammy to connect their class identity or social policy preferences with liberal politics. While individuals at both American churches harbored diverse economic attitudes, their religious networks did not contain diverse *opinion leaders* to counterbalance the culture car captains profiled in chapter 6. As a result, individuals did not always link their progressive policy attitudes to their political identities.

Cosmopolitan Evangelicals

This was even true among more highly educated and politically sophisticated evangelicals like Curtis, an upper-level manager in an insurance company who was also a deacon at Northtown Baptist. Curtis avidly followed global, domestic, and local politics, and was glad to discuss his nuanced positions on a variety of policy issues. But Curtis' political *identity* did not match his diverse political *attitudes*. Throughout the interview, Curtis expressed economic, social, and moral views that political scientists would classify as moderate or liberal.[31] But when Curtis described his political identity, he identified more strongly with conservatives and the Republican Party than one might expect based on his policy attitudes.

As an adult convert to Christianity, Curtis exemplified a more cosmopolitan religious identity, which scholars have found among more highly educated, urban, and professional evangelicals.[32] Curtis identified simply as a Christian. He rejected the label "evangelical" because it had become too closely associated with a particular political perspective:

> The problem I have with the evangelical tag is you have broad-brushed. So the person who stands there at the rainbow parade with a sign that says "God hates fags" is painted as an evangelical. God doesn't hate fags, God loves everybody. . . . To me it's all about Jesus on the throne. I don't like those other tags.

While faith informed his politics, Curtis did not rely on Christian Right advocacy groups and evangelical "experts" on science and history. Instead, he read scholarly works of church history and moderate evangelical publications like "Christianity Today." His primary source of news was National Public Radio on the way to work, and he also watched a variety of news cable shows, including Fox News, MSNBC, and CNN. Among all my American participants, Curtis had the most sophisticated map of politics, informed by his knowledge of international news. For example, he explained that American Democrats would be considered right-wing in most European countries, even though they were often called left-wing in the United States.

Curtis believed that Christians should be involved in politics in ways that expressed tolerance and concern for marginalized people, including gays and lesbians. As a new Christian, Curtis had become involved in running a food pantry at a Nazarene church, which deepened his sense of calling to servant-leadership. Curtis explained, "I've always stood up for the underdog; there was something in me, I don't know where it came from. Long before I knew anything about God." He contrasted his ideal of servant-leadership with the Christian Right approach:

> Well, too many professing religious leaders are intolerant, and nothing will turn off people to Christianity more than intolerance. . . . Jesus was the most tolerant person that walked the face of the planet. He sought out the outcasts of society . . . Even the idea of dining with the hated tax collector . . . touching a leper.

Because of Curtis's concern for marginalized people, he supported civil unions for gays and lesbians, but did not want these unions to be described as "marriage." He understood marriage as a "gift from God," defined in the Bible as a covenant between a man and a woman. If the gay rights movement would accept civil unions, "all those arguments would go away. . . . but they want the word 'marriage'." Nonetheless, Curtis thought that fighting gay marriage was a distraction: "I think the church's response should be less of fighting over that and more of . . . just ministering to the people." Curtis believed that homosexuality was caused by "trauma," and Christians needed to communicate that this trauma could only be overcome "by the healing power of Jesus." He did not feel threatened by the gay rights movement, since for him, homosexuality was "no different than any other sin."

Curtis described himself as a moderately conservative Republican, qualifying that "I've always said that I'm a fiscal conservative and a social moderate." But when he detailed his individual policy attitudes, they were consistently to the left of the Democratic Party. Curtis considered himself a "fiscal conservative" because "I don't believe in the idea of wealth redistribution." However, he supported universal health care because "socially, we do owe people certain basic human needs, we owe them health care. . . . I like the Canadian health care system." Working in the food pantry, he had noticed how many people experienced financial hardship because of illness and lack of health insurance. He also believed that people had a right to decent housing: "Back in the fifties they built all these army barrack looking buildings for public housing which was just terrible . . . People needed a decent place; people need open spaces . . . it has to have a park with grass, not swing sets on the concrete." Curtis described his idiosyncratic vision of "small government," which was driven by a concern for the underdog. For example, the area's school districts should be merged into one, so that everyone had access to the same quality public education. Public services should be centralized so that inner-city Buffalo got the same prompt snow removal that he got in the suburbs. His ideal of "small government" was to cut out unnecessary layers of local bureaucracy that led to disparities between urban and suburban Buffalo.

Curtis also expressed moderate-to-progressive opinions on a variety of other issues: immigration, the environment, and the war in Iraq. He did not see immigrants as threats to the country's moral fabric, because he believed that they shared the "common values" that held America together. Like many evangelicals, Curtis believed that the nation could only be held together by common values but he also emphasized that these values "need to be redefined . . . and discussed." Immigrants shared these common values of "hard work and the importance of family," even "illegal immigrants from Mexico . . . they come here to send money back to their family." Curtis also believed that Christians had a responsibility to protect the environment, because "God gave it to us to manage and not to destroy." Curtis was ambivalent about President Bush and the war in Iraq, stating that Bush had gotten himself "in over his head" and he was unsure how the conflict would turn out.

However, Curtis's more progressive policy attitudes did not inform his political identity and voting behavior. When I asked him why he felt closer to the Republican Party, he explained: "It's just the idea of smaller government, less intrusion. Elect people who know how to run things; do things better." Considered objectively, his social policy attitudes directly conflicted with conservative, small-government ideology. But Curtis did not identify subjectively with liberals or Democrats as a social group. Even though Curtis did not vote straight-ticket, voting for Democrats was not a particularly viable option for him. Curtis could recall one occasion when he had voted for a Democrat, for a local judge who he knew personally. When he disliked the Republican on the ballot, he preferred to make a protest vote rather than vote Democratic. For example, Curtis had voted for a write-in candidate in the 1996 presidential election, because he thought that Bob Dole was "the meanest, nastiest person," but he also disliked Bill Clinton.

Curtis did not associate his policy attitudes with Democrats, because he defined his ideological identity by opposition to the "liberal standpoint." Throughout the interview, he defined American "liberals" in two ways: liberals supported "economic redistribution," and liberals disregarded the role of faith and individual responsibility. Curtis did not associate universal healthcare with economic redistribution, because it involved government services instead of cash payments.[33] He also disagreed with liberals because they wanted "the government to solve all their problems," and ignored the role of "the church or private individuals." For example, Curtis felt that liberals failed to appreciate international charities like World Vision, who helped governments dispense international aid. Liberals also discounted the service work that he did with a faith-based food pantry, and the value of Catholic hospitals, which were "more efficient" and did a better job than "government hospitals." Yet Curtis did not want private charities to take over basic government services, nor did he desire cutbacks in social welfare programs. He simply felt that liberals ignored the existing contributions of churches and Christians like himself.

As a result, Curtis felt closer to conservatives and the Republican Party. This identification may seem surprising, if we assumed that people rationally choose their party identification on the basis of their policy preferences. But it makes perfect sense if we consider that Curtis was immersed in a religious subculture where he was constantly bathed in negative cues about liberals. Curtis had developed progressive ideas about social policy by watching diverse news sources and volunteering among poor people. But in his church, people defined their subcultural identity by contrasting "our" charity work with the godless "liberal" approach to poverty. Furthermore, Curtis had never expressed his opinions about universal healthcare and affordable housing within his religious networks. While Curtis loved to consider new political ideas, he reported that no one at church was interested in debating politics with him. He was also hesitant to bring up topics that might be controversial. Because his progressive ideas were never reinforced socially, his loyalty to conservatives—and sense of distinction from liberals—remained undisturbed. Curtis was aware that some of his ideas put him in tension with other conservatives, but in his mind, that just made him a "social moderate" Republican. As a Christian who stood up for the underdog, Curtis experienced a thin coherence between his values and conservative politics.

This illustrates the social dynamics that limited political diversity in both American churches. As a politically sophisticated individual, Curtis could readily find common ground on issues like homosexuality; for example, he supported civil unions but not marriage. But it was more difficult for him to bridge the symbolic boundary that separated Christians from political liberals. Even though he did not subscribe to conservative policy attitudes, he still defined his political identity by reference to a culture war map.

This was also true for Alice, a physical therapist who worked part-time in the public schools while she raised her two-year-old daughter. She had joined Northtown Baptist two years ago, because they encouraged her to take leadership in community outreach. At first glance, Ann represented a type of cosmopolitan evangelical who might be held up to debunk the culture war myth: she got her news from NPR, she supported more generous social policy, and she was critical of the Christian Right. Alice believed that right-wing politics misrepresented the Christian faith, stating, "I really am disturbed at how much Christians have pigeon-holed themselves to the Republican Party." By supporting an immoral political agenda, Christians had rightly earned hostility from non-Christians, which undermined their ability to witness. As Alice explained:

> Republicans have done a lot to hurt the middle class and the poor people. The tax laws haven't really been beneficial to the poor. They rarely ever vote any legislation that is actually going to help the environment. It's going to help . . . the rich people get richer.

She thought it was unfortunate that evangelical Christians let the abortion issue make the "final judgment which political party we pick," since "we really don't have the party that represents Christianity." Alice believed that "there are a lot of areas where the Democrats have acted in ways that are really consistent with the Bible's teaching about loving your neighbor." After all, Alice pointed out that it was Democrats who stood up for poor people, who signed the Civil Rights Legislation, and "who fight for cleaning up the environment, which is God's creation, you know." Based on her experience in public education, Alice was convinced that schools needed to be equitably funded and that there needed to be more generous programs to help poor families.

Alice also rejected the idea that liberals were somehow to blame for the country's coarsening media climate. Like other people in her church, Alice actively shielded her child from coarse language and violence, because children should "guard their heart." For example, she was frustrated that Disney movies often contained developmentally inappropriate content that was too scary for small children. She blamed this problem on secular culture, reasoning that "most of people making children's movies in Hollywood are not Christians and they don't care about guarding the children's hearts, so they are not coming from a Christian perspective." But she blamed the profit motive for the poor quality of children's media. Her solution was to support PBS, which produced commercial-free children's media with developmental goals in mind. From working in the private sector, she had learned that big business was an amoral environment that constantly tested her Christian integrity. She blamed these corporate interests, not liberal elites, for the family-unfriendly media climate.

But Alice did not identify as a Democrat, or even as an Independent who leaned Democratic. Instead, she thought of herself as apolitical. Alice's political disempowerment was striking, since she avidly followed political news, held detailed opinions about social policy, and described herself as a community leader. When I asked Alice which party she identified with most, she simply restated their pros and cons from a biblical perspective:

> Republicans are reaching more to the unborn and to preserving the family and that's a particular ministry, that's biblical. And the Democrats are doing more to reach out to the very poor and that's very biblical, also.

But as a Christian, Alice distanced herself from both political parties. She felt that Republicans were morally corrupted by corporate interests. On the other hand, Alice felt that "a lot of what [Democrats] are doing is really bad, when it comes to Pro-Choice and . . . they're really pushing towards accepting homosexuality as a God-given way of life." Torn between two unacceptable options, Alice thought that Christians should avoid politics and express their values through personal faithfulness and community service. If only Christians would "focus on doing the good work that He wants us to do," then God's light would "shine through us and hopefully we can overcome . . . the bad political tensions." In her opinion, American Christians did not need to be involved in politics at all.

Why couldn't Alice identify as a morally conservative Democrat, much as Curtis identified as a "socially moderate" Republican? To understand why Alice felt so politically alienated, it is important to consider her social context as well as her theological beliefs. As an educated and thoughtful individual, Alice could readily *imagine* alternatives to the current culture war divide. In her mind, a consistently Christian agenda combined moral conservatism with liberal stances on social policy, racial justice, and the environment. But given her social networks and institutional context, it was practically impossible for her to develop an alternative political identity that transcended the culture war.

In theory, Alice believed that abortion and homosexuality did not automatically trump all other issues, because "creation care" and poverty were also "biblical" issues. Alice had a nuanced perspective on how her traditional morality should inform her politics. She was passionately pro-life, a concern that she had developed in college by joining a Christian pro-life group on campus. Since then, she had regularly engaged in intercessory prayer to end abortion. But she preferred to combat the social barriers that drove women to choose abortion, and help pregnant women who were experiencing crisis pregnancies. For her, the abortion issue was linked to larger economic questions, particularly God's concern for the orphan. Alice had helped found Northtown's adoption ministry to encourage Christians to adopt "unwanted" children and model practical alternatives to abortion. She believed that "God wants to change the way Christians think about parenting," to recognize that all children are a "blessing from the Lord," not just their biological children. Alice's pro-life beliefs were closer to the Catholic "consistent ethic of life," a tradition that stresses the connection between abortion and economic justice.[34]

Furthermore, Alice was willing to support civil unions for same-sex couples, even though she believed that homosexuality was wrong. Like Curtis, she felt that it was wrong to treat homosexuals differently from heterosexual "sinners," who were free to get married even if they engaged in promiscuity, infidelity, or divorce. If same-sex couples could obtain civil unions, they would have the same rights as "sinful" heterosexuals. But if same-sex couples used the term *marriage*, it sent the message that homosexuality was acceptable to God. Alice wanted to protect "marriage" as a biblical ideal that informed the broader culture, even if it was imperfectly realized in practice. Because she considered the term "marriage" to be inherently biblical, she felt that changing the definition of marriage would undermine the authority of Scripture. Yet despite her moral conservatism, Alice agreed in theory with the prevailing Democratic position, which in 2007 was to support civil unions but not marriage for same-sex couples.[35]

Like Curtis, Alice was immersed within a religious subculture that constantly reinforced the symbolic boundary that separated Christians from Democrats as a social group. Furthermore, Alice was keenly aware that many Democratic activists held negative attitudes toward people like her. In fact, Alice was even more keenly aware of these negative attitudes because she actively followed liberal priorities like welfare policy and the environment. Unlike the culture warriors in chapter 6, Alice did not feel embattled by secular liberals because she got her news from partisan, conservative sources. Rather, she felt embattled because she regularly heard *liberal* culture warriors on NPR attacking Christian opposition to abortion and homosexuality.

Listening to the news on NPR, Alice felt particularly attacked by a subgroup of secular Democrats, "who are very liberal, totally atheist or agnostic" who referred to Christians as "Fundamentalists." When liberal activists used "Fundamentalist" as a derogatory term, Alice felt it was intended to dismiss her beliefs as a Christian who "believes in the Bible." Alice resented the claim that she was anti-gay, anti-woman, or hateful as a theologically conservative Christian. This liberal rhetoric made her feel sad and isolated, even though she reminded herself that Christians partly bore the responsibility for these negative stereotypes. To calm her emotions, she usually switched to Christian radio for a few minutes to listen to uplifting worship music. Despite these negative feelings, Alice continued to listen to NPR every day, because she felt that Christian radio did not provide the same quality, in-depth coverage or policy analysis. Alice felt pushed away from the Democratic Party by *liberal* culture war rhetoric, more than she felt drawn to the Republican Party by conservative rhetoric.

It was *theoretically* possible for Alice to vote Democratic, based on her theologically nuanced understanding of abortion and homosexuality. But it was not *socially* possible for her identify as a Democrat, because of her social networks and institutional context. In Alice's church, group members defined a shared map of subcultural identity that opposed Christians to liberals. What would happen if someone publicly defined their Christian identity by opposition to conservatives, as Alice had done privately in our interview? Drawing an alternative map would have violated her church's group style and come across as too political for church. Alice's private map could not become part of the church's public discourse.

Nor did Alice provide an alternative perspective as a political opinion leader, in a way that might counter the conservative voices profiled in chapter 6. Alice reported that she regularly talked with church friends about political news that affected the legality of abortion. In these conversations, she publicly voiced her disagreement with the Democratic stance and support for pro-life Republicans. But she had never publicly expressed her indignation against Republicans for cutting the social safety net, even though she privately felt this went against biblical values. Alice privately disagreed with the notion that faith-based charity was a superior substitute for government social programs, but she did not share these opinions at church. Even though Alice was a prominent lay leader, she felt too alienated from Democrats to provide a counterbalance to conservative opinion leaders at Northtown Baptist.

In Alice's experience, top-down media messages were not the only forces making it difficult for her to overcome culture war politics. Alice was already exposed to top-down framing from alternative evangelical elites that opposed the Christian Right. She had adopted the frame that poverty and environmentalism were moral issues. She could privately imagine ways to transcend the culture war divide. But where could she find social support for this alternative political identity? Her local congregations set limits on how she could publicly locate herself on a cultural map of politics.

YOUNG ADULT EVANGELICALS

I found the same pattern among younger evangelicals: while some individuals held diverse political *attitudes*, their church context made it difficult to develop alternative political *identities*. Younger evangelicals grew up in an era where homosexuality was more accepted and have never known a time before *Roe v. Wade*. There have been many claims in the popular media about evangelicals under age thirty, who are being heralded as more environmentally aware, more critical of the Christian Right, more tolerant of homosexuality, and more interested in engaging the culture in positive ways.

But my fieldwork points to a different picture. In both American churches, young adults actually fit surprisingly well into the culture war narrative of their parents, for two reasons. First, these young people had been socialized into culture war politics from childhood, by parents and other adults in their church, and often looked to this older generation as political opinion leaders. Furthermore, they came of age during the 2004 presidential election, which pitted the evangelical favorite George Bush against a relatively secular John Kerry. "Moral values" became central to the election, as conservatives rallied evangelicals to the polls to support state-level referenda against same-sex marriage. According to research on political socialization, young adults consolidate their political identity and voting habits in their first election cycles.[36]

Second, many younger evangelicals had been influenced by a new generation of Christian Right messaging that specifically targeted their age group. For evangelicals under thirty, an older generation of aging culture warriors like Jerry Falwell, Pat Robertson, or James Dobson was no longer relevant. But this did not necessarily mean that they embraced a more progressive, post–Christian Right identity, focused on environmentalism or concern for the poor instead of moral issues. Instead, they were far more influenced by youth-oriented streams of the pro-life movement.

These individuals also resonated with a softer version of the anti–gay rights message, packaged for a more tolerant generation.

This is consistent with survey findings on the politics of younger evangelicals. Using National Election Survey data, David Campbell found that in 1980, a highly religious eighteen-year-old was 8 percentage points less likely to be a Republican than someone forty-two years his senior. By 1998, that situation had reversed—now the highly religious eighteen-year-old was 12 percentage points more likely to identify with the Republican Party.[37] If younger evangelicals are distancing themselves from the Republican Party, this trend is too recent to speak about with any certainty.

For example, Kevin had just graduated from the University of Buffalo, after growing up at Northtown Baptist and attending there throughout college. At twenty-one, Kevin identified strongly as a Republican, an identity that became clear to him when he turned eighteen, right in time for the 2004 election. For him, the choice was straightforward: "Democrats and liberals were supporting gay marriage, abortion and things like that, things I don't agree with . . . so the Republican side was against that." Kevin did not see homosexuality as a deviant subculture, because he had grown up surrounded by tolerant media portrayals of gays and lesbians. Instead, he saw Christians as the deviant minority, resisting a permissive, sexualized mainstream culture. Kevin described the liberal culture that he saw on TV shows, commercials, and advertising:

> Everything is ok, it is very open, very liberal. I put this in terms of materialism. . . . every commercial says that . . . you got to have money, you got to have a girlfriend or a boyfriend, or you got to have the best . . . that kind of thing.

Within this dominant culture, Kevin felt that the prevailing messages were "Do what you want" and "Whatever you think is good and works for you." He described the two major parties in terms of how much they capitulated to this dominant culture: "I guess I'd say that the Republican side is more conservative . . . and I guess the Democrats are more liberal, trying to please everyone." By voting Republican, he drew symbolic boundaries against the mainstream American culture. Abortion and homosexuality were central issues for him because they symbolized the permissive, self-indulgent mainstream culture, which he associated with the Democratic Party.

At Lifeway Assembly, another young man named Andy had also come of age during the 2004 election. During high school and college, he had attended Lifeway Assembly and been involved in their young adult small group. Andy did not recall hearing any political messages from the pulpit, besides general statements that Christians had a civic obligation to vote.

Instead, Andy had heard the most explicit partisan cues through informal interaction. Andy was not particularly interested in politics, and actively avoided the news during election years; he relied on older, trusted people in his church for political information.

For example, Andy had often heard about politics from Chris and Cheryl, a married couple who led his small group during college. As the group's lay leaders, Chris and Cheryl made it clear that they were "as far on the conservative side of things that you can go, and even further beyond that, and they'll tell you that." As an Air Force officer, Chris regularly talked about "why it was so important to have President Bush as President" and praised the administration's decision to go to war. During the 2004 election, Andy recalled that his young adult small group had talked about why it was so important to elect Christian leaders with integrity like Bush, who would "uphold Christian standards" in the country. During this discussion, Chris and Cheryl explained to the group how President Bush held "Christian" stances on abortion and same-sex marriage, while John Kerry opposed these moral values. In conclusion, the couple encouraged them to get out and vote for "Christian leaders." Because of interactions like this, Andy assumed that no one at his church was a Democrat, unless they were a "very conservative Democrat."

Beyond his local church, Andy did not identify meaningfully with his denomination, the Assemblies of God, nor with any political interest groups. Instead, he identified with charismatic Christian groups like the International House of Prayer (IHOP), a parachurch ministry that conducted round-the-clock prayer and worship in Kansas City. Since its founding in 1999, IHOP has attracted crowds of young pilgrims from all across the country to its 24/7 prayer meetings. Last year, Andy had travelled to Kansas City to worship with them, where he had prayed for "government leaders everywhere: locally, nationally, and internationally . . . for the infiltration of Christians there so righteousness can be upheld." According to IHOP, upholding righteousness meant banning abortion, opposing same-sex marriage, and supporting Israel in its struggle against radical Islam. Andy explained that IHOP also sponsored direct service to poor people, both domestically and internationally.

Andy did not think of IHOP as a "political" group, since they focused on intercessory prayer and direct service to the poor. However, the Southern Poverty Law Center and People for the American Way have expressed concern that IHOP promotes an authoritarian theology known as Dominionism. Dominionist theology calls on believers to seize political power, in anticipation of the return of Christ.[38] IHOP founder Mike Bickle has denied that his ministry teaches Dominionism. But his ministry has regularly thrown its support behind "godly" politicians who can further a Christian "infiltration" of government. For example, Mike Bickle served as the emcee for a 2011 prayer service in Houston, Texas, sponsored by then-presidential candidate Rick Perry. As a member of IHOP's audience, Andy did not believe that Christians should impose a theocratic political regime. But he understood that when IHOP talked about "upholding righteousness," that meant voting for conservatives.[39]

Andy was particularly interested in global poverty, having travelled to Africa to do volunteer work as an engineer. Like other younger evangelicals, Andy was energized by his concern for poor people. But he did not see poverty as a political issue. In his perspective, serving the poor was biblical, but working to end poverty was unrealistic and unbiblical. Like other members of his church, he also contrasted the "deserving" global poor with the lazy and entitled American poor. Even though Andy had a passion for poverty and community service, he mapped his political identity in terms of a culture war narrative.

These two examples provide an important corrective to the claim that younger evangelicals are rejecting the Christian Right. Intergenerational church contexts constrain the kinds of subcultural identities that younger evangelicals can legitimately construct. For young evangelicals to explore an alternative political identity, they may need to seek out new religious networks or congregational contexts to provide a plausibility structure for such a project. For example, Christa was a thirty-one-year-old regular attendee at Lifeway Assembly during my fieldwork, but when I interviewed her, she was considering leaving for another church. She grew up in Assemblies of God and Four Square Gospel churches, both part of the Pentecostal tradition. Christa and her husband had attended Lifeway Assembly for four years, because they liked the free, "spirit-filled" worship. Christa particularly appreciated their emphasis on prophesy: making room for individuals to share "a word from the Lord" during the worship service, as they felt moved by the Spirit. However, she and her husband were looking for a church that talked more about positive ways to engage their neighbors, who couldn't relate to the "Christianese" at Lifeway Assembly.

Christa had become convinced that the church could be doing more to reach out to the community, particularly on issues of poverty. I asked her to explain how she wanted the church to address poverty:

> I think they should be doing a lot, I feel like that's one of my issues. It just seems like in the Bible, God talks so much about the poor. You know, especially in the New Testament but even in the Old Testament, there is just a constant caring for the poor.

Growing up poor in the church, Christa had experienced warm generosity on an interpersonal level, "Like even for our family, I remember how different people in the church bought us winter boots . . . or . . . shoes. And that was nice." But Christa felt that personal charity was not enough. Poverty should be a primary focus, because it was "really close to God's heart: the poor and the needy and hurting." Christa's family had depended on Food Stamps and Unemployment benefits when her father was unemployed, and so she supported social programs that helped people like her family "to help get unstuck." Christa knew that Lifeway Assembly did charitable outreach to the poor, but she did not feel that the church addressed the larger question of how poverty related to their faith. Last week, she had visited a newly planted church, where the pastor talked about global poverty in his sermon. That had confirmed her decision to switch to this new church.

Christa was also looking for a better way to engage with gay and lesbian people that she knew. She had just taken a part-time job at Starbucks after staying home with her kids, and one of her co-workers was a recently divorced gay man. He often talked about his ex-wife, calling her a "fundamentalist Christian" who thought he was "the devil." This led to interesting conversations, since her co-workers knew that she was a Christian. Christa hope that her gay co-worker might change, but she also had doubts about whether it was possible to change sexual orientation:

> I would rather, somehow . . . he would realize what he was doing was just. . . . I don't know . . . I don't like his lifestyle, I wish that he saw things differently. But I just don't know. It makes me wonder if people ever change. . . . But I know from God, of course they can. But it's just . . . I don't know that I really see that happening.

Christa did not have "an agenda, other than that I care about him and I want to be friends with him." She was concerned that the gay community felt "Christians don't like them. And I don't think that's right, and I think that we should love them and be friends with them."

Christa blamed the church for this tension between the gay community and evangelical Christians, because "the way that we express our beliefs about things is sometimes really harsh and not caring." She agreed that homosexuality was a sin, "but there are a lot of other sins that we don't go around saying, 'You are a sinner!'" Christa felt ambivalent about gay marriage: "I've kind of gone both ways." She was wary of "legislating morality," but on the other hand, she was concerned that legalizing gay marriage might lead society to become "more cynical—having more than one wife or two husbands . . . I think it's important for the society to stand for things. But on the other hand, Christa recognized that "it's hard because different people have different beliefs, and things they want to stand for. Like . . . my daughter is totally into global warming, I don't know where she got it from. She wants to take care of the earth so that it won't be hurting the animals."

In summary, Christa recognized that "moral values" went beyond abortion and homosexuality, to include poverty and environmental concern. But this recognition left her ambivalent and politically demobilized. She knew that Democrats were for "government getting more involved" and the Republicans were for "moral issues," but she did not feel closer to either party. While she held objectively liberal views on poverty, she lacked a clear map of politics that linked her concern for the poor to the Democratic Party, leaving her ambivalent and politically demobilized.

In conclusion, both continuity and change can be found among young evangelicals. But my fieldwork shows that change is socially difficult for young evangelicals in an intergenerational church context. In order to explore a post–Christian Right identity, Christa had to seek out a newly planted church composed almost exclusively of people in their 20s. It is not easy for younger evangelicals to jump ship to the Democratic Party, just because they have new concerns about poverty, the environment, and the way the church has treated gay people. Her experience is consistent with the experience reported by many young "post-partisan" evangelical leaders, who protest that there is no room for intergenerational dialogue within existing evangelical churches and parachurch infrastructure.

CONCLUSION

While evangelicals exhibited diverse political attitudes as *individuals*, this diversity was not equally represented in social space within the congregation. Evangelicals who fit the "culture warrior" mold had greater power to set the political tone in their churches than people who did not. By locating individuals in their social context, I show how these dynamics played out in the field of local congregations.

CHAPTER 8

....

PRACTICING CIVILITY IN TWO CANADIAN CONGREGATIONS

After three decades of culture war politics, it is hard for Americans to imagine a theologically conservative evangelical church where Democrats and Republicans worship side by side. Everything about evangelicalism seems to generate lockstep political conformity: rigid theology, absolute moral beliefs, strong subcultural boundaries. But I contend that culture war polarization does not flow naturally from evangelicals' strong moral beliefs, nor from their collective efforts to advocate for those beliefs as a distinctive subculture. Following Georg Simmel, I define an integrated society as one characterized by mediating interests and cross-cutting ties, that allow for broader solidarity in spite of strong differences.[1] A polarized society lacks settings for the development of mutual recognition and broader solidarity between people who hold opposite interests and beliefs. American evangelical churches do not contribute to polarization because they promote strong, shared moral beliefs. The real problem is that American evangelical churches do not make space for cross-cutting identities and concerns that might bridge or transcend the culture war divide.

It may be hard to imagine an evangelical church that bridges political diversity through practices of mutual recognition. But I found that both Canadian evangelical churches made space for opposing partisan affiliations, though they reinforced conformity on the "moral issues" of abortion and homosexuality. In this chapter, I describe the practices of civility by which members acknowledged cross-cutting political affiliations within group interaction. As in American churches, both Canadian churches contained lay leaders who connected their religious identity to conservative politics, and tried to mobilize the church around the "moral issues" of abortion and gay marriage. But their church's unspoken norms of civility made it difficult for them to send partisan cues. These conservative opinion leaders were also counter-balanced by a second set of lay leaders, who embodied alternative political identities that were silenced or nonexistent in the two American churches. Without clear social cues that connected religious identity to partisanship, less politically engaged members lacked a clear map to connect their moral concerns to politics.

OPINION LEADERS FOR MORAL ISSUES AT HIGHPOINT BAPTIST

During my fieldwork at Highpoint Baptist in Hamilton, Ontario, Janice and Walter stood out as two of the most politically active lay leaders. As a stay-at-home mom in her early forties, Janice was recognized by other members from a variety of age groups as a knowledgeable political source, who worked to keep the church informed about the "moral issues." As a recently retired doctor in his mid-sixties, Walter was a well-respected deacon who was considered particularly knowledgeable about politics from a Christian perspective. Both of these political opinion leaders encouraged fellow church members to traditional stances on abortion and homosexuality. Yet both of these politically engaged lay leaders sounded very different from the culture war captains introduced in both U.S. churches.

Both Janice and Walter felt that Christians were culturally embattled, and that it was necessary to defend their values in the public square. But neither of them defined this embattlement in partisan terms, by opposition to a particular political adversary. Instead, they felt that Christians were embattled by "the world," as a theological category that did not map onto partisan differences. While both of them felt that the Conservative Party was the most friendly to Christians on the moral issues, they defined their political identities and religious identities in very separate terms.

In chapter 5, I described how Janice helped other laypeople to get involved in their community by taking them on a prayer walk around their neighborhood. At the end of the prayer walk, Janice invited the group to pray over a local public school, as their school district made revisions to their sexual education curriculum. Like American culture war captains, Janice helped other laypeople to connect their faith to political issues, by bringing the world of School Board politics into the world of everyday religious practice. And like American political opinion leaders, Janice developed a more politicized understanding of her faith through parachurch groups *outside* her local church.

Janice had developed an interest in moral issues by participating in the Hamilton-Wentworth Family Action Council, a local coalition of Christian parents. About ten years ago, an organizer from the group recruited Janice at a school fair, handing her a flier and chatting with her for several minutes. Initially, Janice went to the first meeting because her children had just started school and she wanted to learn more about moral influences there. Initially, her motives to participate were narrowly spiritual: she wanted practical advice on parenting her school-age children. But by participating in the group, Janice had become a confident civic activist, by attending City Council and School Board meetings with other Christian parents. As a member of the Family Action Council, Janice made several announcements in Highpoint Baptist about sex education and pro-life issues, and passed around petitions at church about what she described as "moral issues." When her children were older, Janice decided to redirect her efforts to work with the Parent Council at her children's public school instead. Her parent involvement was still informed by a particular sensitivity to moral influences on her children, which she had developed by working with the Family Action Council.

By getting involved in the Council, Janice had gained a more ecumenical sense of Christian witness in the public sphere. But even after Janice became a pro-family Christian activist, she did not map her religious identity in partisan or political terms. She emphasized how exciting it was to build relationships with other parents from a variety of Christian denominations. Janice had grown up in a fairly self-enclosed Baptist world, but in this group she met "Catholics and Pentecostal and Alliance and a lot of them, all rolling together." What brought their group together was that they "dealt with moral issues. Not doctrinal, right?" Though other members did not necessarily share her theology, Janice found that they shared common values and interests as Christian parents. Significantly, when she described what brought their group together, she did not use culture war language or define their identity in opposition to a particular political adversary.

Even when I pushed Janice to identify the group's opponents, she defined the differences between "us" and "them" in strictly religious terms. Although Janice identified both Planned Parenthood and gay rights activists as countervailing influences on sex education, she did not link these two groups on a larger map of politics. Instead, Janice explained that "we" approached these issues from a "biblical" or "Christian" perspective, while "they" did not. Unlike the American evangelicals, Janice did not make sense of abortion and gay marriage by drawing symbolic boundaries between "liberal" and "conservative" sides.

Throughout the interview, Janice used only narrowly religious language to explain how her beliefs about abortion and birth control differed from those of other people. For example, Janice had taken her church youth group on a field trip to Birthright, a pro-life ministry in Hamilton that provided housing to women during crisis pregnancies. Her stated goal was to counter the messages that her students received about abortion from school and Planned Parenthood. During the trip, Janice taught them "what the Bible says" about sex: that "abortion was wrong" and that staying sexually "pure" was the only reliable way to prevent disease and pregnancy. Janice contrasted Birthright's approach with that of Planned Parenthood, a group that went into schools to talk about birth control. Janice disagreed with Planned Parenthood because they supported abortion and they didn't teach abstinence.

When I pushed Janice to explain why these two groups took different approaches, she did not use a culture war schema. Instead, she talked about their cultural *differences*: both groups wanted to prevent teen pregnancy, but Birthright did so from a Christian perspective. Janice agreed with Planned Parenthood's underlying goal, which she described as preventing "poor children . . . from being raised . . . in a non-structured home, in a dysfunctional home." But this group did not go about this goal "in the way that I would have done it." Janice described their cultural differences:

> I think [Planned Parenthood is] trying to do it in the best way that they know how, by pushing the old "use a condom, use a condom. . . . But Birthright's done a better job because they've said, 'There is only one way that you can be sure . . . and that's abstinence." Planned Parenthood doesn't teach abstinence.

Janice did not describe Birthright and Planned Parenthood in partisan terms, as adversaries in a culture war, even when I prompted her to draw symbolic boundaries between the two groups. Instead, she talked "civic-ly" about their differences, by emphasizing their shared concern for the common good.[2] Her nonpartisan, fairly sympathetic description of Planned Parenthood was also in keeping with this organization's different role in Canada's abortion debate. Unlike its American counterpart, the Canadian affiliate does not have a history of litigating for abortion rights, even though it refers women to abortion providers.[3]

Janice was opposed to homosexuality on biblical grounds, and she felt that Christians should make their voices heard on the issue. As an activist with the Family Action Council, she had tried to stop Hamilton-area schools from talking openly about homosexuality as part of their sexual education curriculum. But when I pushed Janice to define this boundary between supporters and opponents of gay rights, she talked about the cultural differences that separated Christians from the world. For example, Janice described how "the schools" wanted to "bring in a curriculum that says that we need to accept lesbians and homosexuals and accept what they do and say it's ok." Janice disagreed because "my way of thinking is, you need to accept them, but I don't have to say it's ok. Right? I don't have to say it's right." Janice stressed that she cared about gay and lesbian individuals, "I will love them and they shouldn't be discriminated

against, but it's wrong . . . And then, that's what I want my kids to learn."
Her problem with the curriculum is that it was "quite open, to the opposite extreme of pushing it and saying that it's a good thing." Like American evangelicals, it was important for Janice to talk about homosexuality
in a "loving" way, even while drawing moral boundaries based on her
understanding of biblical sexuality.

But unlike American evangelicals, Janice made sense of gay rights
through a nonpartisan lens, even though the gay marriage debates had
been central to the last federal elections in Canada.[4] This was surprising,
since Janice praised the Family Action Council's work on issues like gay
marriage, because "they find out about these bills that they are passing,
and they get the word out to people so that they can write their letters,
and express their opinions and make it known." In the last election, Janice voted Conservative because they had made symbolic gestures of support for traditional marriage. But though she personally identified with
the Conservative Party, she did not describe herself in partisan or ideological terms as a "conservative" at war with "liberals," but simply in theological terms, as a Christian engaging the world. Throughout the interview, Janice lacked a general term to describe her political adversaries:
"they" were simply representatives of "the school" or "the culture." Janice did not describe Christians as victims who were being attacked by the
gay rights movement; she took it for granted that Christians were a small
minority within a secular, diverse society. Through her political activism,
she modestly sought to reproduce this Christian subculture through her
children, rather than to reclaim a "Christian" Canada.

As a prominent lay volunteer, Janice also served as a political opinion
leader, who helped other church members to connect their faith to particular political causes. But Janice did not transmit the kind of culture war
cues that I observed in both American churches. She did not see economic
or social policy issues as part of a "Christian" political agenda. She had
only positive things to say about social programs that helped poor Canadians and immigrants, and she did not draw the same kind of symbolic
boundaries between "Christian" and "liberal" approaches to social policy that I found in the two American churches. Even in a personal interview, Janice defined her political and religious identities in very different
terms. Though she sent clear cues about the correct Christian stances on
"moral issues," she did send partisan cues to define the "correct" political
identity for Christians.

This was also true for Walter, a deacon in his mid-60s, who was considered particularly influential among older members of the congregation. As a respected opinion leader, Walter helped raise awareness within
his church network about the moral issues of abortion and homosexuality. Walter felt extremely threatened by gay civil rights, and held an even

more hard-line position than others in his church. But when I asked Walter to describe his own political identity, he thought of himself as a swing voter, willing to vote for Conservative or Liberal parties depending on the quality of their candidates. Yet Walter held traditional beliefs about moral issues, followed the work of Christian advocacy groups on these issues, and identified himself as ideologically conservative.

Walter closely followed political news, particularly as it affected Canada's moral climate and the rights of Christians. He often brought up these political issues with his friends at church at small group gatherings and "in the hallways" there. Among his network of church friends, he often circulated emails from Christian advocacy groups, urging them to call their M.P.s on issues like abortion, homosexuality, and freedom of religion. Over the last year, Walter had asked his friends to "pray about" the case of Christian Horizons, a faith-based organization that was accused of discriminating against an employee after she came out as a lesbian. That year, Christian Horizons was defending itself against these charges before the Human Rights Commission of Ontario.[5] Walter was following the case closely, because the founder of Christian Horizons had once been an interim pastor at his church.

For his perspective, this court case showed Canada's moral decline, which made it "much harder to be a Christian and keep your values." Christians were embattled because "Satan is ruling, this is his territory, and things are coming to the end. . . . obviously, it's affecting us as Christians, and . . . it's affecting schools, 'cause you can't say the prayers, and you can't have Bible clubs on the grounds." Walter blamed this moral decline on spiritual forces, but he also pointed out the political forces at work, particularly the Charter of Rights and Freedoms. For Walter, the strongest political attacks on Christian morality had happened in the last ten years. During that decade, the Supreme Court had ruled for gay marriage and the Human Rights Commission of Ontario had regularly handed down rulings against Christians who discriminated against homosexuals for religious reasons. Walter saw the Charter as a "license to do anything you want. And it seriously hampered our whole legal structure . . . it gave responsibility for law and order to the Supreme Court rather than to the parliament of Canada."

Walter felt that there was a zero-sum relationship between the rights of Christians and the rights of homosexuals, two mutually exclusive categories. In Walter's mind, these courts were not defending equal rights for homosexuals; instead, they were defending a "libertarian opinion" that Canada had no shared moral standards:

> The court is giving more rights to the gays than they're giving to the ordinary people. The gay people had all of the rights that we did,

from the beginning. They just wanted more. They just wanted to be free to do anything they want.

In the Christian Horizons case, he believed that homosexuals were encroaching on Christian institutions to undermine their moral beliefs: "now, the homosexuals are coming to them, saying we want to be on staff, and they're saying, no, we don't want you on staff." Ironically, court records show that the lesbian woman fired from Christian Horizons was herself an evangelical Christian, who had experienced years of spiritual angst before acknowledging her sexual orientation.[6] But this aspect of the narrative was lost on Walter, since he defined homosexuals as people who rejected God's rules: "we're not free to do anything we want, why should they be?"

Walter did not even acknowledge that faithful Christians might "struggle with" homosexuality as a form of "sexual brokenness."[7] By contrast, Walter's wife repeatedly contested his "us-versus-them" framing of gay rights during the interview. When Walter complained that now gay couples could receive each other's pension benefits, his wife Margaret pointed out, "Although, I must say, if the person has a pension that is basically his, he should be able to give it to whoever he wants!" But even though homosexuality was an extremely salient moral issue to Walter, he did not identify as politically conservative.

Walter explained that he and his wife talked about politics "more freely than some people can, because we don't consider ourselves politically attached." Walter and Margaret particularly liked to "toss back and forth ideas" with two other couples from church about political matters. Walter explained that these conversations were enjoyable because they didn't get too partisan:

> We try and take an objective point of view. And there are some people who are tied to a party, or tied strongly to a candidate, and so it's hard to them to debate or to discuss things objectively. We vote, but we don't always vote the same way, we don't always support the same party.

Over his lifetime, Walter had voted for both the Conservative Party and the Liberal Party, depending on which candidate seemed like "an honest broker," and how well the previous government had performed. He considered this typical among other Christians that he knew, even though his church friends shared his traditional beliefs about abortion, same-sex marriage, and Canada's "moral decline."

Walter's nonpartisan approach to politics was remarkable, since he described himself as ideologically conservative, and he blamed the Liberal Party for gay marriage in Canada. He pointed out that it was their prime minister, Pierre Trudeau, who pushed forward the Charter of Rights and Freedoms in 1982. Because the Liberal Party appointed a "very libertarian, liberal court. . . . we got rulings from the Supreme Court in favor of gay marriage." Walter felt a certain affinity with the Conservative Party because they had tried to "rule back some of the libertarian influences" like gay marriage and unregulated abortion. When I pressed Walter about whether he felt closer to any particular party, he mused, "You know, there are lots of Christians in every party. . . . I would probably consider myself closer with the Conservative Party, although I have not voted for them in any means." But when I asked Walter when he first started identifying with the Conservative Party, he stressed, "I wouldn't say I'm close to them even today." Walter was still amenable to voting for Liberal candidates, and he was not sure which party he would support even if an election was held this year.

Like many American evangelicals, Walter identified as morally and ideologically conservative, but his "conservative" principles were closer to the European tradition of counter-Enlightenment thought. Walter did not describe the differences between liberals and conservatives as a culture war between godly and godless views of moral authority. Instead, he traced this conflict back to Europe:

> The gay marriage issue . . . it's an example of what I call the license of the libertarian approach that we have inherited through the Charter of Rights and Freedoms in Canada. And you know historically, they did the same thing in France. The French Revolution . . . off with his head! So a few years later, they started cutting the heads of the guys that would cut the head of the king. So that was libertarianism in excess, right? Voltaire and Rousseau, well, all those guys and their libertarian philosophies, who espoused the rights of individual above the rights of society.

For Walter, politics was about finding the "right balance" between the rights of the individual and society's need for "law and order." Historically, Canadians like Walter have been described as Red Tories, a distinctively European type of conservative who prioritizes social stability over individual freedom in both moral and economic affairs.[8]

By American standards, Walter expressed liberal attitudes in support of generous social welfare programs. Yet Walter's support for the welfare state ultimately flowed from his "conservative" desire to safeguard the social order:

> I'm in favor of social policy that strives to neutralize the differences between the rich and the poor. Well I guess I'm a realist, and the Bible says the poor you'll always have with you, so I guess that's the

reality of it. But I think aiming to control that, and improving the lot of the poor, is something that I personally would favor.

Walter distanced himself from the utopian goals that he associated with the Social Gospel, but he felt that extreme social inequality would ultimately undermine Canada's stability. He did not connect his faith to themes of social justice, but neither did he see the welfare state as inherently anti-Christian like many American evangelicals. After all, Canada's welfare state was a symbol of national pride, which helped to uphold shared values. When I asked Walter if anything united Canadians from all walks of life, he described his vision of a common patriotism:

> We're slowly becoming more nationalistic, the flag is becoming more to us than it used to be. I think social justice is a strong factor in Canadian unity. We like to see people treated fairly and honorably. . . . Access to education. Being treated equally for the law like everybody. If you are in need, being able to have your needs met, a social network of some sort, in health care or financial need. Being given fair wages for fair work. And having a legal system that's fair.

In short, Walter was concerned that the "liberal, libertarian" trends like gay marriage would unravel the fabric of Canadian society. But he also imagined this "traditional" social order as a set of institutions, which embodied Canada's shared values of social justice. Hence, defending the social order also meant defending social programs that alleviated poverty, Medicare, and other national institutions.

Unlike many American evangelicals, Walter did not imagine the unregulated free market as a force for moral discipline. Instead, he described big corporations as unruly, amoral forces that threatened democracy:

> We're gonna have to take control of those big corporations that prevent us from doing the things we need to do. The big gas companies. Bring us a new engine that's more efficient than gasoline—they'd buy it up and prevent you from implementing the new motor cause it's bad for their business.

He also expressed a concern that Canadians were becoming "very materialistic . . . the economy is booming. . . . we still have a lot of needy people, whose needs are not being met by our social services, as good as they are. I guess goes along with being capitalistic at this stage, you know." Walter shared a moralistic concern about "materialism" with U.S. evangelicals, but he blamed these cultural trends on capitalism and a lack of social solidarity, rather than on "liberal" cultural elites. Walter did not look for the hand of God in the invisible hand of the market. Big government did not cause moral decadence. Instead, he saw government as a steward of the moral order.

Hence, Walter described voting as a balancing act between the strengths of Liberals and Conservatives. Walter admired the Conservative Party for "balancing the budgets" and being "economically responsible and frugal" in their approach to government. The Conservative Party was "more oriented towards successful business, so successful economy," while the Liberal Party tried to "run a middle course, balancing with social issues and economic." In Walter's opinion, Liberal government tended to "run nice big debts," while the Conservative governments specialized in balancing budgets. Walter saw no virtue in cutting government spending as an end in itself; he simply wanted the best quality social services that Canada could sustainably afford.

In summary, both Janice and Walter served as key political opinion leaders at Highpoint church, both in their capacity as lay leaders and in their personal networks. Like politically engaged American lay leaders, they worked to foster Christian greater awareness and involvement on these moral issues. But neither could be described as "captains" for culture war politics in their church. Though Janice privately voted Conservative, she did not signal this partisan identity in church leadership. Likewise, Walter drew a political map that located "lots of Christians in all three parties." Neither of them defined "Christian" as an all-encompassing political identity, defined by opposition to a partisan out-group. Instead, they both described Christians as a tiny cultural minority in a pluralistic society, who lived in tension with "the world" in general. Their goal was not to defeat a specific political adversary, but rather to carve out enough institutional space to safely reproduce their subculture. As a result, both of these lay leaders actively fostered political civility within their congregation, even as they tried to maintain strong boundaries on the "moral issues."

By contrast, I found that the Canadian Pentecostal church, Grace Pentecostal, contained a more partisan network of opinion leaders who sounded more like American culture warriors. But these individuals still struggled to exercise political influence within the church, because partisan cues violated church norms that proscribed political civility.

POLITICAL OPINION LEADERS FOR MORAL
ISSUES AT GRACE PENTECOSTAL

At Grace Pentecostal, Michael tried to rally fellow Christians behind the Conservative Party in his capacity as a lay leader. But his efforts were frustrated by the church's norms regarding political civility. As a forty-seven-year-old, college-educated corrections officer, Michael thought that all Christians should vote Conservative as a bloc. He self-consciously sent clear partisan cues within his church networks to this effect:

> Christians need to stick together and pick the best one, that'll at least get something in there. That's Conservative . . . The church should all go Conservative and freeze that in, or our country will go down the tubes.

I asked Michael if he ever talked politics with people at church, and he answered, "Oh yeah, all the time. I don't think you should, but I just like to debate." But at the same time, Michael made a point of recognizing that not all Christians were Conservative: "There are some Liberals that are Christian and are anti-abortion, and are good people, there are some NDP." His wife often "shushed" him when she realized that he was arguing with someone who voted Liberal. Michael told her that he didn't care: "Yeah, but they need to know the truth: the truth will set them free, and vote Conservative!" Michael recognized that he was breaking his church's unspoken rule against talking politics, and joked self-deprecatingly about how much he embarrassed his wife in the process.

For Michael, abortion defined his political identity, much as it did for culture warriors in the United States. Michael's conservative political leanings began in the 1990s, a period when the Reform Party appealed to Christians by promising to raise the abortion issue. Even after Reform dropped the abortion issue, the party still contained many prominent evangelicals and kept its reputation as a Christian-friendly party. Since then, Michael had volunteered for two local candidates who had unsuccessfully sought nominations for the Conservative Party. Even though Stephen Harper and the Conservative Party had never made any promises to change abortion laws, Michael felt that voting Conservative at least supported people who shared his values. For him, abortion symbolized his general concern that the country was "going down the tubes" morally. But Michael also acknowledged that good Christians could vote Liberal or NDP: "I don't think they're unsaved for voting Liberal." Michael assumed that Christians who voted Liberal had reasoned that, "whether it's Conservative or Liberal, the world is going down the tubes." Michael acknowledged that "to some extent they're right."

In part, Michael was forced to acknowledge political diversity within his church because it was a practical reality. But he also defined the boundaries of Christian identity and partisanship in different terms, which made it easier for him to accept political diversity within the church. Unlike American evangelicals, Michael never defined Christian identity by opposition to liberals, as an ambiguously political and religious term. Instead, he defined evangelical identity by opposition to the world and to secular Canadians. Michael never blamed Canada's moral decline on political forces; instead, he interpreted cultural change as evidence of greater "worldliness" within the church and greater secularism in society as a whole:

> When I grew up, sex outside of marriage was very uncommon, in the secular world, it wasn't questioned. People might do it, but they knew it wasn't godly. Now on TV this guy's having sex with that girl and that's it. . . . TV keeps bombarding their views. . . . The world is good at putting it on.

When I asked Michael why these changes occurred, he explained that "Satan's doing his job well and we're falling for it. The church isn't committed like it was." Too many Christians had become complacent in their personal morality, trusting in the doctrine that they were "once saved, always saved." Like American culture warriors, Michael felt that his religious beliefs were a natural fit with conservative politics. But Michael never identified an out-group that was analogous to the American "liberal elite": a political adversary who could be blamed for Canada's moral decline. Instead, he blamed the evangelical subculture for failing in its witness to "the secular world."

For Michael, being a true Conservative meant two things: "You don't waste money. You don't have abortions."[9] Being politically conservative was about showing "tougher love." As among American evangelicals, the theme of self-discipline linked his beliefs about moral issues and social policy issues. But though fiscal discipline was part of Michael's conservative identity, he was not actually opposed to a generous welfare state. In fact, he expressed stronger support for redistributive social policy than all but the most progressive American evangelicals in my study. For example, when I asked Michael if the government had a responsibility to reduce the gap between rich and poor, he was confused that I would even ask such a question. Looking at me incredulously, he replied, "You *have* to understand why it is important to lessen that gap." The government "would be foolish not to" help poor people, "because society will go back to the stone age, this section is so poor, they have to help them . . . or then you go back to slums."

Unlike many American evangelicals in this study, Michael did not talk about poor people as a separate moral category defined by a refusal to work. Instead, he thought of poor people as workers who paid taxes and so deserved benefits if they fell on hard times. When Michael talked about cutting "wasteful spending," he actually wasn't thinking of programs that benefitted poor Canadians. Instead, he wanted to cut benefits to immigrants who got "all these benefits" and "free health care," taking resources away from Canadians. Immigrants drained resources from *worthy* recipients of government benefits, whom Michael described as "people on welfare, or people that just don't make welfare . . . and you know, there's no reason that person shouldn't be on welfare. . . . they've been paying the system for ten years." It particularly bothered him that immigrants got more government benefits than native Canadians who worked hard, but earned just enough money to not qualify for welfare.[10] His resentment toward immigrants, and defense of poor Canadians, reflects an alternative right-wing rhetoric found outside the United States. In other national contexts, radical right-wing parties often favor a rhetoric of welfare chauvinism rather than small government retrenchment.[11]

Though Michael identified as a political conservative and as a Christian, he did not define small-government, anti-welfare attitudes as part of a coherent Christian political package. This made it easier for him to accept Christians who voted Liberal or NDP for economic reasons, since their differences of opinion on social policy were not charged with religious meaning. When Christians voted Liberal, it was because "they believe it will help them financially, as opposed to voting for the moral reasons." Michael understood why some Christians were attracted by Liberal policies, for example, reasoning that a new child benefit would "save me $100 a month, I'll vote for them." He would personally rather receive a tax cut, but he understood the economic appeal.[12] Being liberal or voting for the Liberal Party did not say anything about a person's moral character or standing as a Christian.

This was even true for Connie, a 57-year-old member of Grace Pentecostal, who was one of only two Canadians interviewed who used American-style culture war rhetoric. Like the politically conservative captains in the American evangelical churches, Connie saw conservative politics as the natural expression of her born-again faith. She described how her Christian beliefs informed her conservative attitudes on every political issue she could think of: she was pro-life, anti–gay marriage, anti-welfare, economically conservative, pro-Israel, and pro-war. Like the American culture warriors, Connie had adopted this framing of Christian identity by watching conservative American news sources and engaging with parachurch ministries and pro-life activism outside of church. But Connie's church interactions did not reinforce this polarized political map; instead, she learned to recognize that other evangelical Christians did not combine religion and partisanship in the same way.

If Connie sounded more like an American culture warrior, it was because she had lived briefly in the United States in the late 1970s, during her formative years as a young Christian. Connie became a born-again Pentecostal in 1977, and moved to the United States with her new husband around 1980. Living briefly in the United States as a new believer, she found her inspiration in Pat Robertson and Ronald Reagan. Connie had relied on Robertson's show *The 700 Club* as her primary source of news, during a period when Robertson covered political events from a consistently conservative perspective.[13] Before her born-again experience at twenty-seven, Connie reported that she had never voted. But in 1980, Connie begged her apolitical American husband to go out and vote for Reagan on her behalf, because he "was a Christian." Connie could not vote for Reagan herself because she was Canadian, but this was the first election when she became interested in politics, because of her newfound "faith in Christ": "Knowing that He purchased his freedom for me, then I needed to be prayerful about who I voted for. And I needed to have people in government as close to my values as possible." After returning to Canada in the early 1980s, Connie became involved in Hamilton's pro-life movement.

Connie had been involved in pro-life causes long before she converted to evangelicalism, since she was raised in the Catholic Church and grew up attending the publicly funded Catholic schools in Hamilton. After graduating high school, she volunteered with Birthright, a nonsectarian, nonpartisan charity that was originally founded in Toronto in 1968.[14] As a young Catholic, she saw an announcement about Birthright in the paper, and decided to volunteer out of a general sense that "that would be something that I would be interested in doing." During her year-long volunteering experience, Connie "saw all the films" that circulated about the pro-life cause, and she became solidly convinced that "well, if it's not a baby, just leave it there for nine months, and if it's just a tissue, then a tissue will come out." After her born-again conversion, Connie was inspired to vote pro-life, taking her cues from the nascent U.S. Christian Right.

Then around 1988, Connie started engaging in more confrontational pro-life protest, with a small group of friends at Grace Pentecostal. Connie shared fond memories of that "season of my life," when she brought her toddler along in the stroller while she picketed outside of Henderson General Hospital in Hamilton. Sometimes people would be "downright ignorant and rude" and give them "the finger as they were driving by." But Connie "didn't care because I knew that . . . that's just something that God wants me to do for now." Even with public opposition, Connie felt that pro-life picketing was generally a "good experience, because I was with friends . . . you weren't all alone." That "season" of her life had ended, but Connie still considered herself "a little bit more politically active in stuff like that."

Abortion remained "the one issue" that motivated Connie to "vote conservative," because "If you're pro-abortion, I don't vote for you." Connie even researched the candidates' abortion stances for municipal elections, even though local governments had no power to regulate abortion:

I asked the guys that were running municipally, like just in the Hamilton area, and they say, "well, what does that have to do with anything?" And I say, "'because if you're against life, you're not gonna be the kind of person that I want running my affairs. So if you're pro-life, you're the kind of person I want, 'cause . . . I know everything else will settle in.

While the Conservative Party had made only symbolic gestures toward limiting abortion, this was enough to show their more "Christian" character.[15] Voting for the Liberals and NDP was unthinkable because those parties "definitely are pro-abortion, and the Conservative Party is not."

Moreover, Connie felt that the Conservative Party represented biblical values on social policy and fiscal issues, as well as moral issues. She tied moral and fiscal conservatism together in a coherent Christian bundle. Connie felt that Conservatives stood for "what the Bible teaches" on social welfare issues, because they believed that "if you don't work, you don't eat, right? And Liberal and NDP parties are more like, 'Well, let's give everybody a hand-out,' you know?" Connie preferred "workfare" because it forced people to develop individual responsibility, while "welfare" promoted "generational poverty." Like American culture warriors, Connie saw economic conservatism as biblical because it fostered individual responsibility, and also because it imposed authority on unruly people.

Connie held an authoritarian ideal of Christian leadership: godly leaders would impose order and moral conformity on a chaotic world. For example, Reagan was not just a Christian leader because he opposed abortion, but also because he stood up to the air traffic controllers:

I liked [Reagan] because he proclaimed to be a Christian . . . he was saying stuff that I liked. Stuff like, "You know what? You air controllers, you think you're gonna go on strike? You can forget it, you're all fired! You're losing your jobs, 'cause you don't go on strike . . . it will disrupt everybody. So you think you're gonna be smart?" They went on strike and he fired them all!

Connie wanted strong Christian leaders to "stand up to" everyone who threatened the social order: striking workers, pro-abortion groups, people dependent on welfare, and especially Muslims. For example, Connie admired George W. Bush as a Christian leader, who was bold enough to recognize the truth about Islam: "They hate us, and so when they say that the Muslim faith is a faith of peace, it's not a faith of peace and the Koran does not teach that." She praised Bush's decision to invade Iraq, because she saw Saddam Hussein as a Muslim leader who persecuted Christians and opposed Israel. Throughout the interview, Connie repeatedly used this language of "standing up" to describe how a Christian solved political problems.

But even though Connie defined her political identity in culture war terms, her local congregation forced her to recognize cross-cutting political identities among Christians. Around elections, Connie made a point of announcing that she wouldn't vote for anyone who supported abortion, and that meant voting Conservative. As a would-be culture war captain, she sought to exercise political influence through the many informal, small group settings that her church provided. But her attempts to exercise political influence always led to an argument from people who voted Liberal or NDP. When I asked Connie why fellow church members felt differently about politics, she struggled to explain, "I don't know, I just don't know." Her husband Jerry chimed in, "We believe in the same nucleus, but surrounding that . . . there's too many variables on the politics." Connie added, "And I think also, as mature Christians, we try to major on the things we have in common, as opposed to things we don't have in common." As an individual, Connie had trouble understanding other political viewpoints among Christians. But at her church, she could not send partisan cues without hearing immediate disagreement from other members, who felt empowered to defend an alternative political identity. By contrast, none of the conservative opinion leaders at either U.S. evangelical churches ever described an argument ensuing as a result of their efforts to influence others.

In summary, both Connie and Michael made regular attempts to send partisan cues at church, much like culture war captains in both U.S. evangelical churches. But when they did so, they were consciously violating the unspoken speech norms of their church. Michael's wife "shushed" him in embarrassment, while Connie found herself in a political argument. Both of these would-be culture warriors were swimming upstream against their church's group style, the unspoken norm that members acknowledge political diversity within their group.

POLITICAL DIVERSITY AMONG LEADERSHIP

These conservative opinion leaders were also counter-balanced by a second set of lay leaders, who embodied alternative political identities that were rendered implausible in both American churches. Members with diverse political views were seen as legitimate in their faith and qualified for leadership, as long as they did not challenge traditional moral beliefs in matters of personal behavior and church discipline. Because of these practices of civility, individuals found it possible to combine traditional morality with left-leaning politics, without being demobilized by social cross-pressures.

For example, Donald and Rose organized the church's outreach to a local nursing home. At seventy-five, Donald had served as an ordained Pentecostal minister for over fifty years. In 1964, they immigrated from England to Atlanta, Georgia, where they were horrified by the particular race relations of the South. Rose remembered how they had trouble getting white church members to pray with black people, who came forward on altar calls to receive prayer. Soon, they started going to civil rights meetings, and formed a strong sense that justice was central to what it meant to be Christian. After they moved to Canada, Donald and Rose went on to become active in the New Democratic Party. In their ministry, they continued to lead evangelistic outreach to poor and marginalized communities through the Pentecostal Assemblies of Canada.

At the same time, Donald and Rose were distressed by the legalization of abortion and new developments like gay marriage. Rose worked for many years as a social worker at a local hospital, and she vividly remembers that after Canada's abortion laws were struck down, her hospital had to install a second incinerator to dispose of fetal remains. It deeply grieved them that Canada had no regulation on abortion, even in the third trimester. Despite their NDP commitments, the couple had occasionally supported Conservative Party candidates who championed the pro-life cause. Donald and Rose rarely discussed politics at church, but not because they felt that their politics were particularly unusual or marginal within their religious milieu. While their faith informed their politics, they felt that voting was an extremely private matter of conscience.

Like the conservative culture warriors from chapter 6, Donald and Rose had formed their strong social justice commitments through a separate stream of religious practice outside of a church setting, a stream provided by the civil rights movement. While their left-leaning, social justice concerns were not reinforced by their local Pentecostal church, neither were they rendered implausible by a constant stream of partisan cues. Unlike Alice in chapter 7, this couple had not withdrawn from politics or become paralyzed by ambivalence. Grace Assembly provided different niches for political identity, where economic populists like Donald and Rose could worship side-by-side with culture warriors like Connie and Michael.

These practices of civility were greatly appreciated by Ryan, a twenty-five-year-old member of Grace Assembly who usually voted for the New Democratic Party. Ryan contrasted his experience in Canadian churches with the partisan climate of American evangelicalism: "I would fear in America becoming a Christian, because that would mean that I would have to be a Republican." Ryan explained, "I don't want parties to be Christian and non-Christian" where "if you're Christian you vote Republican and if you're a Christian and you don't, you are looked down upon."

He valued this separation between religious identity and partisanship as an important part of being a Christian in Canada. Ryan felt free to support the New Democratic Party, even though he described himself as "theologically conservative" and fervently pro-life.

Ryan also felt empowered as a lay leader to initiate group discussion about politics and current events. He was grateful that his church avoided the kinds of partisan cues that he associated with the American Christian Right. But he felt dissatisfied that his church was so focused inward on the spiritual needs of its members. Ryan wanted to see the church "speaking more from our pulpits about current events issues that are relevant. Not our stands on same sex marriages, but how are we going to change things?" For example, Ryan pointed out that "there is an issue with homelessness in the city, there's an issue with child poverty in the city. What are we going to do about it?"

Earlier that year, Ryan had organized a group discussion around the theme "Faith and Politics," as part of a series of young adult social gatherings. At this event, Ryan stood up with a young female associate minister, who introduced the discussion topic with evident embarrassment, "Today we'll be talking about faith and politics. That's something we don't usually delve into . . . unless we're passionate like Ryan." Ryan introduced the topic by acknowledging that "faith and politics is sticky, there are no right or wrong answers. We're going to look at two sides of the issue and develop new ways of looking at it." He encouraged everyone to be considerate of other people's opinions and "join the conversation in love and grace and mercy and all that Jesus stuff." Ryan had prepared a discussion guide with a quote from Gregory Boyd that criticized the U.S. Christian Right. In small group discussion, it was assumed that all Christians should be opposed to abortion and same-sex marriage, but participants also expressed concern about fusing religion and partisanship in a way that they saw as "American." Like conservative culture war generals in both American churches, Ryan set the tone for political talk among young adults at Grace Assembly in his role as a lay leader.

Ironically, Ryan had developed this interest in politics after he participated in a socially conservative prayer rally in Ottawa called *The Cry.* This series of prayer rallies was organized by Faytene Kryskow, a controversial charismatic leader who has been accused of Dominionist theology and strong connections to the Conservative Party. On July 15, 2006, a group of young adults from Grace Assembly had caravanned to Ottawa to attend one of these worship events, where they prayed for Canada to return to "righteousness," an end to abortion, and national revival. During this period, Kryskow used these worship events to recruit young evangelicals for lobbying and campaign volunteering through 4MyCanada. While this Ottawa organization identified as nonpartisan, it focused exclusively on strengthening ties among Conservative M.P.s and evangelical churches.[16]

Yet these partisan cues were lost on the young adults from Grace Assembly who attended The Cry in 2006. Ryan experienced The Cry primarily as a social event: "It's a fun day for me: you get to worship, you get to dance, you get to have a good time, go on a road trip." He and his girlfriend had gone to support a friend who was leading worship at The Cry as a musician. For Ryan, the most meaningful part was "when we pray for our leaders, because . . . too often, we spend time condemning our leaders for what they're doing." Ryan felt it was "very important" to show support for all of Canada's leaders, whether or not "you agree with everything they do."

> We're still called to support them and pray for them and let them know that their job is ridiculously hard. And I'm sure they're doing the best they can . . . for what they think is best. Go and pray, and show support to leaders, regardless of whether it's a Conservative or Liberal or NDP government. . . . And that's my favorite part of The Cry, that's why I like to go.

Outside observers have criticized The Cry for featuring overwhelmingly Conservative Party figures as speakers and guests.[17] But Ryan had not noticed such a partisan bias, as someone who was strongly opposed to the idea of mixing religion with a partisan agenda. On the contrary, The Cry resonated with Ryan because it seemed truly nonpartisan, unlike the American Christian Right.

Ryan also found the event to be meaningful because it celebrated a multicultural narrative of Christian nationalism that he found familiar. Ryan was not disturbed by the use of Christian nationalism at The Cry, because he interpreted it as a celebration of Canadian multiculturalism: "We do some French stuff, we do some native Canadian things, we pray for the different areas and . . . provinces . . . and territories." Ryan described The Cry as "Christians that are Canadian coming together and supporting Canada . . . different parts of the world, too." Celebrating cultural diversity was central to celebrating Canada: "we pray for different immigrants and different cultures . . . we welcome them, and we say, 'that's awesome, we appreciate it, and it makes [Canada] a better place'." Ryan did not perceive this use of nationalism as authoritarian. Instead, he perceived it as civil religion, which affirmed the common principles that bound Canada together, albeit practiced from a distinctly subcultural, Pentecostal perspective.[18]

The Cry inspired Ryan to get involved in politics, by giving him a sense of common purpose with young Christians all across the country. Ryan believed that he was part of a "movement of Christ-followers forming that want to make a change, and want to make a world different and want to make this city of Hamilton different." He was unaware of Faytene Kryskow's ties to the Conservative Party. Ryan's vision of Christian influence in politics was more forward-looking: "I do believe that God has something special for Canada and I believe that we are going to be a part of that."

During the Faith and Politics discussion, three other Grace members mentioned their worship experience at The Cry as a touchstone for their interest in politics. For example, one young man told the group about his experience at The Cry on Parliament Hill: "It was phenomenal, worshipping like that and praying for your country. And they told us about the bills that they were trying to get passed. And they had speakers blasting through the whole capital! You should really go next year." Although The Cry had kindled their interest in politics, none of these youth had come to link their faith to a conservative political identity. Faytene Kryskow had sought to rally them for a culture war, but in their immediate religious community, Ryan promoted a more nonpartisan, justice-minded narrative of Canadian Christian identity. This underscores the role of local opinion leaders like Ryan in bridging the worlds of politics and local religious practice.

In both American churches, it was difficult for young evangelicals to develop a more liberal or left-leaning political identity, without becoming alienated from an intergenerational church setting. But in both Canadian churches, young adults described their incredulity that religion might be rigidly linked to partisanship. At a young adult gathering at Highpoint Baptist, one recent college graduate told me how her friend had gone to a Christian conference in the United States. When her friend described herself as politically liberal to her new American acquaintances, "She got attacked so fast!" Another male lay leader shook his head in amazement, and told me that he had voted for both the New Democratic Party and the Conservative Party in recent elections: the NDP for their "values" and the Conservative Party to stand up for traditional marriage.

At Highpoint Baptist, one young lay leader described in detail how Canadian churches differed from the partisan climate of American evangelicalism. Jesse was a thirty-year-old, college-educated sales representative, who taught Sunday school to elementary school students at Highpoint Baptist. He grew up in the Plymouth Brethren, dropped out of church during college, and then came back to the church after volunteering at a homeless shelter. There, Jesse was moved to "see God working outside of the church" in the lives of homeless people, and he started attending Highpoint Baptist. During my fieldwork, Jesse also became involved with an evangelical movement called TrueCity, which brought together churches and faith leaders interested in urban ministry. He usually voted for the New Democratic Party:

> They seem to have a social conscience, and when I voted NDP, I felt there was a powerful conservative push, whether from the Conservatives or Liberals, economically right-leaning, so it needed some sort of balance.

Jesse had also voted for the Liberal Party for strategic reasons, to keep Conservatives out of power and protect social programs. Since Jesse identified as pro-life and theologically conservative, he felt some ambivalence toward the NDP as "the most socially liberal party. I don't know if I agree with all of that, so it's hard." But Jesse had never felt that his political views were out of place at Highpoint Baptist, even though the church took clear stands on abortion and homosexuality.

Jesse recalled one exception to this rule: two years ago, a guest preacher implied that Christianity was associated with a particular political perspective. One of his Christian friends from college was visiting his church with him that day, and they were both surprised:

> So we were sitting in service and we had a guest pastor, I can't remember his name. But he made a couple references to George Bush, in a favorable light. And I could see her shivering every time. It's weird. I guess people don't follow simple lines of liberal and conservative, but in politics she's socialist, almost. And another comment about Steven Harper, about him not openly displaying his Christianity and that was okay because . . . to stay in power he had to downplay that, in order not to scare off the general population. And she was just losing it, I could tell. And she said, "Oh wow, this church is really American." I guess there must have been something going on that day as well; maybe it could have been Remembrance Day. It was very American patriotism-esque.

The guest speaker had violated the practices of civility that Jesse expected in church. While American churches might mix patriotism and partisanship with religious identity, Jesse and his "socialist" friend took it for granted that Canadian churches recognized multiple political perspectives. This vignette sheds light on why it was so difficult for American evangelicals to develop liberal or left-leaning political identities in their local churches. For Jesse, these partisan cues were a jarring departure from normal religious practice. But in both American evangelical churches, it was impossible to escape a partisan, "patriotism-esque" narrative as a reference point for religious identity.

Both Canadian churches were able to negotiate this political diversity, even though they institutionally endorsed a traditional, patriarchal model of "family values." Significantly, the recognition of multiple political identities did not entail the recognition of multiple perspectives on homosexuality, abortion, or sexual morality. Highpoint and Grace Pentecostal both struck a compromise on gender roles that John Bartkowski has documented in American evangelical churches.[19] While church leaders taught an authoritative, "biblical" model of male headship, they balanced the logic of authority with the logic of compassion, to accommodate more egalitarian marriages or childcare arrangements. In personal interviews, congregants varied in how much emphasis they put on headship/submission or egalitarian relationships. But public church discourse never acknowledged legitimate disagreement among "true" Christians on homosexuality or abortion.

For example, Todd was one of the youngest deacons at Highpoint, who, at the age of thirty-six, encouraged the church to adopt a more forward-looking narrative of evangelical identity. Todd and Clara, his thirty-three-year-old wife, had grown up during the years of the Reform movement, which attempted to rally Canadian evangelical churches around the pro-life issue. Todd told me how his father, a Baptist pastor, had tried to rally his church to vote Reform in the early 1990s, right about the time that he became eligible to vote.[20] When Todd and Clara first married, they both believed that the Bible taught male headship and female submission. But over the last five years, they had decided that the Bible supported an egalitarian position on gender roles, and so they disagreed with the church's refusal to ordain women. Furthermore, they wanted to reconsider the church's opposition to gay marriage.

Todd told me how Robert, a friend from work, had recently "come out" to him as gay, and how it had challenged his conservative perspective on the issue. Though his friend had been raised Catholic, he and his partner had been hurt by the church. Clara added, "To hear it hurts . . . I just never thought about it, you believe mostly what you read." She was moved by their stories of "how hurtful" it was to "never be understood, starting when they were little." Now, Todd thought that homosexuality was "a red herring, a total red herring." Three weeks ago, the pastor had mentioned homosexuality in a sermon, and Clara thought, "Ok, here we go again, homosexuals in the back row, or someone in the church, they are just gonna let them leave. . . . I think people forget that when you are reading those verses, it doesn't just say homosexuals, it includes all those other people . . . there's not degrees of sin, you know: gossiping, blasphemy, all those other sins." Todd had begun to wonder if perhaps "they could live a committed relationship with each other, as gay men, and feel right with God and live a full complete life. . . . Being in a gay relationship, and being a Christian." He and Clara thought that gay people should be eligible for the same rights to have their relationship recognized, get partner benefits, and adopt children.

However, this position was beyond what could be publicly articulated at Highpoint Baptist. So far, Todd and Clara had only talked about their concerns with other people their age in the church, a select group of people who were privately sympathetic because they had friends or family members who were gay. Recently, Todd and Clara had announced to their Bible study that they planned to attend Robert's marriage ceremony to his partner, and several people expressed concerns that this might be seen as condoning sin. Todd pointed out that no one would disapprove if he attended the wedding of a friend who had committed adultery, divorced, and remarried, even though that was also wrong. But he knew that it was not possible for him to challenge the church's stance on homosexuality without jeopardizing his leadership role as a deacon. Public disagreement about the "moral issues" was suppressed by unspoken customs of group life, as well as by institutionalized statements about official church orthodoxy. Highpoint Baptist recognized multiple political identities among Christians on the basis of other issues and interests, not on the basis of multiple interpretations of sexual morality.

ELITE CUES AND LOCAL RELIGIOUS INTERACTION

Without clear social cues that connected religious identity to partisanship, less politically engaged members were unsure about how to connect their moral concerns to politics. For example, Clifford and Shirley, a lower-middle-class couple, described many of the same concerns about moral decline as American evangelicals in their generation. Since Clifford was fifty-eight and Shirley was forty-nine, they had experienced Canada's cultural changes more dramatically than Todd and Clara. Clifford and Shirley told me that they used to be "more for the Conservatives." But now, Clifford told me that they don't know who to vote for anymore:

> I don't think [Canada's political parties] are any different. Basically they got the Left, the Center and the Right. And one is Liberal and one is Conservative. It seems in this climate, to be quite honest with you, I don't know who to vote for right now, because there seems to be a melding of all of them. There is a bit of social in all three of them, and there is a bit of liberalism in all three of them, and I just don't know.

Shirley explained that the Conservatives "used to be more conservative and morally more into our beliefs . . . like abortion, they used to stand up against that choice. Now it doesn't seem that way anymore. I think you have to ask the individuals."

Since Clifford and Shirley paid little attention to politics, they relied on cues from elites and their social environment to connect their values and religious identity to political parties. In previous decades, this couple had tried to vote on the basis of their concerns about abortion and family values. But as discussed in chapter 2, these issues had been systematically excluded from Canada's political agenda. Because all three major parties avoided overt appeals to their religious values, Clifford and Shirley did not see either of Canada's current parties as their champion. By contrast, Americans were constantly reminded which party was "for them" and their values, based on campaign messages and partisan cues from political opinion leaders at church.

Neither Clifford nor Shirley could place themselves on a left-right continuum, nor could they describe clear social policy preferences. On their map of politics, they located parties along two dimensions: "the moral" and "the social." They knew that their values were more "conservative" on moral issues. But in their experience, most politics was about "the social," or getting things done. On the social dimension, they evaluated parties and candidates by how well they "made things happen." Clifford tried to "vote for the man," and he didn't think it mattered which of the political parties got in. The only exception was when the NDP was in power in Ontario ten years ago: "When we had the NDP in power in Ontario ten years ago or so, a lot of things did change, a lot of things happened." Clifford and Shirley did not hesitate to express their admiration for the left-leaning NDP, because they did not reason about politics in structured, ideological terms. Instead, they relied on partisan cues in their social environment to map their relationship to electoral politics. But unlike the American evangelicals described in chapter 7, their social context did not help them link conservative morality and Christian identity to being politically "conservative."

Clifford and Shirley were not just exposed to fewer cues from campaigns and candidates that linked their religion and traditional morality to partisanship. Their religious identity was also kept more separate from partisanship within local religious practice. As lay leaders at Highpoint Baptist, Clifford and Shirley had wrestled with what Canada's "moral decline" meant for the mission of their local church, and they had helped launch an intensive discipleship program at Highpoint. Clifford's goal was to equip believers to be like missionaries to their own society: "You listen to a TV program, that requires people to go to a certain country [as a missionary], and yet there is so much need back here at home ... And as the discipleship program progresses, it allows people to be all that Christ intended them to be. Then God can mobilize these people and so that they can go out and do and be what God wants them to be. We are working together as a full body." The challenge for Christians was to accept the fact that they were a cultural minority, so they could reach Canada as a post-Christian mission field. Within this missional narrative, Christians were not locked into an adversarial relationship with political out-groups like "liberals." Rather, they were in tension with their society as a whole.

When I asked Clifford to clarify how Christians could make a difference in the larger society, he gave an example of civic, nonpartisan leadership. In the nearby city of Caledonia, a First Nations community had occupied property in response to a dispute over land rights. A group of ministers had organized a series of prayer sessions. Clifford contrasted this approach with the way that a nonbeliever might respond to this situation:

> If a person, a believer, is truly following the ways of the Lord, then their response would probably be different than the non-believer, who basically has to rely on his own strength . . . With the world situation right now, with the unrest in the world, unrest in our own community, there are different ways that a believer would respond. How a non-believer would respond, how they should solve the problem—well, I think it's more "bring in the army," and not solve the problem.

By comparison, Clifford thought that Christians had exemplified a more godly approach in Caledonia: "They sit at a table, and they dialogue at the table, as opposed to going storming the place, and taking over." Among American evangelicals, the phrase "godly leadership" had become so charged with partisan meaning, that liberals and Democrats could not be godly leaders by definition. By contrast, Clifford imagined godly leadership in thoroughly nonpartisan, civic terms, as someone who practiced dialogue, problem-solving, and ethnic reconciliation.

At Highpoint Baptist, Brandon and Leah also exemplified this missional, nonpartisan construction of evangelical identity. In their mid-thirties, this couple met while running a Christian camp in Western Canada. Brandon was recently named a deacon at Highpoint Baptist Church, and Leah helped lead the youth group. I asked Leah, "How does life as a Christian feel to you in our society these days?" In response, she described the symbolic boundaries that separated her as a Christian from people outside her subculture.

> I feel abnormal sometimes. . . . A big difference between me and the society in general, is that I have very distinct convictions on things, and a lot of people don't have convictions on anything. It's like, "whatever goes." And I'm not like "whatever goes" because it just doesn't work.

Her husband Brandon added, "And the foundation for those convictions . . . because secular people have beliefs, but it's the foundation of why those people have those beliefs and why we have ours." Leah and

Brandon drew boundaries between themselves and "secular people," while many of the American evangelical respondents drew similar boundaries in terms of "liberal" and "conservative."

Leah went on to describe the challenge of ministering to her neighbors in a post-Christian culture. Three years ago, she and her husband moved to Hamilton after working and living at a Christian summer camp for many years. When they were at the camp, they had lived in an "all-Christian environment" that they called "the bubble." But since they'd moved to Hamilton, Leah had "really come to understand a little bit more of what 'salt and light' means." Now, she lived in a neighborhood where the people next door had a "pot flag in their windows—it looks just like the Canadian flag except it's a marijuana leaf." One of her neighbors had a Mormon background, another had a Catholic background and hadn't gone for years, and her friends around the corner were "nominal Christians . . . they just don't go to church anymore." Leah described her neighborhood as her "biggest sphere of influence," other than her two girls. Getting outside the Christian bubble, she had realized that "The world's a pretty dark place . . . a lot of people are without hope, a lot of people are scarred by what goes on with them. A lot of people just are oblivious to spiritual things."

Leah considered herself pro-life, and she had briefly worked as a counselor at a crisis pregnancy center. When I asked Leah how she was involved with the pro-life movement now, she told me that she expressed her pro-life commitments by sponsoring girls in Africa and Sri Lanka to go to school, "because man, there's no life for girls in other Third World Countries." Leah was particularly excited about supporting a female missionary who worked with women and girls:

> [B]ecause I know the crisis that women and girls face and India and China and . . . just everywhere, they are second class citizens. So I guess from that point of view it's not pro-life in the way that people would think in North America, but it certainly is pro-life for women and girls.

In sum, Leah and Brandon talked about "moral issues" in nonpartisan terms, to describe how the church should deal with personal sin, draw moral boundaries, and witness to the larger society.

In the last election, Leah and Brandon had supported the Conservatives because they took a more conservative stance on gay marriage, and they were glad to see a party standing up for their moral values. They appreciated that Stephen Harper was an evangelical Christian. However, they did not see voting Conservative as an expression of their religious identity, and they reported having voted Liberal in the past. Brandon told me that he simply voted for "whoever would do a good job." Leah preferred the Liberals or the Conservatives: the NDP was a little too "out there" for her, although she was glad that they stood up for the poor and the environment.

In summary, Leah and Brandon sounded very much like many of the American evangelicals in this study: they held conservative positions on the "moral issues" of gay marriage and abortion, they were concerned about the moral climate, and they identify as religiously conservative. Yet they had a more *civic, nonpartisan* way of mapping their relationship to their sociocultural environment. In part, this is a story about top-down political mobilization: when major parties do not distinguish themselves on the basis of religious identity and moral issues, individual voters are less likely to make those issues central to their political priorities.[21] This couple responded to elite cues about religion and traditional morality when the gay marriage issue was salient, but moral issues had not become central to their political identity.

But this is also a story about how Leah and Brandon constructed evangelical identity in local religious practice. Partisanship was not tightly woven together with their religious identity, because they drew on different narratives to understand their relationship to Canada and diverse out-groups in their social environment. While religious identity informed their politics, they defined their religious and political identities in different terms.

CONCLUSION

Partisan polarization is not a natural state for evangelicals, even for churches that exhibit conservative theology, strict moral beliefs, and strong in-group distinction. In both Canadian churches, members with diverse political views were seen as legitimate in their faith and qualified for leadership, as long as they held to conservative morality in their personal behavior. While the moral issues were treated as non-negotiable as standards for internal church discipline, political diversity was accepted as a matter of private conscience. These Canadian evangelical churches engaged in practices of civility to allow for broader solidarity among Christians in spite of political differences.

By comparing churches across the border, we gain insight on how the evangelical subculture has deepened political polarization in the United States. In chapter 7, a Northtown member named Alice described an ideal Christian political platform that transcended the culture wars: morally traditional on abortion and sexuality, but progressive on issues of poverty and the environment. But it was *socially* difficult for her to embrace this kind of cross-cutting political identity, because she lived in a church environment where political liberals were defined as an out-group. This is how American evangelicalism contributes to political polarization: not just by taking strong stances on moral issues, but by making it socially impossible for individuals to hold cross-cutting political identities based on other issues.

By comparison, an integrated civil society is one where conflict is expressed through *non-encompassing identities*, so that the boundaries of religious identity and political identity need not coincide.[22] In a Canadian context, both evangelical churches were able to bridge political divisions instead of amplifying them. By engaging in these daily practices of mutual recognition, local churches contribute to a more integrated Canadian civil society.

CONCLUSION
Politics and Lived Religion

Here is the real core of the religious problem: Help! Help!
No prophet can claim to bring a final message unless
he says things that will have a sound of reality in the
ears of victims such as these.

—William James, *Varieties of Religious Experience*, 1902[1]

The Christian Right is no longer the only public voice speaking for American evangelicals. Since 2004, alternative leaders and advocacy groups have stepped out of the shadows to broaden the evangelical agenda. New voices appeal to evangelicals to consider poverty, creation care, and racial reconciliation as important moral issues. But this broadened political agenda will only gain traction with rank-and-file evangelicals if it becomes part of local religious practice. It is not enough to engage in top-down messaging about moral values. If these elites seek to challenge the hegemony of the Christian Right, they need to find substitutes for the powerful identity-work that goes on every week in evangelical congregations.

CONNECTING PEOPLE AND POLITICS

When Christian Right frames resonate, it is because they are woven into everyday religious practice, reinforcing a powerful connection between religious identity and partisanship. There has always been a divide between the religious worlds of rank-and-file evangelicals and the halls of power, where interest groups and parties operate. The challenge for Christian Right elites has been to bridge this gap between politics and lived religion, so that rank-and-file evangelicals experienced their agenda as an authentic, sacred expression of their faith.

In two American churches, I found that evangelicals connected their personal testimony to political engagement using narratives of Christian nationalism. As Michael Young has shown, confessional protest has a long history in American social movements.[2] In the abolitionist and temperance movements, participants shared their own testimony about renouncing personal sin, and resolved to bear witness to the "special sins" of the nation. Instead of slavery or alcohol, these national sins were named as abortion and sexual immorality. Both American churches invoked Christian nationalism to rally members for discipleship and service, rather than for collective political action. Yet it was precisely this polysemy between the personal and political meanings of Christian nationalism that made these narratives so powerful. When partisanship and faith became interwoven within an individual's personal testimony, voting Republican became a public witness against national sin.

In both American churches, political influence operated through a broad set of opinion leaders, who modeled a conservative political identity and sent partisan cues in informal church interactions. This subset of lay leaders fit James Hunter's ideal-type of the "culture warrior": they defined both religious and political differences as a struggle between two views of authority, which they termed "liberal" and "conservative." These schemas did not come from church involvement, but from sources outside the local congregation: parachurch ministries, interest groups, and Christian and conservative news sources. For culture war captains, parachurch and interest groups served as important agents of religious *socialization*, rather than as a vehicle to act on preexisting religious commitments.

Ironically, lay leaders did not perceive these interest groups and media sources as "political," nor did they describe themselves as political activists. Parachurch groups exercised *political* influence by actively engaging laypeople in *spiritual* disciplines like prayer, Bible study, and family devotion. For example, Buffalo's pro-life movement recruited activists through church networks, but did not rely on congregations to socialize people into a deep religious opposition to abortion. Rather, the pro-life movement recruited laypeople through a parallel stream of religious practice, similar to that provided by evangelical churches.[3] These lay leaders served as captains for culture war politics within their congregations, helping less politically engaged members connect their faith to conservative politics. This two-step model helps us understand how Christian Right generals have been so successful at building a conservative political consensus among rank-and-file evangelicals.

WHAT MAKES TRADITIONAL MORALITY SO POLARIZING?

This book provides a new perspective on why traditional moral concerns have become so polarizing in the United States. Political commentators are wrong to blame political conflict on an essential evangelical worldview. Evangelical congregations draw on a varied cultural toolkit to address the practical needs of real families, unlike culture war elites who defend family values in structured ideological terms. But it is just as wrong to blame the culture wars completely on political elites who manufacture conflict from above. This political mobilization account misses the interplay between top-down elite framing and bottom-up lived religion. Evangelicals inhabit an expanded universe of moral intuitions about authority, purity, and loyalty that many secular Americans do not experience.[4] My contribution is to de-exotify these traditional moral concerns, and to show how they become linked to conservative politics in local religious practice and social networks.

Future work should recognize these traditional moral intuitions, but without assuming that they are part of a coherent ideology or worldview. Social scientists have too often ignored traditional morality except in the context of authoritarian or ethnocentric political movements, which has obscured the enduring, mundane role of traditional morality in modern, pluralistic democracies. For example, my findings suggest that it is more productive to consider moral intuitions about authority as something separate from authoritarianism.[5]

All four churches in this study fostered *authority-mindedness*, not authoritarianism, because they consistently held the logic of judgment together with the logic of compassion.[6] While all four churches drew strong moral boundaries against the outside world, they also equipped members to engage across those boundaries. Angry expressions of outgroup resentment were curtailed by a "loving" group style. It was only appropriate to draw symbolic boundaries between "us" and "them" if one promptly expressed one's intentions to engage across those boundaries. All four churches advocated an authority-minded approach to parenting, but placed an equally strong emphasis on positive emotion work: praise, encouragement, and physical affection toward children. This combination of high standards and high support resembled an authoritative style of parenting, rather than an authoritarian one.

In each church, a handful of individuals expressed sentiments that could be described as authoritarian, and justified these feelings in religious terms. But significantly, their churches actively discouraged expressions of anger, resentment, and disgust as un-Christian. For example, a Lifeway member named Ronald expressed resentment toward liberals, minorities, big government, and undeserving poor people, in terms that fit George Lakoff's model of "strict father" morality. At Lifeway Assembly, Connie praised Ronald Reagan for "standing up" to deviants who threatened the social order: lazy people, Muslims, striking air traffic controllers. Both of these individuals justified their resentment toward outgroups using religious language. Yet after a year of observation, it was apparent that their local church discouraged this kind of punitive talk about out-groups. Instead, these individuals had actively sought out media sources, parachurch ministries, and experiences that would reinforce their fears and resentments. This complex relationship between religious subcultures and authoritarianism merits further research.

Groups, Civic Life, and Partisan Coalitions

Throughout the book, I challenge the Tocquevillean assumption that evangelical churches are pre-political spaces, where citizens acquire values and civic skills for life in a democracy. The American evangelical churches in this study did more than teach moral beliefs; they also sent clear partisan cues about which political identities were appropriate for Christians, and which were not. American evangelicals did not just learn valuable civic skills like running a meeting; they learned to identify themselves as godly leaders, locked into a conflict with godless liberals. Within the American evangelical subculture, religious identity and partisanship have become mutually constitutive identities, and this is a central dynamic in the culture wars. Yet social scientists ignore this dynamic when they study churches as part of "civil society," imagined as a separate sphere from state, family, and market.[7]

Evangelical churches can fuel either partisan polarization or civic integration, depending on whether their associational life sustains cross-cutting relationships based on other social identities. In Canada, both evangelical congregations practiced mutual recognition between Christians with different political identities. In the United States, religious identity was so closely intertwined with partisanship that it was socially impossible for evangelicals to identify with the Democratic Party.[8] These churches taught the same theology, shared the same traditional morality, focused their members' friendships within the subculture, and drew strong boundaries between themselves and the outside world. What varied was the relationship between group identity and partisanship, and the extent to which cross-cutting and partial identities were acknowledged within group life.[9]

These findings show why sociologists should not abandon the study of partisanship and partisan coalitions to political scientists. While religious identity can inform partisan conflict, histories of partisan conflict can also shape the content of religious identity. The Christian Right has not just "represented" the values and policy priorities of evangelicals; it has served as an internal movement to shape what these values and policy priorities should be. This has critical implications for cultural sociologists, who have come to conceptualize culture as an internally heterogeneous toolkit. In the field of cultural sociology, scholars often ask how and why cultural elements become bundled together in stable ways. To answer this question, sociologists should consider how cultural elements become bundled together through strategic negotiation between groups as they seek to expand or maintain partisan coalitions.[10]

For example, why is the U.S. evangelical tradition tied to laissez-faire economics? Most sociologists would answer this question by looking at the internal dynamics of the religious field itself: for example, looking for relationships between theology and economic individualism, or tracing how evangelicals have re-defined their subcultural boundaries over time. By contrast, I find that economic conservatism and evangelical identity became linked in the United States after two groups of organized elites recognized their shared interest in building a new partisan coalition. Starting in the 1940s, businessmen who opposed the New Deal forged an alliance with theologically conservative Protestants. Together, these two groups built new institutions to socialize evangelicals as loyal "conservatives" to fight big government and defend America's Christian identity. Over the course of four decades, these activist networks promoted a narrative of Christian nationalism that linked laissez-faire economics to traditional morality.

In both American churches, this narrative of Christian nationalism informed how evangelicals talked about poverty and the role of government. By contrast, evangelicals in Canadian churches did not associate small-government conservatism with their theology or religious identity. In comparative perspective, we see that evangelicalism became bundled with small-government conservatism through a historical process of partisan coalition-building. While theological reflection and religious meaning-making arguably played a role in this process, it was powerfully driven by strategic considerations. Thus, sociologists should consider the formation of inter-group partisan coalitions as an anchoring mechanism that links elements of political culture.[11]

LOOKING TO THE FUTURE OF EVANGELICAL POLITICS

This book provides a framework to make sense of the increasingly diverse role of evangelicals in public life. At the start of the twenty-first century, left-leaning and moderate evangelical voices gained the visibility and institutional leverage to challenge the Christian Right. New leaders and advocacy groups have stepped forward to define poverty, creation care, and racial reconciliation as equally important moral issues. It has become apparent that the Christian Right is a movement with two faces: one face that represents evangelicals in public debates and electoral politics, and another face that seeks to promote its particular vision of orthodoxy within the evangelical movement. Comparing the United States and Canada, I illuminate this internal struggle to define evangelical identity as a critical dynamic in the culture wars.

In a Canadian context, the Conservative Party has appealed to evangelicals using dog-whistle tactics, to rally traditional voters against same-sex marriage without alienating secular Canadians. But Canada's would-be Christian Right has not been able to link religious identity to partisanship at the level of religious practice. Canadian evangelicals are as morally traditional as American evangelicals, as staunchly opposed to abortion and to homosexuality. But they make sense of their subcultural identity using different narratives of Christian nationalism: less charged with partisan meaning, more akin to Robert Bellah's classic ideal of civil religion. Canadian evangelicals appreciate Stephen Harper's private faith and his subtle gestures toward "family values." But with the gay marriage issue settled, it will be increasingly difficult to rally Canadian evangelicals for a culture war—as long as Liberal and New Democratic Party elites avoid demonizing evangelicals as an out-group.

Since 2004, American pundits have advised progressives to overcome the "God Gap" by framing their issues in the language of moral values. This book provides a different answer. If other movements want to challenge the Christian Right for their own constituency, it will not be enough to engage in top-down messaging about faith and values. New moral issues will only take on a sacred quality if they become part of the lived religion of rank-and-file evangelicals, who are embedded in local congregations. The challenge for young, politically moderate, and left-leaning evangelicals is not just to establish a public face for their political vision. They face a much greater challenge: disentangling evangelical identity from partisanship at the level of religious practice.

METHODOLOGICAL APPENDIX
Ethnographic Methods

I began my fieldwork by introducing myself and my project to pastors and lay leaders in all four churches, and asking for their permission to participate in my study. I described the project as a study of religion and "civic engagement," because my preliminary key informant interviews revealed that "politics" was a dirty word in local churches. I did not want research participants to be more self-conscious about bridging public issues than they normally would. During my year in the field, I conducted participant-observation in these churches' weekly activities, including worship, Sunday school, mid-week small groups, and young adult social gatherings. I took detailed notes about the ways that rituals and personal interactions invoke themes of civic engagement, moral boundaries, cultural tension, and the nation. During this period, I also conducted a total of sixty semi-structured interviews with a cross-section of laity within these four churches, to probe deeper into how individuals constructed their subcultural identity and thought about politics and civic engagement. I also inquired as to the media and community involvements outside of the church that inform their thinking.

This research method required no small quantity of social flexibility and cultural fluency. As the daughter of a Baptist minister, I was able to introduce myself readily into these new church settings. As I gained entrée, I was granted a certain level of acceptance as a religious "insider": by honestly answering questions about my intentions and personal history, I was able to avoid being seen as a target for conversion or as a hostile secular academic. I did not fit popular stereotypes of the hostile, secularist academic. For example, one respondent declared that it was a major victory that my advisor "let me" study religion, and gave me a congratulatory high-five. The implication was that my research was subverting Harvard's hostility to Christianity. A common interpretation of my fieldwork was that I was embattled as a Christian in academia, studying a presumably despised subject, and church members were naturally obliged to show support for my project.[1] I never offered this interpretation myself, so I found it theoretically relevant that this interpretation emerged spontaneously so many times. At the same time, I never actively contradicted this interpretation, which helped me bridge the boundary between Ivy League academia and popular evangelicalism.

But this is not to say that I adopted an unproblematic insider stance with regard to the research participants. In many ways, I was very much an outsider to the evangelical subculture of all four of the congregations that I studied. On many doctrinal and political issues, I hold very different views than many of the research participants. I also grew up on the fringes of evangelicalism in the American Baptist Churches, USA: this denomination is closer to mainline Protestantism at the elite level, although the congregations that I grew up in were closer to evangelicalism. Most of my adult religious participation has been within mainline Protestant circles—a fact that I often emphasized to maintain a partial outsider status. I participated unobtrusively in worship, discussion, and group prayer, following a common ethnographic rule of thumb: to speak only as much as the least active person in the group. I made an effort to dress modestly, although dress was not as important a religious marker as it might have been in more Fundamentalist Protestant churches. I did not represent myself as believing all the same things as other church members, nor did I lead public prayer or take on leadership roles. When research participants voiced political positions that I disagreed with, I neither expressed my opinion nor signaled my assent. In Pentecostal churches, I did not speak in tongues or exhibit more demonstrative worship practices that were unfamiliar to me. I frequently announced myself as a researcher, in accordance with research ethics requirements.

During my fieldwork, I negotiated an ambiguous insider/outsider status in relationship to multiple boundaries: the boundary evangelical and mainline, academia and popular evangelicalism, popular categories of liberal and conservative. I also negotiated an ambiguous relationship to national boundaries: since I am a dual citizen of Canada and the United States, I could honestly claim to be both an insider and an outsider on both sides of the border, which gave me greater latitude to probe about taken-for-granted matters of political culture.[2] Other sociologists of religion have noted that the relationship between "insider" and "outsider" is particularly problematic in research on religion. Ethnographers of religion often feel a particular burden to emphasize their objectivity or distance from their research participants. However, I think that this "blurred" identity was particularly well-suited to access the answers to the particular questions that I set out to study.

For some research purposes, it is reasonable to hope that participants will eventually "let down their guard" in the presence of an "outsider" ethnographer. But I do not think that is reasonable in the case of North American evangelicals, many of whom have been coached from childhood to monitor their social environment for "unsaved" individuals and to accommodate their interactions accordingly.[3] For example, if my respondents had perceived me as "unsaved," they would probably not have admitted to feelings of anger or frustrations toward non-Christians, because of their concern to share a loving witness. Unknown to me, small groups within the church might have kept praying for my salvation for the duration of my fieldwork. When I observed small, casual conversations, participants would have stopped performing identity in ways that assumed all present were Christians.

Multi-site ethnography is particularly well-suited to understand how evangelical identity has become linked to partisanship. The political valence of congregational life is clearly more than the sum of its member's private views. Survey research tends to perpetuate a deceivingly thin model of political socialization, in which religion is reduced to a set of beliefs, which then directly produce political effects. It is particularly important to study subcultural identity using participant-observation, because identity is constructed in daily interaction whenever people tell stories to each other about who they are, or coordinate action by invoking a story about relationships across an *us–them* boundary.[4] While evangelical subcultural identity has been profitably studied by in-depth interviews and surveys, it is important to note that identities are not something that exist only inside people's heads. This relational notion of identity calls for relational data-gathering strategies that analyze the social settings in which these identities are constructed and performed.

I also conducted fifteen in-depth interviews with laity in each church to supplement the participant-observation, to build a dataset of sixty interviews. I initially used the church's membership directory to randomly select fifteen members of each church, used church informants to learn more about the selected individuals, and then adjusted the samples purposefully to match them by gender, socioeconomic status, education, and age. In addition to this semi-random sample, I relied on three to five key informants in each church to help me navigate the ethnographic observation. In-depth interviews helped me identify variation within each church, as well as spot disparities between the public content of discussion and individual's private concerns and opinions. Interviews also provided a venue for respondents to construct personal narratives that connect their own biography to political events and social trends.[5] Interviews were also useful as a "stimulus" for respondents to perform "boundary work," to define themselves as a moral person by making distinctions between themselves and relevant out-groups.[6] If evangelical identity has different political consequences in Canada and the United States, we can understand this by probing for the stories that evangelicals use to explain who they are, who they aren't, how they relate to people across the boundary—and how the government and the nation play a part in these relations. The interviews with laity were designed to supplement, and triangulate, the findings of the ethnographic investigation.

CHOOSING CITIES AND REGIONS TO COMPARE

In choosing these cities, I faced the challenge that evangelicalism is quite diverse in each country, and that there is great regional variation in how this religious tradition has engaged public life. To inform my choice of cities, I also conducted preliminary interviews in Texas and Alberta, to ascertain how regional context mattered for evangelical identity. Texas evangelicalism has a distinct profile, influenced both by Southern and Western histories. Alberta is often considered the "Texas" or "Bible Belt" of Canada, and the home province of many evangelical activists within the Reform Party. However, I decided not to include a Texas-Alberta comparison in this ethnographic study for two reasons. First, multi-site ethnography in four cities was logistically unfeasible. Second, I discovered through preliminary fieldwork that many of the leading pastors and laypeople in Albertan churches were American expatriates, because of the close linkages between evangelicals and "oil patch" culture in Alberta and Texas.[7] In designing this study, I also considered two other pairs of cities: Chicago and Toronto or Seattle and Vancouver. Chicago and Toronto were ruled out on theoretical grounds as being too large, since the so-called Red State/Blue State divide has pitted small and medium-size cities against major cosmopolitan centers. Seattle and Vancouver have served as theoretically interesting sites for other comparative researchers.[8] The Pacific Northwest was also judged as less theoretically useful, since social scientists have nicknamed this region "The None Zone" for its unusually high percentage of religiously unaffiliated people.[9] By process of elimination, Buffalo and Hamilton were judged to be the best comparison for this purpose.

CHOOSING CONGREGATIONS

To isolate the effects of cross-national differences, as opposed to differences between churches, I matched two congregations in each city as closely as possible along a number of important dimensions. Sociologists of religion have documented how religious tradition, denomination, race, national origin, socioeconomic class, lifestyle, level of strictness, size, and internal organization can serve to distinguish institutions in a multicongregational field.[10] While an exact match along all these dimensions was impossible, I worked to match churches that occupy the same niche within the available religious options of the Buffalo and Hamilton areas, which share similar denominational traditions, socioeconomic and ethnic profile, and suburban location. I mapped these religious options by using publicly available registries of congregations, consulting denominational lists, conducting web searches, and by using key informants in each city who were familiar with local evangelical congregations.

DATA ANALYSIS AND VERIFICATION

I carried out ongoing data analysis simultaneously with data collection, using a "constant comparative process" associated with grounded theory.[11] After each period in the field, I took detailed notes of the exchanges I observed. I wrote theoretical memos at least once a week, to note possible trends in the data and suggest areas where I should probe further. Following each interview, I wrote a memo highlighting the most important themes of the interview and noting any theory-generating quotes. After leaving the field, all interviews were transcribed and coded inductively using the software Atlas.ti, using a coding scheme that had emerged from coding the fieldnotes and reviews of the relevant literature.

I focused these fieldnotes, memos, and coding on how evangelicals in these four congregations conducted "identity work." Following Lichterman, I define "identity work" as interactions where "people use words and gestures collectively and individually to articulate who they are and who they are not, making themselves 'social objects' in the civic arena, which they and others can then recognize and evaluate."[12] I coded fieldnotes to compare the U.S. and Canadian churches on two dimensions of collective identity: 1. *mapping* and 2. *public narrative*.

Evangelicals engage in mapping when they draw the symbolic boundaries of group identity to define "us" in opposition to "them."[13] Mapping also means locating the group's relationship to other groups.[14] Smith and colleagues argue that moral issues like abortion and homosexuality are used by evangelicals to draw symbolic boundaries of religious identity and map their group's relationship to other groups.

Collective identities are not just constructed by drawing boundaries between "us" and "them," but also by telling stories that cast a group within an unfolding plot that relates them to other characters, forces, and challenges.[15] For ethnic or subcultural minorities like evangelicals, these public narratives often elaborate the story of the group's relationship to the nation's story.[16] For example, Smith and Emerson describe how American evangelicals rally around the public narrative of America as a chosen nation that must be rescued from moral decline. This myth of a Christian nation helps evangelicals build a strong subcultural identity by mobilizing commitment and reinforcing group boundaries.[17] I coded the public narratives that evangelicals told in group interaction and interviews, looking for how Canadian narratives were similar or different from American ones.

I used the personal interviews to understand individual-level variation within each church in how people related these public narratives to their lives. First, I coded the interviews for instances of "boundary work," where respondents made distinctions between people like them and people not like them. Second, I analyzed each individual's biographical narrative, to see how they made sense of their current religious and political identity in terms of specific events, emotional experiences, and choices in their lives.[18] This life-course approach was important, since party identification tends to form in the first ten years of one's political life.[19] People are generally most influenced by political events that occur in their teenage years and young adulthood, and afterwards, change their partisanship much more rarely.[20] I used these biographical narratives to understand how different cohorts within this sample were formed by different experiences in this formative period. Third, I coded each individual's attitudes on a variety of issues, to see what moral intuitions they used to justify their positions and how they related to their religious identity and party identification.[21]

By coding along all three of these dimensions, I developed a typology of how different individuals mapped their religious identity in relationship to their party identification. Here, I bring together two very different uses of the "mapping" concept from political science and cultural sociology. In political science, Campbell's classic study of public opinion used the concept of "cognitive and affective maps" to describe how people felt closeness to or distance from different political parties.[22] More recent work has argued that party identification works much like other forms of group identity.[23] More recently, cultural sociologists have used this mapping metaphor to study the "social mindscapes"[24] of ethnic identity, national identity, and religious identity. I extended this approach to study how people map their party identification in group interaction and interviews.

Ethnography's strength is that it allows one to test and refine new theoretical frameworks, in an ongoing iteration between theory and data. However, a common criticism of ethnographic findings is that ethnographers are free to select anecdotes to support their preferred conclusions. To ensure that my theoretical conclusions were valid and not just plausible, I incorporated the following verification tactics into my research practice.[25] The first tactic was *checking for representativeness* by coding my fieldnotes and interviews and counting the frequency of different events and themes. The second verification tactic was *methodological triangulation*, combining ethnographic observation and in-depth interviews. Conducting interviews with a purposive sample of the congregational membership allowed me to gauge the representativeness of the attitudes and events that I noted during participant-observation (though the group dynamics of a congregation are more than the sum of its members' private views). The third tactic was *replicating findings* by checking whether patterns held across settings and over time. Since I observed at least five different group settings in each congregation, and two congregations in each country, I was able to query my fieldnotes and count the frequency of an event across settings or over time. The fourth tactic was looking for *negative evidence*, which suggested that there are no significant differences in how Canadian and American Evangelicals construct subcultural identity, or that Canadians exhibited characteristics that I attributed only to American evangelicals. The final tactic was to check out *rival explanations* for any causal relationships or cross-national differences that I thought I may have discovered in the field. This meant looking for ways that these patterns might be largely driven by top-down differences in political mobilization in Canada and the United States, or by media sources or institutions outside of the local congregation. This also meant constantly evaluating the role of other well-documented sources of individual variation in political skills and attitudes, including socioeconomic status, other political or civic affiliations, and sector of employment.[26]

Notes

Introduction

1. Balmer 2006, p. ix.
2. Wallis 2005.
3. Sullivan 2008.
4. Gushee 2008.
5. Guth et al. 2006. Evangelical support for the Republican Party was largely unchanged in 2008, although Obama lost evangelicals by a smaller margin than John Kerry did in 2004.
6. Smidt et al. 2010. It seems unlikely that this evangelical-conservative coalition will break up anytime soon, since white evangelicals were more important than ever to the Republican coalition in 2008. As other Republican constituencies shrink, particularly the white working class, conservatives are sure to fight even harder to keep evangelicals loyal.
7. Green 2008; Lugo et al. 2008.
8. Ammerman and Farnsley 1997; Bartkowski 2001; Becker 1999; Edgell 2006; Wellman 2008.
9. Beyerlein and Chaves 2003.
10. This recurring finding has never sunk in among pundits: that many of the iconic figures of the Christian Right have long been relatively unpopular, even among people who agree with their stands on many issues (Hunter 1987; Jelen 1992; Smith 2000).
11. Beyerlein and Chaves 2003.
12. Beyerlein and Chaves (2003) suggest several possible explanations for these differences: the nature of the issues that different religious groups are concerned with, the preferred political strategies of national leaders within different traditions, long-term religious differences of political style and strategic repertoire, variations across religious traditions in clergy-lay relations, or in differences among religious groups in proximity to political establishments. I will explore these different possibilities further in chapter 4.
13. William Sewell first coined the phrase "thin coherence" in his essay (1999). Paul DiMaggio discusses a similar concept using the term "limited coherence" (DiMaggio 1997, p. 277). This middle position in the study of culture draws together multiple streams from psychology, social movement research, and cultural sociology, as discussed by Amin Ghaziani and Delia Baldassarri (2011).
14. Mehta and Winship 2010.
15. Wuthnow 1988.

16. Farr and Moscovici 1984; Herberg 1955.

17. Dionne and Galston 2010.

18. Djupe 2000; Hoge, Johnson and Luidens 1995; Lazerwitz 1995; Loveland 2003; Sherkat 2001. It should be noted that the main source of evangelical vitality in the late twentieth century has been this group's higher birth rate and higher retention rate than mainline denominations. More Americans are not switching from mainline to conservative Protestant churches than they did earlier in the twentieth century. Religious identity in the United States is increasingly understood as a personal choice rather than an ascribed ethnoreligious membership. However, most people who "choose" evangelicalism as teenagers and adults were raised in this tradition (Hout, Greeley, and Wilde 2001).

19. Bebbington 1989.

20. Woodberry and Smith 1998. Since this book addresses the complex relationship between theological conservatism and political conservatism within everyday religious practice, using the term "conservative Protestant" would require me to constantly clarify this distinction.

21. White evangelicals stand out as the most conservative Christian group, with the exception of Mormons, whose complex relationship to American Protestantism deserves to be considered separately (Layman and Green 2005).

22. Campbell 2007.

23. Here, I am referring to three classic ways of measuring the impact of religion: Believing, belonging, and behaving (Leege and Kellstedt 1993). Throughout the book, I follow the typology of religious traditions developed by Steensland et al. (2000). This typology distinguishes white Conservative Protestants from Catholics, mainline Protestants, and Black Protestants. Unlike Steensland et al., I use the term "evangelical" as an umbrella term for theologically conservative Protestants, to avoid confusion between the theological and political meanings of conservatism.

24. This contrast between "thin" and "thick" coherence comes from the work of William Sewell at the overlap between anthropology and cultural sociology (Sewell 1999). Political scientists use the analogous concept of "constraint" to describe different levels of coherence within political ideology and attitudes (Converse 1964). Some individual's political attitudes exhibit high constraint (e.g., internal structure and coherence), while others exhibit low constraint (e.g., incoherence, ambivalence, and lack of internal structure). For example, a patriarchal model of the nuclear family may be linked to economic attitudes for some individuals but not others (Barker and Tinnick 2006).

25. Mehta and Winship 2010.

26. Hunter 1991, 1994.

27. This summary is a direct paraphrase of Hunter's original formulation, drawing particularly on pp. 108–14 (1991).

28. On page 118, Hunter (1991) argues that these differences in political philosophy cannot be reduce to social rank, because this new divide pits two groups of "new class" knowledge workers against itself. "In this sense, the conflict is prepolitical and it precedes class. What ultimately explains the realignment in America's public culture are allegiances to different formulations and sources of

moral authority." This idea has been extended in cultural sociology by drawing on new findings in cognitive science (Vaisey 2008).

29. Williams 2007.

30. Swidler 1986, 2001.

31. This body of literature includes congregational fieldwork, survey research, and community-level case studies (Greeley and Hout 2006; Djupe and Gilbert 2009). The same phenomenon is found in international contexts. For example, David Smilde rejects the notion of evangelicalism as a coherent "moral order," showing how individuals exercise cultural agency in their own religious conversions (Smilde 2007). He finds that the evangelical "toolkit" or "repertoire" can be assembled into different political combinations, as in the case of Venezuelan evangelicals who support Hugo Chavez as a godly man, even as evangelical-based parties in their country attempt to mobilize their churches for a competing candidate (Smilde 2004).

32. Gallagher and Smith 1999; Gallagher 2003.

33. Throughout the book, I will use the term "pro-life" to describe movements that seek to criminalize the practice of abortion, and "pro-choice" to describe movements that support access to this medical procedure. It is difficult to describe these movements in neutral terms, so I simply use the terms that participants themselves use to describe their movement's goals.

34. Williams and Blackburn 1996. In subsequent chapters, I show how Christian nationalism works as a shared schema or cultural anchor that links religion to conservative politics for different individuals. However, individual evangelicals pour their own meanings into this general narrative, by relating it in different ways to their personal experience or religious testimony. This parallels the way that the pro-life movement itself promotes a particular set of shared schemas, but individual pro-life activists pour their own meanings into them to give them particular resonance.

35. Dillon 1996.

36. Luker 1984.

37. Multiple studies of the pro-life movement have reached this conclusion, e.g., Munson (2008).

38. Shields 2009.

39. Davis and Robinson 1996; Wolfe 1998. A recurring finding in voting research is that only the most politically sophisticated voters make choices in terms of coherent worldviews or political ideologies, and even then inconsistently (Campbell et al. 1960; Converse 1964; Delli Carpini and Keeter 1996; Miller and Shanks 1996).

40. Smith 2000; Wolfe 1998.

41. At the level of individual attitudes, polarization is defined as constraint across issue domains, building on the classic work of Philip Converse (1964). Politically active individuals, often serving as opinion leaders, exhibit higher ideological constraint than other Americans (Abramowitz and Saunders 2008; Layman and Carsey 2002). This distinction figures heavily in this book's sociological account of opinion leadership.

42. Emerson and Smith 2000; Greeley and Hout 2006.

43. Andersen and Heath 2003.

44. Political scientists describe the processes that link religion and politics in terms of horizontal and vertical constraint. *Horizontal constraint* connects different elements of beliefs, values, and policy preferences to one another in a socially constructed package. *Vertical constraint* links people's values, beliefs, identities, and experiences to their policy preferences and evaluation of political parties and candidates, and ultimately to their political behavior (Carmines and Stimson 1989; Converse 1964). Political sociologists call these "cognitive" and "relational" mechanisms, respectively (McAdam, Tarrow, and Tilly 2001; Tilly 2001).

45. This critique is informed by Schattschneider's classic treatise on how elites determine which social boundaries and material struggles become politicized, and by extension, which political "preferences" become most salient for individuals (Schattschneider 1960).

46. Fiorina, Abrams, and Pope 2006; Layman 2001; Leege 2002.

47. Layman and Green 2005.

48. Regnerus, Sikkink, and Smith 1999; Wuthnow 1988. The role of special interest groups is central to Wuthnow's classic account of religious restructuring.

49. Beyerlein and Chaves 2003; Guth et al. 1997; Guth et al. 2003; Rozell and Wilcox 1997; Welch et al. 1993.

50. Wilcox and Larson 2006.

51. Hunter 1991, p. 160.

52. Political scholars are increasingly realizing that political divides may actually be driving religious trends, rather than the other way around (Patrikios 2008).

53. Balmer 2006.

54. Ammerman 1990.

55. Though denominations matter within evangelicalism, power within these denominations runs along lines of congregational clout: the most powerful churches are the largest churches. For example, even the Southern Baptist Convention, the nation's largest Protestant denomination, is largely organized within autonomous local churches. When conservative activists took over the denomination, their largest advantage against liberals and moderates was that they had better connections to local congregations. See Ammerman 1990.

56. Bartkowski 2004; Gallagher and Smith 1999; Hendershot 2004. Historian Robert Orsi influentially illuminated the worlds of lived religion as a topic of study (Orsi 1998).

57. This point is made by studies of how people become converted to deviant religious groups or the kind of new religions formerly known as cults. A recurring finding is that people come to accept cultic or deviant belief following a long process of growing social involvement with the group's members (Balch 1984; Stark and Bainbridge 1985). As new participants learn to perform roles associated with group membership, their beliefs gradually change to fit the group's ideology (Finney 1978). Ongoing commitment to these beliefs is reinforced by regular social interaction with group members, which provide therapies to still doubts, rituals that reiterate beliefs, and ideological legitimations that confirm beliefs. Together, these elements compose what Berger calls a "plausibility structure" (Berger 1970).

58. Here I draw on the symbolic-interactionist tradition in sociology. This research tradition insists that people actively make sense of their social worlds, in ways that are not fully determined by their structural roles, larger cultural discourses, or institutional settings (Becker 1982; Fine 2003).

59. My approach draws on a classic insight of symbolic-interactionism that if people define situations as real, they are real in their consequences (Garfinkel 1967). But I also deviate from the symbolic-interactionist tradition, in seeking to explain stability within social life, rather than contingency in the negotiation of meaning.

60. The work of James K. Wellman is particularly enlightening on this regard. Even in the Pacific Northwest, he found that even when evangelicals expressed political attitudes that diverged from the Republican Party, they still felt compelled to vote Republican on the basis of non-negotiable moral issues (Wellman 2008).

61. As a result, symbolic systems can still have a constraining effect on individual agency, even if they are not perfectly coherent or consensually shared (Sewell 1999, pp. 50–51).

62. Here, I borrow from Anne Kane's (1991) framing of the analytic autonomy of culture, and the relationship between culture, structure, and agency.

63. Jelen 1992, 1993.

64. Iannaccone 1988.

65. In sociology, important work on network homophily includes Hogg and Hains 1996; Ragin 2000; McPherson, Smith-Lovin, and Cook 2001. This book's ethnographic approach differs from the survey-based tradition in political science that was pioneered by the Columbia school (Hayward and Elliott 2011; Quintelier, Stolle, and Harell 2011).

66. Harrington and Fine 2000; Williams 2005. Scott McClurg has argued that the political content of social interaction is an important predictor of political participation; not just civic skills or resources or the structural characteristics of networks, but the content of group interactions that occur within networks and civic organizations (McClurg 2003, 2006). Traditional network analysis is limited by an oversocialized view of human beings, in which people are acted on by networks rather than acting on and through them (Gould 1995; Pachucki and Breiger 2010). For nuanced analyses of churches and political action, see Djupe and Gilbert 2009; Pattillo-McCoy 1998; Smith 2008.

67. Bean, Gonzalez, and Kaufman 2008.

68. Lipset 1990, p. xiii.

69. Berger, Davie, and Fokas 2008; Norris and Inglehart 2004.

70. Elliott and Miller 1987.

71. Margoshes 1999; McLeod and McLeod 1987; Shackleton 1975; Stewart 2003.

72. Noll 2007.

73. Bibby 1999.

74. Beyer 1997.

75. This range acknowledges that different studies in each country have operationalized evangelicals in different ways using available survey questions and different datasets. Using a 1998 module from the International Social Survey

Program, my co-authors and I found that 18.5 percent of Americans are regularly attending evangelicals, compared to 9 percent of Canadians. This represents a more conservative, lower-end estimate, because it incorporates views of the Bible, reports of a born-again experience, and regular church attendance (at least three times a month). Higher estimates include those who identify with theologically conservative traditions, even if they do not attend church regularly or report a born-again experience (Greeley and Hout 2006; Steensland et al. 2000).

76. In most modern Western democracies, secularization has undermined historic religious cleavages in politics, as religion has become marginalized within public life and religious identity has become less salient (Bruce 2003).

77. Bibby 2000, 2002.

78. Evangelicals consider themselves called to be "in but not of the world" (Smith 1998).

79. Reimer 2003.

80. Hoover et al. 2002.

81. Like Jonathan Malloy, I find that the prospects for an American-style Christian Right are over-exaggerated. For an updated comparison of evangelical politics in the United States and Canada, see Malloy (2009). But secular commentators have also tended to underestimate the sustained public role of evangelicalism in Canadian life, hence are repeatedly startled with this religious movement makes a public appearance. Based on what social scientists have learned since the 1980s about the ongoing public role of religion, it should not be surprising that Canada's largest group of active Protestants should have some kind of public role in Canadian public life. The question is not whether evangelicals will have a place at the table, but whether this place will be as a loyal voting block for a particular political party.

82. Gruending 2011; McDonald 2010.

83. Throughout this book, I use the term "religious nationalism" broadly, to refer to expressions of national identity that invoke the sacred, define cultural membership in "the nation" in religious terms, or justify the nation's founding principles in terms of religious authority. This usage differs from that of Robert Bellah, who initiated a flourishing debate over civil religion before abandoning the concept because of intractable definitional problems (Bellah and Hammond 1980). Bellah's concept of civil religion is defined in inherently normative terms, as a nonsectarian tradition that potentially unites Americans across sectarian and partisan divides, but also serves as the basis for prophetic critique. I find the term "religious nationalism" to be preferable because it does not carry the same normative baggage as the term civil religion. In some situations, religious nationalism can function as civil religion in Bellah's sense: as a sacred canopy that unites diverse groups across particular sectarian divides, to allow for democratic civility in spite of ongoing partisan divides. In others, religious nationalism is an ideology that one group uses to express cultural hegemony over other groups (Williams 2013). See also Cristi 2001b.

84. Here, I follow Dennis Owen, Kenneth Wald, and Samuel Hill's distinction between authoritarian and authority-minded cognitive commitments (Owen, Wald, and Hill 1991).

85. Gold and Russell 2007.

86. Carsey and Layman 2006; Hout and Fischer 2002.

87. Fifty years ago, political scientists were intensely concerned about group conformity as a force in political behavior, but this emphasis was lost as the field became increasingly individualistic and influenced by rational choice theory (Katz and Lazarsfeld 1955).

88. This helps us interpret a recurring quantitative finding that evangelical church membership is associated with Republican Party identification, in ways that are not explained by moral traditionalism, even though moral traditionalism is an important predictor of political conservatism. Based on their analysis of NES data, Steve Brint and Seth Abrutyn conclude that churches establish more commonsensical links between religion and partisanship independent of the kinds of thick moral worldviews that Hunter describes (Brint and Abrutyn 2010).

89. Lipset and Rokkan 1967.

90. Throughout the book, I will use the term "cultural map of politics" interchangeably with Campbell et al.'s more cumbersome phrase "cognitive and affective map of politics."

91. In political science, Campbell et al. famously articulated this insight by referencing the individual's "cognitive and affective map of politics." In their classic study *The American Voter*, the authors described this concept:

> In casting a vote the individual acts towards a world of politics in which he perceives the personalities, issues, and the parties and other groupings . . . The elements of politics that are visible to the electorate are not simply seen; they are evaluated as well . . . This mixture of cognition and evaluation, of belief and attitude, or percepts and affect is so complete that we will speak of the individual's cognitive and affective map of politics." (Campbell et al. 1960, p. 15)

See chapters 5 and 6 for further discussion of this concept.

92. Partisanship is more than the sum of one's policy preferences or a "running tally" of political assessments; it is a perceptual screen on how one interprets political "facts" and how one evaluates the performance of elected officials and parties (Bartels 2002). The same basic point is made by psychologists, who coined the term "cultural cognition" to describe how identity and culture shape how people evaluate seemingly objective, scientific facts like the scientific consensus around climate change (Kahan and Braman 2006).

93. This map can sometimes take on a geographical dimension, as among low- and moderate-income conservative voters in small cities who define "us" in opposition to urban minorities and elites (Walsh 2012).

94. Walsh 2004.

95. This connects to a larger debate in political science about whether party identification can serve as an "unmoved mover" of political behavior, or whether it is simply the sum of one's policy preferences (Johnston 2006). My qualitative approach does not directly engage this debate, but my findings are consistent with the notion that party identification works as a "moved mover," that it is informed by policy preferences, but it can also systematically bias how a voter evaluates new issues.

96. Following Green et al., I conceptualize party identification as a form of

group identity that works in a similar way to religious identity (Green, Palmquist, and Schickler 2002), based not simply on an evaluation of the political parties, but also a sense of identification as a member of a partisan group. Like Kathy Cramer Walsh (2004), I explore the subjective content of partisanship, and its social meaning in the lives of voters, rather than simply considering party identification as a variable. Throughout the book, I consistently use this concept of partisanship to refer to this cultural map of politics. This concept is broader than party identification, as an enduring self-identification with a particular party.

97. Malka and Lelkes 2010; Stimson 2004; Treier and Hillygus 2009.

98. In both countries, there are roughly similar levels of stable identification with a particular party, although it is an open question whether partisanship has the same meaning in Canada's multi-party system (Blais et al. 2001). In both countries, the overall percentage of voters who express party identification depends on how the question is asked, and there are important differences in how this variable is generally measured in each country.

99. Sewell's approach to the problem of coherence is enriched by Neil Gross's more recent formulation of mechanisms as practices (Gross 2009). Gross argues that "social mechanisms—the nuts and bolts processes by which cause and effect relationships in the social world come about—are best thought of as chains or aggregations of problem situations and the effects that ensue as a result of the habits actors use to resolve them" (p. 375) .

100. Ganz 2001; Polletta 1998a; Somers 1994. Public narrative emplots social action in a temporal, story-like cultural framework. Narratives typically contain sequential ordering, claims about causality, a cast of characters, a point of view, and normative evaluations.

101. This genre of storytelling helps to build urgency to act, by linking small, personal acts of piety to a larger plot. Michael Young finds that basic form of storytelling has long been a hallmark of evangelical social movements, on both the Right and the Left, as a template of "confessional protest" (Young 2006).

102. In the language of social movement research, this is classified as "diagnostic framing" (Benford and Snow 2000).

103. Lamont and Molnar 2002. Also see Smith et al. 1998.

104. These practices of identity-mapping are also found in social movements, and in social-psychological studies of small group interaction (Schwalbe and Mason-Schrock 1996; Snow et al. 1986, p. 1200).

105. Ann Mische has profitably examined civic leadership as a project: a creative process of imagining multiple futures for oneself, one's potential constituencies, and a broader social vision (Mische 2001).

106. These findings validate Elihu Katz and Paul Lazarsfeld's classic argument that there is a two-step process of influence between elites and mass publics, mediated by opinion leaders who reinforce elite messages within their personal networks (Katz and Lazarsfeld 1955).

107. I use the concept of "cultural anchors" to refer to narratives and schemas that organize internal heterogeneity within cultural toolkits (Ghaziani and Baldassarri 2011).

108. Beatty and Walter 1989; Djupe and Gilbert 2002; Verba, Schlozman, and Brady 1995.

109. Here, I build on an established body of work that examines the dynamics of political influence within local congregations and religious social networks. My contribution is to identify the cultural meanings at work within this political influence. Quantitative work has shown that these "network effects" or "congregational context effects" exist. Examples include Djupe and Gilbert 2009. Qualitative work is useful to understand the relational and cultural mechanisms at work within these networks and congregational contexts that produce these effects. I am indebted to the work of Roger Gould (1995) for this way of thinking about network effects.

110. Bellah and Hammond 1980; Bellah 1991, 1992.

111. Multiple literatures converge on this theme, leading to a confusing set of conceptual debates and competing typologies. In political science, a similar phenomenon is studied under the topic of "political religion" (Cristi 2001b). This political religion concept overlaps with the concept of Christian nationalism in the study of religion (Zubrzycki 2006, 2012). The fracturing of American religious nationalism into liberal and conservative narratives has been carefully documented by Wuthnow (1989).

112. Billig 1995.

113. Here, I build on an argument put forward by Delia Baldassarri and her collaborators (Baldassarri and Bearman 2007; Baldassarri and Gelman 2008; Baldassarri 2011).

114. Berry and Sobieraj 2013; Clifton 2004; Gibson 2004; Green, Rozell, and Wilcox 2001, 2000; Heaney 2010; Hetherington 2001; Teles 2008.

CHAPTER 1
COMPARING EVANGELICALS IN THE UNITED STATES AND CANADA

1. Fieldnotes, Highpoint Baptist trip to Mission Fest, Toronto, March 3, 2007.

2. Franklin is known in evangelical circles for his charity work through Samaritan's Purse, but is better known outside of evangelicalism for his close ties to the American Christian Right and his inflammatory statements about Islam.

3. Even the National Association of Evangelicals does not serve this function, although it was founded as an alternative to the Mainline National Council of Churches.

4. Guth and Fraser 1998.

5. Lipset and Rokkan introduced the idea of "social cleavages" to describe how party systems have developed around different lines of group-based conflict. These cleavages emerged from historical conflicts over industrialization, the consolidation of a national identity, urbanization, and church-state relations (Lipset and Rokkan 1967).Once party conflict becomes organized around one or more social cleavages, this cleavage shapes the construction of group identities, party competition, and linkages between major social institutions (Bartolini and Mair 1990; Brooks, Nieuwbeerta, and Manza 2006).

6. Inglehart 1990; Norris and Inglehart 2004.

7. Flanagan and Lee 2003.

8. For a discussion of out-of-wedlock births and divorce, see Mintz and Kel-

logg (1989). For historical analysis of how sexual norms changed rapidly in the late 1960s, see Allyn (2001) and Bailey (1999). For a discussion of American anxieties about the family in the 1970s, both inside and outside the evangelical subculture, see Zaretsky (2007). For a parallel discussion of cultural and generational change in the 1960s in Canada, see Owram (1996). This shift was particularly dramatic in Quebec, which started out more culturally traditional and ended up swinging far further toward secularism and changing family forms, becoming one of the most secular places on the planet (Gauvreau 2005).

9. Using oral histories of Lawrence, Kansas, Beth Bailey argues convincingly that the pill itself did not drive these sexual changes; rather, an important cultural shift occurred before the pill became widely available, that made doctors more willing to prescribe the pill to unmarried women—even doctors in smaller cities in states like Kansas (Bailey 1997).

10. Banaszak, Beckwith, and Rucht 2003; Brodie 1985; Wolbrecht 2002.

11. In 1962, the state of Illinois removed penalties for consensual sodomy from its criminal code. These developments shocked many North Americans, who grew up an era when homosexuality was treated as a crime that justified discrimination. The *Diagnostic and Statistical Manual of Mental Disorders* is published by the American Psychiatric Association; the first edition appeared in 1952 (Kane 2007).

12. Thirteen other states followed suit by 1972. Reforms in Colorado and other states were based on model legislation from the American Law Institute (Benson Gold 1990).

13. Trudeau's omnibus bill introduced major changes to the Criminal Code of Canada. Prior to 1969, taking steps to cause an abortion was an offense punishable by life imprisonment. *Criminal Code of Canada–Part VIII.3 Offences Against the Person and Reputation*, 287: "Every one who, with intent to procure the miscarriage of a female person, whether or not she is pregnant, uses any means for the purpose of carrying out his intention is guilty of an indictable offence and liable to imprisonment for life." After 1969, abortion was permitted in Canada if a three-doctor therapeutic abortion committee determined that the pregnancy endangered a woman's health (Brodie, Gavigan, and Jenson 1992).

14. Chaves 1994.

15. In August 1968, two prominent American evangelical leaders, Harold Ockenga and Harold Lindsell, invited twenty-five evangelical scholars to a Protestant Symposium on the Control of Human Reproduction. The consensus was that "therapeutic" abortion was acceptable in some cases, although "abortion-on-demand" was sinful (Williams 2012). Likewise, when the Canadian Federation of Evangelical Baptists campaigned against Bill C-150 in 1968 for decriminalizing sodomy, they said little about legalizing therapeutic abortion (Spraggett 1968).

16. Francis Schaeffer and his son launched a national campaign to get evangelicals to take an unequivocal pro-life position, overcoming large cultural and institutional obstacles to this position change (Williams 2010). In California, Darren Dochuk suggests that once this new position was forcefully articulated, it found strong support from the pews in California. For California evangelical pastors and laypeople who were already politicized around opposition to gay

rights and communism, it was intuitive to link abortion to a broader secular humanist agenda (Dochuk 2011).

17. Republican partisanship took a central role from the start of the Christian Right (Dochuk 2011). This point is also driven home by Williams (2010). Social movement scholars often remark on the internal cultural tensions and conflicts that threaten to tear movements apart. But within internally diverse social movements, it is still possible to coordinate action based on a more "thin" cultural coherence, provided by "cultural anchors" that hold together quite diverse concerns, issues, and frames (Ghaziani and Baldassarri 2011). My analysis here draws on the familiar social movement distinction between "diagnostic" and "prognostic" frames (Benford and Snow 2000).

18. Haussman 2005; Tatalovich 1997.

19. The more overtly right-wing expressions of evangelicalism were often ignored by academic researchers during this period, who tended to draw sharper contrasts between the United States and Canada. But this story is well-told by right-wing activists like Michael Wagner (2007). These gaps in the literature are understandable, given that both religion and right-wing politics are understudied topics in Canadian academia. Notable exceptions include Hoover (1997b).

20. Ganiel (2008) adapted the term "mediating" from Noll's characterization of Canadian evangelicals as a group that have "moderated extremes" in Canadian politics, interacting with government and non-evangelical groups with an "accommodating spirit" (Noll 2001, p. 253).

21. Smith et al. 1998, p. 97. For a comparative theory of evangelical politics, see Bruce 1998.

22. Working within the secularization paradigm, researchers often treat evangelicalism as a monolithic "orthodoxy" which reacts to the onslaughts of "modernity" through "Fundamentalist" political movements. But in Casanova's analysis, the U.S. Christian Right was a constructive reformulation of the evangelical tradition for a new modern context, more than a futile backlash against the inexorable forces of secularizing modernity (Casanova 1994).

23. This is a point cogently made by Christian Smith et al. (1998). For a comparative analysis of how different religious traditions have formulated their public presence as a majority, minority, or in a multi-faith setting, see Jelen and Wilcox 2002.

24. Ammerman 1990.

25. Though denominations matter within evangelicalism, power within these denominations runs along lines of congregational clout: the most powerful churches are the largest churches. For example, even the Southern Baptist Convention, the nation's largest Protestant denomination, is largely organized within autonomous local churches. When conservative activists took over the denomination, their largest advantage against liberals and moderates was that they had better connections to local congregations. See Ammerman 1990.

26. Bruce 1985. Steve Bruce concludes that this propensity to fission is ultimately a driver of secularization and the loss of religious authority in modern life (1990).

27. Wilcox 1992.

28. Throughout this narrative, I stress the proactive, rather than reactive, na-

ture of the post-1960s conservative revival. In their long-term vision to rally evangelicals and build a new political coalition, conservatives were not engaged in short-term, emotional "backlash." The New Christian Right of the 1980s was the product of decades of careful strategy and long-term institution-building, guided by a narrative of reclaiming America for Christian values. This narrative was backwards-looking to an ideal founding moment, but it was also increasingly forward-looking, particularly for neo-evangelicals who rejected the pessimistic, end-times prophetic preoccupations of their Fundamentalist forbears. See Dochuk 2006.

29. The concept of "abeyance structures" refers to how movements wait out disadvantageous periods of time, to re-emerge when circumstances are more favorable or new threats emerge (Schwartz 2006). The Christian Right grew stronger in abeyance, because their response was to build stronger parallel institutions and mobilize their grassroots constituency in preparation for a long-term political struggle. This long-term focus was likely helped by their dual concerns for building a religious subculture and for building a partisan coalition.

30. Handy 1966.

31. Kazin 2007.

32. Noll 1992.

33. Boyer 1992.

34. Shields 2011.

35. Carpenter 1980.

36. This point is made by Joel Carpenter: that withdrawal did not mean giving up a sense of rightful ownership (1980).

37. Even the New Deal became a Satanic plot in some more conspiratorial Fundamentalist theories (Sutton 2012). In a different religious stream, Pentecostals also called America back to God, and denounced political forces seen to advance a secularizing agenda. In 1934, California Pentecostal evangelist Aimee Semple McPherson launched a national tour of revival meetings that turned out one in fifty Americans (Sutton 2007). During this period of national fame, Semple McPherson privately considered alliances with particular politicians, indicating that the turn to politics among Pentecostals began long before the 1960s (Sutton 2005).

38. Hendershot 2007.

39. Balmer 1989.

40. Miller 2009, pp. 69–74.

41. See Darren Dochuk's analysis of "plain-folk religion" in southern evangelicalism. Many Southern evangelicals did not see themselves as "poor," but valorized their material struggles, celebrated egalitarianism, and defended their "plain-folk" identity in opposition to proud, elitist rich people (Dochuk 2011).

42. *Engel v. Vitale* (1962) and *Abington v. Schempp* (1963) (Williams 2010, pp. 64–66).

43. Southern Baptists enjoyed unquestioned dominance in their region's public schools; indeed, school prayer continued throughout the South long after these Supreme Court rulings. Given their cultural hegemony, Southern Baptists supported the separation of church and state doctrine as a firewall against Catholic influence. See Williams 2010, chap. 3.

44. The anti-semitism and far-right rhetoric of some Southern Fundamentalists also conflicted with the NAE's more respectable vision of engaged orthodoxy (Miller 2009).

45. Dochuk 2011, pp. 274–81. This colorblind evangelical language has continued to stymy cooperation between black and white American evangelicals (Emerson and Smith 2000). However, unlike Smith and Emerson, I do not trace this problem to evangelical theology or strictly theological resources like "accountable individualism." Colorblind conservatism resonated with an enduring theological focus on personal conversion, but it is impossible to understand their widespread appeal apart from the racialized history of white evangelicalism. These theological tools evolved as a spiritualized way to justify white privilege. They did not come from a racially neutral theological heritage—they were bundled together through the cultural brokerage performed by Billy Graham and a host of California-based evangelical elites who worked to find a compromise position on race that could satisfy both northern, southern, and Californian evangelical sensibilities. Billy Graham was often willing to make compromises with Southern racist sensibilities that he found personally offensive, in part because he was strongly motivated to broker a new partisan coalition that required support from southern evangelicals. Graham's complex role in brokering this evangelical compromise position on race is told by Miller (2009). The historical story presented here is more consonant with the critique of Emerson and Smith provided by Eric Tranby and Douglas Hartmann (2008).

46. Williams 2010.

47. By highlighting this collaboration between wealthy anti–New Deal businessmen and evangelicalism, I do not mean to suggest a crude Marxian analysis. Many of these businessmen shared the evangelical theology and moral traditionalism of the ministries that they sponsored. The relationship was more akin to Weber's "elective affinity" between class interest and religious ideas.

48. See Martin (1966, p. 152) for a discussion of the Christian Freedom Foundation and its hand in the early days of the Christian Right. See also Philips-Fein 2010 and Lichtman 2008.

49. See in particular Dochuk (2011, chap. 3) for specific examples of evangelical leaders who pitched their ministry ideas to donors by promising to make evangelicals into responsible conservatives. This was not entirely a cynical proposition, since many of these philanthropists were evangelicals who were true believers in the Gospel of Wealth. This long-term strategic vision is well-documented among conservative philanthropists of this era, who were forced to take a long-term view under conditions where they seemed doomed to be in a permanent minority position (Teles 2008).

50. Hendershot 2004.

51. Hendershot 2007.

52. Sara Diamond highlights the critical role of Christian radio in far-right politics; see chapter 1 (Diamond 1989).

53. Robertson, Falwell, and Dobson were all deeply influenced by the right-wing currents coming together in California. Despite their sectarian and regional differences, their shared ideology came from their shared cultural connec-

tions to Southern California's right-wing evangelical empire. See Dochuk 2011, pp. 303–4.

54. Like the nineteenth-century anti-vice crusades described by Nicola Beisel, these struggles were both symbolic and material, since they addressed parents' desires to reproduce desired attributes in children. Passing on Christianity morality was also a way of ensuring social and economic success, since young people gained entry to middle-class networks by establishing their good character (Beisel 1990, 1997).

55. It is overly simplistic to characterize white movement to the suburbs in the 1960s as "white flight." In the South, white Fundamentalist churches formed Christian academies after their vocal opposition to desegregation failed. For small-town evangelicals in the Deep South, private Christian schools may have symbolized a rejection of racial equality. But for suburban white evangelicals in California and the Sun Belt, this defense of a suburban, private, Christian world was understood through a discourse of racial innocence and alleged colorblindness, a discourse pioneered by leaders like Billy Graham and Ronald Reagan (Lassiter 2006; Self 2003).

56. Dochuk offers a sensitive, qualitative account of how Fundamentalists became suburban, and how they made sense of urban and suburban space in religious terms (Dochuk 2003).

57. Dochuk 2003, pp. 147–49.

58. Martin 1996, p. 173.

59. Griffith 2000.

60. For example, Tim and Beverly LaHaye started a travelling series of "Family Life Seminars" to "enrich good marriages, salvage bad ones, and prepare young people for marriage and lead people to Jesus Christ." Undated workshop advertisement for Family Life Seminars cited in Dochuk (2011, p. 351).

61. The anti-ERA movement was able to mobilize so quickly because it co-opted a well-established network of Christian women's ministries that provided social and religious support to traditional women across California, Texas, the Deep South, and the North (Brady and Tedin 1976; Critchlow 2005; Tedin 1978).

62. Fejes 2008.

63. Williams 2010, pp. 118–20.

64. Hunt, Benford, and Snow 1994.

65. It would be simplistic to say that this struggle between Southern Baptists was about abortion and theology; it was also a battle about whether the denomination could be enlisted in the culture war or whether it would remain politically diverse and nonpartisan in tone (Ammerman 1990, 1993; Leonard 1990; Sadler 1991).

66. Swartz 2012.

67. Martin 1996, p. 234. This is not to downplay the role of cultural change and meaningful theological disagreements over the role of women and biblical literalism in Southern Baptist conflict (Ammerman 1990, 1993). However, it is likely that these cultural, moral, and theological divides could have continued to co-exist within a diverse denominational context, without the strategic intervention of political activists who recognized their need for the SBC's infrastructure to mobilize evangelicals as a voting bloc.

68. Indeed, Christian Right often marshaled resources and strategic advice from the secular conservative world to attack its critics within evangelicalism and mainline Protestantism. For example, the Institute for Religion and Democracy framed itself as a conservative Christian alternative to the misguided politics of the mainline's National Council of Churches. However, the impetus and the money for the IRD came from secular conservative sources like the Smith Richard Foundation (Diamond 1989, p. 152).

69. Hankins 1998.

70. Throughout the book, I refer to each of these decades in more detail. Martin (1996) and Lienesch (1993) provide a comprehensive history of the Christian Right from the late 1970s to the early 1990s. Another wave of scholarship follows the Christian Right through the 1990s and early 2000s (Gilgoff 2008; Green, Rozell, and Wilcox 2000; Rozell and Wilcox 1997).

71. For a discussion of Protestant moral reform movements during this period, see Valverde 1991.

72. Christie and Gauvreau 1996. While American Protestants sorted themselves into a two-party system after the Fundamentalist-liberal controversy, the divide between Canadian modernists and fundamentalists was less severe, and Canadian Protestants did not sort completely into two rival camps.

73. Gauvreau and Christie 2003.

74. For example, A. B. Simpson, the Canadian founder of the Christian Alliance, began his ministry with a strong interest in Christian social work. But by 1911, Simpson had embraced a pessimistic, premillennial view of the end-times, and taken up ranting against socialism as an expression of modernist theology (Simpson 1966 [1911], cited in Elliot 1994).

75. McLeod and McLeod 1987.

76. By contrast, California's labor movement developed an adversarial relationship with Southern Baptist and Pentecostal migrants to their state after World War II. California's progressive establishment quickly labeled southern migrants as a threat, rather than as a potential constituency. For a discussion of this unfolding culture war between labor and evangelicals in 1940s California, see chapter 4 of Dochuk (2011). For cross-regional comparisons in this antagonism between radical labor and traditional religion, see Christiano (1988). Canadian organized labor did not come into direct conflict with evangelicals in the same way that labor movements did in California, parts of the Northern United States, and in the South during Operation Dixie.

77. Cywinski 2011. In Quebec, labor unions developed around a Catholic identity, based on papal encyclicals rather than secular ideologies (Barnes 1958).

78. Quoted by Althouse 2009, p. 73.

79. From the 1930s through the 1950s, the United Church of Canada supported both social reforms and mass evangelism, and in 1958, welcomed a Billy Graham crusade. During this period, many theologically conservative Protestant groups continued to build separate institutions from the United Church of Canada, including fundamentalists, Mennonites, Pentecostals, Plymouth Brethren, and various Baptists. But there were few institutional connections that bridged these sectarian divides, to foster an alternative "evangelical" identity. When these

institutional connections existed, they were moderate and irenic in tone, following the pattern of British evangelicalism (Stackhouse 1991).

80. Schweitzer 2011.

81. Hoover 1997a.

82. This contrast between mediating versus partisanship leadership draws on Ann Mische's ethnography of Brazilian activists (Mische 2008). In theory, American evangelical organizations like the National Association of Evangelicals would also claim to be nonpartisan. Likewise, Billy Graham sought to avoid being labeled as a political operative, instead preferring to position himself as a purely spiritual figure. But when historians look at the behind-the-scenes behavior of NAE founders and Graham, they find that building a Republican-evangelical coalition was always a central goal for these leaders. Accordingly, the political issues taken up by the NAE and Billy Graham have been consistently cut to fit the needs of that partisan coalition. As a social scientist, I do not offer a moral critique that being part of a partisan coalition necessarily invalidates religious claims. But in the history of the Christian Right, it is clear that claiming to be "above" partisan politics is often used to enhance a leader's moral power or spiritual authority, regardless of their partisan commitment as revealed in behavior and behind-the-scenes leadership. See in particular Williams 2010 and Dochuk 2011.

83. History of the Evangelical Fellowship of Canada, published on the organization's website, http://www.evangelicalfellowship.ca/Page.aspx?pid=286. Accessed 11/14/2012.

84. Ganiel 2008. Ganiel adapted the term "mediating" from Noll's characterization of Canadian evangelicals as a group that have "moderated extremes" in Canadian politics, interacting with government and non-evangelical groups with an "accommodating spirit" (Noll 2001, p. 253). This concept is also adopted by Malloy 2009.

85. Brodie, Gavigan, and Jenson 1992.

86. Hoover 1997a.

87. Canadian multiculturalism did not threaten the cultural privilege of Anglo Protestant Canadians, because it enshrined them as the unmarked category who generously tolerated the diverse cultures of Quebec, First nations, and non-Anglo immigrants—with Quebec demoted to being one of three founding societies, more like an immigrant minority than a separate nation (Miedema 2005).

88. Kim 1993; Lipset 1990.

89. The EFC brought together a different mix of theologically conservative Protestants than American umbrella organizations like the National Association of Evangelicals (Hoover 1997a). For ethnic traditions like the Mennonites and Dutch Reformed, it was not so strange to engage in public life as one voice among many, because they had always been a countercultural minority. Mennonites and Dutch Reformed also had strong social justice traditions that had outlived the nineteenth century (Kniss 1996; Stackhouse 1991).

90. Author interview with Richard Cizik, December 20, 2012.

91. From the 1940s to the 1960s, the NAE played a critical role in the construction of the evangelical movement, by building a new coalition of denominations and parachurch ministries. But this membership strategy depended on rela-

tionships among organizations, and lacked a way to reach evangelicals in the pews directly. In both the U.S. and Canada, mainline Protestant groups fought to exclude evangelicals from the airwaves in the early twentieth century. The difference was that Canadian mainline groups were more successful in maintaining a monopoly over Protestant broadcasting. The history of American Christian broadcasting was shaped by federal regulatory battles (Boyer 1992, p. 106; Hangen 2002; Ward 1994).

92. These potential rivals included Renaissance Canada, the Canadian Family Action Coalition, the Canadian Center of Law and Justice, the Centre for Renewal of Public Policy, and Citizen Impact (Hoover 1997b).

93. Canadian evangelicals had tried to build sectarian Christian TV and radio empires throughout the twentieth century, but their efforts were consistently blocked by the Canadian Radio-television and Telecommunications Commission. From 1928 to 1993, the Canadian Radio-television and Telecommunications Commission had a strict policy of denying broadcasting licenses to sectarian religious broadcasters. Evangelical programs on Canadian radio and TV had to find their place within a multifaith or ecumenical lineup, rather than on a dedicated Christian station. In 1993, the CRTC reconsidered this policy and began considering licenses for single-faith broadcasting. But these licenses were quite restrictive and involved extensive government oversight. Canada still maintains "balance" regulations on radio and TV broadcasting that make it difficult for evangelicals to use these mediums for political advocacy. For example, many local evangelical broadcasters were denied the ability to use commercial advertising to finance their activities. These restrictive licenses seem intended to concede some rights to freedom of speech and religious expression, while keeping evangelicals from creating American-style media empires in Canada (Brooks 2003). The enforcement of "balance" has been a controversial issue for evangelical broadcasters, who object to the ways that religion is treated as an inherently controversial subject and target of regulation (Simpson 1985). In Canada, anxieties over national identity have played a role in these regulatory battles since the 1970s, as negative images of American televangelists were frequently mentioned by Canadian regulators as a threat to national unity (Cook and Ruggles 1992; Faassen 2011; Zolf and Taylor 1989).

94. Hoover and den Dulk note this cross-national difference in the relationship between Christian legal advocacy groups and Christian media empires, but consider it an anomaly rather than a significant piece of the puzzle (Hoover and den Dulk 2004). Focus on the Family radio programs had already taken on a partisan edge in the early 1990s, which attracted investigations by the Internal Revenue Service about their political lobbying activities. In 1992, James Dobson's Focus on the Family spun off the Family Research Council as a separate think tank to champion a conservative "family values" agenda. In 2004, James Dobson founded Focus Action as a separate 401(c)(4) to protect himself from IRS concerns about his political activities (Gilgoff 2008).

95. Layman, Carsey, and Horowitz 2006.

96. Schattschneider 1960.

97. Smith 2008; Staggenborg and Meyer 1998.

98. Ronald Landes describes two examples of these different federal arrange-

ments. For example, Calgary attempted to restrict prostitution in 1983, and Saskatchewan attempted to restrict abortion in 1984, but both of these efforts were ruled unconstitutional on jurisdictional grounds. This has hampered the ability of Christian Right forces to take advantage of areas of demographic strength, for example, in rural British Columbia or Alberta (Landes 1995).

99. Herman 1994. This laid the groundwork for the Supreme Court ruling in 2004 that legalized same-sex marriage, with no opportunity for provincial governments to resist the ruling (Smith 1999). Likewise, sexual education curricula are handled at the provincial level in Canada, instead of resting with local school boards as in the United States (Smylie, Maticka-Tyndale, and Boyd 2008).

100. While Canadian evangelicals mobilized to fight these rulings in court, they had few opportunities to follow up with electoral mobilization (Hoover and den Dulk 2004).

101. Smith and Tatalovich 2003; Studlar and Christensen 2006; Tatalovich 1997.

102. Grabb and Curtis 2005.

103. Secular voters in Canada document that they were a force earlier on in Canadian politics, whereas only now are they becoming a force in the United States (Hout and Fischer 2002).

104. This Christian Right infiltration was part of a more general far-right takeover of the Republican Party, which until the 1960s was solidly controlled by moderates (Kabaservice 2011). For a state-by-state comparison of the relationship between the Christian Right and moderate Republicans, see Green, Rozell, and Wilcox (2000) and Rozell and Wilcox (1997). In some states, Christian Right activists were embraced by state Republican Party organizations as welcome allies; in others, their involvement was perceived as a hostile takeover.

105. Horowitz 1966.

106. Farney (2009) analyzes how Progressive Conservative elites thought of moral issues as a matter of conscience, not as a legitimate subject for political debate. Comparing the United States to Great Britain, Steve Bruce and Christopher Soper point to Westminster systems that give greater power to party leaders that allow them to discipline dissenting voices (Bruce 1998; Soper 1994).

107. From 1969 to 1988, access to abortion was uneven across Canadian provinces and cities, as some committees would consider psychological health, while other committees refused almost all requests. After these regulations were struck down, the Progressive Conservative bill proposed to limit abortion in a more permissive form that was intended to satisfy both pro-life and pro-choice activists. In the end, the abortion bill cleared the House of Commons by nine votes, but was defeated by a tie vote in the Senate (Pal 1991).

108. Polls 2012.

109. Jelen and Chandler 1994; Meyer and Staggenborg 1996.

110. Herman 1994.

111. Hexham 2002.

112. Andersen and Fetner 2008; Grabb and Curtis 2005.

113. Gidengil et al. 2005; Guth and Fraser 2001; Lusztig and Wilson 2005.

114. McTague 2010.

115. Both Paul Martin and his Liberal predecessor, Jean Chretien, publicly

changed their stance on gay marriage, in response to a series of court decisions that declared existing laws discriminatory (Malloy 2009).

116. Clarke et al. 2005.

117. Malloy 2011.

118. Malloy 2009.

119. Gidengil et al. 2009.

120. For an in-depth discussion of Harper's religious biography and how it informs his political views, see Mackey (2005b). As an adult convert with a relatively flexible approach to orthodoxy, Harper resembles many elite evangelicals studied in an American context (Lindsay 2007).

121. McDonald 2010.

122. Clarke et al. 2006.

123. This perspective on politics-as-spectacle has a long history in political science, and has also been influential in social movement research (Edelman 1964).

124. This is a more general pattern in the Harper government, to mix centrism with highly strategic efforts to polarize Canadians using issues like crime (Martin 2010). Here, the Canadian Right takes a page from the American Right's playbook, which has been intentional in pushing beyond the boundaries of current public opinion (Hacker and Pierson 2005).

125. Curry and MacDonald 2008; Dauda 2010; El Akkad 2008; Libin 2010; Warner 2010.

126. Dennis Gruending (2011) has documented the ways that Stephen Harper and Conservatives have made consistent use of "strict father" metaphors and dismissed their opponents as morally weak. His analysis is based on the influential work of George Lakoff (2002), who highlighted the role of family metaphors. Lakoff is discussed in more detail later in chapter 2.

127. From the 1970s to the 1990s, institutional barriers prevented Christian Right activists from mobilizing Canadian evangelicals along partisan, ideological lines as they did in the United States. Until Canada's adoption of the Charter in 1982, there were few access points for interest groups, since the Canadian government structure has historically concentrated power in the cabinet and bureaucracy. Because abortion and other so-called moral issues were kept off the political agenda, it was difficult for Christian Right organizations to mobilize resources, gain media attention, or build a constituency (Pross 1975; Tatalovich 1997).

128. Many Canadians were startled by the emergence of Christian Right interest groups to oppose gay marriage, because they assumed that evangelical activism was not part of their country's political culture. But Canadian evangelicals have a long history of political engagement, including efforts to ally this religious subculture with right-wing politics. This underscores a basic point of historical institutionalism: that political culture is contested, internally diverse, and channeled by trajectories of institutional development. Morality politics have followed different paths in the United States and Canada, but not because Canada's political culture rendered a culture war impossible.

129. Campbell 2007.

130. Smith 2008b.

131. In 2006, the NDP captured 27 percent of the evangelical vote in On-

tario, compared to the Conservative Party's 40 percent. Evangelical support for the Green Party more than doubled between 2003 and 2008 (Hutchinson and Hiemstra 2009).

132. Bruce 1998; Hoover 1997a; Noll, Bebbington, and Rawlyk 1994; Reimer 2003; Soper 1994.

133. Armstrong and Bernstein 2008.

134. As political scientist David Karol has pointed out, the relationship between parties and groups requires coalition management, carried out by interlocking networks of partisan and interest group activists. Indeed, it is more fruitful to think of "parties" as composed of these broader networks of interest groups, rather than distinguishing rigidly between the party apparatus and organized group interests (Karol 2009).

CHAPTER 2
THE BOUNDARIES OF EVANGELICAL IDENTITY

1. McRoberts 2004. Ganiel and Mitchell have written a thoughtful comparison of the advantages of religious "insider" and "outsider" ethnography. Both women have done ethnographic research on evangelicalism in Northern Ireland, one as a practicing American evangelical and the other as an agnostic from an Irish evangelical home (Ganiel and Mitchell 2006).

2. For an in-depth discussion of site selection, see the Methodological Appendix.

3. Hoover et al. 2002; Reimer 1995, 2003; Smith et al. 1998.

4. Ammerman and Farnsley 1997; Eiesland 2000; Stark and Finke 2000; Warner 1993.

5. Ammerman 1990, 1993; Rozell and Wilcox 1997.

6. This was an important consideration as I chose congregations. Many important churches in Hamilton were eliminated because they belonged to Canadian denominations that lacked a significant presence in American public life (for example, the Christian and Missionary Alliance). Likewise, there are many American denominations that lacked an obvious Canadian counterpart.

7. Wilcox and Larson 2006.

8. Lugo et al. 2006.

9. In obtaining informed consent, I agreed to change all names and identifying information of individuals and local churches. Accordingly, I describe the four congregations and individuals using pseudonyms.

10. For example, Omar McRoberts found that store-front churches in the same high-poverty neighborhood reworked the same holiness theology in different ways as they navigated their relationship to both "the world" and "the street" (McRoberts 2003).

11. For example, this generic "conservative Christianity" is constructed in similar ways in Christian schools that bring together various denominations with non-denominational and Independent churches (Wagner 1997).

12. Ammerman and Farnsley 1997; Ammerman 2005.

13. Becker 1999.

14. Ammerman 1993; Dougherty 2004; Finke 1994.

15. From personal experience, I could think of at least three Southern Baptist churches with similarly expressive, contemporary worship, so I interpreted these remarks as clues to how they defined their congregational identity, rather than empirical facts about their differences from Southern Baptists nationwide.

16. Becker 1999, p. 103.

17. Edgell 1999, p. 104.

18. Royal Rangers and Missionettes are generally gender-segregated, and are similar in format to the Boy and Girl Scouts. The main difference is that they are expressly evangelistic and teach children to identify with the global missions movement.

19. I quietly shuffled out of the room at this point, since the official class time was over. At the time, I was worried that if I stayed, they might somehow find out that I lacked this gift and ask to pray for me with the laying on of hands. A few months later, I determined that these fears had been unfounded. During my field-work, no one in either of the Pentecostal churches pushed me toward these kinds of practices or implied that I was less of a Christian because I lacked the "evidence of tongues."

20. I describe this emphasis as "positive" because leadership and members described homeschooling in hopeful and constructive terms, as a way of advancing the "kingdom," and not in terms of strict separation. I do not mean to claim that the consequences were uniformly positive, since that determination goes beyond the scope of my research. These projects of intensive parenting often had a sectarian flavor as well; in interviews, parents often expressed a concern to shield their children from negative influences in the public schools, and spoke of "the world" as a dangerous place. But I want to emphasize that homeschooling and Christian education were most commonly described as part of the church's positive mission as a self-described "family."

21. Williams and Blackburn 1996: 558–60.

22. This missional language has become increasingly common within Canadian evangelicalism; see Reimer 2012.

23. McCarthy 1993.

24. De Valk 1989.

25. Herman 1994.

26. Wells 2008.

27. Eyal Press describes this period of conflict over abortion in Buffalo, and the events leading up to Slepian's assassination. I rely on his historical reconstruction of events, but I am more critical of his interpretation of the religious organizations and motivations involved. Without empirical evidence, Press describes Pentecostal churches as a "refuge" from cultural change and as functional equivalents of labor unions—coming very close to a "religion as opiate of the masses" interpretation (Press 2006). Contrast Press's theoretical account of working-class religion with the empirical account of working-class religious lives recounted throughout the book.

28. Bibby 1993, p. 23; Bramadat and Seljak 2005.

29. Beyer 2005; Bramadat and Seljak 2005.

30. Smith et al. 1998.

31. Bielo 2009a; Smith 2011.

32. It is not uncommon for evangelical churches to negotiate mutual tolerance between premillennial and amillennial views of the end-times, even though this debate was quite divisive in decades past (Marti 2009, pp. 84–85).

33. Cox 2001; Wilkinson 2009.

34. Wilcox, Chaves, and Franz 2004; Wilcox 2004.

35. Within rational choice approaches to religion, it is theorized that strictness and resulting social stigma of such behavioral norms contributes to the strength of conservative churches (Iannaccone 1994). However, there is a loose coupling between sexual purity aspirations and sexual behavior of evangelical youth (Regnerus 2007).

36. Here, my findings duplicate the work of other scholars who have documented this loose coupling between gender discourse and practice within evangelicalism (Bartkowski 2001; Gallagher and Smith 1999; Gallagher 2003; Griffith 2000; Wilcox 2004).

37. Bartkowski and Ellison 1995.

38. Ellison, Bartkowski, and Segal 1996; Wilcox 1998.

39. Each of these three dimensions brings together diverse conceptualizations of overlapping concepts in social psychology, social movement theory, and organizational theory (Lichterman 2009, p. 851).

40. Erving Goffman (1967) pioneered this approach to the "interaction order," revealing how groups work to maintain a surface consensus in face-to-face interaction.

41. This finding parallels Dawn Moone's ethnography of two Methodist congregations, both of which avoided "political" talk about human sexuality. Rather, each congregation practiced an "everyday theology" of sexuality that could not be explicitly challenged without threatening the atmosphere of consensus that members associated with spirituality (Moon 2004).

42. Becker 1999.

43. Guth et al. 1997; Kellstedt and Green 2003.

44. Here, my findings duplicate those of James Wellman, who found this more complicated dynamic of pastoral "authority" in twenty-four evangelical churches in the Pacific Northwest (Wellman 2008).

45. Welch et al. 1993.

46. But it is also a mistake to think that evangelicals simply "use" their religious tools in instrumental terms, as they suit particular lines of action. In embracing the culture-as-toolkit paradigm, cultural sociologists have been too quick to reject the idea that culture motivates behavior, that culture can guide *ends* as well as *means*. This paradigm makes it difficult to explain why evangelicals are more strongly motivated by "moral issues" than by schemas that they share with other Americans. As Steven Vaisey has pointed out, people clearly internalize some cultural schemas more deeply than others. Culture can guide *ends* as well as *means*, when schemas shape the intuitive, moral intuitions that guide a person's conscious use of cultural repertoires. These unconscious habits of moral perception are part of what Pierre Bourdieu called the *habitus*, a cognitive-motivational system that shapes perception and choice (Vaisey 2009).

47. Edgell 2006; Gallagher and Smith 1999; Griffith 2000.

48. George Lakoff popularized the idea that conservative evangelical religion

teaches a "strict father" model of the parenting that leads to authoritarian political values (Lakoff 2002). Here, I agree with Brad Wilcox's assessment that evangelical Protestants are authoritative in their childrearing, rather than authoritarian (Wilcox 1998). Lakoff's framework does not stand up to empirical scrutiny, when I observe how self-identified religious and political conservatives actually practice parenting.

49. Surveying experimental evidence, Jonathan Haidt finds that people rarely make moral judgments on the basis of rational reflection, by considering their choices in light of abstract moral principles. Instead, most judgments are made in a flash of moral intuition, a gut-level, emotional response that occurs before our rational faculties have time to engage. When people engage in rational moral deliberation, then, it is usually to justify this initial flash of moral intuition. These gut-level moral intuitions motivate individuals to respond, even before they have time to engage in moral reasoning. But when anthropologists and other social scientists compare across societies, cultures, and groups, they find that not everyone relies on the same set of moral intuitions (Haidt 2007).

50. Haidt and his collaborators argue that people from modern, Western, secular backgrounds tend to rely on just two moral intuitions: *harm* and *fairness*. For example, moral intuitions about harm and care might be triggered if one saw a small child dart out in front of a car. Moral intuitions about fairness and reciprocity might be triggered if a basketball player breaks the rules, or if a free-riding co-worker does not carry their fair share of the workload (Haidt and Graham 2007).

51. D'Andrade 1995; Douglas 1970; Friedland 2002.

52. For example, American political conservatives are motivated by intuitions about harm and fairness. But they have other concerns about authority or in-group loyalty that potentially override these intuitions or motivate them to reason about harm and fairness differently.

53. Concerns about purity can motivate evangelicals to advocate for abstinence-only sex education that cultivates intuitions about purity in children, rather than relying solely on intuitions about harm and care (Luker 2006).

54. Hence, evangelicals respond emotionally to arguments that same-sex unions are wrong because they violate a sacred ideal, or because they undermine the authority of scripture. Anyone can understand these arguments in the abstract, but they only make intuitive sense if one has been socialized to rely upon traditional moral intuitions.

55. Reimer and Park 2001; Wolfe 1998. Throughout this book, I will argue that evangelicals are also deeply ambivalent about gay rights, in ways that already make it difficult for Christian Right elites to rally their core constituency against the expansion of marriage rights.

56. Here, I find that Sewell's general approach to the problem of coherence is enriched by Neil Gross's more recent formulation of mechanisms as practices (Gross 2009). Gross argues that "social mechanisms—the nuts and bolts processes by which cause and effect relationships in the social world come about—are best thought of as chains or aggregations of problem situations and the effects that ensue as a result of the habits actors use to resolve them" (375).

CHAPTER 3
TWO AMERICAN CHURCHES: PARTISANSHIP WITHOUT POLITICS

1. Lichterman 2009, p. 851. Here, I am indebted to Nina Eliasoph's analysis of how Americans "avoid politics" in a variety of local civic contexts (Eliasoph 1998).

2. Smith 2000, p. 6.

3. Eliasoph and Lichterman 2003. The notion of "culture in interaction" builds on Ann Swidler's insight that people draw on their cultural "repertoires" or "toolkits" in the course of practical action, in ways shaped by their social and institutional contexts (Swidler 1986). This way of studying culture is compatible with the "strong program" in cultural sociology in that it acknowledges the analytic autonomy of collective representations (Alexander 2003; Kane 1991). But instead of analyzing the internal content of these collective representations, I look at how these symbols, narratives, and frames are actually used in concrete interactions. This approach also builds on Alan Fine's ethnographic work in the tradition of small group research (Fine 1995).

4. Eliasoph and Lichterman 2003; Lichterman 2009.

5. Ammerman 1990; Martin 1996.

6. John 15: 18:20 in the Holman Christian Standard Bible, the version cited by the Southern Baptist Convention's Lifeway Curriculum: "If the world hates you, understand that it hated Me before it hated you. If you were of the world, the world would love [you as] its own. However, because you are not of the world, but I have chosen you out of it, the world hates you. Remember the word I spoke to you: 'A slave is not greater than his master.' If they persecuted Me, they will also persecute you. If they kept My word, they will also keep yours."

7. The phenomenon of "moral minimalism" in American life is a recurring theme in cultural sociology (Baumgartner 1988; Bellah et al. 1985; Eliasoph 1998).

8. In chapter 4, I will extend this analysis of Christian nationalism (Friedland 2001; Gorski 2000; Zubrzycki 2006), using Somers' notion of public narrative (Somers 1994).

9. Eliasoph and Lichterman's concept of group boundaries is informed by the social identity perspective in social psychology (Farr and Moscovici 1984; McCall and Simmons 1978; Stets and Burke 2000; Tajfel 1981), and its further elaboration by cultural sociology (Lamont and Molnar 2002; Pachucki, Pendergrass, and Lamont 2007).

10. This is a common theme in public discourse over teen pregnancy (Luker 1996).

11. Theologian Stanley Hauerwas has drawn connections between the prolife stance and the inclusion of people with disabilities, but this dimension is often absent from public debates over abortion (Hauerwas 1981).

12. These attributes arguably characterize mainstream American congregations more generally: pragmatism, focus on local concerns, conflict-avoidance, and a therapeutic, individualistic orientation toward religion. See Becker 1999; Madsen 2009; and Moon 2004.

13. Erzen 2006.

14. In June 2012, Exodus International, the national organization with which Ann was affiliated, formally announced that they would break ties with any efforts that claimed to "cure" homosexuality. This field of evangelical ministry has continued to rapidly evolve. Even within the evangelical community, there is a growing recognition that "reparative" therapy is rarely successful in changing sexual attraction toward the same sex. "Evangelicals Fight Over Therapy to 'Cure' Gays." National Public Radio, All Things Considered, July 6, 2012.

15. Fieldnotes, October 29, 2006. It was common for Lifeway to use different artifacts as aids to prayer. For example, they also hung photos of people from around the world, representing different nations that needed prayer. Inspired by a scene from the Christian movie *Facing the Giants*, they also hung drawings of lockers on the sanctuary walls to use as aids to prayer for different teenagers in the youth group.

16. For example, journalists like Michelle Goldberg (2006) have terrified secular readers with their descriptions of spiritual warfare.

17. These territorial practices of spiritual warfare are also described by Bartkowski and Regis (2003).

18. This anti-Masonism has a long history, carried forward more recently with Pentecostal discourses about "spiritual warfare" against cults (Ellis 2000; Kutolowski 1984).

19. Here, Jonathan referred to the story of Joshua, who led the Israelites into Canaan and laid siege to the town of Jericho (Joshua 6: 1–27).

20. In my fieldwork, Pentecostal and charismatic Christians often made a distinction between "the natural" and the "supernatural" dimensions of reality. "Seeing in the natural" means only seeing the material dimension of things, as opposed to seeing the supernatural reality made possible by God.

21. Fieldnotes, April 15, 2007.

22. Friedland and Hecht 1996.

23. Fieldnotes, May 20, 2007.

24. Harvey Cox calls this "radical embodiment," and it takes on a distinctive flavor within Pentecostal and charismatic traditions (Cox 2001; McRoberts 1999).

25. Alexander 2001.

26. I borrow the term "special sin" from Michael Young, who argues that the American social movement form has evangelical roots in the language of bearing witness against "special sins" like alcohol and slavery (Young 2006).

27. Because these stories involve personal information about "closeted" people who wish to remain unidentified within evangelical churches, I have respected my participants' requests for greater anonymity by not associating them to a particular participant. This is more than a methodological matter—it also demonstrates the practical challenges of talking publicly about homosexuality within the evangelical subculture.

28. There is growing scholarly interest in gay Christian identities, as well as the identity-conflict that these individuals and communities experience in relation to American religious institutions (Mahaffy 1996; Rodriguez and Ouellette 2000; Wilcox 2002).

29. Eliasoph and Lichterman 2003.

30. Erving Goffman coined this distinction between "front-" and "backstage" settings (Goffman 1959).

31. Lichterman 2008.

32. Group influence can work in the absence of reasons or deliberation. Elizabeth Suhay (2011) presents experimental evidence that people adjust their attitudes upon receiving cues about appropriate group attitudes, in the absence of rational persuasion.

33. Ideological identity (a self-categorization) is conceptually distinct from ideology (an integrated value system). In this case, participants may hold a strong "conservative" identity, even though they show a limited grasp of conservative ideology (Malka and Lelkes 2010).

34. Fieldnotes, May 15, 2007.

35. The history and continued reality of religious nationalism has been influentially discussed by Phil Gorski (2000), Anthony Smith (2003a), and Genevieve Zubrzycki (2006).

36. Djupe and Gilbert 2003; Smidt et al. 2003.

37. The National Sanctity of Human Life Day was first recognized by executive proclamation, issued by President Ronald Reagan in 1984. It was discontinued by President Clinton, and renewed by President George W. Bush in 2007. "Bush declares National Sanctity of Human Life Day." CNN.com. 2007–01–15. Retrieved 2007–10–05.

38. According to the National Congregations Study, about 10 percent of conservative Protestant churches circulate Christian Right voter guides. By comparison, mainline and Black Protestant churches are far more likely to host discussions about political issues and host candidates, whereas Catholic churches are far more likely to engage in collective protest (Beyerlein and Chaves 2003). See also Putnam and Campbell 2010.

39. Elacqua 2007–2008.

40. Before the 2004 elections, James Dobson had never endorsed a presidential candidate (Djupe and Olson 2008 [2003]). John C. Green (2006) has discussed the mobilization of "Patriot Pastors" in Ohio in the 2004 election.

41. Becker 1999; Djupe and Gilbert 2008.

42. Burack (2008) discusses the complexity of anti-gay rhetoric within Christian Right interest groups, and the diverse audiences and constituencies to which it is directed.

43. Tina Fetner (2008) describes how the gay rights movement has formed its identity in reaction to conservative Protestant activism. The Christian Right has become locked into an antagonistic relationship to the gay rights movement, where each side's moves are driven by the moves of the other, and where each side perceives the other as the aggressor and the initiator of the conflict.

44. For example, James Wellman (2008) discusses liberal Protestant disgust with "hate the sin, love the sinner" rhetoric toward gays and lesbians.

45. Fifty years ago, political scientists were intensely concerned about group conformity as a force in political behavior, but this emphasis was lost as the field became increasingly individualistic and influenced by rational choice theory.

46. This helps us interpret a recurring quantitative finding that evangelical church membership is associated with Republican Party identification, in ways

that are not explained by moral traditionalism, even though moral traditionalism is an important predictor of political conservatism. Churches establish more commonsensical links between religion and partisanship independent of the kinds of thick moral worldviews that Hunter describes (Brint and Abrutyn 2010).

CHAPTER 4
TWO CANADIAN CHURCHES: CIVIL RELIGION IN EXILE

1. In chapter 1, I discussed how the introduction of the "New Curriculum" was a lightning rod in the United Church, which alerted theologically conservative Protestants that this denomination could no longer be trusted as the steward of Canadian Protestant values (Schweitzer 2011).

2. Fieldnotes, Highpoint Baptist, March 14, 2007.

3. This metaphor of a "cognitive and affective map" of partisanship comes from the classic political science study "The American Voter" (Campbell et al. 1960).

4. In theological terms, this is referred to as a "missional" stance toward the culture, advocated by figures like Lesslie Newbigin (Guder and Barrett 1998; Newbigin 1989; Newbigin and Weston 2006).

5. Interestingly, the Quiet Revolution was not seen as a loss by evangelicals in this study. One former missionary recalled his memories as an evangelist to a formerly Catholic Quebec, where he was regularly jailed and had eggs thrown at him. When Quebec experienced rapid secularization in the 1960s, the influence of the Catholic Church declined—but so did the institutional barriers to evangelism. On balance, the Quiet Revolution created greater opportunities for Protestants in Quebec, not fewer (Gauvreau 2005; Grabb and Curtis 2005).

6. Wang 2006.

7. Fieldnotes, Highpoint Baptist, July 27, 2007.

8. "Day favours case-by-case approach to Canadians facing death penalty," the Canadian Press (reprinted by CBC News), March 14, 2008 (retrieved on December 14, 2008).

9. This network of evangelical elites is discussed in the Introduction and Conclusion. There is a divide between the social worlds of these evangelical conservative leaders and the worlds of local congregations where most rank-and-file evangelicals make sense of their religious identity. For a focused discussion on the separate world of evangelical Christian Right activists, see Mackey (2005a). To understand the theology and religious identity of figures like Stockwell Day and Stephen Harper, Canadian scholars might benefit from engagement with Michael Lindsay's work on evangelical elites (Lindsay 2007).

10. Fieldnotes, January 14, 2007.

11. Goldberg 2006; Hedges 2006.

12. McDonald 2010.

13. In Aristotle's terms, this image functions as an enthymeme, standing in for a larger historical narrative or collective memory that would be familiar to a Canadian evangelical audience (Aristotle 2007, p. 219).

14. Olick and Robbins 1998; Schwartz and Schuman 2005a; Zerubavel 2003.

15. In the social movement literature, this process is referred to as "boundary

framing" or "adversarial framing" (Gamson 1995; Hunt, Benford, and Snow 1994).

16. This metaphor of a "cognitive and affective map" of partisanship comes from the classic political science study "The American Voter" (Campbell et al. 1960).

17. In 2004, the Canadian Radio-television and Telecommunications Commission approved an application to bring Fox News to Canada. "CRTC approves Fox News for Canada," cbc.ca. 2004–11–18. Archived from the original on 2010–11–22. Retrieved 2012–03–25.

18. Anti-Mormon attitudes are common in American evangelicalism, despite the strong political alliances between evangelicals and Mormons within the Republican coalition (Introvigne 1994). This internal conflict had to be skillfully bridged during the 2012 presidential candidacy of Mitt Romney. For example, the Billy Graham Evangelistic Association scrubbed its website of anti-Mormon statements promptly before expressing support for Romney as a man of God (Haws 2013).

19. Barker, Hurwitz, and Nelson 2008; Froese and Mencken 2009.

20. Fieldnotes, November 12, 2006.

21. Even the most liberal or left-leaning of my respondents expressing pride in Canada's military efforts, particularly Canada's identity as a "peacekeeper."

22. This pattern has been documented in other American evangelical churches. For example, both U.S. congregations sounded very much like City Church, a majority-white Baptist church congregation that Penny Edgell studied in Oak Park, Illinois. City Church adapted to changing neighborhood demographics by drawing on their history of global missions, and finally developed a new congregational identity around the model of a "New Testament church" that bridged ethnic and cultural differences. Like City Church, both American churches had "mined their tradition" to bridge ethnic, racial, and national boundaries, though both remained majority white, located in majority-white neighborhoods. Both American churches engaged in active outreach to immigrants in their communities, which involved talk about respecting diversity and loving people across cultural boundaries. Both American churches hosted visiting missionaries, to encourage members to take a transnational perspective on the work of Christians all over the globe (Becker 1999).

23. Indeed, themes of national identity are more readily linked to broader civic engagement and political issues outside the church, when compared to interpersonal or relational projects (Huddy and Khatib 2007). In the United States, there is a niche for multicultural churches like Mosaic in Los Angeles (Marti 2009). This is different in Canada—it is not a niche, it is the predominant narrative that white evangelicals are getting from the wider field of Canadian evangelicalism. This was not a "niche" identity specific to the congregation, defined by contrast with other evangelical churches. This was a narrative they took from the wider field of Canadian evangelicalism.

24. Examples include Asian American evangelicals (Ecklund 2005; Emerson and Woo 2006) and Hispanic evangelicals (Martínez 2011).

25. Marti 2009.

26. Miedema 2005.

27. Wuthnow 1988, pp. 241–67. A contrasting trend in Canada has been noted by other observers of contemporary Canadian civil religion (Hiller 2000; Miedema 2005). Highlighting how Canadian Anglo evangelicals practice Christian nationalism, I challenge the idea that Canada has no civil religion at all (Kim 1993).

28. Important exceptions include the now-defunct Reform Party, which sought to make culture a private choice, to be carried out with personal resources rather than government support (Laycock 2002). The debate over multiculturalism also looks completely different in Quebec, where there is a perceived conflict between official bilingualism and the "dilution" of Quebec's unique status with other cultural claims (Kymlicka 1998).

29. Reimer and Wilkinson (under review). The "Canadian Evangelical Churches Study" (CECS) included interviews with the lead pastors (the senior pastor or only pastor) of 478 evangelical congregations by phone in 2009. These phone interviews were completed by Advitek, a data collection firm in Toronto, in both English and French (the English version of the survey is given below. The response rate for these interviews was roughly 40 percent. Advitek also performed 100 youth and children's pastor phone interviews in these same congregations. The congregations contacted were randomly selected from lists of congregations provided by denominational leaders. The denominations were the Pentecostal Assemblies of Canada (PAOC), the Christian Reformed Church (CRC), the Mennonite Brethren (MB), the Christian and Missionary Alliance (CMA), and the four Baptist Conventions—the Convention of Atlantic Baptist Churches (CABC), the Baptist Convention of Ontario and Quebec (CBOQ), the Canadian Baptists of Western Canada (CBWC), and the French Baptist Union/Union D'églises Baptistes Françaises au Canada (FBU). Prior to the phone interviews, the authors conducted face-to-face interviews with fifty other lead pastors in major regions across Canada (Maritimes, Toronto area, Calgary area, and Vancouver area). Finally, they interviewed the national leaders from the denominations in our study.

30. Reimer 2011. While these comparisons use different survey questions, this is the best comparison that is possible given existing longitudinal sources. It is particularly significant that U.S. and Canadian attitudes have diverged since 2000, in response to the gay marriage debates in their respective countries.

CHAPTER 5
EVANGELICALS, ECONOMIC CONSERVATISM, AND NATIONAL IDENTITY

1. Olasky 2000; Sager 2010.
2. Barker and Carman 2000; Brooks 2006.
3. Andersen and Heath 2003; Norris and Inglehart 2004.
4. Bean, Gonzalez, and Kaufman 2008; Hoover et al. 2002; Malloy 2009; Reimer 2003.
5. Emerson and Smith 2000.
6. Hart 1992; McRoberts 2003; Steensland 2002.
7. Barker and Carman 2000; Greeley and Hout 2006; Pyle 1993.
8. Layman and Green 2005.
9. Will and Cochran 1995; Wilson 1999.

10. Hempel and Bartkowski 2008.

11. Brooks 2006; Regnerus, Smith, and Sikkink 1998.

12. Swidler 2001, p. 206.

13. Ghaziani and Baldassarri 2011.

14. Edgell and Tranby 2010; Edgell 2012. Building on debates about social capital, many scholars have investigated the bridging role of religion (Beyerlein and Hipp 2006; Brown and Brown 2003; Putnam and Campbell 2010. But it is also important to acknowledge the exclusionary consequences of religion (Beyerlein and Hipp 2005; Blanchard 2007; Edgell, Gerteis, and Hartmann 2006.

15. Bellah and Hammond 1980l; Cristi 2001a; Friedland 2001; Gorski 2000; Zubrzycki 2006.

16. Brubaker 1994; Lamont and Molnar 2002. Instead, the subfield has focused on measures of religious *belief, belonging,* and *behavior* as the primary mechanisms that shape civic engagement or political attitudes. See Leege and Kellstedt 1993.

17. DiMaggio 1997, p. 277; Sewell 1999, pp. 49–50.

18. Hartz 1955.

19. Lipset 1990.

20. Almond and Verba 1963; Lipset 1963a.

21. Berezin 1997; Orloff 1993; Skocpol 1992.

22. Alexander 2003; Kane 1991.

23. Swidler 1986.

24. Boychuk 2008; Kaufman 2009; Smith 2008c.

25. Olick and Robbins 1998; Schwartz 1982.

26. Lamont and Thévenot 2000.

27. Grabb and Curtis 2005, p. 192.

28. Grabb and Curtis 2005, p. 182.

29. Andersen and Curtis 2011.

30. Inglehart and Baker 2000.

31. Brooks and Manza 2007.

32. Ghaziani and Baldassarri 2011.

33. Spillman 1997, 1998.

34. Olick and Robbins 1998; Schwartz and Schuman 2005b.

35. Béland and Lecours 2005; Brooks and Manza 2007.

36. Larsen 2006; Rothstein 1998.

37. Gilens 1999; Mettler 2002; Schneider and Ingram 2005; Schram, Soss, and Fording 2003.

38. Anderson 1983; Handler and Hasenfeld 1991; Lamont and Molnar 2002; Lamont 2000.

39. Esping-Andersen 1990.

40. Banting, Hoberg, and Simeon 1997; Myles 1998.

41. Mohr 1994; Steensland 2006.

42. Rothstein 1998; Schneider and Ingram 2005.

43. Hays 2003.

44. Soss and Schram 2007.

45. Hudson and Coukos 2005; Morone 2003; Somers and Block 2005.

46. Brodie 2002.
47. Béland and Lecours 2005, p. 222.
48. Maioni 1998.
49. DeWitt, Béland, and Berkowitz 2008; Howard 2007.
50. Rice and Prince 2000.
51. Zuberi 2006.
52. Fraser and Gordon 1998; Katz 1986.
53. Brubaker 2006; Lamont 2000.
54. Bellah 1975; Edgell and Tranby 2010; Wuthnow 1988, pp. 241–67.
55. Gorski 2000; Smith 2003a; Zubrzycki 2006.
56. Smith 2000; Wolfe 1998.
57. Edgell and Tranby 2010; McDaniel, Nooruddin, and Shortle 2011.
58. More commonly, researchers use measures of religious networks, congregational attendance, and civic activities to assess whether religious participation generates "bonding" or "bridging" forms of social capital (Campbell 2004). As Paul Lichterman has demonstrated, we should not assume that particular meanings about "bonding" or "bridging" will naturally emerge from particular kinds of religious networks or civic activities (Lichterman 2005). By comparing similar groups in different national contexts, we gain greater analytical leverage on how religious traditions imagine broader forms of cultural membership (Zubrzycki 2012).
59. Chaves and Tsitsos 2001; Sider and Unruh 2001; Wuthnow 1999.
60. Ammerman 2005; White and Hopkins 1976.
61. Elisha 2008.
62. Lichterman 2008.
63. Elisha 2008.
64. Kymlicka and Banting 2006.
65. Fine 1995.
66. See Ammerman 2007.
67. Chaves 2004; Wuthnow 2004.
68. Zerubavel 2003.
69. Mettler 2002; Mettler and Soss 2004; Schneider and Ingram 2005; Steensland 2006; Zerubavel 2003.
70. Cnaan and Handy 2000.
71. Billig 1995.
72. Hinojosa and Park 2004.
73. Edgell and Tranby 2007; Tranby and Hartmann 2008.
74. Cromartie 2003, Olasky 1992; Olasky and Gingrich 1996.
75. Skocpol 1997.

CHAPTER 6
CAPTAINS IN THE CULTURE WAR

1. Eveland and Kleinman 2013.
2. The role of lay leaders has been documented in state-level studies of party activists; for example, lay leaders played an important role in the Christian Coa-

lition's local strategy (Green, Rozell, and Wilcox 2000; Rozell and Wilcox 1997). What is missing is the relationship between more politically engaged lay activists, who operate within party politics or social movements, and their local churches.

3. Haidt 2007; Vaisey 2009.

4. Both Wuthnow and Hunter highlighted the role of parachurch ministries in the culture wars.

5. David Smilde shows that this is a common conversion narrative among Venezuelan evangelicals. One common narrative follows the form "I was lost but now am found": the convert emphasizes his or her previous sin and trouble, to create a dramatic contrast between the previous "lostness" and current transformed life. But evangelicals often use a second kind of conversion narrative, where they emphasize God's agency in miraculously bringing them into the fold. (Smilde 2007).

6. Munson 2008.

7. Spitzer had not yet been implicated in a prostitution scandal, which broke after my fieldwork had concluded.

8. These individuals can be considered closer partisans (Dennis 1992; Keith et al. 1992).

9. Ann does not identify as "ex-gay" for two reasons: first, she never "came out" as a lesbian, even to her close friends, and second, her same-sex attraction has not gone away. Rather, Ann believes that God intervened to keep her from becoming entrenched in a gay lifestyle. This is consistent with Erzen's findings on the complexity of religious identity within the "ex-gay" movement (Erzen 2006).

10. Biographical narrative can become linked to public narratives, when individuals situate a personal story of transformation within a broader public story about a movement, community, group, or nation (Ganz 2001; McAdams 2006).

11. Young 2002. Michael Lienesch has documented the same confessional narrative structure among Christian Right elite activists (Lienesch 1993, chap. 1).

12. Smilde 2007. For example, David Smilde argues that people sometimes put themselves in religious subcultures because they already want to quit alcohol, and so put themselves in a setting that will reinforce that. This instrumentality is hidden from themselves, however, through narratives that posit God's irresistible call to them that precedes their own choice.

13. Here I am describing Ann's own attributions of "compassion" within her biographical narrative, rather than making a normative judgment about what constitutes a "truly" compassionate response. Supporters of gay rights might identify other factors contributing to Ann's distress: for example, the anticipated rejection of family and friends, the lack of legal recognition for same-sex relationships, or the absence of pro-gay faith communities which could have affirmed moral boundaries against infidelity. However, these factors are not part of Ann's narrative construction of her experience, and so are not considered as part of what constitutes "compassion" from her perspective.

14. As evangelical historian has commented, this miracle motif has been a barrier to evangelical social concern, by occluding the need for systemic change (Nash 1972).

15. If we think of the Christian Right as a movement to shape the content of

evangelical orthodoxy and identity, then it does not particularly matter if most evangelicals express ambivalence about the limits of Christian political engagement. The Christian Right has succeeded to the extent that rank-and-file evangelicals define their religious identity by opposition to political "liberals." To the extent that evangelicals map their religious and political identity in terms of an imagined culture war, the Christian Right has broad influence.

16. Dombrowski 2001; Habermas and Mendieta 2002.

17. Nielsen 2001.

18. Audrey's approach to "spiritual warfare" may strike readers as anti-modern and authoritarian. However, her way of thinking would be quite unremarkeable within her social milieu, and is shared by Pentecostals from many cultures all over the world, regardless of their political proclivities or relationship to modernity. Charles Taylor has argued that this kind of collective, territorial way of practicing religion is a feature of pre-modern "social imaginaries" (Taylor 2003). Contemporary charismatic and Pentecostal practices often carry these so-called pre-modern elements into contemporary practice, but blending them with a thoroughly modern or even post-modern approach to the authority of personal experience (Singleton 2001).

19. Through his experience with the emerging Christian Right in California, Reagan learned to cast himself as a godly leader within this Christian nationalist narrative. (Dochuk 2011, chap. 10).

20. Spielvogel 2005; Froese and Mencken 2009.

21. For a discussion of internal diversity within the homeschooling movement, see Stevens 2001.

22. In fact, during my fieldwork, I learned that there were at least two individuals involved with Lifeway Assembly who "struggled with homosexuality." However, I could not incorporate more details on these situations due to the sensitive nature of the topic.

23. This theme of social reproduction—"protecting children"—has been noted by other studies of socially conservative activism. For examples, see Beisel's comparative account of Victorian-era anti-obscenity crusades (Beisel 1997), and Luker's account of conflict over sexual education (Luker 2006).

24. Hunter and Wolfe 2006, p. 98.

25. Sandel 2009, p. 249.

26. Nunberg 2006.

27. Stephens and Giberson 2011.

28. Lakoff 2002.

29. Munson 2007.

30. For a sociological and theological discussion of evangelical uses of the Bible to enforce theological boundaries, see Smith 2011 and Bielo 2009a.

31. The Pentecostal tradition has been more centered on vivid, emotional practices of prayer and worship, unlike the conservative Southern Baptist model of biblical exegesis (Cox 2001).

32. Collins 2004.

33. Taylor 1989.

34. Katz and Lazarsfeld 1955.

CHAPTER 7
PRACTICING CIVILITY IN TWO CANADIAN CONGREGATIONS

1. This is consistent with a large body of work in political science and sociology that shows that political ideology is multidimensional (Treier and Hillygus 2009).

2. Greeley and Hout 2006; McTague 2010.

3. Lindsay 2008; Marti 2009; Schmalzbauer 1993.

4. Bielo 2009b; Kinnaman and Lyons 2007; Wilkinson 2012.

5. Emerson and Smith 2000; Gilbreath 2006.

6. Nicoli 2012.

7. Suhay 2011.

8. McTague 2010.

9. Lareau and Conley 2008.

10. Frank 2004. Frank's thesis is balanced by more scholarly, empirically rigorous accounts of white working-class authoritarianism or symbolic racism (Hetherington and Weiler 2009; Sears, Sidanius, and Bobo 2000). Larry Bartels argues that Frank misses the fact that many working-class voters actually hold economically conservative attitudes, and are actually closer to Democrats on social issues than economic ones (Bartels 2006).

11. Greeley and Hout discuss these class differences among evangelicals (2006). Beyond evangelicalism, multiple scholars have noted that income differences do affect voting, albeit more for people with extremely low income rather than working- or lower-middle class people (Brewer and Stonecash 2007; McCarty, Poole, and Rosenthal 2006).

12. Many political journalists and scholars wonder whether and why the white working class left the New Deal coalition that formerly defined the Democratic Party (Edsall and Edsall 1992; Teixeira and Rogers 2000; Prasad et al. 2009). The exodus of blue-collar men is the primary reason for a widening gender gap between Republicans and Democrats over the last twenty years (Brady, Sosnaud, and Frenk 2009).

13. Lipset 1963b, p. 92.

14. Hetherington and Weiler suggest that, like authoritarians, non-authoritarians operate under a "motivated social cognition," or the notion that people "believe what they believe because to do so serves certain key psychological purposes (pp. 42–43). For authoritarians, the motivated social cognition is a need for order and an aversion to differences, ambiguity, and non-conformity (Hetherington and Weiler 2009).

15. McTague 2010.

16. Kaufmann 2002. The defense of group position involves "beliefs of ingroup superiority, perceptions of out-group distinctiveness, an assumption of proprietary claim on important in-group privileges such as power and material wealth, and a challenge from subordinate groups for greater control of those valued resources" (287).

17. Lamont 2000.

18. Ronald refused to recognize any structural reasons for black-white in-

equality. He shares this characteristic with many white evangelicals (Emerson and Smith 2000; Tranby and Hartmann 2008).

19. Ronald fit a common typology of authoritarianism, expressing his desire to force conformity on deviants. Though Ronald felt these attitudes were justified by his religious faith, it is important to acknowledge that he stood out within his church context in expressing this kind of negative attitude toward out-groups (Barker and Tinnick 2006; Lakoff 2002).

20. Bobo and Smith 1998; Sears, Sidanius, and Bobo 2000.

21. This punitive response to threat is what distinguishes authoritarian beliefs from traditional moral beliefs. Morally traditional people are motivated to sustain a valued way of life, while authoritarian individuals are motivated to punish those who threaten their vision of order (Stenner 2005).

22. This was also a finding of Christian Smith's classic study of American evangelicals: most interview subjects did not express anger toward non-Christians, but rather stressed their concern for others' well-being. Their primary motivation was compassion, rather than righteous rage (Smith 1998).

23. McMath and Foner 1993.

24. As Frank and others have noted, American conservatives have successfully redefined what it means to be "elite," to refer to cultural preferences and lifestyles rather than wealth (Frank 2004; Nunberg 2006).

25. Lamont 2000.

26. Bobo 1999.

27. Ginsburg 1989; Munson 2008.

28. This narrative was found among poor Venezuelan Pentecostals (Smilde 2007).

29. Mettler 2002; Soss and Schram 2007.

30. Green, Palmquist, and Schickler 2002.

31. Treier and Hillygus 2009.

32. Lindsay 2008. Like Curtis, Lindsay's sample also had a higher percentage of adult converts to Christianity than the national average.

33. This is consistent with public opinion research that finds greater support for universal services than toward targeted cash payments, which provoke anti-welfare resentment (Schneider and Ingram 2005; Soss and Schram 2007).

34. Bernardin and Feuchtmann 1988.

35. From 2008 to 2012, the issue of gay marriage became increasingly important, and this intermediate position in support for civil unions but not marriage melted away. The year 2012 could be considered a turning point: Obama made an official statement for gay marriage, reporting that his attitudes were "evolving" on the issue. But during the period of my fieldwork, the Democratic Party remained divided over gay marriage (Karol 2012).

36. Achen 2002; Plutzer 2004.

37. Campbell 2002, pp. 226–27.

38. Hedges 2006.

39. Every year, IHOP organizes a national conference that purports to reach over 100,000 young charismatic Christians. As a single organization, their na-

tional constituency is arguably larger than the entire progressive evangelical movement combined.

CHAPTER 8
PRACTICING CIVILITY IN TWO CANADIAN CONGREGATIONS

1. Simmel 1908 [1955]. This insight was extended by Peter Blau and classic studies of social cleavage politics in Europe. For a review, see Baldassarri and Bearman 2007; Baldassarri 2011.

2. Nina Eliasoph and Paul Lichterman introduced this adverb, "civic-ly," to describe how people map relationships to others as they puzzle through shared problems (Lichterman 2009).

3. Canada's Planned Parenthood recently changed its name to the Canadian Federation for Sexual Health. Available online at http://www.cfsh.ca/

4. Malloy 2011.

5. This time line is taken from the April 15, 2008 Decision of the Human Rights Tribunal of Ontario, 2008 HRTO 22, accessed on 8/30/20012 at: http://www.canlii.org/en/on/onhrt/doc/2008/2008hrto22/2008hrto22.pdf

6. *Ontario Human Rights Commission v. Christian Horizons* 2010.

7. By comparison, two of Walter's retirement-age friends had recently attended a church presentation by Exodus International, where they had learned that even Christians might experience same-sex attraction. While gay rights advocates have criticized this "sexual brokenness" model of homosexuality as harmful and retrogressive, it was a revelation for older evangelicals who grew up before homosexuality was discussed publicly.

8. Lipset 1990. In more recent years, leaders like Stephen Harper have worked with groups like the Frasier Institute to forge what has become known as the "Calgary School" of conservative ideology. Conservative leaders have made new American-style efforts to bind moral conservatism and economic individualism into a neat package: to link the growth of the welfare state to moral decadence, and reframe the market as a force of social discipline and conformity (Mackey 2005a).

9. Michael identified with conservatives because they were "more biblical" and because they "clean up the wasted money." For example, Michael felt that his tax money should not pay for "the waste of money in abortions, all the money wasted. . . . it's from our taxes. Conservatives, say, 'If you want that you're paying from your pocket.'" However, he got frustrated with the Conservative Party, because they were often "as liberal as the Liberals," refusing to raise the abortion issues by saying, "there's freedom, so you can't change that." He felt that the party had strayed from "the true conservative platform" which was ideally "godly-based."

10. Michael sounded very much like the French working-class men interviewed by Michele Lamont in her comparative study of working-class identity in the United States and France. Like many American evangelicals, Michael wanted to restore "biblical" values to social policy, which included "tough love" and "cleaning up wasted funds." But he included other poor Canadians within the

boundaries of cultural membership; his concerns about waste were directed toward immigrants as an out-group (Lamont 2000).

11. Rydgren 2007.

12. Though Michael belonged to a union through his job, he didn't vote with his union because "when the Liberals were in power, they didn't help us, the union." Unlike many American evangelicals, Michael did not use the term "liberal" as a moral category. Instead, he defined "liberals" as people who believed in being "more liberal with money: giving it out for this thing, for that thing."

13. The 700 Club has a Canadian version, distributed through the Vision Network. Vision is a multifaith channel, and overtly partisan speech is regulated in a Canadian framework (Brooks 2003).

14. Birthright International was founded in 1968 by Louise Summerhill in Toronto, Canada. Available online at http://www.birthright.org/htmpages/about .htm

15. This shows how much political mileage the Conservative Party has been able to achieve by making simply symbolic statements of disapproval toward abortion. Connie did not vote Conservative because she believed that they would be able to pass new legislation limiting abortion. Voting "pro-life" was an expression of identity, a way to draw symbolic boundaries against out-groups, and hence the Conservative Party did not need to promise substantive policy changes to get her vote.

16. McDonald 2010.

17. The close relationship between Kryskow and Stephen Harper has been closely scrutinized by the Canadian media (Gravel 2011).

18. Ryan did not interpret the goals of The Cry as authoritarian, even though they had prayed for a revolution of "righteousness" to break out in Canada, which would end abortion and restore sexual purity. When I pressed Ryan to explain exactly how that might happen, he interpreted this revolution in exclusively spiritualized terms, involving better judgment among individuals, rather than structural or legal changes. For example, he recalled praying to "keep the airwaves clean and pure." I asked Ryan if that involved greater censorship, and he explained, "They tend to pray that the leaders that are involved in the media would be responsible. I don't know how that works. . . . most of the prayers are pretty general." The only exception was that they had prayed specifically for "the bills for the abortion issue to make it," and they had also prayed against a bill that "makes it more difficult to have worship." Ryan imagined social change as occurring through individual change. By praying, they would unlock hidden spiritual power, facilitate evangelism, and also exercise moral suasion on leaders to "make wise choices . . . and then somebody will see what happens, we don't pray against them, we pray for them, which I think is important." In this sense, Ryan interpreted the language of spiritual warfare and Christian nationalism in a similar way to American Pentecostals. Unlike American Pentecostals, Ryan did not associate "godly leadership" and greater "Christian" influence with a conservative political agenda.

19. Bartkowski 2001, pp. 168–71.

20. Todd described this period in the interview: "Reform party started in

1990, right about the time I was able to vote, 18 or 19. So that was when churches would get on the political soap boxes, around election time, and basically tell you how you should vote. And they told all of us to vote Reform, because Reform was voting against the legalization of abortion. . . . I remember, my dad as a pastor said, "Ok, we got to mobilize the troops, you're calling your Member of Parliament, make sure to vote for this, because this party will protect the definition of family, and also make sure abortion is illegal."

21. Andersen and Heath 2003; Layman and Green 2005.

22. This definition is based on Georg Simmel, as elaborated by Delia Baldassari's paper (2011, pp. 27–28).

CONCLUSION

1. James 2004, p. 147.

2. Young 2002. Michael Lienesch has documented the same confessional narrative structure among Christian Right elite activists (Lienesch 1993, chap. 1).

3. Here, I build on Ziad Munson's valuable study of pro-life activists, only telling the story from the vantage point of local congregations rather than the pro-life movement. Taken together, these two studies paint a complete picture about how congregations relate to political activism, through streams of recruitment and religious practice (Munson 2008).

4. In embracing the culture-as-toolkit paradigm, cultural sociologists have been too quick to reject the idea that culture motivates behavior, that culture can guide *ends* as well as *means*.

5. Here, I emphasize that traditional moral intuitions about purity, authority, and loyalty often operate in a toolkit-like fashion, as an enduring moral concern that is only loosely coupled with particular political ideologies. Hence, it is a mistake to assume that a concern for sexual purity is necessarily part of some global sexual-nationalistic ideology about controlling female bodies, for example.

6. Hempel and Bartkowski 2008.

7. Baldassarri and Bearman 2007; Baldassarri and Diani 2007; Cohen and Arato 1992.

8. Here, evangelical churches parallel Lipset and Rokkan's description of socialist parties and churches in European social cleavage politics, who "tended to isolate their supporters from outside influence through the development of a wide variety of parallel organizations and agencies: they . . . developed confessionally distinct trade unions, sports clubs, leisure associations, publishing houses, magazines, newspapers, in one or two cases even radio and television stations" (Lipset and Rokkan 1967, p. 15).

9. Like Lipset and Rokkan, I argue that there is nothing inherently democratic about civic associations. Associational life can foster support for democratic or authoritarian regimes, depending on how people partition themselves into groups (Lipset and Rokkan 1967).

10. This argument is consistent with Bawn et al., who argue that particular

configurations of "liberal" or "conservative" ideology take shape through strategic negotiation between groups (Bawn et al. 2012).

11. Ghaziani and Baldassarri 2011.

METHODOLOGICAL APPENDIX

1. Nancy Ammerman reports a similar experience in the methodological discussion for the book *Bible Believers,* an influential case study of an evangelical congregation (Ammerman 1987).

2. Here, I used Michele Lamont's comparative research as a model of how to use an ambiguous national and linguistic identity to "blur" symbolic boundaries and alternate between "insider" and "outsider" stances. Since Lamont is a native Francophone from Quebec, she could position herself as a partial "outsider" to both French and American cultures (Lamont 1992, 2000).

3. In fact, I regularly observed this coaching in the course of my fieldwork. For example, the deacons at one church asked me a set of "diagnostic questions," which I later observed being taught to laypeople in a program on neighbor-to-neighbor evangelism.

4. Tilly 2003.

5. Brown and Brown 2003; Ginsburg 1989; Luker 1984; Polletta 1998b.

6. Lamont 1992, 2000.

7. Dochuk 2012.

8. Zuberi 2006.

9. Killen and Silk 2004.

10. Ammerman and Farnsley 1997; Eiesland 2000; Stark and Finke 2000; Warner 1993.

11. Glaser and Strauss 1967.

12. Lichterman 2008, p. 85.

13. Lamont and Molnar 2002; Turner et al. 1987.

14. Lichterman 2008; Schwalbe and Mason-Schrock 1996.

15. Polletta 2006; Sewell 1992; Smith 2003b; Somers 1994.

16. Ashmore, Deaux, and McLaughlin-Volpe 2004; Eyerman 2004.

17. Morone 2003; Noll, Hatch, and Marsden 1989.

18. Bruner 1986; McAdams et al. 2004.

19. Green, Palmquist, and Schickler 2002.

20. Campbell 2002; Johnston 2006.

21. Haidt 2007.

22. Campbell et al. 1960.

23. Blais et al. 2001; Greene 2002; Greene 2004.

24. Zerubavel 2003.

25. Miles and Huberman 1994.

26. Schmalzbauer 1993; Verba, Schlozman, and Brady 1995.

Bibliography

1958. "A Protestant Affirmation on the Control of Human Reproduction." *Christianity Today*, 11/08/1968, pp. 18–19.

Ontario Human Rights Commission v. Christian Horizons. 2010. Ontario Superior Court of Justice.

Abramowitz, Alan I. and Kyle L. Saunders. 2008. "Is Polarization a Myth?" *Journal of Politics* 70(02):542–55. doi:10.1017/S0022381608080493.

Achen, Christopher H. 2002. "Parental Socialization and Rational Party Identification." *Political Behavior* 24(2):151–70.

Alexander, Jeffrey C. 2001. "Toward a Sociology of Evil: Getting Beyond Modernist Common Sense About the Alternative to 'the Good'." Pp. 153–72 in *Rethinking Evil: Contemporary Perspectives*, edited by M. P. Lara. Berkeley: University of California Press.

———. 2003. *The Meanings of Social Life: A Cultural Sociology*. Oxford: Oxford University Press.

Allyn, David. 2001. *Make Love, Not War: The Sexual Revolution: An Unfettered History*. New York: Routledge.

Almond, Gabriel A. and Sidney Verba. 1963. *The Civic Culture: Political Attitudes and Democracy in Five Nations*. Princeton, NJ: Princeton University Press.

Althouse, Peter. 2009. "Apocalyptic Discourse and a Pentecostal Vision of Canada." Pp. 59–78 in *Canadian Pentecostalism: Transition and Transformation*, Vol. 49, edited by M. Wilkinson. Montreal and Kingston: McGill-Queen's University Press.

Ammerman, Nancy Tatom. 1987. *Bible Believers: Fundamentalists in the Modern World*. New Brunswick, NJ: Rutgers University Press.

———. 1990. *Baptist Battles: Social Change and Religious Conflict in the Southern Baptist Convention*. New Brunswick, NJ: Rutgers University Press.

———. 1993. *Southern Baptists Observed: Multiple Perspectives on a Changing Denomination*. Knoxville: University of Tennessee Press.

———. 2005. *Pillars of Faith: American Congregations and Their Partners*. Berkeley: University of California Press.

———. 2007. *Everyday Religion: Observing Modern Religious Lives*. Oxford and New York: Oxford University Press.

Ammerman, Nancy Tatom and Arthur Emery Farnsley. 1997. *Congregation & Community*. New Brunswick, NJ: Rutgers University Press.

Andersen, Robert and Josh Curtis. 2011. "Public Opinion on Redistribution in Canada, 1980–2005: The Role of Political and Economic Context." In *The*

New Politics of Redistribution in Canada, edited by K. G. Banting and J. Myles. Vancouver: University of British Columbia Press.

Andersen, Robert and Tina Fetner. 2008. "Cohort Differences in Tolerance of Homosexuality: Attitudinal Change in Canada and the United States, 1981–2000." *Public Opinion Quarterly* 72(2):311–30. doi: 10.1093/poq/nfn017.

Andersen, Robert and Anthony Heath. 2003. "Social Identities and Political Cleavages: The Role of Political Context." *Journal of the Royal Statistical Society: Series A (Statistics in Society)* 166(3):301–27. doi: doi:10.1111/1467–985X.00279.

Anderson, Benedict R. 1983. *Imagined Communities: Reflections on the Origin and Spread of Nationalism.* London: Verso.

Aristotle. 2007. *On Rhetoric: A Theory of Civic Discourse.* Translated by G. A. Kennedy. New York, Oxford: Oxford University Press.

Armstrong, Elizabeth A. and Mary Bernstein. 2008. "Culture, Power, and Institutions: A Multi-Institutional Politics Approach to Social Movements." *Sociological Theory* 26(1):74–99. doi:10.1111/j.1467–9558.2008.00319.x.

Ashmore, Richard D., Kay Deaux, and Tracy McLaughlin-Volpe. 2004. "An Organizing Framework for Collective Identity: Articulation and Significance of Multidimensionality." *Psychological Bulletin* 130(1):80–114.

Bailey, Beth. 1997. "Prescribing the Pill: Politics, Culture, and the Sexual Revolution in America's Heartland." *Journal of Social History* 30(4):827–56.

———. 1999. *Sex in the Heartland: Politics, Culture, and the Sexual Revolution.* Cambridge, MA: Harvard University Press.

Balch, Robert W. 1984. "Looking Behind the Scenes in a Religious Cult: Implications for the Study of Conversion." Pp. 309–16 in *Religion: North American Style,* edited by P. H. McNamara. Belmont, CA: Wadsworth.

Baldassarri, Delia. 2011. "Partisan Joiners: Associational Membership and Political Polarization in the United States (1974–2004)." *Social Science Quarterly* 92(3):631–55. doi: 10.1111/j.1540–6237.2011.00785.x.

Baldassarri, Delia and Peter Bearman. 2007. "Dynamics of Political Polarization." *American Sociological Review* 72:784–811.

Baldassarri, Delia and Mario Diani. 2007. "The Integrative Power of Civic Networks." *American Journal of Sociology* 113(3):735–80.

Baldassarri, Delia and Andrew Gelman. 2008. "Partisans without Constraint: Political Polarization and Trends in American Public Opinion." *American Journal of Sociology* 114(2):408–46.

Balmer, Randall Herbert. 1989. *Mine Eyes Have Seen the Glory: A Journey into the Evangelical Subculture in America.* New York: Oxford University Press.

———. 2006. *Thy Kingdom Come: An Evangelical's Lament: How the Religious Right Distorts the Faith and Threatens America.* Minneapolis, MN: Basic Books.

Banaszak, Lee Ann, Karen Beckwith, and Dieter Rucht. 2003. *Women's Movements Facing the Reconfigured State.* Cambridge and New York: Cambridge University Press.

Banting, Keith G., George Hoberg, and Richard Simeon. 1997. *Degrees of Freedom: Canada and the United States in a Changing World.* Montreal: McGill-Queen's University Press.

Barker, D. C. and J. D. Tinnick. 2006. "Competing Visions of Parental Roles and Ideological Constraint." *American Political Science Review* 100(02):249–63.

Barker, David C. and Christopher Jan Carman. 2000. "The Spirit of Capitalism? Religious Doctrine, Values, and Economic Attitude Constructs." *Political Behavior* 22(1):1–27.

Barker, David C., Jon Hurwitz, and Traci L. Nelson. 2008. "Of Crusades and Culture Wars: 'Messianic' Militarism and Political Conflict in the United States." *Journal of Politics* 70(02):307–22. doi: doi:10.1017/S00223816080 80328.

Barnes, Samuel H. 1958. "The Evolution of Christian Trade Unionism in Quebec." *Industrial and Labor Relations Review* 12:568.

Bartels, Larry M. 2002. "Beyond the Running Tally: Partisan Bias in Political Perceptions." *Political Behavior* 24(2):117–50.

———. 2006. "What's the Matter with What's the Matter with Kansas?" *Quarterly Journal of Political Science* 1(2):201–26.

Bartkowski, John P. 2001. *Remaking the Godly Marriage: Gender Negotiation in Evangelical Families*. New Brunswick, NJ: Rutgers University Press.

———. *The Promise Keepers: Servants, Soldiers, and Godly Men*. New Brunswick, NJ: Rutgers University Press.

Bartkowski, John P. and Christopher G. Ellison. 1995. "Divergent Models of Childrearing in Popular Manuals: Conservative Protestants vs. The Mainstream Experts." *Sociology of Religion* 56(1):21–34.

Bartkowski, John P. and Helen A. Regis. 2003. *Charitable Choices: Religion, Race, and Poverty in the Post-Welfare Era*. New York: New York University Press.

Bartolini, Stefano and Peter Mair. 1990. *Identity, Competition, and Electoral Availability: The Stabilisation of European Electorates, 1885–1985*. New York: Cambridge University Press.

Baumgartner, M. P. 1988. *The Moral Order of a Suburb*. New York: Oxford University Press.

Bawn, Kathleen, Martin Cohen, David Karol, Seth Masket, Hans Noel, and John Zaller. 2012. "A Theory of Political Parties: Groups, Policy Demands and Nominations in American Politics." *Perspectives on Politics* 10(3):571–97.

Bean, Lydia, Marco Gonzalez, and Jason Kaufman. 2008. "Why Doesn't Canada Have an American-Style Christian Right? A Comparative Framework for Analyzing the Political Effects of Evangelical Subcultural Identity." *Canadian Journal of Sociology* 33:899–943.

Beatty, Kathleen Murphy and Oliver Walter. 1989. "A Group Theory of Religion and Politics: The Clergy as Group Leaders." *Western Political Quarterly* 42(1):129–46.

Bebbington, David W. 1989. *Evangelicalism in Modern Britain: A History from the 1730s to the 1980s*. London and Boston: Allen & Unwin.

Becker, Howard Saul. 1982. *Art Worlds*. Berkeley: University of California Press.

Becker, Penny Edgell. 1999. *Congregations in Conflict: Cultural Models of Local Religious Life*. Cambridge: Cambridge University Press.

Beisel, Nicola Kay. 1990. "Class, Culture, and Campaigns against Vice in Three American Cities, 1872–1892." *American Sociological Review* 55(1):44–62.

———. 1997. *Imperiled Innocents: Anthony Comstock and Family Reproduction in Victorian America*. Princeton, NJ: Princeton University Press.

Béland, Daniel and Andre Lecours. 2005. "The Politics of Territorial Solidarity: Nationalism and Social Policy Reform in Canada, the United Kingdom, and Belgium." *Comparative Political Studies* 38(6):676–703.

Bellah, Robert Neelly. 1975. *The Broken Covenant: American Civil Religion in Time of Trial*. New York: Seabury Press.

———. 1991. *The Good Society*. New York: Knopf; distributed by Random House.

———. 1992. *The Broken Covenant: American Civil Religion in Time of Trial*. Chicago: University of Chicago Press.

Bellah, Robert Neelly and Phillip E. Hammond. 1980. *Varieties of Civil Religion*. San Francisco: Harper & Row.

Bellah, Robert Neelly, William M. Sullivan, Richard Madsen, Ann Swidler, and Steven M. Tipton. 1985. *Habits of the Heart: Individualism and Commitment in American Life*. Berkeley: University of California Press.

Benford, Robert and David Snow. 2000. "Framing Processes and Social Movements: An Overview and Assessment." *Annual Review of Sociology* 26(1): 611–39.

Benson Gold, Rachel. 1990. "Abortion and Women's Health: A Turning Point for America?" Alan Guttmacher Institute.

Berezin, Mabel. 1997. "Politics and Culture: A Less Fissured Terrain." *Annual Review of Sociology* 23(1):361–83. doi: doi:10.1146/annurev.soc.23.1.361.

Berger, Peter L. 1970. *A Rumor of Angels: Modern Society and the Rediscovery of the Supernatural*. Garden City, NY: Doubleday.

Berger, Peter L., Grace Davie, and Effie Fokas. 2008. *Religious America, Secular Europe?: A Theme and Variation*. Burlington, VT: Ashgate.

Bernardin, Joseph and Thomas Gerhard Feuchtmann. 1988. *Consistent Ethic of Life*. Kansas City, MO: Sheed & Ward.

Berry, Jeffrey M. and Sarah Sobieraj. 2013. *The Outrage Industry: Political Opinion Media and the New Incivility*. New York: Oxford University Press.

Beyer, Peter. 1997. "Religious Vitality in Canada: The Complementarity of Religious Market and Secularization Perspectives." *Journal for the Scientific Study of Religion* 36(2):272–88.

———. 2005. "Religious Identity and Educational Attainment among Recent Immigrants to Canada: Gender, Age, and 2nd Generation." *Journal of International Migration and Integration* 6(2):177–99.

Beyerlein, Kraig and Mark Chaves. 2003. "The Political Activities of Religious Congregations in the United States." *Journal for the Scientific Study of Religion* 42(2):229–46.

Beyerlein, Kraig and John R. Hipp. 2005. "Social Capital, Too Much of a Good Thing? American Religious Traditions and Community Crime." *Social Forces* 84(2):995–1013.

———. 2006. "From Pews to Participation: The Effect of Congregation Activity and Context on Bridging Civic Engagement." *Social Problems* 53(1):97–117.

Bibby, Reginald W. 1999. "On Boundaries, Gates, and Circulating Saints: A Longitudinal Look at Loyalty and Loss." *Review of Religious Research* 41(2): 149–65.

———. 2000. "Canada's Mythical Religious Mosaic: Some Census Findings." *Journal for the Scientific Study of Religion* 39(2):235–39.

Bibby, Reginald Wayne. 1993. *Unknown Gods: The Ongoing Story of Religion in Canada.* Toronto: Stoddart.

———. 2002. *Restless Gods: The Renaissance of Religion in Canada.* Toronto and Niagara Falls, NY: Stoddart.

Bielo, James S. 2009a. *Words Upon the Word: An Ethnography of Evangelical Group Bible Study.* New York: New York University Press.

———. 2009b. "The 'Emerging Church' in America: Notes on the Interaction of Christianities." *Religion* 39(3):219–32. doi: http://dx.doi.org/10.1016/j.religion.2009.02.007.

Billig, Michael. 1995. *Banal Nationalism.* Thousand Oaks, CA: Sage.

Blais, André, Elisabeth Gidengil, Richard Nadeau, and Neil Nevitte. 2001. "Measuring Party Identification: Britain, Canada, and the United States." *Political Behavior* 23(1):5–22.

Blanchard, Troy C. 2007. "Conservative Protestant Congregations and Racial Residential Segregation: Evaluating the Closed Community Thesis in Metropolitan and Nonmetropolitan Counties." *American Sociological Review* 72(3):416–33. doi: 10.2307/25472470.

Bobo, Lawrence D. 1999. "Prejudice as Group Position: Microfoundations of a Sociological Approach to Racism and Race Relations." *Journal of Social Issues* 55(3):445–72. doi: 10.1111/0022–4537.00127.

Bobo, Lawrence and Ryan A. Smith. 1998. "From Jim Crow Racism to Laissez-Faire Racism: The Transformation of Racial Attitudes." Pp. 182–220 in *Beyond Pluralism: The Conception of Groups and Group Identities in America,* edited by W. F. Katkin, N. C. Landsman, and A. Tyree. Urbana and Chicago: University of Illinois Press.

Boychuk, Gerard William. 2008. *National Health Insurance in the United States and Canada: Race, Territory, and the Roots of Difference.* Washington, DC: Georgetown University Press.

Boyer, Paul. 1992. *When Time Shall Be No More: Prophecy Belief in Modern American Culture.* Cambridge, MA: Belknap Press.

Brady, David, Benjamin Sosnaud, and Steven M. Frenk. 2009. "The Shifting and Diverging White Working Class in U.S. Presidential Elections, 1972–2004." *Social Science Research* 38(1):118–33. doi: http://dx.doi.org/10.1016/j.ssresearch.2008.07.002.

Brady, David W. and Kent L. Tedin. 1976. "Ladies in Pink: Religion and Political Ideology in the Anti-ERA Movement." *Social Science Quarterly* 56(4): 564–75.

Bramadat, Paul and David Seljak. 2005. *Religion and Ethnicity in Canada.* Toronto: Pearson Longman.

Brewer, Mark D. and Jeffrey M. Stonecash. 2007. *Split: Class and Cultural Divides in American Politics.* Washington, DC: CQ Press.

Brint, Steven and Seth Abrutyn. 2010. "Who's Right About the Right? Comparing Competing Explanations of the Link between White Evangelicals and

Conservative Politics in the United States." *Journal for the Scientific Study of Religion* 49(2):328–50. doi: 10.1111/j.1468–5906.2010.01513.x.

Brodie, M. Janine. 1985. *Women and Politics in Canada*. Toronto and New York: McGraw-Hill Ryerson.

———. 2002. "Citizenship and Solidarity: Reflections on the Canadian Way." *Citizenship Studies* 6(4):377–94.

Brodie, Janine, Shelley A. M. Gavigan, and Jane Jenson. 1992. *The Politics of Abortion*. Toronto and Oxford: Oxford University Press.

Brooks, Arthur C. 2006. *Who Really Cares: The Surprising Truth About Compassionate Conservatism: America's Charity Divide—Who Gives, Who Doesn't, and Why It Matters*. New York: Basic Books.

Brooks, Clem and Jeff Manza. 2007. *Why Welfare States Persist: The Importance of Public Opinion in Democracies*. Chicago: University of Chicago Press.

Brooks, Clem, Paul Nieuwbeerta, and Jeff Manza. 2006. "Cleavage-Based Voting Behavior in Cross-National Perspective: Evidence from Six Postwar Democracies." *Social Science Research* 35(1):88–128.

Brooks, Richard T. 2003. "The 'Canadian Electric Church': The Development of Single-Faith Broadcasting in Canada." Master of Arts thesis, Department of History, McMaster University.

Brown, R. Khari and Ronald E. Brown. 2003. "Faith and Works: Church-Based Social Capital Resources and African American Political Activism." *Social Forces* 82(2):617–41.

Brubaker, Rogers. 1994. "Rethinking Nationhood: Nation as Institutionalized Form, Practical Category, Contingent Event." *Contention* 4(1):3–14.

———. 2006. *Nationalist Politics and Everyday Ethnicity in a Transylvanian Town*. Princeton, NJ: Princeton University Press.

Bruce, Steve. 1985. "Authority and Fission: The Protestants' Divisions." *British Journal of Sociology* 36(4):592–603.

———. 1990. *A House Divided: Protestantism, Schism, and Secularization*. London and New York: Routledge.

———. 1998. *Conservative Protestant Politics*. Oxford, New York: Oxford University Press.

———. 2003. *Politics and Religion*. Cambridge, UK: Polity Press.

Bruner, Jerome. 1986. *Actual Minds, Possible Worlds*. Cambridge, MA: Harvard University Press.

Burack, Cynthia. 2008. *Sin, Sex, and Democracy: Antigay Rhetoric and the Christian Right*. Albany: State University of New York Press.

Campbell, Angus, Philip E. Converse, Warren E. Miller, and Donald E. Stokes. 1960. *The American Voter*. Edited by University of Michigan Social Research Center. New York: Wiley.

Campbell, David E. 2002. "The Young and the Realigning: A Test of the Socialization Theory of Realignment." *Public Opinion Quarterly* 66(2):209–34.

———. 2004. "Acts of Faith: Churches and Political Engagement." *Political Behavior* 26(2):155–80.

———. 2007. *A Matter of Faith: Religion in the 2004 Presidential Election*. Washington, DC: Brookings Institution Press.

Carmines, Edward G. and James A. Stimson. 1989. *Issue Evolution: Race and the*

Transformation of American Politics. Princeton, NJ: Princeton University Press.

Carpenter, Joel A. 1980. "Fundamentalist Institutions and the Rise of Evangelical Protestantism, 1929–1942." *Church History: Studies in Christianity and Culture* 49(01):62–75. doi: doi:10.2307/3164640.

Carsey, Thomas M. and Geoffrey C. Layman. 2006. "Changing Sides or Changing Minds? Party Identification and Policy Preferences in the American Electorate." *American Journal of Political Science* 50(2):464–77. doi: 10.1111/j.1540-5907.2006.00196.x.

Casanova, José. 1994. *Public Religions in the Modern World*. Chicago: University of Chicago Press.

Chaves, Mark. 1994. "Secularization as Declining Religious Authority." *Social Forces* 72(3):749–74.

———. 2004. *Congregations in America*. Cambridge, MA: Harvard University Press.

Chaves, Mark and William Tsitsos. 2001. "Congregations and Social Services: What They Do, How They Do It, and with Whom." *Nonprofit and Voluntary Sector Quarterly* 30(4):660–83. doi: 10.1177/0899764001304003.

Christiano, Kevin J. 1988. "Religion and Radical Labor Unionism: American States in the 1920's." *Journal for the Scientific Study of Religion* 27(3): 378–88.

Christie, Nancy and Michael Gauvreau. 1996. *A Full-Orbed Christianity: The Protestant Churches and Social Welfare in Canada, 1900–1940*. Montreal and Buffalo: McGill-Queen's University Press.

Clarke, Harold D., Allan Kornberg, John MacLeod, and Thomas Scotto. 2005. "Too Close to Call: Political Choice in Canada, 2004." *PS: Political Science & Politics* 38(02):247–53. doi: doi:10.1017/S1049096505056386.

Clarke, Harold D., Allan Kornberg, Thomas Scotto, and Joe Twyman. 2006. "Flawless Campaign, Fragile Victory: Voting in Canada's 2006 Federal Election." *PS: Political Science & Politics* 39(04):815–19.

Clifton, Brett M. 2004. "Romancing the GOP: Assessing the Strategies Used by the Christian Coalition to Influence the Republican Party." *Party Politics* 10(5):475–98.

Cnaan, Ram A. and Femida Handy. 2000. "Comparing Neighbors: Social Service Provision by Religious Congregations in Ontario and the United States." *American Review of Canadian Studies* 30(4):521.

Cohen, Jean L. and Andrew Arato. 1992. *Civil Society and Political Theory*. Cambridge, MA: MIT Press.

Collins, Randall. 2004. *Interaction Ritual Chains*. Princeton, NJ: Princeton University Press.

Converse, Philip E. 1964. "The Nature of Belief Systems in Mass Publics." Pp. 206–61 in *Ideology and Discontent*, edited by D. E. Apter. New York: Free Press.

Cook, Peter G. and Myles A. Ruggles. 1992. "Balance and Freedom of Speech: Challenge for Canadian Broadcasting." *Canadian Journal of Communication* 17(1).

Cox, Harvey Gallagher. 2001. *Fire from Heaven: The Rise of Pentecostal Spiritu-*

ality and the Reshaping of Religion in the Twenty-First Century. Cambridge, MA: Da Capo Press.

Cristi, Marcela. 2001a. *From Civil to Political Religion: The Intersection of Culture, Religion and Politics*. Waterloo, ON: Wilfrid Laurier University Press. Available online: http://search.ebscohost.com/login.aspx?direct=true&scope=site&db=nlebk&db=nlabk&AN=85584.

———. 2001b. *From Civil to Political Religion: The Intersection of Culture, Religion and Politics*. Waterloo, ON: Wilfrid Laurier University Press.

Critchlow, Donald T. 2005. *Phyllis Schlafly and Grassroots Conservatism: A Woman's Crusade*. Princeton, NJ: Princeton University Press.

Cromartie, Michael. 2003. *A Public Faith: Evangelicals and Civic Engagement*. Lanham, MD: Rowman & Littlefield.

Curry, Bill and Gayle MacDonald. 2008. "Evangelist Takes Credit for Film Crackdown." In *Globe and Mail*, vol. A1.

Cywinski, Adam. 2011. "Christian Labour Association of Canada: Competing from the Outside." Master of Arts thesis, Work and Society, McMaster University, Hamilton, Ontario.

D'Andrade, Roy G. 1995. *The Development of Cognitive Anthropology*. Cambridge and New York: Cambridge University Press.

Dauda, Carol L. 2010. "Childhood, Age of Consent and Moral Regulation in Canada and the UK." *Contemporary Politics* 16(3):227–47.

Davis, Nancy J. and Robert V. Robinson. 1996. "Are the Rumors of War Exaggerated? Religious Orthodoxy and Moral Progressivism in America." *American Journal of Sociology* 102(3):756–87.

De Valk, Alphonse. 1989. "Operation Rescue in Canada." In *The Interim: Canada's Life and Family Newspaper*.

Delli Carpini, Michael X. and Scott Keeter. 1996. *What Americans Know About Politics and Why It Matters*. New Haven, CT: Yale University Press.

Dennis, Jack. 1992. "Political Independence in America, 3: In Search of Closet Partisans." *Political Behavior* 14(3):261–96.

DeWitt, Larry, Daniel Béland, and Edward D. Berkowitz. 2008. *Social Security: A Documentary History*. Washington, DC: CQ Press.

Diamond, Sara. 1989. *Spiritual Warfare: The Politics of the Christian Right*. Boston: South End Press.

Dillon, Michele. 1996. "The American Abortion Debate: Culture War or Normal Discourse?" Pp. 115–32 in *The American Culture Wars: Current Contests and Future Prospects*, edited by J. L. Nolan. Charlottesville: University Press of Virginia.

DiMaggio, Paul. 1997. "Culture and Cognition." *Annual Review of Sociology* 23(1):263–87. doi:10.1146/annurev.soc.23.1.263.

Dionne, E. J., Jr., and William A. Galston. 2010. "The Old and New Politics of Faith: Religion and the 2010 Election." Washington, DC: Brookings.

Djupe, Paul A. 2000. "Religious Brand Loyalty and Political Loyalties." *Journal for the Scientific Study of Religion* 39(1):78–89.

Djupe, Paul A. and Christopher P. Gilbert. 2002. "The Political Voice of Clergy." *Journal of Politics* 64(2):596–609. doi:10.1111/1468–2508.00142.

———. 2003. *The Prophetic Pulpit: Clergy, Churches, and Communities in American Politics.* Lanham, MD: Rowman & Littlefield.

———. 2008. "Politics and Church: Byproduct or Central Mission?" *Journal for the Scientific Study of Religion* 47(1):45–62. doi: 10.1111/j.1468-5906 .2008.00391.x.

———. 2009. *The Political Influence of Churches.* Cambridge and New York: Cambridge University Press.

Djupe, Paul A. and Laura R. Olson. 2008 [2003]. *Encyclopedia of American Religion and Politics.* New York: Checkmark Books.

Dochuk, Darren. 2003. " 'Praying for a Wicked City': Congregation, Community, and the Suburbanization of Fundamentalism." *Religion and American Culture* 13(2):167–203. doi:10.1525/rac.2003.13.2.167.

———. 2006. "Revival on the Right: Making Sense of the Conservative Moment in Post–World War II American History." 4:975–99. doi: 10.1111/j.1478-0542 .2006.00341.x.

———. 2011. *From Bible Belt to Sunbelt: Plain-Folk Religion, Grassroots Politics, and the Rise of Evangelical Conservatism.* New York: W.W. Norton.

———. 2012. "Blessed by Oil, Cursed with Crude: God and Black Gold in the American Southwest." *Journal of American History* 99(1):51–61. doi: 10.1093/ jahist/jas100.

Dombrowski, Daniel A. 2001. "Rawls and Religion: The Case for Political Liberalism." Albany: State University of New York Press. Available online: http:// search.ebscohost.com/login.aspx?direct=true&scope=site&db=nlebk&db =nlabk&AN=67871.

Dougherty, Kevin D. 2004. "Institutional Influences on Growth in Southern Baptist Congregations." *Review of Religious Research* 46(2):117–31. doi: 10 .2307/3512228.

Douglas, Mary. 1970. *Natural Symbols: Explorations in Cosmology.* London: Barrie & Rockliff/ The Cresset Press.

Ecklund, Elaine Howard. 2005. "Models of Civic Responsibility: Korean Americans in Congregations with Different Ethnic Compositions." *Journal for the Scientific Study of Religion* 44(1):15–28.

Edelman, Murray J. 1964. *The Symbolic Uses of Politics.* Urbana: University of Illinois Press.

Edgell, Penny. 2006. *Religion and Family in a Changing Society.* Princeton, NJ: Princeton University Press.

———. 2012. "A Cultural Sociology of Religion: New Directions." *Annual Review of Sociology* 38(1):247–65. doi:10.1146/annurev-soc-071811-145424.

Edgell, Penny, Joseph Gerteis, and Douglas Hartmann. 2006. "Atheists as 'Other': Moral Boundaries and Cultural Membership in American Society." *American Sociological Review* 71(2):211.

Edgell, Penny and Eric Tranby. 2007. "Religious Influences on Understandings of Racial Inequality in the United States." *Social Problems* 54(2):263–88. doi: 10.1525/sp.2007.54.2.263.

———. 2010. "Shared Visions? Diversity and Cultural Membership in American Life." *Social Problems* 57(2):175–204.

Edsall, Thomas Byrne and Mary D. Edsall. 1992. *Chain Reaction: The Impact of Race, Rights, and Taxes on American Politics.* New York: W.W. Norton.

Eiesland, Nancy L. 2000. *A Particular Place: Urban Restructuring and Religious Ecology in a Southern Exurb.* New Brunswick, NJ: Rutgers University Press.

El Akkad, Omar. 2008. "Tax-Credit Crackdown on Films Puts Spotlight on Evangelical Community." In *Globe and Mail,* Tuesday, March 4.

Elacqua, Amelia. 2007–2008. "Eyes Wide Shut: The Ambiguous 'Political Activity' Prohibition and Its Effects on 501(C)(3) Organizations." *Houston Business and Tax Journal* 8:113–41.

Eliasoph, Nina. 1998. *Avoiding Politics: How Americans Produce Apathy in Everyday Life.* Cambridge and New York: Cambridge University Press.

Eliasoph, Nina and Paul Lichterman. 2003. "Culture in Interaction." *American Journal of Sociology* 108(4):735.

Elisha, Omri. 2008. "*Moral Ambitions of Grace: The Paradox of Compassion and Accountability in Evangelical Faith-Based Activism.*" *Cultural Anthropology* 23(1): 154–89. London: Blackwell.

Elliot, David R. 1994. "Knowing No Borders: Canadian Contributions to American Fundamentalism." Pp. 429 in *Amazing Grace: Evangelicalism in Australia, Britain, Canada, and the United States, McGill-Queen's Studies in the History of Religion, 13,* edited by G. A. Rawlyk and M. A. Noll. Montréal: McGill-Queen's University Press.

Elliott, David Raymond and Iris Miller. 1987. *Bible Bill: A Biography of William Aberhart.* Edmonton, Alberta: Reidmore Books.

Ellis, Bill. 2000. *Raising the Devil: Satanism, New Religions, and the Media.* Lexington: University Press of Kentucky.

Ellison, Christopher G., John P. Bartkowski, and Michelle L. Segal. 1996. "Conservative Protestantism and the Parental Use of Corporal Punishment." *Social Forces* 74(3):1003–28.

Emerson, Michael O. and Christian Smith. 2000. *Divided by Faith: Evangelical Religion and the Problem of Race in America.* Oxford and New York: Oxford University Press.

Emerson, Michael O. and Rodney M. Woo. 2006. *People of the Dream: Multiracial Congregations in the United States.* Princeton, NJ: Princeton University Press.

Erzen, Tanya. 2006. *Straight to Jesus: Sexual and Christian Conversions in the Ex-Gay Movement.* Berkeley: University of California Press.

Esping-Andersen, Gøsta. 1990. *The Three Worlds of Welfare Capitalism.* Princeton, NJ: Princeton University Press.

Eveland, William and Steven Kleinman. 2013. "Comparing General and Political Discussion Networks within Voluntary Organizations Using Social Network Analysis." *Political Behavior* 35(1):65–87. doi: 10.1007/s11109–011–9187–4.

Eyerman, Ron. 2004. "The Past in the Present: Culture and the Transmission of Memory." *Acta Sociologica* 47(2):159–69. doi: 10.1177/0001699304043853.

Faassen, Mark. 2011. "A Fine Balance: The Regulation of Canadian Religious Broadcasting." *Queen's Law Journal* 37:303.

Farney, James. 2009. "The Personal Is Not Political: The Progressive Conservative Response to Social Issues." *American Review of Canadian Studies* 39(3):242–52. doi: 10.1080/02722010903146076.

Farr, Robert M. and Serge Moscovici. 1984. *Social Representation*. Cambridge: Cambridge University Press.

Fejes, Fred. 2008. *Gay Rights and Moral Panic: The Origins of America's Debate on Homosexuality*. New York: Palgrave Macmillan.

Fetner, Tina. 2008. *How the Religious Right Shaped Lesbian and Gay Activism*. Minneapolis: University of Minnesota Press.

Fine, Gary Alan. 1995. "Public Narration and Group Culture: Discerning Discourse in Social Movements." Pp. 127–43 in *Social Movements and Culture, Social Movements, Protest, and Contention, vol. 4*, edited by H. Johnston and B. Klandermans. Minneapolis: University of Minnesota Press.

———. 2003. "Towards a Peopled Ethnography: Developing Theory from Group Life." *Ethnography* 4(1):41–60.

Finke, Roger. 1994. "The Quiet Transformation: Changes in Size and Leadership of Southern Baptist Churches." *Review of Religious Research* 36(1):3–22. doi: 10.2307/3511649.

Finney, John M. 1978. "A Theory of Religious Commitment." *Sociology of Religion* 39(1):19–35.

Fiorina, Morris P., Samuel J. Abrams, and Jeremy Pope. 2006. *Culture War?: The Myth of a Polarized America*. New York: Pearson Longman.

Flanagan, Scott C. and Aie-rie Lee. 2003. "The New Politics, Culture Wars, and the Authoritarian-Libertarian Value Change in Advanced Industrial Democracies." *Comparative Political Studies* 36(3):235–70.

Frank, Thomas. 2004. *What's the Matter with Kansas?: How Conservatives Won the Heart of America*. New York: Metropolitan Books.

Fraser, Nancy and Linda Gordon. 1998. "Contract Versus Charity: Why Is There No Social Citizenship in the United States?" Pp. 113–27 in *The Citizenship Debates: A Reader*, edited by G. Shafir. Minneapolis: University of Minnesota Press.

Friedland, Roger. 2001. "Religious Nationalism and the Problem of Collective Representation." *Annual Review of Sociology* 27(1):125–52. doi:10.1146 /annurev.soc.27.1.125.

———. 2002. "Money, Sex, and God: The Erotic Logic of Religious Nationalism." *Sociological Theory* 20(3):381–425.

Friedland, Roger and Richard D. Hecht. 1996. *To Rule Jerusalem*. Cambridge and New York: Cambridge University Press.

Froese, Paul and F. Carson Mencken. 2009. "A U.S. Holy War? The Effects of Religion on Iraq War Policy Attitudes." *Social Science Quarterly* 90(1):103–16. doi: 10.1111/j.1540-6237.2009.00605.x.

Gallagher, Sally K. 2003. *Evangelical Identity and Gendered Family Life*. New Brunswick, NJ: Rutgers University Press.

Gallagher, Sally K. and Christian Smith. 1999. "Symbolic Traditionalism and Pragmatic Egalitarianism: Contemporary Evangelicals, Families, and Gender." *Gender and Society* 13(2):211–33.

Gamson, W. A. 1995. "Constructing Social Protest." *Social Movements and Culture* 4:85–106.

Ganiel, Gladys. 2008. "Explaining New Forms of Evangelical Activism in Northern Ireland: Comparative Perspectives from the USA and Canada." *Journal of Church and State* 50(3):475–93. doi: 10.1093/jcs/50.3.475.

Ganiel, Gladys and Claire Mitchell. 2006. "Turning the Categories Inside-Out: Complex Identifications and Multiple Interactions in Religious Ethnography." *Sociology of Religion* 67(1):3–21.

Ganz, Marshall. 2001. "The Power of Story in Social Movements." Paper presented at the Annual Meeting of the American Sociological Association, August 2001, Anaheim, California.

Garfinkel, Harold. 1967. *Studies in Ethnomethodology*. Englewood Cliffs, NJ: Prentice-Hall.

Gauvreau, Michael. 2005. *The Catholic Origins of Quebec's Quiet Revolution, 1931–1970*. Montreal: McGill-Queen's University Press.

Gauvreau, Michael and Nancy Christie. 2003. *Cultures of Citizenship in Post-War Canada, 1940–1955*. Montréal: McGill-Queen's University Press.

Ghaziani, Amin and Delia Baldassarri. 2011. "Cultural Anchors and the Organization of Differences." *American Sociological Review* 76(2):179–206. doi: 10 .1177/0003122411401252.

Gibson, M. Troy. 2004. "Culture Wars in State Education Policy: A Look at the Relative Treatment of Evolutionary Theory in State Science Standards." *Social Science Quarterly* 85(5):1129–49.

Gidengil, Elisabeth, Patrick Fournier, Joanna Everitt, Neil Nevitte, and André Blais. 2009. "The Anatomy of a Liberal Defeat." In *Annual Meeting of the Canadian Political Science Association* (May 2009), Carleton University, Ottawa/Canada.

Gidengil, Elisabeth, Matthew Hennigar, André Blais, and Neil Nevitte. 2005. "Explaining the Gender Gap in Support for the New Right: The Case of Canada." *Comparative Political Studies* 38(10):1171–95. doi: 10.1177 /0010414005279320.

Gilbreath, Edward. 2006. *Reconciliation Blues: A Black Evangelical's Inside View of White Christianity*. Downers Grove, IL: InterVarsity Press.

Gilens, Martin. 1999. *Why Americans Hate Welfare: Race, Media, and the Politics of Antipoverty Policy*. Chicago: University of Chicago Press.

Gilgoff, Dan. 2008. *The Jesus Machine: How James Dobson, Focus on the Family, and Evangelical America Are Winning the Culture War*. New York: St. Martin's Press.

Ginsburg, Faye D. 1989. *Contested Lives: The Abortion Debate in an American Community*. Berkeley: University of California Press.

Glaser, Barney G. and Anselm L. Strauss. 1967. *The Discovery of Grounded Theory: Strategies for Qualitative Research*. Chicago: Aldine Publishing.

Goffman, Erving. 1959. *The Presentation of Self in Everyday Life*. Garden City, NY: Doubleday.

———. 1967. *Interaction Ritual: Essays in Face-to-Face Behavior*. Chicago: Aldine Publishing.

Gold, Howard J. and Gina E. Russell. 2007. "The Rising Influence of Evangelicalism in American Political Behavior, 1980–2004." *Social Science Journal* 44(3):554–62.

Goldberg, Michelle. 2006. *Kingdom Coming: The Rise of Christian Nationalism.* New York: W.W. Norton.

Gorski, Philip S. 2000. "The Mosaic Moment: An Early Modernist Critique of Modernist Theories of Nationalism." *American Journal of Sociology* 105(5):1428–68.

Gould, Roger V. 1995. *Insurgent Identities: Class, Community, and Protest in Paris from 1848 to the Commune.* Chicago: University of Chicago Press.

Grabb, Edward G. and James E. Curtis. 2005. *Regions Apart: The Four Societies of Canada and the United States.* New York: Oxford University Press.

Gravel, Alain [Director]. 2011. February 10. *À La Droite De Harper.* Available online: http://www.radio-canada.ca/emissions/enquete/2010–2011/Reportage .asp?idDoc=133851&autoPlay=http://www.radio-canada.ca/Medianet/2011 /CBFT/Enquete201102102000_3.asx,%20http://www.radio-canada.ca/Media net/2011/CBFT/Enquete201102102000_4.asx.

Greeley, Andrew M. and Michael Hout. 2006. *The Truth About Conservative Christians: What They Think and What They Believe.* Chicago: University of Chicago Press.

Green, Donald P., Bradley Palmquist, and Eric Schickler. 2002. *Partisan Hearts and Minds: Political Parties and the Social Identities of Voters.* New Haven, CT: Yale University Press.

Green, John. 2008. "A Post-Election Look at Religious Voters in the 2008 Election." In *Faith Angle Conference*: Pew Research Religion and Public Life Project.

Green, John C. 2006. "Ohio: The Bible and the Buckeye State." Pp. 79–97 in *The Values Campaign?: The Christian Right and the 2004 Elections*, edited by J. C. Green. Washington, DC: Georgetown University Press.

Green, John C., Mark J. Rozell, and Clyde Wilcox. 2001. "Social Movements and Party Politics: The Case of the Christian Right." *Journal for the Scientific Study of Religion* 40(3):413–26.

Green, John Clifford, Mark J. Rozell, and Clyde Wilcox. 2000. *Prayers in the Precincts: The Christian Right in the 1998 Elections.* Washington, DC: Georgetown University Press.

Greene, Steven. 2002. "The Social-Psychological Measurement of Partisanship." *Political Behavior* 24(3):171–97.

———. 2004. "Social Identity Theory and Party Identification." *Social Science Quarterly* 85(1):136–53. doi:10.1111/j.0038–4941.2004.08501010.x.

Griffith, R. Marie. 2000. *God's Daughters: Evangelical Women and the Power of Submission.* Berkeley and Los Angeles: University of California Press.

Gross, Neil. 2009. "A Pragmatist Theory of Social Mechanisms." *American Sociological Review* 74(3):358–79. doi: 10.1177/000312240907400302.

Gruending, Dennis. 2011. *Pulpit and Politics: Competing Religious Ideologies in Canadian Public Life.* Cochrane, Alberta: Kingsley Publishing.

Guder, Darrell L. and Lois Barrett. 1998. *Missional Church: A Vision for the Sending of the Church in North America.* Grand Rapids, MI: W.B. Eerdmans.

Gushee, David P. 2008. *The Future of Faith in American Politics: The Public Witness of the Evangelical Center.* Waco, TX: Baylor University Press.

Guth, James L., Linda Beail, Greg Crow, Beverly Gaddy, Steve Montreal, Brent

Nelsen, James Penning, and Jeff Walz. 2003. "The Political Activity of Evangelical Clergy in the Election of 2000: A Case Study of Five Denominations." *Journal for the Scientific Study of Religion* 42(4):501–14. doi:10.1046/j .1468–5906.2003.00199.x.

Guth, James L. and Cleveland R. Fraser. 1998. "Religion and Partisanship in Canada." *Journal for the Scientific Study of Religion* 3:6.

———. 2001. "Religion and Partisanship in Canada." *Journal for the Scientific Study of Religion* 40(1):51.

Guth, James L., John C. Green, Corwin E. Smidt, Lyman A. Kellstedt, and Margaret M. Poloma. 1997. *The Bully Pulpit: The Politics of Protestant Clergy.* Lawrence: University Press of Kansas.

Guth, James L., Lyman A. Kellstedt, Corwin E. Smidt, and John C. Green. 2006. "Religious Influences in the 2004 Presidential Election." *Presidential Studies Quarterly* 36(2):223–42.

Habermas, Jürgen and Eduardo Mendieta. 2002. *Religion and Rationality: Essays on Reason, God, and Modernity.* Cambridge, MA: MIT Press.

Hacker, Jacob S. and Paul Pierson. 2005. *Off Center: The Republican Revolution and the Erosion of American Democracy.* New Haven, CT: Yale University Press.

Haidt, Jonathan. 2007. "The New Synthesis in Moral Psychology." *Science* 316(5827):998–1002. doi: 10.1126/science.1137651.

Haidt, Jonathan and Jesse Graham. 2007. "When Morality Opposes Justice: Conservatives Have Moral Intuitions That Liberals May Not Recognize." *Social Justice Research* 20(1):98–116.

Handler, Joel F. and Yeheskel Hasenfeld. 1991. *The Moral Construction of Poverty: Welfare Reform in America.* Newbury Park, CA: Sage Publications.

Handy, Robert T. 1966. *The Social Gospel in America, 1870–1920.* New York: Oxford University Press.

Hangen, Tona J. 2002. *Redeeming the Dial: Radio, Religion and Popular Culture in America.* Chapel Hill: University of North Carolina Press.

Hankins, Barry. 1998. "Principle, Perception, and Position: Why Southern Baptist Conservatives Differ from Moderates on Church-State Issues." *Journal of Church and State* 40(2):343–70.

Harrington, Brooke and Gary Alan Fine. 2000. "Opening the 'Black Box': Small Groups and Twenty-First-Century Sociology." *Social Psychology Quarterly* 63(4):312–23.

Hart, Stephen. 1992. *What Does the Lord Require?: How American Christians Think About Economic Justice.* New York: Oxford University Press.

Hartz, Louis. 1955. *The Liberal Tradition in America: An Interpretation of American Political Thought since the Revolution.* New York: Harcourt, Brace.

Hauerwas, Stanley. 1981. *A Community of Character: Toward a Constructive Christian Social Ethic.* Notre Dame, IN: University of Notre Dame Press.

Haussman, Melissa. 2005. *Abortion Politics in North America.* Boulder, CO: Lynne Rienner.

Haws, J. B. 2013. *The Mormon Image in the American Mind: Fifty Years of Public Perception.* New York: Oxford University Press.

Hays, Sharon. 2003. *Flat Broke with Children: Women in the Age of Welfare Reform*. Oxford, New York: Oxford University Press.

Hayward, R. David and Marta Elliott. 2011. "Subjective and Objective Fit in Religious Congregations: Implications for Well-Being." *Group Processes & Intergroup Relations* 14(1):127–39. doi: 10.1177/1368430210370041.

Heaney, Michael T. 2010. "Linking Political Parties and Interest Groups." In *The Oxford Handbook of American Political Parties and Interest Groups*, edited by L. S. Maisel and J. M. Berry. New York: Oxford University Press.

Hedges, Chris. 2006. *American Fascists: The Christian Right and the War on America*. New York: Free Press.

Hempel, Lynn M. and John P. Bartkowski. 2008. "Scripture, Sin and Salvation: Theological Conservatism Reconsidered." *Social Forces* 86(4):1647–74.

Hendershot, Heather. 2004. *Shaking the World for Jesus: Media and Conservative Evangelical Culture*. Chicago: University of Chicago Press.

———. 2007. "God's Angriest Man: Carl Mcintire, Cold War Fundamentalism, and Right-Wing Broadcasting." *American Quarterly* 59(2):373–96.

Herberg, Will. 1955. *Protestant, Catholic, Jew; an Essay in American Religious Sociology*. Garden City, NY: Doubleday.

Herman, Didi. 1994. "The Christian Right and the Politics of Morality in Canada." *Parliamentary Affairs* 47(2):268–79.

Hetherington, Marc J. 2001. "Resurgent Mass Partisanship: The Role of Elite Polarization." *American Political Science Review* 95(03):619–31. doi:10.1017/S0003055401003045.

Hetherington, Marc J. and Jonathan Daniel Weiler. 2009. *Authoritarianism and Polarization in American Politics*. New York: Cambridge University Press.

Hexham, Irving. 2002. "Canadian Alliance Changes Leaders." *Christianity Today*, July 8, p. 15.

Hiller, Harry H. 2000. "Civil Religion and the Problem of National Unity: The 1995 Quebec Referendum Crisis." Pp. 166–86 in *Rethinking Church, State, and Modernity: Canada between Europe and America*, edited by D. Lyon and M. Van Die. Toronto: University of Toronto Press.

Hinojosa, Victor J. and Jerry Z. Park. 2004. "Religion and the Paradox of Racial Inequality Attitudes." *Journal for the Scientific Study of Religion* 43(2):229–38. doi: 10.1111/j.1468–5906.2004.00229.x.

Hoge, R., Benton Johnson, and Donald A. Luidens. 1995. "Types of Denominational Switching among Protestant Young Adults." *Journal for the Scientific Study of Religion* 34(2):253–58.

Hogg, Michael A. and Sarah C. Hains. 1996. "Intergroup Relations and Group Solidarity: Effects of Group Identification and Social Beliefs on Depersonalized Attraction." *Journal of Personality and Social Psychology* 70(2):295–309. doi: 10.1037/0022–3514.70.2.295.

Hoover, Dennis R. 1997a. "Conservative Protestant Politics in the U.S. and Canada." Unpublished dissertation, University of Oxford.

———. 1997b. "The Christian Right under Old Glory and the Maple Leaf." Pp. 193–216 in *Sojourners in the Wilderness: The Christian Right in Comparative Perspective*, edited by C. E. Smidt and J. M. Penning. Lanham, MD: Rowman & Littlefield.

Hoover, Dennis R. and Kevin R. den Dulk. 2004. "Christian Conservatives Go to Court: Religion and Legal Mobilization in the United States and Canada." *International Political Science Review/ Revue internationale de science politique* 25(1):9–34.

Hoover, Dennis R., Michael D. Martinez, Samuel H. Reimer, and Kenneth D. Wald. 2002. "Evangelicalism Meets the Continental Divide: Moral and Economic Conservatism in the United States and Canada." *Political Research Quarterly* 55(2):351–74.

Horowitz, Gad. 1966. "Conservatism, Liberalism, and Socialism in Canada: An Interpretation." *Canadian Journal of Economics and Political Science/Revue canadienne d'Economique et de Science politique* 32(2):143–71.

Hout, Michael and Claude S. Fischer. 2002. "Why More Americans Have No Religious Preference: Politics and Generations." *American Sociological Review* 67(2):165–90.

Hout, Michael, Andrew Greeley, and Melissa J. Wilde. 2001. "The Demographic Imperative in Religious Change in the United States." *American Journal of Sociology* 107(2):468–500. doi:10.1086/324189.

Howard, Christopher. 2007. *The Welfare State Nobody Knows: Debunking Myths About U.S. Social Policy.* Princeton, NJ: Princeton University Press.

Huddy, Leonie and Nadia Khatib. 2007. "American Patriotism, National Identity, and Political Involvement." *American Journal of Political Science* 51(1):63–77. doi: 10.1111/j.1540–5907.2007.00237.x.

Hudson, Kenneth and Andrea Coukos. 2005. "The Dark Side of the Protestant Ethic: A Comparative Analysis of Welfare Reform." *Sociological Theory* 23(1):1–24. doi: 10.1111/j.0735–2751.2005.00240.x.

Hunt, Scott A., Robert D. Benford, and David A. Snow. 1994. "Identity Fields: Framing Processes and the Social Construction of Movement Identities." Pp. 185–208 in *New Social Movements: From Ideology to Identity*, edited by Enrique Laraña, Hank Johnston, and Joseph R. Gusfield. Philadelphia: Temple University Press.

Hunter, James Davison. 1987. *Evangelicalism: The Coming Generation.* Chicago: University of Chicago Press.

———. 1991. *Culture Wars: The Struggle to Define America.* New York: Basic Books.

———. 1994. *Before the Shooting Begins: Searching for Democracy in America's Culture War.* New York: Free Press.

Hunter, James Davison and Alan Wolfe. 2006. *Is There a Culture War?: A Dialogue on Values and American Public Life.* Washington, DC, Bristol: Brookings.

Hutchinson, Donald and Rick Hiemstra. 2009. "Canadian Evangelical Voting Trends by Region, 1996–2008." 2(3). *Church and Faith Trends: A Publication of the Centre for Research on Canadian Evangelicalism.*

Iannaccone, Laurence R. 1988. "A Formal Model of Church and Sect." *American Journal of Sociology* 94 (Supplement: Organizations and Institutions: Sociological and Economic Approaches to the Analysis of Social Structure): S241–S68.

———. 1994. "Why Strict Churches Are Strong." *American Journal of Sociology* 99(5):1180–1211.

Inglehart, Ronald. 1990. *Culture Shift in Advanced Industrial Society*. Princeton, NJ: Princeton University Press.

Inglehart, Ronald and Wayne E. Baker. 2000. "Modernization, Cultural Change, and the Persistence of Traditional Values." *American Sociological Review* 65(1):19–51.

Introvigne, Massimo. 1994. "The Devil Makers: Contemporary Evangelical Fundamentalist Anti-Mormonism." *Dialogue: A Journal of Mormon Thought* 27(1):153–69.

James, William. 2004. *The Varieties of Religious Experience: A Study in Human Nature*. New York: Barnes & Noble Classics.

Jelen, Ted G. 1992. "Political Christianity: A Contextual Analysis." *American Journal of Political Science* 36(3):692–714.

———. 1993. "The Political Consequences of Religious Group Attitudes." *Journal of Politics* 55(1):178–90.

Jelen, Ted G. and Martha A. Chandler. 1994. *Abortion Politics in the United States and Canada: Studies in Public Opinion*. Westport, CT: Praeger.

Jelen, Ted G. and Clyde Wilcox. 2002. *Religion and Politics in Comparative Perspective: The One, the Few, and the Many*. New York: Cambridge University Press.

Johnston, Richard. 2006. "Party Identification: Unmoved Mover or Sum of Preferences?" *Annual Review of Political Science* 9(1):329–51. doi:10.1146/annurev.polisci.9.062404.170523.

Kabaservice, Geoffrey. 2011. *Rule and Ruin: The Downfall of Moderation and the Destruction of the Republican Party, from Eisenhower to the Tea Party*. New York: Oxford University Press.

Kahan, Dan and Donald Braman. 2006. "Cultural Cognition and Public Policy." *Yale Law & Policy Review* 24:147.

Kane, Anne. 1991. "Cultural Analysis in Historical Sociology: The Analytic and Concrete Forms of the Autonomy of Culture." *Sociological Theory* 9(1): 53–69.

Kane, Melinda D. 2007. "Timing Matters: Shifts in the Causal Determinants of Sodomy Law Decriminalization, 1961–1998." *Social Problems* 54(2):211–39. doi:10.1525/sp.2007.54.2.211.

Karol, David. 2009. *Party Position Change in American Politics: Coalition Management*. Cambridge and New York: Cambridge University Press.

———. 2012. "How Does Party Position Change Happen? The Case of Gay Rights in the U.S. Congress." Paper presented at the Annual Meeting of the Southern Political Science Association, New Orleans, Louisiana.

Katz, Elihu, and Paul Felix Lazarsfeld. 1955. *Personal Influence: The Part Played by People in the Flow of Mass Communications*, Edited by Bureau of Applied Social Research, Columbia University. Glencoe, IL: Free Press.

Katz, Michael B. 1986. *In the Shadow of the Poorhouse: A Social History of Welfare in America*. New York: Basic Books.

Kaufman, Jason Andrew. 2009. *The Origins of Canadian and American Political Differences*. Cambridge, MA: Harvard University Press.

Kaufmann, Karen M. 2002. "Culture Wars, Secular Realignment, and the Gender Gap in Party Identification." *Political Behavior* 24(3):283–307.

Kazin, Michael. 2007. *A Godly Hero: The Life of William Jennings Bryan*. New York: Anchor.

Keith, Bruce E., D. B. Magleby, C. J. Nelson, E. Orr, M.C. Westlye, and R. E. Wolfinger. 1992. *The Myth of the Independent Voter*. Berkeley: University of California Press.

Kellstedt, Lyman A. and John C. Green. 2003. "The Politics of the Willow Creek Association Pastors." *Journal for the Scientific Study of Religion* 42:547–61.

Killen, Patricia O'Connell and Mark Silk. 2004. *Religion and Public Life in the Pacific Northwest: The None Zone*, Vol. 1. Walnut Creek, CA: Altamira Press.

Kim, Andrew. 1993. "The Absence of Pan-Canadian Civil Religion." *Sociology of Religion* 44(3):257–75.

Kinnaman, David and Gabe Lyons. 2007. *Unchristian: What a New Generation Really Thinks About Christianity—and Why It Matters*. Grand Rapids, MI: Baker Books.

Kniss, Fred. 1996. "Ideas and Symbols as Resources in Intrareligious Conflict: The Case of American Mennonites." *Sociology of Religion* 57(1):7–23.

Kutolowski, Kathleen Smith. 1984. "Antimasonry Reexamined: Social Bases of the Grass-Roots Party." *Journal of American History* 71(2):269–93.

Kymlicka, Will. 1998. *Finding Our Way: Rethinking Ethnocultural Relations in Canada*, Vol. 19. Toronto: Oxford University Press.

Kymlicka, Will and Keith G. Banting. 2006. *Multiculturalism and the Welfare State: Recognition and Redistribution in Contemporary Democracies*. Oxford and New York: Oxford University Press.

Lakoff, George. 2002. *Moral Politics: How Liberals and Conservatives Think*. Chicago: University of Chicago Press.

Lamont, Michèle. 1992. *Money, Morals, and Manners: The Culture of the French and American Upper-Middle Class*. Chicago: University of Chicago Press.

———. 2000. *The Dignity of Working Men: Morality and the Boundaries of Race, Class, and Immigration*. New York and Cambridge, MA: Russell Sage Foundation, Harvard University Press.

Lamont, Michele and Virag Molnar. 2002. "The Study of Boundaries in the Social Sciences." *Annual Review of Sociology* 28(1):167–95. doi:10.1146/annurev.soc.28.110601.141107.

Lamont, Michèle and Laurent Thévenot. 2000. "Introduction: Toward a Renewed Comparative Cultural Sociology." Pp. xv, 375 in *Rethinking Comparative Cultural Sociology: Repertoires of Evaluation in France and the United States, Cambridge Cultural Social Studies*, edited by M. Lamont and L. Thévenot. Cambridge, UK and New York: Cambridge University Press.

Landes, Ronald G. 1995. *The Canadian Polity: A Comparative Introduction*. Scarborough, ON: Prentice Hall Canada.

Lareau, Annette and Dalton Conley. 2008. *Social Class: How Does It Work?* New York: Russell Sage Foundation.

Larsen, Christian Albrekt. 2006. *The Institutional Logic of Welfare Attitudes: How Welfare Regimes Influence Public Support*. Aldershot, UK and Burlington, VT: Ashgate.

Lassiter, Matthew D. 2006. *The Silent Majority: Suburban Politics in the Sunbelt South*. Princeton, NJ: Princeton University Press.

Laycock, David H. 2002. *The New Right and Democracy in Canada: Understanding Reform and the Canadian Alliance*. New York: Oxford University Press.

Layman, Geoffrey C. 2001. *The Great Divide: Religious and Cultural Conflict in American Party Politics*. New York: Columbia University Press.

Layman, Geoffrey C. and Thomas M. Carsey. 2002. "Party Polarization and 'Conflict Extension' in the American Electorate." *American Journal of Political Science* 46(4):786–802.

Layman, Geoffrey C., Thomas M. Carsey, and Juliana Menasce Horowitz. 2006. "Party Polarization in American Politics: Characteristics, Causes, and Consequences." *Annual Review of Political Science* 9(1):83–110. doi:10.1146/annurev.polisci.9.070204.105138.

Layman, Geoffrey C. and John C. Green. 2005. "Wars and Rumours of Wars: The Contexts of Cultural Conflict in American Political Behaviour." *British Journal of Political Science* 36(01):61–89.

Lazerwitz, Bernard. 1995. "Denominational Retention and Switching among American Jews." *Journal for the Scientific Study of Religion* 34(4):499–506.

Leege, David C. 2002. *The Politics of Cultural Differences: Social Change and Voter Mobilization Strategies in the Post–New Deal Period*. Princeton, NJ: Princeton University Press.

Leege, David C. and Lyman A. Kellstedt. 1993. *Rediscovering the Religious Factor in American Politics*. Armonk, NY: M.E. Sharpe.

Leonard, Bill J. 1990. *God's Last and Only Hope*. Grand Rapids, MI: William B. Eerdmans.

Libin, Kevin. 2010. "Grants and Drag Queens Don't Mix." *National Post*, May 11.

Lichterman, Paul. 2005. *Elusive Togetherness: Church Groups Trying to Bridge America's Divisions*. Princeton, NJ: Princeton University Press.

———. 2008. "Religion and the Construction of Civic Identity." *American Sociological Review* 73:83–104.

———. 2009. "Social Capacity and the Styles of Group Life." *American Behavioral Scientist* 52(6):846–66. doi: 10.1177/0002764208327662.

Lichtman, Allan J. 2008. *White Protestant Nation: The Rise of the American Conservative Movement*. New York: Atlantic Monthly Press.

Lienesch, Michael. 1993. *Redeeming America: Piety and Politics in the New Christian Right*. Chapel Hill: University of North Carolina Press.

Lindsay, D. Michael. 2008. "Evangelicals in the Power Elite: Elite Cohesion Advancing a Movement." *American Sociological Review* 73:60–82.

Lindsay, David Michael. 2007. *Faith in the Halls of Power: How Evangelicals Joined the American Elite*. Oxford, New York: Oxford University Press.

Lipset, Seymour Martin. 1963a. "The Value Patterns of Democracy: A Case Study in Comparative Analysis." *American Sociological Review* 28(4):515–31.

———. 1963b. *Political Man: The Social Bases of Politics*. Garden City, NY: Anchor Books.

————. 1990. *Continental Divide: The Values and Institutions of the United States and Canada.* New York: Routledge.

Lipset, Seymour Martin and Stein Rokkan. 1967. "Cleavage Structures, Party Systems, and Voter Alignments: An Introduction." Pp. 1–64 in *Party Systems and Voter Alignments: Cross-National Perspectives, International Yearbook of Political Behavior Research V. 7*, edited by S. M. Lipset and S. Rokkan. New York: Free Press.

Loveland, Matthew T. 2003. "Religious Switching: Preference Development, Maintenance, and Change." *Journal for the Scientific Study of Religion* 42(1): 147–57.

Lugo, Luis, Sandra Stencel, John Green, Gregory Smith, and Allison Pond. 2006. "Spirit and Power: A 10-Country Survey of Pentecostals." Washington, DC: Pew Research Center.

Lugo, Luis, Sandra Stencel, John Green, Gregory Smith, Dan Cox, Allison Pond, Tracy Miller, Elizabeth Podrebarac, Michelle Ralston, and Hilary Ramp. 2008. "U.S. Religious Landscape Study." Pew Research Center: Pew Forum on Public Life. Washington, DC: Pew Research Center.

Luker, Kristin. 1984. *Abortion and the Politics of Motherhood.* Berkeley: University of California Press.

————. 1996. *Dubious Conceptions: The Politics of Teenage Pregnancy.* Cambridge, MA: Harvard University Press.

————. 2006. *When Sex Goes to School: Warring Views on Sex—and Sex Education—since the Sixties.* New York: W. W. Norton.

Lusztig, Michael and J. Matthew Wilson. 2005. "A New Right? Moral Issues and Partisan Change in Canada." *Social Science Quarterly* 86(1):109–28. doi:10.1111/j.0038–4941.2005.00293.x.

Mackey, Lloyd. 2005. *The Pilgrimage of Stephen Harper.* Toronto: ECW Press.

Madsen, Richard. 2009. "The Archipelago of Faith: Religious Individualism and Faith Community in America Today." *American Journal of Sociology* 114(5): 1263–1301.

Mahaffy, Kimberly A. 1996. "Cognitive Dissonance and Its Resolution: A Study of Lesbian Christians." *Journal for the Scientific Study of Religion* 35(4): 392–402.

Maioni, Antonia. 1998. *Parting at the Crossroads: The Emergence of Health Insurance in the United States and Canada.* Princeton, NJ: Princeton University Press.

Malka, Ariel and Yphtach Lelkes. 2010. "More Than Ideology: Conservative-Liberal Identity and Receptivity to Political Cues." *Social Justice Research* 23(2):156–88. doi: 10.1007/s11211–010–0114–3.

Malloy, Jonathan. 2009. "Bush/Harper? Canadian and American Evangelical Politics Compared." *American Review of Canadian Studies* 39(4):352–63.

————. 2011. "Between America and Europe: Religion, Politics and Evangelicals in Canada." *Politics, Religion & Ideology* 12(3):317–33. doi: 10.1080/21567689 .2011.596416.

Margoshes, Dave. 1999. *Tommy Douglas: Building the New Society.* Montréal: XYZ Publishing.

Marti, Gerardo. 2009. *A Mosaic of Believers: Diversity and Innovation in a Multiethnic Church*. Bloomington: Indiana University Press.

Martin, Lawrence. 2010. *Harperland: The Politics of Control*. Toronto: Viking Canada.

Martin, William C. 1996. *With God on Our Side: The Rise of the Religious Right in America*. New York: Broadway Books.

Martínez, Juan Francisco. 2011. *Los Protestantes: An Introduction to Latino Protestantism in the United States*. Santa Barbara, CA: Praeger.

McAdam, Doug, Sidney G. Tarrow, and Charles Tilly. 2001. *Dynamics of Contention*. New York: Cambridge University Press.

McAdams, Dan P. 2006. *The Redemptive Self: Stories Americans Live By*. Oxford and New York: Oxford University Press.

McAdams, Dan P., Nana Akua Anyidoho, Chelsea Brown, Yi Ting Huang, Bonnie Kaplan, and Mary Anne Machado. 2004. "Traits and Stories: Links between Dispositional and Narrative Features of Personality." *Journal of Personality* 72(4):761–84. doi:10.1111/j.0022–3506.2004.00279.x.

McCall, George J. and J. L. Simmons. 1978. *Identities and Interactions: An Examination of Human Associations in Everyday Life*. New York: Free Press.

McCarthy, Molly. 1993. "3 Incumbents in Williamsville Re-Elected; Voter Turnout Is the Highest in Years; $86.8 Million Budget Approved." *Buffalo News*, Buffalo, NY.

McCarty, Nolan M., Keith T. Poole, and Howard Rosenthal. 2006. *Polarized America: The Dance of Ideology and Unequal Riches*. Cambridge, MA: MIT Press.

McClurg, Scott D. 2003. "Social Networks and Political Participation: The Role of Social Interaction in Explaining Political Participation." *Political Research Quarterly* 56(4):449–64.

———. 2006. "The Electoral Relevance of Political Talk: Examining Disagreement and Expertise Effects in Social Networks on Political Participation." *American Journal of Political Science* 50(3):737–54.

McDaniel, Eric Leon, Irfan Nooruddin, and Allyson Faith Shortle. 2011. "Divine Boundaries: How Religion Shapes Citizens' Attitudes toward Immigrants." *American Politics Research* 39(1):205–33. doi: 10.1177/1532673x10371300.

McDonald, Marci. 2010. *The Armageddon Factor: The Rise of Christian Nationalism in Canada*. Toronto: Random House Canada.

McLeod, Thomas H. and Ian McLeod. 1987. *Tommy Douglas: The Road to Jerusalem*. Edmonton: Hurtig.

McMath, Robert C. and Eric Foner. 1993. *American Populism: A Social History, 1877–1898*. New York: Hill and Wang.

McPherson, Miller, Lynn Smith-Lovin, and James M. Cook. 2001. "Birds of a Feather: Homophily in Social Networks." *Annual Review of Sociology* 27(1):415–44. doi:10.1146/annurev.soc.27.1.415.

McRoberts, Omar M. 1999. "Understanding the 'New' Black Pentecostal Activism: Lessons from Ecumenical Urban Ministries in Boston." *Sociology of Religion* 60:47–70.

———. 2003. *Streets of Glory: Church and Community in a Black Urban Neighborhood*. Chicago: University of Chicago.

———. 2004. "Beyond Mysterium Tremendum: Thoughts toward an Aesthetic Study of Religious Experience." *Annals of the American Academy of Political and Social Science* 595(1):190–203. doi: 10.1177/0002716204267111.

McTague, John Michael. 2010. "Contested Populism: The Cross-Pressured White Working Class in American Politics." PhD Dissertation, Department of Government and Politics, University of Maryland, College Park.

Mehta, Jal David and Christopher Winship. 2010. "Moral Power." Pp. 425–38 in *Handbook of the Sociology of Morality*, edited by S. Hitlin and S. Vaisey. New York: Springer.

Mettler, Suzanne. 2002. "Bringing the State Back in to Civic Engagement: Policy Feedback Effects of the G.I. Bill for World War II Veterans." *American Political Science Review* 96(2):351–65.

Mettler, Suzanne and Joe Soss. 2004. "The Consequences of Public Policy for Democratic Citizenship: Bridging Policy Studies and Mass Politics." *Perspectives on Politics* 2(01):55–73.

Meyer, David S. and Suzanne Staggenborg. 1996. "Movements, Countermovements, and the Structure of Political Opportunity." *American Journal of Sociology* 101(6):1628–60.

Miedema, Gary R. 2005. *For Canada's Sake: Public Religion, Centennial Celebrations, and the Re-Making of Canada in the 1960s*. Montréal: McGill-Queen's University Press.

Miles, Matthew B. and A. M. Huberman. 1994. *Qualitative Data Analysis: An Expanded Sourcebook*. Thousand Oaks, CA: Sage Publications.

Miller, Steven P. 2009. *Billy Graham and the Rise of the Republican South*. Philadelphia: University of Pennsylvania Press.

Miller, Warren E. and J. Merrill Shanks. 1996. *The New American Voter*. Cambridge, MA: Harvard University Press.

Mintz, Steven and Susan Kellogg. 1989. *Domestic Revolutions: A Social History of American Family Life*. New York: Simon & Schuster.

Mische, Ann. 2001. "Juggling Multiple Futures: Personal and Collective Project-Formation among Brazilian Youth Leaders." Pp. 137–59 in *Leadership and Social Movements*, edited by C. Barker. Manchester: Manchester University Press.

———. 2008. *Partisan Publics: Communication and Contention across Brazilian Youth Activist Networks*. Princeton, NJ: Princeton University Press.

Mohr, John W. 1994. "Soldiers, Mothers, Tramps and Others: Discourse Roles in the 1907 New York City Charity Directory." *Poetics* 22(4):327–57.

Moon, Dawne. 2004. *God, Sex, and Politics: Homosexuality and Everyday Theologies*. Chicago: University of Chicago Press.

Morone, James A. 2003. *Hellfire Nation: The Politics of Sin in American History*. New Haven, CT: Yale University Press.

Munson, Ziad. 2007. "When a Funeral Isn't Just a Funeral: The Layered Meaning of Everyday Action." Pp. x, 243 in *Everyday Religion: Observing Modern Religious Lives*, edited by N. T. Ammerman. Oxford and New York: Oxford University Press.

Munson, Ziad W. 2008. *The Making of Pro-Life Activists: How Social Movement Mobilization Works*. Chicago: University of Chicago Press.

Myles, John. 1998. "How to Design a 'Liberal' Welfare State: A Comparison of Canada and the United States." *Social Policy & Administration* 32(4):341–64. doi:10.1111/1467–9515.00120.

Nash, Lee. 1972. "Evangelism and Social Concern." Pp. p. 133–55 in *The Cross and the Flag*, edited by R. G. Clouse, R. D. Linder, and R. V. Pierard. Carol Stream, IL: Creation House.

Newbigin, Lesslie. 1989. *The Gospel in a Pluralist Society*. Grand Rapids, MI: W.B. Eerdmans.

Newbigin, Lesslie and Paul Weston. 2006. *Lesslie Newbigin: Missionary Theologian: A Reader*. Grand Rapids, MI: W.B. Eerdmans.

Nicoli, Lisa Thiebaud. 2012. "Half a Loaf: Generosity in Cash Assistance to Single Mothers across US States, 1911–1996." Sociology, PhD thesis, University of Arizona.

Nielsen, Donald A. 2001. "Transformation of Society and the Sacred in Durkheim's Religious Sociology." Pp. 120–33 in *The Blackwell Companion to Sociology of Religion*, edited by R. K. Fenn. Malden, MA: Blackwell.

Noll, Mark A. 1992. *A History of Christianity in the United States and Canada*. Grand Rapids, MI: W.B. Eerdmans.

———. 2001. *American Evangelical Christianity: An Introduction*. Oxford and Malden, MA: Blackwell.

———. 2007. *What Happened to Christian Canada?* Vancouver: Regent College Publishing.

Noll, Mark A., David W. Bebbington, and George A. Rawlyk. 1994. *Evangelicalism: Comparative Studies of Popular Protestantism in North America, the British Isles, and Beyond, 1700–1900*. New York: Oxford University Press.

Noll, Mark A., Nathan O. Hatch, and George M. Marsden. 1989. *The Search for Christian America*. Colorado Springs: Helmers & Howard.

Norris, Pippa and Ronald Inglehart. 2004. *Sacred and Secular: Religion and Politics Worldwide*. Cambridge, UK and New York: Cambridge University Press.

Nunberg, Geoffrey. 2006. *Talking Right: How Conservatives Turned Liberalism into a Tax-Raising, Latte-Drinking, Sushi-Eating, Volvo-Driving, New York Times-Reading, Body-Piercing, Hollywood-Loving, Left-Wing Freak Show*. New York: Public Affairs.

Olasky, Marvin N. 1992. *The Tragedy of American Compassion*. Washington, DC: Regnery Gateway.

———. 2000. *Compassionate Conservatism: What It Is, What It Does, and How It Can Transform America*. New York: Free Press.

Olasky, Marvin N. and Newt Gingrich. 1996. *Renewing American Compassion*. New York: Free Press.

Olick, Jeffrey K. and Joyce Robbins. 1998. "Social Memory Studies: From 'Collective Memory' to the Historical Sociology of Mnemonic Practices." *Annual Review of Sociology* 24:105–40.

Orloff, Ann Shola. 1993. "Gender and the Social Rights of Citizenship: The Comparative Analysis of Gender Relations and Welfare States." *American Sociological Review* 58(3):303–28.

Orsi, Robert. 1998. *Thank You, St. Jude: Women's Devotion to the Patron Saint of Hopeless Causes*. New Haven, CT: Yale University Press.

Owen, Dennis E., Kenneth D. Wald, and Samuel S. Hill. 1991. "Authoritarian or Authority-Minded? The Cognitive Commitments of Fundamentalists and the Christian Right." *Religion and American Culture: A Journal of Interpretation* 1(1):73–100.

Owram, Doug. 1996. *Born at the Right Time: A History of the Baby-Boom Generation.* Toronto: University of Toronto Press.

Pachucki, Mark A. and Ronald L. Breiger. 2010. "Cultural Holes: Beyond Relationality in Social Networks and Culture." *Annual Review of Sociology* 36(1):205–24. doi:10.1146/annurev.soc.012809.102615.

Pachucki, Mark A., Sabrina Pendergrass, and Michele Lamont. 2007. "Boundary Processes: Recent Theoretical Developments and New Contributions." *Poetics* 35(6):331–51.

Pal, Leslie. 1991. "How Ottawa Dithers: The Conservatives and Abortion Policy." In *How Ottawa Spends: 1991–1992*, edited by F. Abele. Ottawa: Carleton University Press.

Patrikios, Stratos. 2008. "American Republican Religion? Disentangling the Causal Link between Religion and Politics in the US." *Political Behavior* 30(3):367–89. doi: 10.1007/s11109–008–9053–1.

Pattillo-McCoy, Mary. 1998. "Church Culture as a Strategy of Action in the Black Community." *American Sociological Review* 63(6):767–84.

Phillips-Fein, Kim. 2010. *Invisible Hands: The Businessmen's Crusade against the New Deal.* New York: W.W. Norton.

Plutzer, Eric. 2004. "Becoming a Habitual Voter: Inertia, Resources, and Growth in Young Adulthood." *American Political Science Review* 96(01):41–56. doi:10.1017/S0003055402004227.

Polletta, Francesca. 1998a. " 'It Was Like a Fever . . .' Narrative and Identity in Social Protest." *Social Problems* 45(2):137–59.

———. 1998b. "Contending Stories: Narrative in Social Movements." *Qualitative Sociology* 21(4):419–46.

———. 2006. *It Was Like a Fever: Storytelling in Protest and Politics.* Chicago: University of Chicago Press.

Polls, Ipsos Global. 2012. "Canadians Assess Key Social-Values Questions Facing the Country." Available online: https://www.ipsos-na.com/news-polls/pressrelease.aspx?id=5690.

Prasad, Monica, Andrew J. Perrin, Kieran Bezila, Steve G. Hoffman, Kate Kindleberger, Kim Manturuk, Ashleigh Smith Powers, and Andrew R. Payton. 2009. "The Undeserving Rich: 'Moral Values' and the White Working Class." *Sociological Forum* 24(2):225–53. doi: 10.1111/j.1573–7861.2009.01098.x.

Press, Eyal. 2006. *Absolute Convictions: My Father, a City, and the Conflict That Divided America.* New York: Henry Holt.

Pross, A. Paul. 1975. *Pressure Group Behaviour in Canadian Politics.* Scarborough, ON: McGraw-Hill Ryerson.

Putnam, Robert D. and David E. Campbell. 2010. *American Grace: How Religion Divides and Unites Us.* New York: Simon & Schuster.

Pyle, Ralph E. 1993. "Faith and Commitment to the Poor: Theological Orientation and Support for Government Assistance Measures." *Sociology of Religion* 54(4):385–401.

Quintelier, Ellen, Dietlind Stolle, and Allison Harell. 2012. "Politics in Peer Groups: Exploring the Causal Relationship between Network Diversity and Political Participation." *Political Research Quarterly* 65(4): 868–81

Ragin, Charles C. 2000. *Fuzzy-Set Social Science*. Chicago: University of Chicago Press.

Regnerus, Mark. 2007. *Forbidden Fruit: Sex & Religion in the Lives of American Teenagers*. Oxford and New York: Oxford University Press.

Regnerus, Mark D., David Sikkink, and Christian Smith. 1999. "Voting with the Christian Right: Contextual and Individual Patterns of Electoral Influence." *Social Forces* 77(4):1375–1401.

Regnerus, Mark D., Christian Smith, and David Sikkink. 1998. "Who Gives to the Poor? The Influence of Religious Tradition and Political Location on the Personal Generosity of Americans toward the Poor." *Journal for the Scientific Study of Religion* 37(3):481–93.

Reimer, Sam. 2011. " 'Civility without Compromise': Evangelical Attitudes Towards Same-Sex Issues in Comparative Context." Pp. 71–86 in *Faith, Politics, and Sexual Diversity in Canada and the United States*, edited by D. M. Rayside and C. Wilcox. Vancouver: UBC Press.

———. 2012. "Pentecostal Assemblies of Canada's Congregations: Vitality, Diversity, Identity and Equity." *Canadian Journal of Pentecostal-Charismatic Christianity* 3(1):41–69.

Reimer, Sam and Jerry Z. Park. 2001. "Tolerant (in)Civility? A Longitudinal Analysis of White Conservative Protestants' Willingness to Grant Civil Liberties." *Journal for the Scientific Study of Religion* 40(4):735–45.

Reimer, Sam and Michael Wilkinson. under review. *Evangelical Churches in Canada*. Book manuscript under review, cited by permission.

Reimer, Samuel H. 1995. "A Look at Cultural Effects on Religiosity: A Comparison between the United States and Canada." *Journal for the Scientific Study of Religion* 34(4):445–57.

Reimer, Samuel Harold. 2003. *Evangelicals and the Continental Divide: The Conservative Protestant Subculture in Canada and the United States*. Montreal and Ithaca, NY: McGill-Queen's University Press.

Rice, James J. and Michael J. Prince. 2000. *Changing Politics of Canadian Social Policy*. Toronto and Buffalo, NY: University of Toronto Press.

Rodriguez, Eric M. and Suzanne C. Ouellette. 2000. "Gay and Lesbian Christians: Homosexual and Religious Identity Integration in the Members and Participants of a Gay-Positive Church." *Journal for the Scientific Study of Religion* 39(3):333–47. doi: 10.1111/0021–8294.00028.

Rothstein, Bo. 1998. *Just Institutions Matter: The Moral and Political Logic of the Universal Welfare State*. Cambridge, UK: Cambridge University Press.

Rozell, Mark J. and Clyde Wilcox. 1997. *God at the Grassroots, 1996: The Christian Right in the American Elections*. Lanham, MD: Rowman & Littlefield.

Rydgren, Jens. 2007. "The Sociology of the Radical Right." *Annual Review of Sociology* 33(1):241–62. doi:10.1146/annurev.soc.33.040406.131752.

Sadler, Paul L. 1991. "The Abortion Issue within the Southern Baptist Convention, 1969–1988." Retrieved from /z-wcorg/.

Sager, Rebecca. 2010. *Faith, Politics, and Power: The Politics of Faith-Based Ini-*

tiatives: The Politics of Faith-Based Initiatives. New York: Oxford University Press.

Sandel, Michael J. 2009. *Justice: What's the Right Thing to Do?* New York: Farrar, Straus and Giroux.

Schattschneider, E. E. 1960. *The Semisovereign People: A Realist's View of Democracy in America.* New York: Holt Rinehart and Winston.

Schmalzbauer, John. 1993. "Evangelicals in the New Class: Class Versus Subcultural Predictors of Ideology." *Journal for the Scientific Study of Religion* 32(4):330–42.

Schneider, Anne L. and Helen M. Ingram. 2005. *Deserving and Entitled: Social Constructions and Public Policy.* Albany: State University of New York Press.

Schram, Sanford, Joe Soss, and Richard C. Fording. 2003. *Race and the Politics of Welfare Reform.* Ann Arbor: University of Michigan Press.

Schwalbe, Michael and Douglas Mason-Schrock. 1996. "Identity Work as Group Process." *Advances in Group Processes* 13:113–47.

Schwartz, Barry. 1982. "The Social Context of Commemoration: A Study in Collective Memory." *Social Forces* 61(2):374–402. doi: 10.1093/sf/61.2.374.

Schwartz, Barry and Howard Schuman. 2005 "History, Commemoration, and Belief: Abraham Lincoln in American Memory, 1945–2001." *American Sociological Review* 70(2):183–203.

Schwartz, Mildred A. 2006. *Party Movements in the United States and Canada: Strategies of Persistence.* Lanham, MD: Rowman & Littlefield.

Schweitzer, Don. 2011. *The United Church of Canada: A History.* Waterloo, ON: Wilfrid Laurier University Press.

Sears, David O., Jim Sidanius, and Lawrence Bobo. 2000. *Racialized Politics: The Debate About Racism in America.* Chicago: University of Chicago Press.

Self, Robert O. 2003. *American Babylon: Race and the Struggle for Postwar Oakland.* Princeton, NJ: Princeton University Press.

Sewell, William H. 1999. "The Concept(s) of Culture." Pp. 35–61 in *Beyond the Cultural Turn: New Directions in the Study of Society and Culture,* edited by V. E. Bonnell, L. Hunt, and H. White. Berkeley: University of California Press.

Sewell, William H., Jr. 1992. "Introduction: Narratives and Social Identities." *Social Science History* 16(3):479–88.

Shackleton, Doris French. 1975. *Tommy Douglas.* Toronto: McClelland and Stewart.

Sherkat, Darren E. 2001. "Tracking the Restructuring of American Religion: Religious Affiliation and Patterns of Religious Mobility, 1973–1998." *Social Forces* 79(4):1459–93.

Shields, Jon A. 2009. *The Democratic Virtues of the Christian Right.* Princeton, NJ: Princeton University Press. Available online: http://public.eblib.com/EBL Public/PublicView.do?ptiID=457910.

———. 2011. "Framing the Christian Right: How Progressives and Post-War Liberals Constructed the Religious Right." *Journal of Church and State* 53(4): 635–55.

Sider, Ronald J. and Heidi Rolland Unruh. 2001. "Evangelism and Church-State Partnerships." *Journal of Church and State* 43(2):267–95. doi: 10.1093/jcs/43 .2.267.

Simmel, Georg. 1908 [1955]. *Conflict and the Web of Group Affiliations*. New York: Free Press.

Simpson, A. B. 1966 [1911]. *The Old Faith and the New Gospels*. Harrisburg, PA: Christian Publications.

Simpson, John. 1985. "Federal Regulation and Religious Broadcasting." Pp. 152–63 in *Religion/Culture: Comparative Canadian Studies*, edited by W. Westfall, L. Rousseau, F. Harvey, and J. Simpson. Ottawa: Association for Canadian Studies.

Singleton, Andrew. 2001. "No Sympathy for the Devil: Narratives About Evil." *Journal of Contemporary Religion* 16(2):177–91. doi: 10.1080/13537900 120040654.

Skocpol, Theda. 1992. *Protecting Soldiers and Mothers: The Political Origins of Social Policy in the United States*. Cambridge, MA: Belknap Press of Harvard University Press.

———. 1997. "The Tocqueville Problem: Civic Engagement in American Democracy." *Social Science History* 21(4):455–79.

Smidt, Corwin, Sue Crawford, Melissa Deckman, Donald Gray, Dan Hofrenning, Laura Olson, Sherrie Steiner, and Beau Weston. 2003. "The Political Attitudes and Activities of Mainline Protestant Clergy in the Election of 2000: A Study of Six Denominations." *Journal for the Scientific Study of Religion* 42(4):515–32. doi:10.1046/j.1468–5906.2003.00200.x.

Smidt, Corwin E., Kevin den Dulk, Bryan Froehle, James Penning, Stephen Monsma, and Douglas Koopman. 2010. *The Disappearing God Gap?: Religion in the 2008 Presidential Election*. Oxford, New York: Oxford University Press.

Smilde, David. 2004. "Contradiction without Paradox: Evangelical Political Culture in the 1998 Venezuelan Elections." *Latin American Politics and Society* 46(1) {AU: PAGE NUMBERS?}.

———. 2007. *Reason to Believe: Cultural Agency in Latin American Evangelicalism*. Berkeley: University of California Press.

Smith, Anthony D. 2003. *Chosen Peoples: Sacred Sources of National Identity*. Oxford, New York: Oxford University Press.

Smith, Christian. 1998. *American Evangelicalism: Embattled and Thriving*. Chicago: University of Chicago Press.

Smith, Christian. 2000. *Christian America?: What Evangelicals Really Want*. Berkeley: University of California Press.

———. 2003. *Moral, Believing Animals: Human Personhood and Culture*. New York: Oxford University Press.

———. 2011. *The Bible Made Impossible: Why Biblicism Is Not a Truly Evangelical Reading of Scripture*. Grand Rapids, MI: Brazos.

Smith, Christian, Michael O. Emerson, Sally Gallagher, Paul Kennedy, and David Sikkink. 1998. *American Evangelicalism: Embattled and Thriving*. Chicago: University of Chicago Press.

Smith, Gregory A. 2008. *Politics in the Parish: The Political Influence of Catholic Priests*. Washington, DC: Georgetown University Press.

Smith, Miriam Catherine. 1999. *Lesbian and Gay Rights in Canada: Social*

Movements and Equality-Seeking: 1971–1995. Toronto and Buffalo, NY: University of Toronto Press.

———. 2008. *Political Institutions and Lesbian and Gay Rights in the United States and Canada.* New York: Routledge. Available online: http://www.net library.com/urlapi.asp?action=summary&v=1&bookid=236583.

Smith, T. Alexander and Raymond Tatalovich. 2003. *Cultures at War: Moral Conflicts in Western Democracies.* Peterborough, ON: Broadview Press.

Smylie, Lisa, Eleanor Maticka-Tyndale and Dana Boyd. 2008. "Evaluation of a School-Based Sex Education Programme Delivered to Grade Nine Students in Canada." *Sex Education* 8(1):25–46. doi: 10.1080/14681810701811795.

Snow, David A., E. Burke Rochford, Jr., Steven K. Worden, and Robert D. Benford. 1986. "Frame Alignment Processes, Micromobilization, and Movement Participation." *American Sociological Review* 51(4):464–81.

Somers, Margaret R. 1994. "The Narrative Constitution of Identity: A Relational and Network Approach." *Theory and Society* 23(5):605–49.

Somers, Margaret R. and Fred Block. 2005. "From Poverty to Perversity: Ideas, Markets, and Institutions over 200 Years of Welfare Debate." *American Sociological Review* 70:260–87.

Soper, J. Christopher. 1994. *Evangelical Christianity in the United States and Great Britain: Religious Beliefs, Political Choices.* Basingstoke, UK: Macmillan.

Soss, Joe and Sanford F. Schram. 2007. "A Public Transformed? Welfare Reform as Policy Feedback." *American Political Science Review* 101(01):111–27.

Spielvogel, Christian. 2005. " 'You Know Where I Stand': Moral Framing of the War on Terrorism and the Iraq War in the 2004 Presidential Campaign." *Rhetoric & Public Affairs* 8(4):549–69.

Spillman, Lyn. 1997. *Nation and Commemoration: Creating National Identities in the United States and Australia.* New York: Cambridge University Press.

———. 1998. "When Do Collective Memories Last? Founding Moments in the United States and Australia." *Social Science History* 22(4):445–77.

Spraggett, Allen. 1968. "Baptists Crusade to Kill Off New Homosexual Law." Pp. 13 in *Toronto Daily Star.* Toronto.

Stackhouse, John G., Jr. 1991. "The Emergence of a Fellowship: Canadian Evangelicalism in the Twentieth Century." *Church History* 60(2):247–62.

Staggenborg, Suzanne and David S. Meyer. 1998. "Counter Movement Dynamics in Federal Systems: A Comparison of Abortion Movements in Canada and the United States." *Research in Political Sociology* 8(2):209–40.

Stark, Rodney and Roger Finke. 2000. *Acts of Faith: Explaining the Human Side of Religion.* Berkeley: University of California Press.

Stark, Rodney and William Sims Bainbridge. 1985. *The Future of Religion: Secularization, Revival, and Cult Formation.* Berkeley: University of California Press.

Steensland, Brian. 2002. "The Hydra and the Swords: Social Welfare and Mainline Advocacy, 1964–2000." In *The Quiet Hand of God: Faith-Based Activism and the Public Role of Mainline Protestantism,* edited by R. Wuthnow and J. H. Evans. Berkeley: University of California Press.

———. 2006. "Cultural Categories and the American Welfare State: The Case of Guaranteed Income Policy." *American Journal of Sociology* 111(5):1273–1326.

Steensland, Brian, Jerry Z. Park, Mark D. Regnerus, Lynn D. Robinson, W. Bradford Wilcox, and Robert D. Woodberry. 2000. "The Measure of American Religion: Toward Improving the State of the Art." *Social Forces* 79(1):291–318.

Stenner, Karen. 2005. *The Authoritarian Dynamic*. New York: Cambridge University Press.

Stephens, Randall J. and Karl Giberson. 2011. *The Anointed: Evangelical Truth in a Secular Age*. Cambridge, MA: Belknap Press of Harvard University Press.

Stets, Jan E. and Peter J. Burke. 2000. "Identity Theory and Social Identity Theory." *Social Psychology Quarterly* 63(3):224–37.

Stevens, Mitchell L. 2001. *Kingdom of Children: Culture and Controversy in the Homeschooling Movement*. Princeton, NJ: Princeton University Press.

Stewart, Walter. 2003. *The Life and Political Times of Tommy Douglas*. Toronto: McArthur.

Stimson, James A. 2004. *Tides of Consent: How Public Opinion Shapes American Politics*. New York: Cambridge University Press.

Studlar, Donley T. and Kyle Christensen. 2006. "Is Canada a Westminster or Consensus Democracy? A Brief Analysis." *PS: Political Science & Politics* 39(04):837–41.

Suhay, Elizabeth. 2011. "Influence without Reason: The Role of Identity and Emotion in Political Conformity." In *Annual Meeting of the American Political Science Association*. Seattle, WA.

Sullivan, Amy. 2008. *The Party Faithful: How and Why Democrats Are Closing the God Gap*. New York: Scribner.

Sutton, Matthew A. 2005. "Clutching to 'Christian' America: Aimee Semple Mcpherson, the Great Depression, and the Origins of Pentecostal Political Activism." *Journal of Policy History* 17(03):308–38. doi:10.1353/jph.2005.0018.

Sutton, Matthew Avery. 2007. *Aimee Semple Mcpherson and the Resurrection of Christian America*. Cambridge, MA: Harvard University Press.

———. 2012. "Was FDR the Antichrist? The Birth of Fundamentalist Antiliberalism in a Global Age." *Journal of American History* 98(4):1052–74.

Swartz, David R. 2012. *Moral Minority: The Evangelical Left in an Age of Conservatism*. Philadelphia: University of Pennsylvania Press.

Swidler, Ann. 1986. "Culture in Action: Symbols and Strategies." *American Sociological Review* 51:273–86.

———. 2001. *Talk of Love: How Culture Matters*. Chicago: University of Chicago Press.

Tajfel, Henri. 1981. *Human Groups and Social Categories: Studies in Social Psychology*. New York: Cambridge University Press.

Tatalovich, Raymond. 1997. *The Politics of Abortion in the United States and Canada: A Comparative Study*. Armonk, NY: M.E. Sharpe.

Taylor, Charles. 1989. *Sources of the Self: The Making of the Modern Identity*. Cambridge, MA: Harvard University Press.

———. 2003. *Modern Social Imaginaries*. Durham, NC: Duke University Press.

Tedin, Kent L. 1978. "Religous Preference and Pro/Anti Activism on the Equal Rights Amendment Issue." *Pacific Sociological Review* 21(1):55–66.

Teixeira, Ruy A. and Joel Rogers. 2000. *America's Forgotten Majority: Why the White Working Class Still Matters*. New York: Basic Books.

Teles, Steven Michael. 2008. *The Rise of the Conservative Legal Movement: The Battle for Control of the Law*. Princeton, NJ: Princeton University Press.

Tilly, Charles. 2001. "Mechanisms in Political Processes." *Annual Review of Political Science* 4(1):21–41. doi:10.1146/annurev.polisci.4.1.21.

———. 2003. "Political Identities in Changing Polities." *Social Research* 70(2):605–20.

Tranby, Eric and Douglas Hartmann. 2008. "Critical Whiteness Theories and the Evangelical 'Race Problem': Extending Emerson and Smith's Divided by Faith." *Journal for the Scientific Study of Religion* 47(3):341–59. doi: 10.1111/j .1468–5906.2008.00414.x.

Treier, Shawn and D. Sunshine Hillygus. 2009. "The Nature of Political Ideology in the Contemporary Electorate." *Public Opinion Quarterly* 73(4):679–703. doi: 10.1093/poq/nfp067.

Turner, John C., Michael A. Hogg, Penelope J. Oakes, Stephen D. Reicher, and Margaret S. Wetherell. 1987. *Rediscovering the Social Group: A Self-Categorization Theory*. Oxford, UK and New York: Blackwell.

Vaisey, Stephen. 2008. "Socrates, Skinner, and Aristotle: Three Ways of Thinking About Culture in Action." *Sociological Forum* 23(3):603–13. doi: 10.1111/j .1573–7861.2008.00079.x.

———. 2009. "Motivation and Justification: A Dual-Process Model of Culture in Action." *American Journal of Sociology* 114(6):1675–1715.

Valverde, Mariana. 1991. *The Age of Light, Soap, and Water: Moral Reform in English Canada, 1885–1925*. Toronto: McClelland & Stewart.

Verba, Sidney, Kay Lehman Schlozman, and Henry E. Brady. 1995. *Voice and Equality: Civic Voluntarism in American Politics*. Cambridge, MA: Harvard University Press.

Wagner, Melinda Bollar. 1997. "Generic Conservative Christianity: The Demise of Denominationalism in Christian Schools." *Journal for the Scientific Study of Religion* 36(1):13–24.

Wagner, Michael. 2007. *Standing on Guard for Thee: The Past, Present, and Future of Canada's Christian Right*: St. Catherines, ON: Freedom Press Canada.

Wallis, Jim. 2005. *God's Politics: Why the Right Gets It Wrong and the Left Doesn't Get It*. San Francisco: HarperSanFrancisco.

Walsh, Katherine Cramer. 2004. *Talking About Politics: Informal Groups and Social Identity in American Life*. Chicago: University of Chicago Press.

———. 2012. "Putting Inequality in Its Place: Rural Consciousness and the Power of Perspective." *American Political Science Review* 106(03):517–32. doi:10.1017/S0003055412000305.

Wang, Jiwu. 2006. *"His Dominion" and the "Yellow Peril": Protestant Missions to Chinese Immigrants in Canada, 1859–1967*. Waterloo, ON: Wilfrid Laurier University Press.

Ward, Mark. 1994. *Air of Salvation: The Story of Christian Broadcasting*. Grand Rapids, MI: Baker Books.

Warner, R. Stephen. 1993. "Work in Progress toward a New Paradigm for the

Sociological Study of Religion in the United States." *American Journal of Sociology* 98(5):1044–93.

Warner, Tom. 2010. *Losing Control: Canada's Social Conservatives in the Age of Rights.* Toronto: Between the Lines.

Welch, Michael R., David C. Leege, Kenneth D. Wald, and Lyman A. Kellstedt. 1993. "Are the Sheep Herding the Shepherds? Cue Perceptions, Congregational Responses and Political Communication Processes." Pp. xv, 319 in *Rediscovering the Religious Factor in American Politics*, edited by D. C. Leege and L. A. Kellstedt. Armonk, NY: M.E. Sharpe.

Wellman, James K. 2008. *Evangelical vs. Liberal: The Clash of Christian Cultures in the Pacific Northwest.* Oxford and New York: Oxford University Press.

Wells, Jon. 2008, *Sniper: The True Story of Anti-Abortion Killer James Kopp.* Mississauga, ON: J. Wiley & Sons Canada.

White, Ronald C. and Charles Howard Hopkins. 1976. *The Social Gospel: Religion and Reform in Changing America.* Philadelphia: Temple University Press.

Wilcox, Clyde. 1992. *God's Warriors: The Christian Right in Twentieth-Century America.* Baltimore: Johns Hopkins University Press.

Wilcox, Clyde and Carin Larson. 2006. *Onward Christian Soldiers?: The Religious Right in American Politics.* Boulder, CO: Westview Press.

Wilcox, Melissa M. 2002. "When Sheila's a Lesbian: Religious Individualism among Lesbian, Gay, Bisexual, and Transgender Christians." *Sociology of Religion* 63(4):497–513. doi: 10.2307/3712304.

Wilcox, W. Bradford. 1998. "Conservative Protestant Childrearing: Authoritarian or Authoritative?" *American Sociological Review* 63(6):796–809.

Wilcox, W. Bradford, Mark Chaves, and David Franz. 2004. "Focused on the Family? Religious Traditions, Family Discourse, and Pastoral Practice." *Journal for the Scientific Study of Religion* 43(4):491–504.

Wilcox, William Bradford. 2004. *Soft Patriarchs, New Men: How Christianity Shapes Fathers and Husbands.* Chicago: University of Chicago Press.

Wilkinson, Katharine K. 2012. *Between God and Green: How Evangelicals Are Cultivating a Middle Ground on Climate Change.* New York: Oxford University Press.

Wilkinson, Michael, ed. 2009. *Canadian Pentecostalism: Transition and Transformation*, Vol. 49, edited by D. H. Akenson. Montreal and Kingston: McGill-Queen's University Press.

Will, Jeffry A. and John K. Cochran. 1995. "God Helps Those Who Help Themselves?: The Effects of Religious Affiliation, Religiosity, and Deservedness on Generosity toward the Poor." *Sociology of Religion* 56(3):327–38.

Williams, Daniel. 2010. *God's Own Party: The Making of the Christian Right.* New York: Oxford University Press.

Williams, Rhys H. 2005. "Introduction to a Forum on Religion and Place." *Journal for the Scientific Study of Religion* 44(3):239–42. doi:10.1111/j.1468 –5906.2005.00281.x.

———. 2007. " 'Religion as a Cultural System': Theoretical and Empirical Developments since Geertz." Pp. 97–113 in *The Blackwell Companion to the Sociology of Culture.* Oxford: Blackwell.

———. 2013. "Civil Religion and the Cultural Politics of National Identity in

Obama's America." *Journal for the Scientific Study of Religion* 52(2):239–57. doi: 10.1111/jssr.12032.

Williams, Rhys H. and Jeffrey Neal Blackburn. 1996. "Many Are Called but Few Obey: Ideological Commitment and Activism in Operation Rescue." Pp. xi, 236 in *Disruptive Religion: The Force of Faith in Social-Movement Activism*, edited by C. Smith. New York: Routledge.

Wilson, J. Matthew. 1999. " 'Blessed Are the Poor': American Protestantism and Attitudes toward Poverty and Welfare." *Southeastern Political Review* 27(3):421–37. doi: 10.1111/j.1747–1346.1999.tb00544.x.

Wolbrecht, Christina. 2002. "Explaining Women's Rights Realignment: Convention Delegates, 1972–1992." *Political Behavior* 24(3):237–82.

Wolfe, Alan. 1998. *One Nation after All: What Middle-Class Americans Really Think About God, Country, and Family, Racism, Welfare, Immigration, Homosexuality, Work, the Right, the Left, and Each Other*. New York: Viking.

Woodberry, Robert D. and Christian S. Smith. 1998. "Fundamentalism et al.: Conservative Protestants in America." *Annual Review of Sociology* 24:25–56.

Wuthnow, Robert. 1988. *The Restructuring of American Religion: Society and Faith since World War II*. Princeton, NJ: Princeton University Press.

———. 1989. *The Struggle for America's Soul: Evangelicals, Liberals, and Secularism*. Grand Rapids, MI: W.B. Eerdmans.

———. 1999. "Mobilizing Civic Engagement: The Changing Impact of Religious Involvement." Pp. 331–63 in *Civic Engagement in American Democracy*, edited by T. Skocpol and M. P. Fiorina. Washington, DC and New York: Brookings Institution Press, Russell Sage Foundation.

———. 2004. *Saving America?: Faith-Based Services and the Future of Civil Society*. Princeton, NJ: Princeton University Press.

Young, Michael P. 2002. "Confessional Protest: The Religious Birth of U.S. National Social Movements." *American Sociological Review* 67(5):660–88.

———. 2006. *Bearing Witness against Sin: The Evangelical Birth of the American Social Movement*. Chicago: University of Chicago Press.

Zaretsky, Natasha. 2007. *No Direction Home: The American Family and the Fear of National Decline, 1968–1980*. Chapel Hill: University of North Carolina Press.

Zerubavel, Eviatar. 2003. *Time Maps: Collective Memory and the Social Shape of the Past*. Chicago: University of Chicago Press.

Zolf, Dorothy and Paul W. Taylor. 1989. "Redressing the Balance in Canadian Broadcasting: A History of Religious Broadcasting Policy in Canada." *Studies in Religion* 18(2):153–70.

Zuberi, Dan. 2006. *Differences That Matter: Social Policy and the Working Poor in the United States and Canada*. Ithaca, NY: Cornell University Press.

Zubrzycki, Geneviève. 2006. *The Crosses of Auschwitz: Nationalism and Religion in Post-Communist Poland*. Chicago: University of Chicago Press.

———. 2012. "Religion, Religious Tradition, and Nationalism: Jewish Revival in Poland and 'Religious Heritage' in Québec." *Journal for the Scientific Study of Religion* 51(3):442–55. doi: 10.1111/j.1468–5906.2012.01666.x.

INDEX

Aberhart, William, 35

abeyance structures, 246n29

abortion, 6–7, 8–9, 32–33, 153, 237n33; avoidance of political talk and, 66–69; Canadian and American evangelical views on, 12, 36, 96–97; combative imagery of spiritual warfare and, 75–76; discussions of grey areas and, 96–98; group boundaries and, 68–69; laws in Canada, 39, 206–7, 244n13, 244n15, 252n107; partial birth, 142; pro-life extremists and, 54; young adult evangelicals' views on, 192. *See also* pro-choice movement; pro-life movement

absolutism, voluntary, 152

accountable individualism, 113, 122, 130

adoption, 55

adversarial framing, 103

Afghanistan War, 54

American Center for Law and Justice, 37

American Council of Christian Churches, 28

American Voter, The, 13, 241n91

Ammerman, Nancy, 26

anchoring mechanisms, 114, 118

anti-structuralism, 113

Armageddon Factor, The, 101

Assemblies of God. *See* Lifeway Assembly of God

"Assignment Life," 141

authoritarianism, 57–58, 73, 223–24, 267n18, 268n14, 269n19, 269n21

authority-mindedness, 223

Bakker, Jim, 31

Baldassarri, Delia, 116

Balmer, Randall, 1

Baptists: discourses about poverty, 119–22, 124–28; evangelical identity, 56–58; Highpoint Baptist Church, 51–52, 88, 90–100, 124–28, 194–202; Northtown Baptist Church, 48–50, 64–73, 79–80, 83–85, 119–22. *See also* Southern Baptist Convention

Barkowski, John, 56–57

Barton, David, 162

Beck, Glenn, 105–6

Bellah, Robert, 90, 96, 226

Beyerlein, Kraig, 2

Bickle, Mike, 189–90

Billings, Robert, 32

birth control, 24

Birthright, 195–96, 206

Blackburn, Jeffrey Neal, 6

Black Protestant churches, 2–3, 113; moral beliefs and political behavior of, 7

Blackwell, Morton, 33

born-again Christians, 45–47

boundaries: between Canadian Christians and society as a whole, 90–100, 217–18; between Christians and liberals, 80–82; civil religion and, 96, 149–50; ethnographic methods for studying, 229; evangelicals as religious minority and, 89; group, 64, 65, 68–69, 258n9; thin coherence between religious and political identity, 167–69; working-class evangelicals and, 169–79

Boyd, Gregory, 210

Breaking Free, 70–71, 72

Bright, Bill, 30

Bryan, William Jennings, 28